Echoes of Thunder

Echoes of Thunder

A Guide to the Seven Days Battles

Matt Spruill III
Matt Spruill IV

The University of Tennessee Press / Knoxville

Copyright © 2006 by The University of Tennessee Press / Knoxville.
All Rights Reserved. Manufactured in the United States of America.
First Edition.

This book is printed on acid-free paper.

Library of Congress Cataloging-in-Publication Data

Spruill, Matt.

  Echoes of thunder : a guide to the Seven Days Battles / Matt Spruill III, Matt
Spruill IV.– 1st ed.
    p. cm.
Includes index.

ISBN 1-57233-547-5 (pbk. : alk. paper)

  1. Seven Days' Battles, Va., 1862.
  I. Spruill, Matt, IV.
  II. Title.

E473.68.S67 2006

973.7'32–dc22   2005036654

For
Kathy, Bonnie, Meagan, and Katie
Our wives, daughters, and granddaughters

Contents

Figures

Maps

Introduction

The spring and summer of 1862 was a defining period in the Civil War. In the western theater Major General Ulysses S. Grant captured Fort Henry and Fort Donaldson and opened the Cumberland and Tennessee rivers as routes of advance, supply, and communication for Union armies into Mississippi, Tennessee, and northern Georgia. In April, Grant's Army of the Tennessee, reinforced by Major General Don Carlos Buell's Army of the Ohio, fought a bloody two-day battle against the Confederate Army of the Mississippi at Shiloh, Tennessee. The fighting on April 6 and 7 produced 23,741 total casualties, a total of 20 percent of all troops engaged. The casualties at Shiloh were greater than the sum of all the casualties American armies had taken in every war prior to the Civil War.

In the spring of 1862 the two main opposing armies in the East faced each other in northeast Virginia. Responding to the calls of "On to Richmond," two courses of action were available to Major General George B. McClellan, the Union army commander. He could pursue an overland route directly to Richmond, some one hundred miles away. As a variation on this he could maneuver his army in a westerly direction to outflank his opponent. A second course of action was to conduct a turning movement by using naval power to move his army from the vicinity of Washington to the tip of the Virginia Peninsula and then move rapidly and reach Richmond before the Confederate army. The second option was decided upon. This decision brought the Union Army of the Potomac to the outskirts of the Confederate capitol and then, in a dramatic turn of events, drove it back to an enclave twenty-five miles southeast of Richmond. These dramatic events are the series of battles in late June and on July 1 that are collectively called the Seven Days Battles.

When the Civil War began in the spring of 1861 many thought it would be a short war. In the model of the Napoleonic wars there would be maneuvering, then one or two large battles that would decide the issue. However, the spring of 1862 began to change the thinking about how long the war might last and what the cost in casualties would be.

The casualties from the Seven Days Battles totaled 35,999—15,795 Union and 20,204 Confederate. These losses came just two months after Shiloh began to develop an understanding on both sides that the war would not be decided by a quick victory of one or two battles. The battles during this period showed just how resilient large armies had become. Armies could now suffer large casualties and still keep going as they recovered their strength and combat power.

Among many on both sides the concept existed that the capture of the Confederate capitol, Richmond, would bring the collapse of the government and a quick end to the war. Developing this theme, many northern newspapers and politicians urged a campaign of "On to Richmond." This was the centerpiece of the Union strategy in the East for the next two years. Although Richmond was an important city and contained the capability of producing much of the equipment and supplies needed to keep Confederate armies in the field, it is debatable that its capture would have brought an end to the war. However, because of its industrial capability, any threat to Richmond by a Union army would bring a Confederate army to its defense.

There was no long-term association with Richmond and the Confederate government as there was with the Federal government and Washington, D.C. The Confederate government had only existed since February 1861, with its first capital at Montgomery, Alabama. On May 21, 1861, Richmond, Virginia, was designated the new capital, with the government moving there in June. The Confederate capital could easily be reestablished in several other southern cities that had good communication capability, such as Atlanta, Augusta, Selma, and others.

A more viable objective was the Confederate army in Virginia. Destroying this force or, what was more likely, rendering it combat ineffective would allow a Union army or armies in Virginia to move wherever they wished and to destroy or capture infrastructure at will. The problem was that this destruction could not be done in one or two battles. It would take a series of battles and many casualties.

U.S. Army doctrine recognizes four types of offensive operations: movement to contact, attack, exploitation, and pursuit. A movement to contact is conducted by a force when the commander is unsure of the exact enemy location and force. An attack, which uses various forms of maneuver, is conducted to destroy or render combat ineffective an enemy force or to capture key terrain. An exploitation often follows a successful attack with the purpose of preventing the enemy from reestablishing the defense and to capture objectives deep in the enemy rear area. A pursuit like the exploitation follows a successful attack or a successful exploitation. Where the exploitation orients on capture of terrain, the pursuit orients on the enemy force. The purpose of the pursuit is to cut off, capture, or destroy an enemy force attempting to escape. [*Field Manual 3-0* (Washington, D.C.: Government Printing Office, 2001), chap. 7. Hereafter cited as *FM 3-0*.]

The Seven Days presents the opportunity to study the attack and the exploitation as two of the types of offensive operations used by *Lee*. *Lee* employed the attack in each of the five battles that he fought from June 26 to July 1. On June 29 and 30 *Lee* was conducting a pursuit as he maneuvered forces to attempt to cut off the Union retreat to the James River.

There are five forms of maneuver that can be used when conducting an attack: envelopment, turning movement, infiltration, penetration, and frontal attack. The envelopment avoids the enemy front and maneuvers against one or both flanks. The single envelopment is against one flank, while the double envelopment is against both flanks. Some authors refer to these as flank attacks. The ultimate purpose of the envelopment is to gain the enemy rear area to isolate it and control its lines of communication. An attacking force uses a turning movement to avoid the enemy's principal defensive position by seizing objectives in the enemy rear and causing it to move out of its current position or to divert major forces against a new threat. The presence of a force in the enemy's rear turns him out of his position. The infiltration is a form of maneuver in which an attacking force moves undetected through or into an area occupied by the enemy to a position of advantage in the enemy rear. The penetration is used to cause a break in the enemy's defensive position. This maneuver creates assailable flanks at the point of penetration and provides access to enemy rear areas. A frontal attack strikes the enemy across a wide front and over the most direct approaches. Success with this form of maneuver depends on achieving an advantage in combat power throughout the attack. It can be the most costly form of maneuver (*FM 3-0*).

Three forms of maneuver were used or planned for by *Lee* in the Seven Days. *Lee*'s operations against the Union flank along Beaver Dam Creek on June 26 was planned to be a turning movement. When *Jackson* was unable to place his force in the rear of the defenses in the planned-for time, the opportunity to complete the turning movement was lost. *Lee* used the frontal attack in the other four battles fought from June 27 to July 1. During one of these, Gaines Mill on June 27, *Hood* was able to turn his frontal attack into a penetration of part of the Union defenses along Boatswain's Creek.

In developing this study and tour of the Seven Days we have concentrated on the battles from June 26 to July 1—Beaver Dam Creek, Gaines Mill, Savage Station, White Oak Swamp, Glendale, and Malvern Hill. Although many consider the action on June 25 at Oak Grove as a part of the Seven Days, we have chosen not to include it. This action was a result of a Union limited objective attack to establish an artillery position from which siege guns could be employed against the Richmond defenses. It had no influence on *Robert E.*

Lee's plan of action, nor did it assist McClellan's army when *Lee* initiated his attack the next day.

In recounting the story of the Seven Days Battles we have relied heavily on the *Official Records of the Union and Confederate Armies*. The gathering and publishing of these records was a monumental task. It was initially begun in 1864 as commanders' reports were collected. In the late 1860s a start was made in putting the reports collected so far into book form. In 1877 Captain Robert L. Scott, a Civil War aide to General Henry W. Halleck, was placed in charge of the project. Scott developed the plan as to how the material would be organized. Until his death in 1887 he supervised the compilation and publication of a large part of the work. The first book of what was to be a series of 128 books was published in 1880 and the last one in 1901. Where *Official Records* were not available, we have used other original source material.

We have left the spelling and capitalization as we found it in anything written by the participants: for example, in 1862 it was re-enforce and Richmond road; today it is reinforce and Richmond Road. For ease of identifying who was Confederate and who was Union, the names of Confederate soldiers and civilians are in italic.

The book is organized so that you may follow the battles from start to finish in a chronological order. Driving instructions direct you from battle to battle along the same routes taken by many of the Union and Confederate units. The complete tour is twenty-six miles. Each chapter is designed to stand-alone, however, so that you may visit only those battles that you wish or have time to.

We have provided three different types of maps in the book. There are forty-four tactical maps that show the terrain as it was in the 1860s and indicate specific unit deployments during a short time frame. Union units are shown in black, and Confederate units are shown in gray. A unit is shown as a bar, which represents the location of the unit's battle line. Unless otherwise indicated all units shown are brigades. If otherwise, the unit designation and size will be indicated. A number officially designated Union brigades, for example First Brigade, First Division. However for clarity and ease of use we have shown them with the commander's name. In mid-1862 Confederate brigades were given numerical designations, while divisions were named after their commanders. This was in the process of evolution and brigades would also be designated by their commander's name. As this is the form most familiar with readers today, we have used commander's names to also designate Confederate brigades. We have used this designation even if someone else was commanding the unit. For example, *Pickett*'s Brigade of *Longstreet*'s Division. After *Pickett* was wounded, Colonel *Eppa Hunton* and then Colonel *John B. Strange* commanded his brigade. On maps and in the text we have continued to designate it as *Pickett*'s Brigade

In addition to the tactical maps there are operational maps showing general situations and planned movements. Each chapter also has a driving map indicating modern-day roads and the location of each stop.

We are greatly indebted to many people for their assistance and support in preparing this book. Dr. Jay Luvaas and Brigadier General Hal Nelson taught us the value of the *Official Records* and how to use them on a battlefield. Without them, the *Guide to the Battle of Chickamauga* and *Storming the Heights: A Guide to the Battle of Chattanooga* would not have been written. This book has been modeled on those and similar books that have written for the Army War College. We wish to express our appreciation to Dr. John G. Selby of Roanoke College for reading the manuscript and providing many valuable suggestions. Scot Pawlowski of the National Park Service, Denver Service Center, was immensely helpful in locating and providing movement maps of the battles. Jennifer McDaid of the Library of Virginia helped with the Lee-Davis correspondence. Our thanks go to the University of Tennessee Press director Jennifer Siler and her production and marketing team. Foremost among them are Scot Danforth, who has guided and supported us in the publication process; Gene Adair and Monica Phillips, who worked on the editing and final manuscript preparation; and Tom Post and Cheryl Carson, who have provided support and encouragement. To our son and brother, Lee Spruill, special thanks for reading and providing suggested changes to the manuscript.

We wish to express our appreciation to Brian Deal for permission to park in the grass and gravel area, Stop 11, at Old Cold Harbor, and to Edwin Adams for permission to drive and park on the Old Quaker Road, a private road, at Stop 13.

Our greatest thanks go to our wives, Kathy and Bonnie, without whose constant support and encouragement this work would not have moved from concept to book.

One final but very important comment. Of the 4.1 million who wore the blue and the gray from 1861 to 1865, a little over 600,000 gave their lives in a war that determined what the United States would become. What our country is today is because of their commitments and sacrifices.

Those veterans who survived have passed on. The generation that followed them, who personally knew them, has also gone. The personal contact that later generations had to these veterans and their war is now gone forever. The only contact we and future generations have are the writings, the artifacts, and the ground upon which they stood, fought, and died. The most direct contact we can have with those veterans and the Civil War is the battlefields themselves. One of the reasons this and other guidebooks are written is to provide that connection with past events on the actual spot where they happened.

Fortunately national, state, and local governments have preserved some of this ground. However, a crisis in battlefield preservation is upon us. Urban development in our country is growing at an exponential rate. In the past, where we may have had a generation or a decade to protect battlefields, we now have only a few years, or in some very threatened places only a few months. If you believe in saving this vital part of our heritage we encourage you to become active in battlefield preservation.

One of the most successful organizations in preserving battlefields is the nonprofit Civil War Preservation Trust (CWPT). We strongly urge you to become a member of the CWPT and leave a legacy that will be passed to future generations of your family. The CWPT can be contacted by writing Civil War Preservation Trust, 1331 H Street NW, Suite 1001, Washington, DC, 20005, or by calling (202) 367-1861, or via the Internet at http://www.civilwar.org.

It is our hope that as you read this book in the comfort of your home or on the battlefield, especially on the battlefield, that you will be able to see the events being described by those who were there. And perhaps across the years you will hear, if faintly, the roar of cannon and crack of rifle fire—echoes of thunder from the past.

Matt Spruill III   Matt Spruill IV
Littleton, Colorado   Chesapeake, Virginia

MAP LEGEND

Union unit - a brigade unless specified

Confederate unit - a brigade unless specified

Union unit attacking

Confederate unit attacking

Union unit in march column

Confederate unit in march column

Artillery position

3, 3B or B   **Stop and Position indicator**

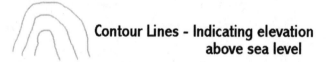

Contour Lines - Indicating elevation above sea level

Chronology

The Peninsula Campaign and the Seven Days Battles
March–August 1862

March 17	The Union Army of the Potomac began movement by ship to Fort Monroe at the tip of the Virginia Peninsula
April 2	Headquarters Army of the Potomac was established at Fort Monroe
April 5–May 4	Union siege of Yorktown
April 17	Confederate reinforcements from northern Virginia under General *Joseph E. Johnston* reached the Peninsula
May 4	Confederates evacuated Yorktown
May 5	Battle of Williamsburg
May 6	*Johnston*'s army retreated up the Peninsula
May 10	Major General George B. McClellan established his major supply depot at White House on the Pamunkey River
May 24	Army of the Potomac closed up to the defenses of Richmond with half the army south of the Chickahominy River and half north of the river
May 31–June 1	Battle of Fair Oaks (Seven Pines)
May 31	*Johnston* wounded at Battle of Fair Oaks

June 1	General *Robert E. Lee* assumed command of *Johnston*'s army and renamed it the Army of Northern Virginia
June 5	*Lee* began to formulate plans to go on the offensive against the right of McClellan's army, which was north of the Chickahominy River
June 12–15	Brigadier General *J. E. B. Stuart*'s reconnaissance around the Army of the Potomac
June 18	Major General *Thomas J. (Stonewall) Jackson* began moving his command from the Shenandoah Valley to reinforce *Lee*
June 18	Franklin's Sixth Corps moved south of the Chickahominy River leaving Porter's Fifth Corps the only Union force north of the river
June 23	*Lee* met with *Jackson, Longstreet, A. P. Hill,* and *D. H. Hill* to finalize the plan for the attack on June 26
June 25	Battle of Oak Grove

June 25–July 1   The Seven Days Battles

June 26	Beaver Dam Creek
June 27	Gaines Mill
June 29	Savage Station
June 30	Glendale
July 1	Malvern Hill

June 27 (Night)	McClellan issued orders for his army to abandon positions in front of Richmond and retreat south to the James River
July 2	Union army retreated to Harrison's Landing on the James River
July 8	*Lee* moved back from the Union army to positions covering the roads into Richmond
July 12	*Lee* moved *Jackson* with two divisions to vicinity of Gordonsville to face another Union threat

August 3	McClellan ordered to withdraw his army from the Peninsula
August 13	*Lee* began redeploying the remainder of his army to positions in the vicinity Gordonsville
August 26	The last units of the Army of the Potomac leave the Peninsula

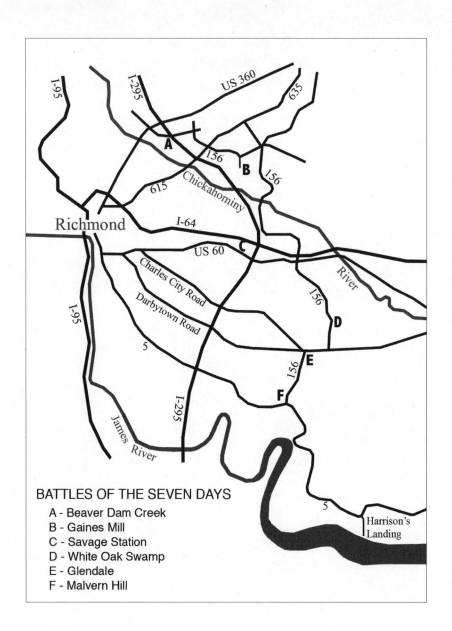

BATTLES OF THE SEVEN DAYS

A - Beaver Dam Creek
B - Gaines Mill
C - Savage Station
D - White Oak Swamp
E - Glendale
F - Malvern Hill

Chapter 1

Prelude

From Interstate 295, take the 37B exit for U.S. Highway 360 West. Drive west on Highway 360 for 2.4 miles. In 1.1 miles you will go through Mechanicsville and in another 0.5 mile you will cross the Chickahominy River. After you cross the river you will go up a hill. Near the top of the hill look for the National Park sign "Chickahominy Bluff" on your left. Turn left onto the park road and drive to the parking area. Park and get out of your car.

Stop 1—*Lee* Develops a Plan

You are located on the Chickahominy Bluffs in the area where General *Robert E. Lee* and his staff were on June 26, 1862. The earth works around you are the northern part of the Confederate defensive position east of Richmond. The sequence of events that brought *Lee* to this place began in March 1862 when he was not yet the commander of the Army of Northern Virginia.

Under the command of General *Joseph E. Johnston* the main Confederate army in Virginia had spent the winter of 1861–62 in entrenchments just south of Washington, D.C. Its Union opponent, the Army of the Potomac, had spent the winter in fortifications around Washington. During this time it had received reinforcements and had been reorganized and trained by its new commander, Major General George B. McClellan.

With the coming of spring McClellan began to develop his operational plans for an offense to capture Richmond, the Confederate capital. He basically had two options. McClellan could conduct a campaign overland from Washington directly toward Richmond,

or he could use the Union's naval mobility and move his army by
water to a position along the Virginia coast that placed him close
to Richmond. An offensive overland would bring the Union army
into direct contact with the Confederate army and would develop
into a prolonged series of battles in northern Virginia. The second
option had the potential for McClellan to outflank *Johnston*'s army
and put the Union army closer to Richmond than the Confederate
army. McClellan decided on the second option and in a letter to the
secretary of war outlined his plan of campaign.

Report of Maj. Gen. George B. McClellan, USA, Commanding Army of the Potomac

HEADQUARTERS ARMY OF THE POTOMAC,
Theological Seminary, Va., March 19, 1862.

SIR: I have the honor to submit the following notes on the proposed operations of the active portion of the Army of the Potomac.

The proposed plan of campaign is to assume Fort Monroe as the first base
of operations, taking the line of Yorktown and West Point upon Richmond as
the line of operations, Richmond being the objective point. It is assumed that
the fall of Richmond involves that of Norfolk and the whole of Virginia; also
that we shall fight a decisive battle between West Point and Richmond, to
give which battle the rebels will concentrate all their available forces, understanding, as they will, that it involves the fate of their cause. It therefore
follows -

1st. That we should collect all our available forces and operate upon adjacent lines, maintaining perfect communication between our columns.

2d. That no time should be lost in reaching the field of battle.

The advantages of the Peninsula between York and James Rivers are too
obvious to need explanation. It is also clear that West Point should as soon as
possible be reached and used as our main depot, that we may have the shortest
line of land transportation for our supplies and the use of the York River.

There are two methods of reaching this point:

1st: By moving directly from Fort Monroe as a base, and trusting to the
roads for our supplies, at the same time landing a strong corps as near Yorktown as possible, in order to turn the rebel lines of defense south of Yorktown;
then to reduce Yorktown and Gloucester by a siege, in all probability involv-
ing a delay of weeks, perhaps.

2d. To make a combined naval and land attack upon Yorktown the first
object of the campaign. This leads to the most rapid and decisive results. To

accomplish this, the Navy should at once concentrate upon the York River all their available and most powerful batteries. Its reduction should not in that case require many hours. A strong corps would be pushed up the York, under cover of the Navy, directly upon West Point, immediately upon the fall of Yorktown, and we could at once establish our new base of operations at a distance of some 25 miles from Richmond, with every facility for developing and bringing into play the whole of our available force on either or both banks of the James.

It is impossible to urge too strongly the absolute necessity of the full co-operation of the Navy as a part of this programme. Without it the operations may be prolonged for many weeks, and we may be forced to carry in front several strong positions, which by their aid could be turned without serious loss of either time or men.

It is also of first importance to bear in mind the fact, already alluded to, that the capture of Richmond necessarily involves the prompt fall of Norfolk, while an operation against Norfolk, if successful, as the beginning of the campaign, facilitates the reduction of Richmond merely by the demoralization of the rebel troops involved, and that after the fall of Norfolk we should be obliged to undertake the capture of Richmond by the same means which would have accomplished it in the beginning, having meanwhile afforded the rebels ample time to perfect their defensive arrangements; for they would well know, from the moment the Army of the Potomac changed its base to Fort Monroe, that Richmond must be its ultimate object.

It may be summed up in few words, that for the prompt success of this campaign it is absolutely necessary that the Navy should at once throw its whole available force, its most powerful vessels, against Yorktown. There is the most important point—there the knot to be cut. An immediate decision upon the subject-matter of this communication is highly desirable, and seems called for by the exigencies of the occasion.

I am, sir, very respectfully, your obedient servant,

GEO. B. MCCLELLAN,
Major General.

Hon. E. M. STANTON,
Secretary of War

[*War of the Rebellion: A Compilation of the Official Records of the Union and Confederate Armies* (Washington D.C.: Government Printing Office, 1881), vol. 5 (hereafter cited as *OR 5*), pp. 57–58.]

On March 17, 1862, McClellan's Army of the Potomac began loading on ships and ferries at Alexandria, Virginia, sailed down Chesapeake Bay, and landed at Fort Monroe, Virginia. By early

April the majority of McClellan's army had moved to Fort Monroe. It was only seventy-three miles from Richmond.

On April 5 McClellan moved his army forward less than twenty miles and began a siege of the Confederate position at Yorktown and along the Warwick River. Through skillful use of deception Major General *John B. Magruder* was able to make his Confederate force of approximately ten thousand appear much larger. This deception held McClellan in check in front of Yorktown for a month and allowed *Johnston* to move the majority of his army from northern Virginia to the Peninsula, where he assumed overall command of Confederate forces. He then abandoned Yorktown, which McClellan occupied on May 4.

Johnston had retreated to Williamsburg where the Confederate rear guard clashed with the advancing Union force on May 5. The next day *Johnston* continued his retreat up the Peninsula and by May 17 had entered the old defensive work just four miles from Richmond. The Army of the Potomac continued to follow at a slow pace, but now McClellan had a supply base at White House on the Pamunkey

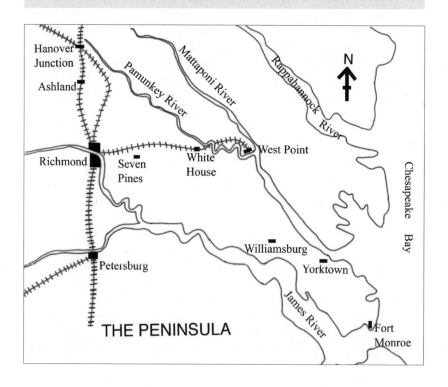

THE PENINSULA

River. From here a railroad ran toward Richmond and was used to supply the Union army.

In the later half of May the Army of the Potomac had closed up to the Confederate defensive positions at Richmond. However, a serious situation had developed in its deployment. Half of the Union army was north of the Chickahominy River while the other half was south of the river. Seizing upon this situation *Johnston* launched an attack against the Union positions south of the river. The result was the Battle of Fair Oaks (also called Seven Pines) fought May 31 and June 1. Late in the afternoon of May 31 *Johnston* was wounded. The next day *Robert E. Lee* was appointed to command the army. *Lee* immediately began to look for opportunities to take the initiative and go on the offense. His plans changed the character of the combat operations being conducted in front of Richmond.

Lee's first move was to create defensive positions that could be occupied by a minimum of force. This freed a large force that he could use to maneuver against McClellan's flank. The creation of a defensive work was begun with the dispatch of a letter of instruction to his chief engineer:

HEADQUARTERS,
Dabbs House, Va., June 3, 1862.

Maj. *W. H. STEVENS*
Chief Engineer Army of Northern Virginia:

MAJOR: I desire you to make an examination of the country in the vicinity of the line which our army now occupies, with a view of ascertaining the best position in which we may fight a battle or resist the advance of the enemy. The commanding points on this line I desire to be prepared for occupation by our field guns and the whole line strengthened by such artificial defenses as time and opportunity may permit. My object is to make use of every means in our power to strengthen ourselves and to enable us to fight the enemy to the best advantage. It is not intended to construct a continuous line of defense or to erect extensive works. Having selected the line and put the works in progress of construction, I desire you to resume the examination and see what other positions can be taken nearer Richmond in case of necessity. You will please make requisitions upon the commanders of divisions in the vicinity of the works to be constructed for such working parties as may be necessary. You must also make arrangements to collect such tools as may be with the army, and I have to request that you will push forward the work with the utmost diligence.

I am, very respectfully, your obedient servant,

R. E. LEE,
General

[*War of the Rebellion: A Compilation of the Official Records of the Union and Confederate Armies* (Washington D.C.: Government Printing Office, 1884), vol. 11, part 3, pp. 571–72 (hereafter cited as *OR* 11, pt. 1, 2, or 3).]

After receiving Major *Stevens*'s report *Lee* issued the order for his army to begin constructing the defensive works.

GENERAL ORDERS
No. 62.

HDQRS. DEPT. OF NORTHERN VIRGINIA
June 4, 1862

Division commanders will have 300 men from their respective divisions detailed as pioneers, who, under engineer officers, may be employed as working parties, to throw up earthworks, dig rifle pits, and construct lines of abatis. These men will be borne upon their company rolls and paid as extra-duty men, retaining their arms and equipments. Regimental officers in proportion to details from their regiments—at least 1 to every 35 men—will accompany these details, descriptive rolls being furnished with each company detail. Mechanics, bridge-builders, and laborers volunteering for this duty will be preferred. Officers so detailed will report to Maj. *W. H. Stevens*, Engineer Corps, for duty with their details. Maj. *W. H. Stevens*, engineer department, will make the necessary requisition on his own or the quartermaster's department for implements and material required.

By command of General *Lee:*

R. H. CHILTON,
Assistant Adjutant-General

[*OR* 11, pt. 3, p. 573.]

Although the Army of Northern Virginia created defensive works, *Lee*'s intention was not to stay on the defense but to go on the offense as early as possible. In a letter to President *Jefferson Davis* he outlined what he saw as McClellan's tactic of placing Richmond under siege. *Lee* knew that if he tried to defend against a siege that he would eventually lose to the overwhelming Union numbers.

Confederate defensive earthworks at Chickahominy Bluffs.

Headquarters near Richmond
June 5, 1862

His Excellency President *Davis*,

. . . McClellan will make this a battle of post. He will take position from position, under cover of his heavy guns, and we can not get at him without storming his works, which with our new troops is extremely hazardous. . . . It will require 100,000 men to resist the regular siege of Richmond, which perhaps would only prolong not save it. I am preparing a line that I can hold with part of our forces in front, while with the rest I will endeavour to make a diversion to bring McClellan out. He sticks under his batteries and is working day and night. He is obliged to adhere to the [Richmond and York River] railroad unless he can reach the James River to provision his army.

R. E. Lee
General

[*Lee-Davis* Correspondence, 1862–65, Personal Paper Collection, The Library of Virginia, Richmond, Va.]

Lee had understood McClellan's operational plan exactly. Throughout the last half of May and into June, McClellan continued to bring up forces and establish a supply base at White House on the Pamunkey River. He planned on using the Richmond and York River Railroad to move forward his heavy siege guns and to supply his army.

In military tactics, attacks against a position are categorized as main and supporting attacks. The main attack is the one the commander designs to capture the enemy's position or to achieve the overall objective. Usually it has the majority of troops assigned to it and has priority of supporting artillery fire. The reserve is normally placed so as to be able to support or exploit the success of the main attack. Supporting attacks are designed to bolster the main attack by causing the enemy to disperse his forces and fight in several locations, pin enemy forces in position, cause a premature and incorrect commitment of the enemy's reserve, and confuse the enemy as to which is the main attack. So, it was with *Lee*'s plan to attack McClellan's army. *Lee*'s concept as of mid-June called for part of his army at Richmond to conduct a supporting attack, while Major General *Thomas J. (Stonewall) Jackson* brought his three-division command from the Shenandoah Valley and joining with part of the Army of Northern Virginia conduct the main attack against the north flank of the Army of the Potomac. To increase *Jackson*'s combat power *Lee* sent him units from the Richmond area. This also had a secondary benefit of appearing that *Jackson* was being reinforced for another operation down (north) the Shenandoah Valley. *Lee*'s thinking to this point in time is contained in a letter he sent to *Jackson*.

HEADQUARTERS,
Near Richmond, Va., June 11, 1862.

Brig. Gen. *THOMAS J. JACKSON,*
Commanding Valley District:

GENERAL: Your recent successes have been the cause of the liveliest joy in this army as well as in the country. The admiration excited by your skill and boldness has been constantly mingled with solicitude for your situation. The practicability of re-enforcing you has been the subject of earnest consideration. It has been determined to do so at the expense of weakening this army. Brigadier-General *Lawton* with six regiments from Georgia is on the way to you, and Brigadier-General *Whiting* with eight veteran regiments leaves here to-day. The object is to enable you to crush the forces opposed to you. Leave your enfeebled troops to watch the country and guard the passes covered by your cavalry and artillery, and with your main body, including *Ewell*'s division and *Lawton*'s and *Whiting*'s commands, move rapidly to Ashland by rail or otherwise, as you may find most advantageous, and sweep down between the Chickahominy and Pamunkey, cutting up the enemy's communications, &c., while this army attacks General McClellan in front. He will thus, I think, be forced to come out of his intrenchments, where he is strongly posted on the Chickahominy, and apparently preparing to move by gradual approaches on Richmond. Keep me advised of your movements, and, if practicable, precede your troops, that we may confer and arrange for simultaneous attack.

I am, with great respect, your obedient servant,

R. E. LEE,
General.

[*OR* 11, pt. 3, pp. 589–90.]

After deciding on a basic plan of operations, *Lee* now began to refine it. To do this he needed specific information on the location of the Union right flank north of the Chickahominy River. To obtain this information he ordered a cavalry reconnaissance.

HEADQUARTERS,
Dabbs Farm, Va., June 11, 1862.

Brig. Gen. *J. E. B. STUART,*
Commanding Cavalry:

GENERAL: You are desired to make a secret movement to the rear of the enemy, now posted on Chickahominy, with a view of gaining intelligence of his operations, communications, &c., of driving in his foraging parties, and securing such grain, cattle, &c., for ourselves as you can make arrangements to have driven in. Another object is to destroy his wagon trains, said to be daily passing from the Piping Tree road to his camp on the Chickahominy. The utmost vigilance on your part will be necessary to prevent any surprise to yourself, and the greatest caution must be practiced in keeping well in your front and flanks reliable scouts to give you information.

You will return as soon as the object of your expedition is accomplished, and you must bear constantly in mind, while endeavoring to execute the general purpose of your mission, not to hazard unnecessarily your command or to attempt what your judgment may not approve but be content to accomplish all the good you can without feeling it necessary to obtain all that might be desired. I recommend that you only take such men and horses as can stand the expedition, and that you take every means in your power to save and cherish those you do take. You must leave sufficient cavalry here for the service of this army, and remember that one of the chief objects of your expedition is to gain intelligence for the guidance of future operations.

Information received last evening, the points of which I sent you, lead me to infer that there is a stronger force on the enemy's right than was previously reported. A large body of infantry, as well as cavalry, was reported near the [Virginia] Central Railroad. Should you find upon investigation that the enemy is moving to his right, or is so strongly posted as to render your expedition inopportune—as its success, in my opinion, depends upon its secrecy—you will, after gaining all the information you can, resume your former position.

I am, with great respect, your obedient servant,

R. E. LEE,
General.

[OR 11, pt. 3, pp. 590–91.]

Stuart, with a cavalry force of about 1,200 troopers and a section (two guns) of artillery, on June 12 moved to a location just north of Ashland, which is about twelve miles north of where you are located. The next day he began his reconnaissance of the Union right (north) flank. *Stuart*'s movement carried his cavalry in an easterly direction along the south bank of the Pamunkey River to a location about eighteen miles east of where you are now. Here he crossed the Union supply line along the Richmond and York River Railroad just two miles from the supply base at White House.

Having reached this point *Stuart* had the information that *Lee* needed. Instead of returning the way they had traveled he turned his cavalry south and marched across the rear of the Union army to the James River. Here he turned west and paralleled the north bank of the James River back to Richmond. He arrived there in the early morning hours of June 15.

Lee now knew generally where the right (north) flank of the Army of the Potomac was and completed his plan for going over to the offense. A complete tour and study of *Stuart*'s reconnaissance and ride around the Union army is contained in Appendix V.

In mid-June *Lee* began making preparations to shift part of his army off the defensive lines in front of Richmond. These units were to be used in the attack on the Union right flank. At the same time he dispatched another letter to Jackson. This letter contained *Lee*'s assessment of McClellan's army and his probable future plans. *Lee* also provided *Jackson* with additional details of his own plan and issued instructions for him to leave the Shenandoah Valley and move his force to a location in the vicinity of Ashland prior to attacking the Union right.

HEADQUARTERS,
Near Richmond, Va., June 16, 1862.

Maj. Gen. *THOMAS J. JACKSON,*
Commanding Valley District:

GENERAL: . . . Fremont and Shields are apparently retrograding, their troops shaken and disorganized, and some time will be required to set them again in the field. If this is so, the sooner you unite with this army the better. McClellan is being strengthened; Burnside is with him, and some of McDowell's troops are also reported to have joined him. There is much sickness in his ranks, but his re-enforcements by far exceed his losses. The present, therefore, seems to be favorable for a junction of your army and this. If you agree with me, the sooner you can make arrangements to do so the better. In moving your troops you could let it be understood that it was to pursue the enemy in your front. Dispose those to hold the valley so as to deceive the enemy, keeping your cavalry well in their front, and at the proper time suddenly descending upon the Pamunkey. To be efficacious, the movement must be secret. Let me know the force you can bring, and be careful to guard from friends and foes your purpose and your intention of personally leaving the valley. The country is full of spies, and our plans are immediately carried to the enemy. Please inform me what arrangements you can make for subsisting your troops. Beef-cattle could at least be driven, and if necessary we can subsist on meat alone.

Unless McClellan can be driven out of his intrenchments he will move by positions under cover of his heavy guns within shelling distance of Richmond. I know of no surer way of thwarting him than that proposed. I should like to have the advantage of your views and be able to confer with you. Will meet you at some point on your approach to the Chickahominy. . . .

I am, with great respect, your obedient servant,

R. E. LEE,
General

[*OR* 11, pt. 3, p. 602.]

On June 23 *Lee* held a meeting at his headquarters in the Dabbs House. Four of the most significant subordinates in his plan were there. Present at the meeting were *"Stonewall" Jackson,* who had ridden in from the Shenandoah Valley, and Major Generals *Daniel Harvey Hill, James Longstreet* and *Ambrose Powell Hill.* These generals commanded the maneuver forces in *Lee's* plan. The next day *Lee* issued General Orders Number 75 and placed into motion his plan of offense by using a turning movement against the flank of the Army of the Potomac.

GENERAL ORDERS
No. 75

HDQRS. ARMY OF NORTHERN VIRGINIA,
June 24, 1862

I. General *Jackson's* command will proceed to-morrow from Ashland toward the Slash Church and encamp at some convenient point west of the [Virginia] Central Railroad. *Branch's* brigade, of *A. P. Hill's* division, will also to-morrow evening take position on the Chickahominy near Half Sink. At 3 o'clock Thursday morning, 26th instant, General *Jackson* will advance on the road leading to Pole Green Church, communicating his march to General *Branch*, who will immediately cross the Chickahominy and take the road leading to Mechanicsville. As soon as the movements of these columns are discovered, General *A. P. Hill*, with the rest of his division, will cross the Chickahominy near Meadow Bridge and move direct upon Mechanicsville. To aid his advance, the heavy batteries on the Chickahominy will at the proper time open upon the batteries at Mechanicsville. The enemy being driven from Mechanicsville and the passage across the bridge opened, General *Longstreet*, with his division and that of General *D. H. Hill*, will cross the Chickahominy at or near that point, General *D. H. Hill* moving to the support of General *Jackson* and General *Longstreet* supporting General *A. P. Hill*. The [three] divisions, keeping in communication with each other and moving *en échelon* on separate roads, if practicable, the left division in advance, with skirmishers and sharpshooters extending their front, will sweep down the Chickahominy and endeavor to drive the enemy from his position above New Bridge, General *Jackson* bearing well to his left, turning Beaver Dam Creek and taking the direction toward Cold Harbor. They will then press forward toward the [Richmond and] York River Railroad, closing upon the enemy's rear and forcing him down the Chickahominy. Any advance of the enemy toward Richmond will be prevented by vigorously following his rear and crippling and arresting his progress.

II. The divisions under Generals *Huger* and *Magruder* will hold their positions in front of the enemy against attack, and make such demonstrations Thursday [June 26] as to discover his operations. Should opportunity offer, the feint will be converted into a real attack, and should an abandonment of his intrenchments by the enemy be discovered, he will be closely pursued.

III. The Third Virginia Cavalry will observe the Charles City road. The Fifth Virginia, the First North Carolina, and the Hampton Legion (cavalry) will observe the Darbytown, Varina, and Osborne roads. Should a movement of the enemy down the Chickahominy be discovered, they will close upon his flank and endeavor to arrest his march.

IV. General *Stuart*, with the First, Fourth, and Ninth Virginia Cavalry, the cavalry of *Cobb's* Legion and the *Jeff. Davis* Legion, will cross the Chicka-

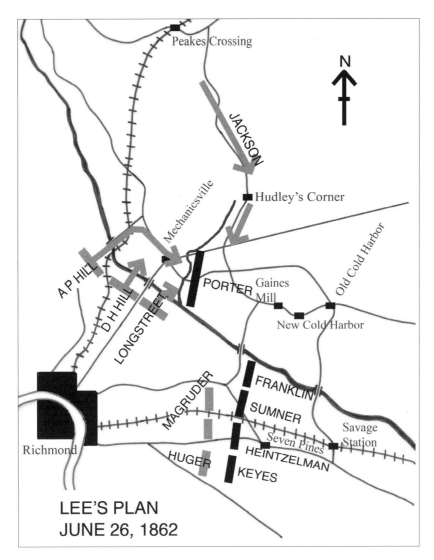

Peakes Crossing

JACKSON

N

Mechanicsville

Hudley's Corner

Old Cold Harbor

A P HILL

D H HILL

LONGSTREET

PORTER

Gaines Mill

New Cold Harbor

MAGRUDER

FRANKLIN

SUMNER

Savage Station

Richmond

HUGER

Seven Pines

HEINTZELMAN

KEYES

LEE'S PLAN
JUNE 26, 1862

hominy to-morrow and take position to the left of General *Jackson*'s line of march. The main body will be held in reserve, with scouts well extended to the front and left. General *Stuart* will keep General *Jackson* informed of the movements of the enemy on his left and will co-operate with him in his advance. The Tenth Virginia Cavalry, Colonel *Davis*, will remain on the Nine-mile road.

V. General *Ransom*'s brigade, of General *Holmes*' command, will be placed in reserve on the Williamsburg road by General *Huger*, to whom he will report for orders.

VI. Commanders of divisions will cause their commands to be provided with three days cooked rations. The necessary ambulances and ordnance trains will be ready to accompany the divisions and receive orders from their respective commanders. Officers in charge of all trains will invariably remain with them. Batteries and wagons will keep on the right of the road. The chief engineer, Major *Stevens*, will assign engineer officers to each division, whose duty it will be to make provision for overcoming all difficulties to the progress of the troops. The staff departments will give the necessary instructions to facilitate the movements herein directed.

By command of General *Lee:*

R. H. CHILTON,
Assistant Adjutant-General.

[*OR* 11, pt. 2, pp. 498–99.]

What *Lee* intended was no less than to force a complete abandonment of the Union position by conducting a turning movement against McClellan's right flank and cutting off his supply line to White House. This would force McClellan to abandon the siege of Richmond and bring his army out of its fortifications into open ground where it could be destroyed by maneuver and attack.

Lee's plan called for *Jackson*'s force to move south from the vicinity of Ashland and turn the right of the Union position north of the Chickahominy River. As *Jackson* approached the rear of the Union position he would communicate his location to *A. P. Hill*, who was then to cross his division over the Chickahominy River at Meadow Bridge. Today this is the bridge over the river on the Richmond-Henrico Turnpike, State Road 627.

After crossing the river *A. P. Hill* was to turn southeast and proceed along the north bank of the Chickahominy River to Mechanicsville. The purpose of *A. P. Hill*'s march to Mechanicsville was to open the crossing of the Chickahominy River by the bridge over the river on the Mechanicsville Turnpike for *D. H. Hill*'s and *Longstreet*'s Divisions. These two division were to cross the river and join with *A. P. Hill*. Then all three divisions would move parallel with the river in a southeast direction.

When the sweep of *A. P. Hill*, *D. H. Hill*, and *Longstreet* had proceeded about three miles from Mechanicsville it would have reached New Bridge. There the attacking force could make contact with the Confederates south of the Chickahominy River.

Jackson in the meantime was to continue his attack toward Old Cold Harbor in the rear of the Union flank. This attack was designed to take *Jackson* across the Union railroad and road supply lines that came out of White House.

While the main attack was developing north of the Chicka-hominy River the forces of Major Generals *John B. Magruder* and *Benjamin Huger* were to occupy the defensive positions in front of Richmond and conduct demonstrations to hold Union forces in position on the south side of the river. If the opportunity presented itself they were to attack the Union force as they retreated.

The majority of the cavalry, under *Stewart,* was to cover *Jackson*'s left (east) flank as he came down upon the rear of the Union position.

A recapitulation of the situation as Lee saw it and his operation concept are contained in his report of the campaign.

Report of General *Robert E. Lee,* CSA, Commanding Army of Northern Virginia

After the battle of Seven Pines the Federal Army, under General McClellan, preparatory to an advance upon Richmond, proceeded to fortify its position on the Chickahominy and to perfect communications with its base of supplies near the head of York River. Its left was established south of the Chickahominy, between White Oak Swamp and New Bridge, defended by a line of strong works, access to which, except by a few narrow roads, was obstructed by felling the dense forests in front. These roads were commanded for a great distance by the heavy guns in the fortifications. The right wing lay north of the Chickahominy, extending beyond Mechanicsville, and the approaches from the south side were strongly defended by intrenchments. Our army was around Richmond, the divisions of *Huger* and *Magruder,* supported by those of *Longstreet* and *D. H. Hill,* in front of the enemy's left, and that of *A. P. Hill* extending from *Magruder*'s left beyond Meadow Bridge.

The command of General *Jackson,* including *Ewell*'s division, operating in the Shenandoah Valley, had succeeded in diverting the army of McDowell at Fredericksburg from uniting with that of McClellan. To render this diversion more decided, and effectually mask his withdrawal from the valley at the proper time, *Jackson,* after the defeat of Frémont and Shields, was re-enforced by *Whiting*'s division, composed of *Hood*'s Texas brigade and his own, under Colonel *Law,* from Richmond, and that of *Lawton,* from the south.

The intention of the enemy seemed to be to attack Richmond by regular approaches. The strength of his left wing rendered a direct assault injudicious, if not impracticable. It was therefore determined to construct defensive lines, so as to enable a part of the army to defend the city and leave the other part free to cross the Chickahominy and operate on the north bank. By sweeping down the river on that side and threatening his communications with York River it was thought that the enemy would be compelled to retreat or give battle out of his intrenchments. The plan was submitted to His Excellency the President, who was repeatedly on the field in the course of its execution.

While preparations were in progress a cavalry expedition, under General *Stuart,* was made around the rear of the Federal Army to ascertain its position and movements. This was executed with great address and daring by that accomplished officer. As soon as the defensive works were sufficiently advanced General *Jackson* was directed to move rapidly and secretly from the valley, so as to arrive in the vicinity of Ashland by June 24.

The enemy appeared to be unaware of our purpose, and on the 25th attacked General *Huger* on the Williamsburg road, with the intention, as ap-

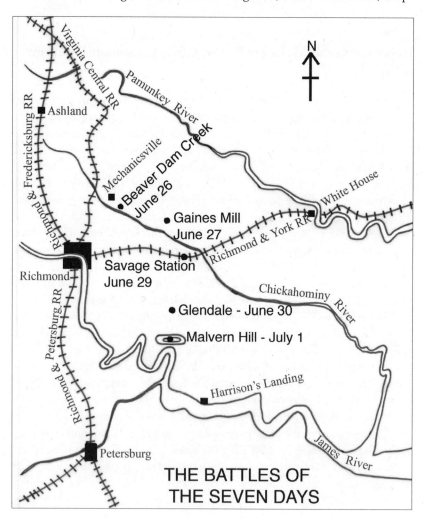

THE BATTLES OF
THE SEVEN DAYS

peared by a dispatch from General McClellan, of securing his advance toward Richmond. The effort was successfully resisted and our line maintained.

According to the general order of battle, a copy of which is annexed, General *Jackson* was to march from Ashland on the 25th in the direction of Slash Church, encamping for the night west of the [Virginia] Central Railroad, and to advance at 3 a.m. on the 26th and turn Beaver Dam Creek. *A. P. Hill* was to cross the Chickahominy at Meadow Bridge when *Jackson*'s advance beyond that point should be known and move directly upon Mechanicsville. As soon as the Mechanicsville Bridge should be uncovered *Longstreet* and *D. H. Hill* were to cross, the latter to proceed to the support of *Jackson* and the former to that of *A. P. Hill*. The four commands were directed to sweep down the north side of the Chickahominy toward the [Richmond and] York River Railroad, *Jackson* on the left and in advance, *Longstreet* nearest the river and in the rear. *Huger* and *Magruder* were ordered to hold their positions against any assault of the enemy, to observe his movements, and follow him closely should he retreat. General *Stuart*, with the cavalry, was thrown out on *Jackson*'s left to guard his flank and give notice of the enemy's movements. Brigadier-General *Pendleton* was directed to employ the Reserve Artillery, so as to resist any approach of the enemy toward Richmond, to superintend that portion of it posted to aid in the operations of the north bank, and hold the remainder ready for use when it might be required. [*OR* 11, pt. 2, pp. 489–90.]

From this location you will now follow the attack of *A. P. Hill*'s Division as it moved on Mechanicsville and the strong Union position at Beaver Dam Creek

Before you leave this position you may wish to look at what remains of some of the earthwork dug by *Lee*'s army.

Return to your car for the drive to Stop 2.

Chapter 2

Battle of Beaver Dam Creek
Thursday, June 26, 1862

Drive back to Highway 360, Mechanicsville Turnpike. Make a left turn onto Highway 360 and drive for 0.4 mile to the intersection with East Laburnum Avenue. Turn right onto East Laburnum Avenue and drive for 1.6 miles to the Richmond-Henrico Turnpike, State Highway 627. Turn right on to the Richmond-Henrico Turnpike and drive for 1.9 miles. Pull off to the side of the road just after you cross the railroad tracks at the end of this 1.9-mile segment. There is a historical placard to the left directly across the road.

Stop 2—Meadow Bridge

Here is the area where *A. P. Hill*'s Division was concentrated on the morning of June 26. The Chickahominy River is 0.4 mile ahead. There was a road and bridge where the current road and bridge are today. In 1862 the bridge was called Meadow Bridge. The tracks of the Virginia Central Railroad also crossed the river at this location but on the opposite side of the bridge from where the railroad tracks are now. A Union outpost line occupied the ground on the other side of the river. Stop 1 and *Lee*'s position is 3,900 yards, 2.2 miles, to the right.

Lee's plan was for *A. P. Hill*'s Division to cross the Chickahominy River and initially march to Mechanicsville. When *A. P. Hill* reached Mechanicsville, the divisions of *James Longstreet* and *Daniel H. Hill*, located in the area of Stop 1, would move forward and cross the river on or in the vicinity of the Mechanicsville Bridge. The signal for the movement of *A. P. Hill* was to be the arrival of *Jackson*'s command on the right rear of the Union force at Beaver Dam Creek.

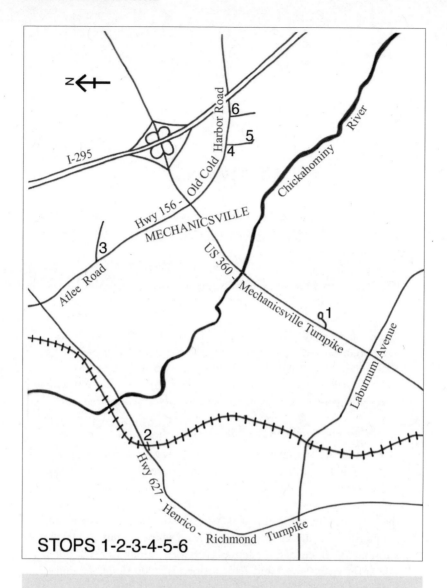

STOPS 1-2-3-4-5-6

The Confederate forces should have crossed the river sometime in the morning of June 26. However, *Jackson* was late in arriving behind the Union flank. In mid-afternoon *A. P. Hill* decided rather than risk a complete breakdown of the plan he would cross the Chickahominy and move to Mechanicsville.

Report of Maj. Gen. *Ambrose P. Hill*, CSA, Commanding Light Division (*Hill's* Division), Army of Northern Virginia

In obedience to orders, received from the general commanding, on Wednesday night, June 25, I concentrated my division near the Meadow Bridge, viz: The brigades of *J. R. Anderson, Gregg, Field, Pender,* and *Archer,* the brigade of General *Branch* having been directed to move to the bridge some 7 miles above, where the Brooke turnpike crosses the Chickahominy. . . .

My orders were that General *Jackson,* moving down from Ashland, would inform General *Branch* of his near approach. As soon as *Jackson* crossed the Central Railroad, *Branch* was to cross the Chickahominy, and, taking the river road, push on and clear the Meadow Bridge. This done, I was to cross at Meadow Bridge, and, sweeping down to Mechanicsville, open the way for General *Longstreet* [and *D. H. Hill*]. It was expected that General *Jackson* would be in the position assigned him by early dawn, and all my preparations were made with the view of moving early. General *Branch,* however, did not receive intelligence from General *Jackson* until about 10 o'clock, when he immediately crossed and proceeded to carry out his instructions. He was delayed by the enemy's skirmishers and advanced but slowly.

Three o'clock having arrived, and no intelligence from *Jackson* or *Branch,* I determined to cross at once rather than hazard the failure of the whole plan by longer deferring it. General *Field,* already selected for the advance, being in readiness, seized the bridge, and the Fortieth Virginia, Colonel *Brockenbrough,* leading, his brigade passed over, meeting but slight opposition, the enemy falling back to Mechanicsville. . . . [*OR* 11, pt. 2, pp. 834–35.]

> *A. P. Hill's* orders to his brigade commanders was for their brigades to cross Meadow Bridge and move on the road to Mechanicsville, in the order of *Field's, Anderson's, Archer's, Pender's,* and *Gregg's* Brigades. Brigadier General *Charles W. Field* the night before had placed one of his regiments on picket duty overlooking the bridge.

Report of Col. *Francis Mallory,* CSA, Commanding Fiftyfifth Virginia Infantry, *Field's* Brigade, *A. P. Hill's* Division, Army of Northern Virginia

On the night of Wednesday, June 25, the regiment was on picket near the Little Meadow Bridge. About 3 p.m. Thursday, June 26, it being reported

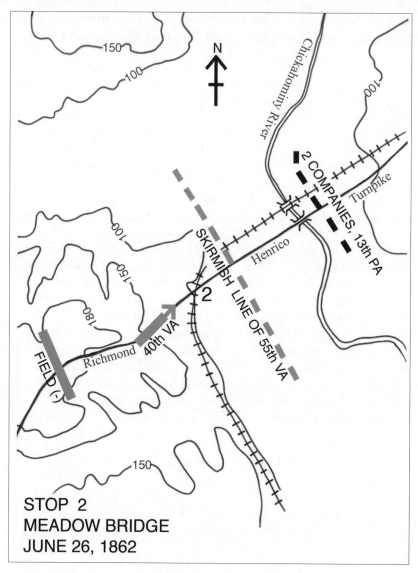

STOP 2
MEADOW BRIDGE
JUNE 26, 1862

that the enemy's picket had been withdrawn, I immediately took possession of the bridge which he had held. Our brigade, being in advance, was soon ordered to cross. The Fortieth Virginia crossed first, followed by the Fifty-fifth Virginia and the other regiments composing the brigade. A mile or more beyond the swamp [river] the regiment was formed in line of battle across the road, where the first prisoner was taken by Capt. *J. F. Alexander*'s company. It was here that we received a few shots from the enemy's picket, who retreated in haste. [*OR* 11, pt. 2, p. 846.]

The pickets near Meadow Bridge were two companies of the Thirteenth Pennsylvania Reserves. Once the bridge had been secured, the Fortieth Virginia Regiment crossed over the river and became the leading element of *Field*'s Brigade. Departing this location you will now follow *Field*'s Brigade as it moved on the Union positions in and around Mechanicsville.

Continue driving on the Richmond-Henrico Turnpike for 1.6 miles to Atlee Road. Turn right on Atlee Road and drive for 0.6 mile to Rose Hill Drive. Turn left on Rose Hill Drive and drive for 0.1 mile. Pull off to the side and stop.

Stop 3—*Field*'s Brigade Deploys

Field's Brigade did not follow the road over Meadow Bridge all the way to the intersection as you did. Instead, his regiments took a shortcut using farm roads and emerged on Atlee Road just prior to where you turned onto Rose Hill Drive. About here *Field* was forced to deploy his brigade into a line of battle. The ground to your front was an open farm field with a rise in the ground at about one thousand yards. On this rise were posted Union artillery and infantry. Also in Mechanicsville were a Union skirmish line and Battery B, First Pennsylvania Artillery. This artillery opened fire on *Field*'s Brigade as it marched down the Atlee Road toward Mechanicsville, which is 0.9 mile away.

Report of Brig. Gen. *Charles W. Field*, CSA, Commanding *Field*'s Brigade, *A. P. Hill*'s Division, Army of Northern Virginia

It was 3 p.m. on the 26th when Maj. Gen. *A. P. Hill*, commanding the division, directed me to wait no longer, but to cross and attack the enemy at Mechanicsville. The enemy made no opposition to my passage of the Chickahominy, but, posting skirmishers in a thick wood about a mile beyond, fired on the advance, wounding 1 man, and himself losing 1 captured.

From this point [Meadow Bridge] to Mechanicsville the road was open, but as I approached that place a heavy fire from several batteries on my left and front and from sharpshooters, all behind intrenchments, was opened. Forming my brigade in line of battle, the Fifty-fifth and Sixtieth Virginia on the right of the road and the Fortieth and Forty-seventh Virginia and Second Virginia Battalion on the left and *Pegram*'s battery in the center, we steadily

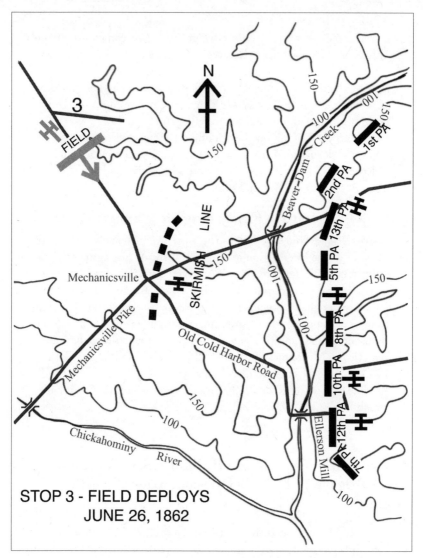

STOP 3 - FIELD DEPLOYS
JUNE 26, 1862

and in perfect line advanced upon the enemy, the infantry and artillery occasionally halting for a moment to deliver fire. Gaining the cross-roads, where
it was known batteries had been posted and were supposed still to be, it was
found to be unoccupied. Meanwhile an active and vigorous fire was opened
on us from the batteries situated on the [east] side of Beaver Dam Creek. I
changed front to the left by throwing forward the right wing, and advanced
to attack them, directing Captain *Pegram* to take position and open fire on
the enemy's batteries, a part of General *Archer*'s brigade having been ordered
by General *Hill* to support me. [*OR* 11, pt. 2, p. 841.]

Mechanicsville in the 1860s. Library of Congress.

Depart this location by turning around and driving back to Atlee Road. Turn left on Atlee Road and drive for 0.9 mile to the intersection with the Mechanicsville Turnpike, where there is a stoplight and Atlee Road becomes the Old Cold Harbor Road and State Highway 156. Continue through the intersection and drive for 0.7 mile, at which point there will be a road to the right that goes to Beaver Dam Creek. Look for a National Park sign—"Beaver Dam Creek, Richmond National Battlefield Park, NEXT RIGHT"—just before the bridge. Before the intersection with this park road, pull to the side and stop. Get out of your car and position yourself so you can see the bridge and the ground on either side of Beaver Dam Creek. Be careful of traffic.

Stop 4—Beaver Dam Creek

Atlee Road from Stop 3 to this location was here in 1862. This side of Mechanicsville it was called the Old Cold Harbor Road. In 1862 the road you are on made a right turn where the park road is today. From there it continued on for 0.2 mile, where it crossed Beaver Dam Creek. After it crossed the creek it went through the Union defensive position then turned left and came back out to join this road on the other side of the modern bridge, about where you see a road coming from the right. The part of the road from where you are to the intersection on the other side of the bridge was not there in 1862. Beaver Dam Creek is in the low ground directly in front of you. Although there were woods to your left and rear, much of the ground was open and provided good fields of fire and observation.

The divisions of Brigadier General Fitz John Porter's Fifth Corps were deployed along the high ground east of Beaver Dam Creek. As you look at the Union position, Brigadier General George A. McCall's division was deployed from the north side of today's Highway 360, to your left, in a southern direction for approximately 3,100 yards. The brigade of Brigadier General John Reynolds held the right of the Union line. This brigade's right (north) flank was north of today's Highway 360. Reynolds's line extended south to just north of where the millpond was in 1862. This is to your left front. Brigadier General Truman Seymour's brigade held the left of the Union position. Seymour's brigade was astride the old road as it climbed up onto the high ground east of the creek. Supporting artillery, with good fields of fire, was deployed with the defending infantry. The division reserve, Brigadier General George G. Meade's brigade was deployed just behind the center of the defensive line. A supporting force consisting of Brigadier General George W. Morell's division was located east of the defensive position.

Report of Brig. Gen. George A. McCall, USA, Commanding Third Division, Fifth Corps, Army of the Potomac

On the afternoon of the 19th June I received your [Porter's] orders requiring the "greater part" of my division to move forward from Gaines' farm, where I was then encamped, about 2½ miles from Mechanicsville, and relieve Taylor's brigade, of [Slocum's] division, at the above-named village, then the extreme right of the Army of the Potomac. In accordance with this order I directed the First and Third Brigades, commanded respectively by Brig. Gens. J. F. Reynolds and T. Seymour, to proceed to Beaver Dam Creek, 1 mile this side of Mechanicsville, and occupy a strong position on its left bank near its junction with the Chickahominy, and thence to throw forward to the heights in front of Mechanicsville one regiment and a battery to relieve Taylor, and to post a strong line of pickets from the Mechanicsville Bridge to the Meadow Bridge. The position selected on the Beaver Dam Creek was naturally a strong one, the left resting on the Chickahominy and the right extending to thick woods beyond the upper Mechanicsville road, which were occupied. The passage of the Beaver Dam Creek was difficult throughout the greater part of my front, and, with the exception of the roads crossing at Ellison's [Ellerson] Mill and that above mentioned, impracticable for artillery. On the right of the last-named road an epaulement calculated for four pieces of field artillery was thrown up and rifle pits for a regiment each were constructed in advance of each brigade. Cooper's battery of six 10-pounder Parrott guns on the right of the upper road and Smead's battery (regular) of four 12-pounder guns on the left commanded that approach. De Hart's battery (regular) of six 12-pounder guns was near the front-center, commanding a more distant view of the same road and also the lower road direct to Mechanicsville. I held in reserve the Second Brigade (Meade's) in front of Gaines' farm, ready to act either in support of Reynolds and Seymour or to oppose the crossing at New Bridge should the enemy attempt it.

At about noon on the 26th the enemy was discovered to be in motion, and at 12.30 p.m. our pickets at Meadow Bridge were driven in by the advancing column of the enemy, and those along the road were ordered to fall back. Soon afterward, when the head of his column approached, my infantry and artillery in front of Mechanicsville were recalled. I now ordered forward Meade's brigade, and directed them to occupy ground in rear of the line, where they would be out of the range of musketry and at a practicable distance for support of any part of the field. [*OR* 11, pt. 2, pp. 384–85.]

It was not *Lee*'s plan for *A. P. Hill* to attack the Union position at Beaver Dam Creek. *Jackson*'s arrival on the right rear of the Union position was designed to cause the defenders to retreat or face being cut off. However, *Jackson* did not arrive as planned, and *A. P. Hill* was committed to a frontal attack against a formidable defensive position.

The lead brigade, *Field*'s, of *A. P. Hill*'s division, had deployed astride this road north of Mechanicsville and moved southeast. When *Field*'s Brigade reached that location it turned to the left in response to the Union fire from the other side of Beaver Dam Creek. *Hill*'s next brigade in the order of march was Brigadier General *Joseph R. Anderson*'s brigade. *Anderson*'s Brigade turned off the Atlee Road while still north of Mechanicsville, deployed into a battle line and attacked towards the north flank of the Union position. Brigadier General *James J. Archer*'s brigade was third in the line of march. This brigade was deployed in a line of battle and moved up on *Field*'s left, so as to be between *Anderson* and *Field*. *Archer's* Brigade was directly north of where you are. Its left flank was just south of where Highway 360, the Mechanicsville Turnpike, is today.

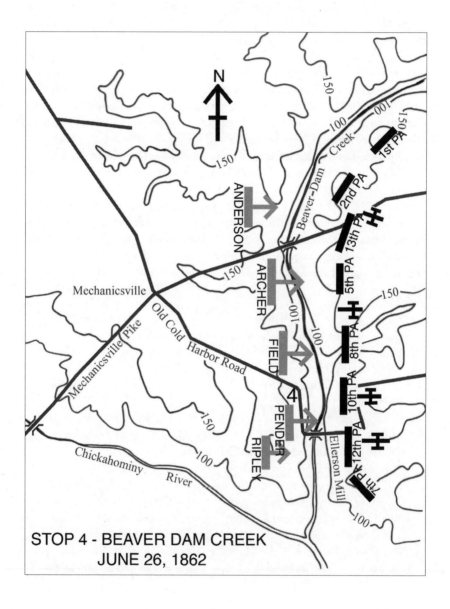

STOP 4 - BEAVER DAM CREEK
JUNE 26, 1862

Report of Brig. Gen. *James J. Archer*, CSA, Commanding *Archer*'s Brigade, *A. P. Hill*'s Division, Army of Northern Virginia

I have the honor to report that [on] the evening of June 26, by direction of Maj. Gen. *A. P. Hill,* I marched my brigade, 1,228 strong, into Mechanicsville and thence up the Mechanicsville turnpike in line of battle, the left flank guided by the line of the turnpike (today Highway 360); the Nineteenth Georgia (Lieut. Col. *T. C. Johnson*) on the left, the First Tennessee (Lieut. Col. *J. C. Shackelford*) on the right, the Fifth Alabama Battalion (Captain *Van de Graaff*) and Seventh Tennessee (Col. *John F. Goodner*) supporting. The Fourteenth Tennessee (Col. *W. A. Forbes*) became separated from me during the movement, and becoming involved with General *Field*'s brigade, did not join me until night.

The brigade moved on steadily to the Beaver Dam Creek under a heavy fire of artillery and rifles from the batteries and strongly intrenched positions of the enemy on the opposite bank. Night closed in before a crossing could be effected. We remained through the night in possession of the ground we had gained and the next morning the enemy abandoned their works.

My loss in this action was 43 killed and 171 wounded; among the former was Lieutenant-Colonel *Johnson,* commanding Nineteenth Georgia, who fell gallantly cheering his men in battle; and among the latter the gallant and efficient Captain *Van de Graaff,* commanding the Fifth Alabama Battalion. [*OR* 11, pt. 2, p. 897.]

Maneuvering on *Archer*'s right, *Field*'s Brigade attacked across the ground to the left.

Report of Brig. Gen. *Charles W. Field,* CSA (Continued)

About a mile of open ground was to be gotten over, most of which was swept by three or four batteries, but the brigade in the original order gallantly moved forward, though their ranks were momentarily thinned by the most destructive cannonading I have yet known. Our only safety from this fire lay in pushing forward as rapidly as possible and getting so close to the enemy's infantry as to draw the fire upon his own troops should it be continued. He occupied a wooded hill-side overlooking Beaver Dam Creek. Gaining a dense thicket on this side, the stream only separating us, both sides opened with the musket and continued it until about 9 o'clock at night. [*OR* 11, pt. 2, p. 841.]

The Sixtieth Virginia Infantry was the regiment on the extreme right of *Field*'s line of battle. As the brigade wheeled to the left, this regiment passed just to your left and attacked the Union position on the other side of the creek.

Report of Col. *William E. Starke*, CSA, Commanding Sixtieth Virginia Infantry, *Field*'s Brigade, *A. P. Hill*'s Division, Army of Northern Virginia

Advancing steadily [along Atlee Road] we forced the enemy to abandon Mechanicsville. Immediately beyond this point we encountered a severe fire from their batteries in crossing an open field in their front.

In obedience to orders the direction was changed to the left, and marching by that flank we reached the cover of the woods [behind you], where we were halted. Here we were exposed for a few moments to a most galling fire from the enemy's batteries, under which fire I was wounded in the hand, and turned over the command of the regiment to Lieut. Col. *B. H. Jones,* to whom I am indebted for the facts connected with the report from that time until I resumed the command.

Proceeding through this wood another field was crossed and another wood again entered, where the enemy were drawn up in line of battle on the crest of a hill on the opposite side of a small branch in the ravine in front of us. Advancing through this wood [to your left], the regiment having been wheeled into line of battle, we moved down the side of the hill, took our position in rear of the forces of a brigade immediately in our front, and opened fire upon the enemy. Here for at least two hours the battle raged most violently.

Our loss here was considerable, Lieut. *S. Lilly,* of Company I, being killed; Capt. *John L. Caynor* and Lieut. *P.M. Paxton,* of Company F, and Lieut. *S. D. Pack,* of Company A, being wounded, and many privates both killed and wounded. [*OR* 11, pt. 2, p. 849.]

Report of Maj. Gen. *Ambrose P. Hill*, CSA (Continued)

Beaver Dam Creek curves around Mechanicsville, the high banks being on the [east] side and in possession of the enemy. This naturally strong line of defense had been made very much stronger by rifle pits and earthen epaulements for guns.

The enemy opened a concentric fire of artillery on the head of *Field*'s column, who, throwing his brigade into line of battle, with *Pegram* in the center, steadily advancing, drove the enemy from Mechanicsville.

Anderson was ordered to make a flank movement to the left, and take in reverse a battery, which was spiteful in its activity, while *McIntosh* [Battery] was sent forward to attract its attention and keep it employed. *Archer* was moved up to the support of *Field,* and formed line on his (*Field's*) left, with his own left resting on the turnpike. *Braxton* [Battery] was sent in to the assistance of *McIntosh*. *Gregg* and *Pender* approached the village in line of battle over the hills and open fields from the direction of the river. *Field* had driven the enemy from the village and its surroundings across Beaver Dam Creek to his stronghold. *Archer* swept along to his left, and with the same result. *Pender* was ordered to support these brigades already engaged, and to take position on the right of *Field.* This was gallantly done in the face of a murderous fire. *Andrews* [Battery] galloped up to the assistance of *Pegram.*

The battle now raged furiously along my whole line; the artillery fire from the enemy was terrific. Their position along Beaver Dam Creek was too strong to be carried by a direct attack without heavy loss, and expecting every moment to hear *Jackson's* guns on my left and in rear of the enemy, I forbore to order the storming of their lines. General *Branch,* having come up, was ordered forward as a support to the brigades already engaged, and *Johnson's* battery took position near *McIntosh* and *Braxton*. *Gregg* was held in reserve near Mechanicsville. The Thirty-eighth North Carolina, Colonel [*William J.*] *Hoke,* and the Thirty-fourth North Carolina, Colonel [*Richard H.*] *Riddick,* of *Pender's* brigade, made a gallant but abortive attempt to force a crossing. [*OR* 11, pt. 2, p. 835.]

Return to your car. Make an immediate right on to the old road. Drive for 0.2 mile to the parking lot, park, get out of your car, and face east.

Stop 5, Position A—Ellerson Mill

Directly in front of you is Beaver Dam Creek. The ground behind you and in front of you, except for scrub growth along the creek, was more open in 1862 than it is today. Ellerson Mill was located just on the other side of the creek. In 1862 this road continued across the creek and up onto the high ground to your front. From there it made a left turn, then a right turn, and then continued on to Old Cold Harbor. The Union Fifth Corps used part of this road when it retreated from this position on the morning of June 27. Confederate forces moving to attack the Union position near Gaines Mill also used the road.

The Union defense at this point were elements of Brigadier General Truman Seymour's brigade. The defensive line was located 125 yards from here. Brigadier General *William Dorsey Pender* commanded the Confederate brigade that was deployed in a battle line that ran from Stop 4 to this location. It attacked the Union position directly in front of you.

Pender's Brigade was fourth in *A. P. Hill*'s order of march and was the next brigade of *A. P. Hill*'s Division to be committed to the fight. *Pender* had crossed the Chickahominy River at Meadow Bridge and moved along the road to Mechanicsville. As he approached Mechanicsville *Pender* was ordered by *A. P. Hill* to move into line to the right of *Field* and support his brigade. As he began deploying he came under artillery fire from the Union position south of Ellerson Mill. *Pender* moved his brigade farther to the right to confront this part of the Union position. Where you are standing was the center of *Pender*'s right regiment, the Thirty-fourth North Carolina.

Report of Brig. Gen. *William D. Pender*, CSA, Commanding *Pender*'s Brigade, *A. P. Hill*'s Division, Army of Northern Virginia

Upon reaching Mechanicsville I was ordered by you [*A. P. Hill*] to support General *Field*. I at once made my dispositions to do so, but soon found that by taking the direction General *Field* was going [it] left his right much exposed to a heavy fire of artillery, which was playing at the same time on *Pegram*'s battery with great effect. This artillery was obliquely to the right and lower down Beaver Dam Creek than I saw any troops going. I at once changed the direction of two of my regiments, so as to bring them to the right of this artillery, and succeeded in getting within 150 or 200 yards of it before we were opened upon, but when they did open upon us it was destructive, and the obstacles so great in front, the creek and mill-dam, that after the Thirty-eighth North Carolina had reached these obstacles, and within less than 100 yards of the enemy's rifle pits, they had to fall back. This regiment here advanced boldly and maintained its ground well. The Thirty-fourth North Carolina—the other regiment that had been led by me to the right—had made too much of a detour, and did not come up until the Thirty-eighth had been repulsed. After bringing it up I sent it farther to the right, to make as much diversion as possible in that direction.

General *Ripley* at this time came up with his brigade, advancing over part of the same ground, which had been passed by the Thirty-eighth North

Carolina, directly in front of the mill. The Thirty-fourth North Carolina advanced to the creek and there maintained its position until after dark, when I had it withdrawn, so that with this and General *Ripley* with part of his brigade we held the extreme right of our position until about daylight next morning, when I was relieved. General *Ripley* had been relieved before.

Other brigades came up during the night. The Twenty-second North Carolina, which had followed to support General *Field,* when getting to the creek near him, came suddenly upon a regiment of the enemy, just across the run, and after some little parley opened fire, driving the enemy quickly away, but found it impossible to cross. The loss of this regiment here was also very heavy; among others its brave colonel (*Conner*) received a severe wound in the leg.

I should state, while relating the incidents of this day's fight, that Colonel *Hoke* (Thirty-eighth North Carolina) was also wounded and had to leave the field. The adjutant of the Thirty-eighth was wounded also, but nobly maintained his position until after dark. [*OR* 11, pt. 2, p. 899.]

> The Thirty-fourth North Carolina and Thirty-eighth North Carolina Infantry Regiments had fought where you are and to your left. The majority of the casualties in *Pender*'s Brigade were in these two regiments.
>
> The divisions of Major Generals *James Longstreet* and *Daniel H. Hill* were concealed behind the high ground, in the vicinity of Stop 1, on the other side of the Chickahominy River. As *A. P. Hill*'s Division attacked south from Meadow Bridge it captured the ground east of Mechanicsville Bridge. This was to allow *Longstreet*'s and *D. H. Hill*'s Divisions to cross the Chickahominy, but *A. P. Hill*'s brigades opened the Mechanicsville Bridge too late in the afternoon for both divisions to be committed to the fight. However, *D. H. Hill* was able to cross over Brigadier General *Roswell S. Ripley*'s brigade and send it to support the right of *Pender*'s Brigade.
>
> Two regiments of *Ripley*'s Brigade, the Forty-fourth Georgia and First North Carolina, attacked over the ground to the right of where you are standing. Both regiments suffered severe casualties.

Report of Brig. Gen. *Roswell S. Ripley,* CSA, Commanding *Ripley*'s Brigade, *D. H. Hill*'s Division, Army of Northern Virginia

I have the honor to report that on the morning of Thursday, June 26, the brigade under my command, consisting of the First and Third Regiments North Carolina troops and Forty-fourth and Forty-eighth Regiments of

Georgia Volunteers, marched from its position near the Williamsburg road, about 5 miles from Richmond, to a point in the vicinity of the batteries commanding the bridge over the Chickahominy River, on the Mechanicsville turnpike.

With other troops at that point the brigade lay waiting orders until near 4 p.m., when it was ordered to cross the Chickahominy in advance of the division, and effect a junction with the troops of Maj. Gen. *A. P. Hill*'s command, then moving down the Chickahominy in the direction of Mechanicsville. The order was executed and the infantry crossed at once, forming line of battle across the road leading to the village, about half a mile in advance of the bridge. Upon communicating with General *A. P. Hill* I was informed that the enemy had a strong and well-served battery and force in position near Ellison's [Ellerson's] Mill, something over a mile to the east of the road, to attack which he had sent Brigadier-General *Pender*'s brigade by the right and other troops to the left, and it was arranged that my brigade was to cooperate. The enemy had opened on the Mechanicsville road and was rapidly verifying the range. My brigade changed front and advanced to the brow of the hill opposite the enemy's battery, expecting, if possible, to use artillery in the attack. While the troops were in motion I received orders to assault the enemy from General *Lee* and also from Maj. Gen. *D. H. Hill*, the latter of whom directed me to send two regiments to support General *Pender*, on my right, and attack the battery in front with the remainder of my force. The Forty-fourth Georgia, under Col. *Robert A. Smith*, and the First North Carolina, under Colonel [*M. S.*] *Stokes*, marched at once to the right, while the Forty-eighth Georgia, under Colonel [*William*] *Gibson*, and Third North Carolina, under Colonel [*Gaston*] *Meares*, moved to a position in front of the enemy on their left.

Meanwhile the passage of the Chickahominy by the artillery had been impeded by the broken bridges, and night coming on and it being deemed important to attack the position at once, the advance was ordered along the whole line. General *Pender*'s brigade and the two regiments of my own advanced rapidly on the right, while the remainder of my command moved against the front, driving back the enemy from his advanced positions and closing in upon the batteries and their heavy infantry supports, all of which poured upon our troops a heavy and incessant fire of shell, canister, and musketry. The ground was rugged and intersected by ditches and hedges and covered with abatis a short distance in front of the position to be assaulted. A mill-race, with scarped banks, and in some places waist-deep in water, ran along the front of the enemy at a distance ranging from 50 to 100 yards. To this position our troops succeeded in advancing, notwithstanding the fire of the enemy was exceedingly heavy and our loss extremely severe. Of the Forty-fourth Georgia Col. *Robert A. Smith* and Lieutenant-Colonel [*John B.*]

Estes fell wounded, the former mortally, besides 2 captains and 10 lieutenants killed and wounded. Of the First North Carolina Colonel *Stokes* was mortally wounded, Lieutenant-Colonel [*John A.*] *McDowell* severely wounded, and Major [*T. L.*] *Skinner* killed, with 6 captains and lieutenants of the regiment killed and wounded, including the adjutant. The Forty-eighth Georgia and Third North Carolina had a more advantageous position, and suffered less severely than the former regiments, although the Third lost its major (*Edward Savage*), wounded. The loss of non-commissioned officers and privates was heavy in the extreme, amounting in the Forty-fourth Georgia to 321 and in the First North Carolina to 133.

Near dark Capt. *A. Burnet Rhett*'s battery of artillery, attached to my command, succeeded in crossing the broken bridges over the Chickahominy, and was located directly in front of the enemy at about 1,200 yards' distance. Captain *Rhett* opened an effective fire, and soon relieved our infantry from the storm of shell and canister which had been poured upon them. It was soon re-enforced by another battery, and a fire was kept up on the enemy until late in the evening.

Some time after night-fall, under cover of the cannonade, our troops were withdrawn to a point of woods a few hundred yards' distance, near the angle of our line of battle, which position was held by the Third North Carolina and Forty-eighth Georgia and a portion of General *Pender*'s brigade. The fragments of the First North Carolina and Forty-fourth Georgia were rallied some distance in the rear under some difficulty, owing to the loss of all their field and many of their company officers, who fell while gallantly performing their duty. [*OR* 11, pt. 2, pp. 647–48.]

Walk to the footbridge over Beaver Dam Creek. Cross the bridge and follow the walking path for one hundred yards. Walk twenty-five yards past the park tablet "The Pennsylvanians Stand Firm" stop; turn around and face the way you just came. You are now looking to the west. There is a marker next to the park tablet that gives the general location of where Ellerson Mill was located.

If the footbridge is not usable there is an alternate route to Position B. Drive back to Highway 156, turn right, and drive 0.2 mile to Harbor Hill Road. Turn right on Harbor Hill Road and drive 0.2 mile to Old Cold Harbor Road. Take a right on Old Cold Harbor Road and drive to the bottom of the hill. Park, get out of your car, and walk west down the trail to just before the park tablet "The Pennsylvanians Stand Firm."

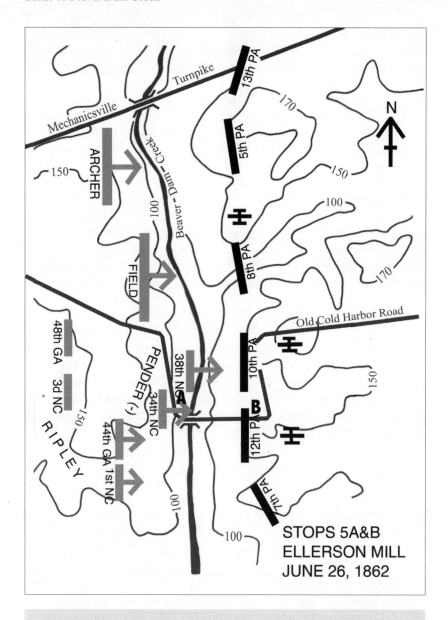

STOPS 5A&B
ELLERSON MILL
JUNE 26, 1862

Position B—The Union Defense at Ellerson Mill

You are in the south center part of the Union defensive position. This position was 3,100 yards long. It went from a point 2,300 yards to your right (north) to a point 800 yards to your left (south). The infantry was generally on the same line as you are on now, with the artillery higher up on the ridge. Brigadier General George A. McCall's

Old Cold Harbor Road at Ellerson Mill today. Stop 5B and Union line was about where the fence is across the road.

Third Division, Fifth Corps, defended the position. Known as the Pennsylvania Reserves, the division was composed of thirteen Pennsylvania infantry regiments that were divided into three brigades. Four artillery batteries supported the infantry regiments. Within the ranks of this division were a future army commander, two corps commanders, and numerous brigade commanders.

The regiment to the right of where you are was the Tenth Pennsylvania Reserves. The regiment's left flank was located about fifty yards to your right (north) on the other side of a small draw. The Tenth's line extended north to the other side of today's Highway 156.

The Union regiment defending the road was the Twelfth Pennsylvania Reserves. You are standing in the right part of the regiment's position. This regiment's right flank touched the draw fifty yards to your right. The regiments left flank was two hundred yards to your left. A two-gun section of artillery from Captain James H. Cooper's Battery B, First Pennsylvania Light Artillery, under command of First Lieutenant James S. Fullerton, was positioned on higher ground about one hundred yards to your left rear. From that location the artillery could safely fire over the heads of the defending infantry.

A defensive position of the Pennsylvania Reserves at Ellerson Mill. *Century Magazine.*

Report of Col. John H. Taggart, USA, Commanding Twelfth Pennsylvania Reserves, Third Brigade, Third Division, Fifth Corps, Army of the Potomac

In anticipation of an attack, rifle pits had been dug on the slope of the hill on both sides of the Cold Harbor road leading from Mechanicsville, which commanded the approaches by the road in that direction. On the afternoon of the 26th it was reported that the enemy were advancing in force, when eight companies of the regiment were at once posted in the rifle pits on both sides of the road, and two companies, B, Captain Mathewson, and C, Captain Gustin, were posted at a rifle pit near Ellison's grist-mill, in advance on the right of the road, which commanded the meadow which lay between our position and the advance of the enemy. Two pieces of artillery of Cooper's battery, under command of First Lieut. James S. Fullerton, were also posted on the brow of the hill in rear of the road over which the enemy were expected to pass. These dispositions made, it was not long before the enemy appeared in large force marching from Mechanicsville. Fire was immediately opened upon them by the two pieces of artillery and by the infantry in the rifle pits, which was returned with great spirit and determination by the advancing force.

The battle raged for an hour with great fury, when I discovered that the enemy were attempting to turn our left flank, two full regiments being deployed along the hill opposite us for that purpose, whose skirmishers had advanced to the creek on the west side of the meadow and were endeavoring to cross some distance to our left. I instantly communicated the fact to Brigadier-General Seymour, who ordered the Seventh Regiment Pennsylvania Reserve Volunteer Corps, Colonel Harvey, a battery of three pieces of artillery, and a Massachusetts regiment into a position on our left, which fortunately prevented the accomplishment of the movement.

The action continued until after dark, lasting some five hours, during which we maintained our ground and kept at bay an overwhelming force of the enemy. The firing at dark closed by mutual consent, the enemy occupying the woods on the hill fronting our position, while the men under my command retained possession of the rifle pits, in which they remained during the night. The loss of the enemy must have been very heavy, as they were in full view of our infantry and artillery at short range while the action lasted and in great force. The cries of their wounded were heard plainly all through the night from our position. [*OR* 11, pt. 2, p. 426.]

Return to your car for the drive to Stop 6. Depart the parking lot and drive 0.2 mile back to the intersection with Highway 156. Turn right on to Highway 156 and drive for 0.2 mile to Harbor Hill

Ellerson Mill and Beaver Dam Creek as seen from the Union defensive position. Stop 5A is in the center of the picture, just across the creek. Stop 5B is to the right of where the picture was taken. *Century Magazine.*

Road, just across the bridge. Turn right on Harbor Hill Road and immediately pull off to the side of the road. Leave your car and face back in the direction you just came from so that you can see the bridge. Be careful of traffic.

If you used the alternate route to Stop 5, Position B, drive back to the intersection of Harbor Hill Road and Highway 156. Just before you reach the intersection, pull off to the side of the road and

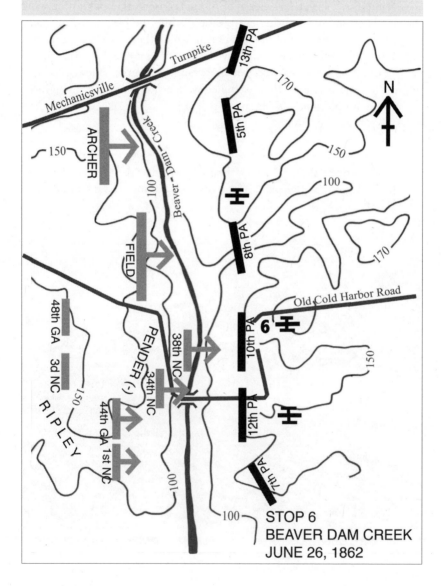

STOP 6
BEAVER DAM CREEK
JUNE 26, 1862

stop. Leave your car and face west so that you can see the bridge. Be careful of traffic.

Stop 6—Beaver Dam Creek

You are located in the center of the defensive position of the Tenth Pennsylvania Reserves. The left flank of this regiment position was just to the north of Stop 5, Position B, at Ellerson Mill, to your left. A section of guns from Battery K, Fifth U.S. Artillery, commanded by Lieutenant William Van Reed, was located to your left rear. Toward the west, from where you just came, the left of *Pender's* Brigade attacked on the left of the road you just drove over and the right of *Field's* Brigade on the right of the road.

Report of Col. James T. Kirk, USA, Commanding Tenth Pennsylvania Reserves, Third Brigade, Third Division, Fifth Corps, Army of the Potomac

I have the honor to report that on Thursday, June 26, 1862, at 4 o'clock p.m., the Tenth Regiment Pennsylvania Reserve Volunteer Corps, according to orders of the general, was formed in line of battle on the "color front." Firing immediately commenced on our right. I threw forward, by the general's order, Companies A and B, in command of Captain McConnell, to the rifle pits in front of a section of De Hart's battery. These companies were supported by Companies F and G, all under command of Major Smith. Company K was sent to support Easton's battery on the hill in rear of De Hart's battery. The remaining companies, in charge of Lieutenant-Colonel Warner, were deployed through the woods on the right as skirmishers, to pick off the enemy's gunners, and to prevent his crossing the swamp. Companies A and B held their positions in the pits until their ammunition was exhausted, when they were relieved by Companies E, F, and G. Company E was afterward relieved by Company K. The rifle pits were thus held until 10 o'clock p.m., when, by the general's orders, I withdrew my command, the ground being occupied by the Eighth Regiment Pennsylvania Reserve Volunteer Corps. It is, perhaps, but justice to state that while in no part of the field was the enemy in greater force or more determined in his efforts to gain our lines than in the road in front of the rifle pits, he was every time repulsed with heavy loss. Our loss was 3 killed and 2 wounded, including Captain McConnell. [*OR* 11, pt. 2, p. 424.]

Although the Union defenses here and farther north along Beaver Dam Creek had been successful it became necessary for the force here to abandon their position for a new one farther east. The report of the Fifth Corps commander explains his rationale for abandoning this position.

Report of Brig. Gen. Fitz John Porter, USA, Commanding Fifth Corps, Army of the Potomac

The firing ceased about 9 p.m. and the men lay on their arms in ranks as they had stood during the day, while exertions were being made by their officers to refill their exhausted cartridge boxes and to bring food to such men as had none in their haversacks, and by the medical department to care for and remove to the rear the wounded, happily not very numerous on our side. All was made ready for a renewal of the contest on the old ground, or an advance toward Richmond via the bridges which the enemy had crossed, should our success warrant it. During the night, however, as the commanding general (who had joined me at an early hour in the afternoon and remained until about 10 o'clock at night) is aware, numerous and unvarying accounts came in from our outposts and scouts toward the Pamunkey which tended to corroborate the previously received intelligence of the advance of the whole of *Jackson's* force from the direction of Gordonsville, whereby our right was to be effectually flanked without at all weakening the force in the immediate front of the army.

It was thus rendered necessary to select which side of the Chickahominy should be held in force, there being on each side an army of our enemies equivalent (in connection with their breastworks) to the whole of our own, and these two armies and defenses well connected with each other, and with Richmond, their base. But for the conception of the idea of a flank movement, changing our base by the left flank to the James River, our position would have left but one alternative—a hasty abandonment of our attack on Richmond and a retirement by the way we had advanced. The former plan, however, now so happily accomplished, which was made safe by its very boldness, necessitated the gradual withdrawal of our right. The commanding general, however, left me, with the intention of deciding, on information he should receive on arrival at his own headquarters, whether I should remain where I was and hold Beaver Creek, or retire to a position selected by General Barnard near Gaines' Mill. General Barnard remained with me to conduct my command to the new position, if decided upon to withdraw from Mechanicsville.

Immediately after pointing out to me the new ground, General Barnard left me, to represent the state of affairs to the major-general commanding and the necessity for additional troops, and also to send me axes, that the proper defenses might to some degree be prepared. In accordance with the orders of the major-general commanding for this end, received about 2 a.m. on the 27th, the retirement from Mechanicsville was begun at daylight of Friday, the 27th June. The brigade of General Seymour was the last to start, and that force, under its gallant and skillful commander, most coolly retired, covering the march of the other forces, occupying the attention of the foe so perfectly that ample time was allowed for all, horse, foot, and artillery, wagons and wounded, to reach their designated posts in the line where a new stand was to be made before crossing the Chickahominy. The guns of position were safely removed from the works we were about to abandon—works overlooking New Bridge—and during the action of the same afternoon did us good auxiliary service by the fire from [Brigadier General William F.] Smith's position beyond the Chickahominy. On the open plain near those works were posted Tidball's [Battery A, Second U.S. Artillery] and Robertson's [Batteries B and L, Second U.S. Artillery] Horse Batteries, which carefully watched the road and secured the retiring troops from the enemy, now pressing upon Seymour's brave band. All finally got securely back within the lines selected for the next stand, near the upper bridges, in use by our forces. [*OR* 11, pt. 2, pp. 222–23.]

The Union defenses along Beaver Dam Creek were successful for two reasons. First, it was a naturally strong defensive position. The creek with the undergrowth and swampy land provided a natural barrier that aided the defenders. This made it difficult for *A. P. Hill*'s brigades to coordinate their attacks and in many instances prevented the full combat power of individual brigades from being brought against the defenses.

Second, although several brigade attacks were pushed to the maximum, *A. P. Hill* and his commanders knew *Lee*'s plan called for *Jackson* to march to the right and rear of the Union Fifth Corps defensive line. This would cause the collapse of the defense along Beaver Dam Creek. By the time it was apparent that *Jackson* would not be in position to attack on June 26 it was rapidly becoming dark and further attacks by *A. P. Hill*, even with reinforcements, were not possible.

During the night of June 26 and into early morning the next day an opportunity was presented to McClellan to regain the initiative. *A. P. Hill*'s Division had been fought to a standstill. *Longstreet* and *D. H. Hill* did not get their divisions across the Chickahominy River until after dark and *Jackson* was still off to the north. Union reinforcements could have been brought over to the north side of the Chickahominy River. Part of these reinforcements could have protected the Union right flank while the rest joined with the Fifth Corps in an attack on *A. P. Hill*'s, *Longstreet*'s, and *D. H. Hill*'s divisions that were along Beaver Dam Creek and around Mechanicsville. However, McClellan refused to believe that he still outnumbered *Lee* and the opportunity was allowed to pass.

Chapter 3

Battle of Gaines Mill
Friday, June 27, 1862

Return to your car for the drive to Stop 7, Gaines Mill. You will be following the route taken by *A. P. Hill*'s Division on June 27. Make a U-turn and drive back to Highway 156. Turn right on to Highway 156 and drive for 1.1 miles to Walnut Grove Church and park on the right side of the road.

In 1862, Walnut Grove Church was also to your left across the road. Here on the morning of Friday, June 27, 1862, *Lee* met with *Jackson* and *A. P. Hill* and issued orders for the continued movement of their units. The outcome of these instructions was the Battle of Gaines Mill.

Drive forward 0.1 mile to the intersection with Highway 643, *Lee–Davis* Road. Turn right onto Highway 156. This part of the road was called Telegraph Road in 1862. Drive for 1.9 miles to Old Millstone Road and turn left. Drive to the first road on the left (Old Meadow Court), make a U-turn, and pull off to the side of the road, facing Highway 156.

To your left is Powhite Creek, and Gaines Mill is on the other side of it. Deployed on the high ground across the creek as part of the rear guard were Battery A, Second U.S. Artillery, and the Ninth Massachusetts Infantry. The artillery was to the left of the road, while the infantry was deployed to the right of the road. A detail from the artillery destroyed the bridge. The advance guard for *A. P. Hill*'s Division was *Gregg*'s Brigade. This brigade marched over the same road you just drove over, and as they approached this position they were fired upon from the other side of Powhite Creek.

Walnut Grove Church.

Report of Brig. Gen. *Maxcy Gregg*, CSA, Commanding *Gregg*'s Brigade, *A. P. Hill*'s Division, Army of Northern Virginia

The enemy [rear guard] made some stand at Gaines' Mill, and here our skirmishers, *Cordero*'s and *Haskell*'s companies of the First [South Carolina] and *Miller*'s of the Twelfth [South Carolina], became sharply engaged. The enemy were sheltered by trees; our riflemen availed themselves of the inequalities of the ground, where they could fire and load lying down. This exchange of fire having continued for some short time, while the First and Twelfth were preparing to advance in line, and judging that a rapid charge of the skirmishers would dislodge the enemy with least loss to our troops, I ordered them forward at the double-quick. At the word of command the riflemen sprang to their feet, and advancing impetuously drove the enemy before them. The First and Twelfth now followed in line of battle, and after the bridges over the creek and mill-race, torn up by the enemy, had been re-laid by a working party, under directions of Lieutenants *Johnston* and *Izard* of the Engineer Corps, crossed the stream and again formed line of battle on the brow of the hill, to advance, supported as before by the other two regiments. It was now nearly 2 p.m. [*OR* 11, pt. 2, p. 854.]

Return to Highway 156, turn left, and continue to drive on Highway 156 for another 0.7 mile to the intersection with the road to the Watt House. Look for the National Park sign "Gaines Mill Unit." At this intersection Highway 156 will make a sharp left turn and the road you want to follow will continue to the right. When you reach this intersection, turn right on Watt House Road and pull to the side of the road and stop.

Stop 7—*Lee* Deploys

You are at the location where the first Confederate division to reach the battlefield began deploying. *Lee* was still attempting to execute his original plan to cut McClellan off from his supply base at White House on the Pamunkey River. *Lee,* therefore, issued instructions that had *Jackson* and *D. H. Hill* march on routes that were north then east of *A. P. Hill.* This would place them in position to cut the Union supply line and cut off the Union Fifth Corps north of the Chickahominy River. The divisions of *A. P. Hill* and *Longstreet* were to keep the pressure on the Fifth Corps by advancing from the west.

You have followed the route *A. P. Hill* took to reach this location. To his right was the division of Major General *James Longstreet. Longstreet's* Division advanced parallel to *A. P. Hill* over a series of country lanes and roads, many which do not exist today.

The division of *D. H. Hill* marched the longest distance. The route of this division using modern-day road numbers and names was as follows. From Mechanicsville *D. H. Hill* marched east on Highway 360, Old Church Road in 1862, for 4.6 miles to the intersection with Highway 615, Walnut Grove Road. Here *Hill* turned right and marched southwest for one mile to a road intersection where he turned left on to Colt's Neck Road and marched southeast for 0.7 mile to the intersection with Highway 635, Sandy Valley Road. At this intersection *Hill's* Division turned left and marched northeast for 0.5 mile to the intersection with Highway 633, Beulah Church Road, where it turned right and marched southeast for 1.5 miles to Old Cold Harbor and the intersection with Highway 156. At that location *D. H. Hill* deployed into attack formation. When deployed his division was aligned along Highway 156 to the west and facing south. This placed his division on the extreme left end of the Confederate line opposite the Union Fifth Corps right.

Jackson's force marched from Hudley's Corner and after it passed Walnut Grove intersection marched between the divisions of *D. H. Hill* on its left and *A. P. Hill* on its right. The route of *Jackson*'s force using modern-day road numbers and names was as follows. *Jackson* started at Hudley's Corner, which is located today at the intersection of Highway 787, Rural Point Road, and Highway 642, Meadow Bridge Road. From there *Jackson* marched west on Highway 642 for 0.3 mile to the intersection of Highway 643, *Lee-Davis* Road. Here he turned left and marched south on Highway 643 for 1.8 miles to the intersection with Highway 360, Old Church Road in 1862. He marched through the intersection and continued on Highway 643 for 0.8 mile to the intersection with Highway 636, Walnut Grove Road, where he met with *Lee*. At this intersection he turned left and marched northeast 2.0 miles to an intersection where he turned right on to Creighton Road and marched south for 0.7 mile to Highway 635, Sandy Valley Road. At this point he turned left and marched northeast for 1.5 miles to Highway 633, Beulah Church Road. After

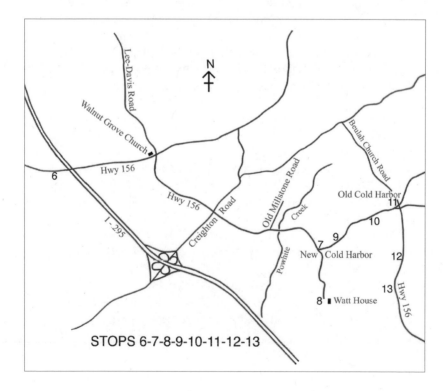

STOPS 6-7-8-9-10-11-12-13

marching about 0.5 mile on Highway 635, Sandy Valley Road, the lead units turned right down a country lane and moved toward Gaines Mill. After a short distance they were countermarched back to Highway 635, where they continued in a northeast direction. At the intersection with Highway 633, Beulah Church Road, *Jackson* turned right and southeast for about 0.7 mile where his lead element, *Ewell*'s Division, began to deploy on the right (west) side of the road. His other two divisions, *Winder*'s and *Whiting*'s, began deploying south from Highway 635.

The first division to deploy was *A. P. Hill*'s Light Division. The center of the division was about where you are now. As you look south down the road to the Watt House, the division line stretched to your right front in a southwesterly direction for one thousand yards. To your left the line extended seven hundred yards along Highway 156. The second Confederate division to arrive was *Longstreet*'s. His division had been to the south paralleling the route of *A. P. Hill*'s Division. *Longstreet* deployed his division to the right of *A. P. Hill*'s.

Old Cold Harbor is located 1.3 miles down Highway 156 from where you are. When *D. H. Hill*'s Division reached Old Cold Harbor it was the third Confederate division to arrive in the battle area.

The next Confederate division to arrive and deploy was that of Major General *Richard S. Ewell*. *Ewell* began deploying his division shortly after it turned south on Highway 633 (Beulah Church Road). The division worked its way south and deployed on *A. P. Hill*'s left flank. This placed it along Highway 156 to your left. The space between *Ewell* and *D. H. Hill* was filled with part of *Jackson*'s Division, commanded by Brigadier General *Charles S. Winder*.

The last Confederate division to arrive came into position in the area where you are located. It was the two-brigade division of Brigadier General *W. H. C. Whiting*. This division deployed behind the center of *A. P. Hill*'s line just to the right of you.

In 1862 three roads intersected were you are. To your left Highway 156 continued east for 1.3 miles to Old Cold Harbor. The road you are stopped on went directly south 0.7 mile to the Watt House. Between these two roads a third road went southeast for 0.8 mile then turned east and went 0.5 mile, where it intersected with Highway 156, near the McGehee House, as it came south from Old Cold Harbor. That segment of the road ran across part of the battlefield. It does not exist today; however, the eastern part that intersects with Highway 156 does.

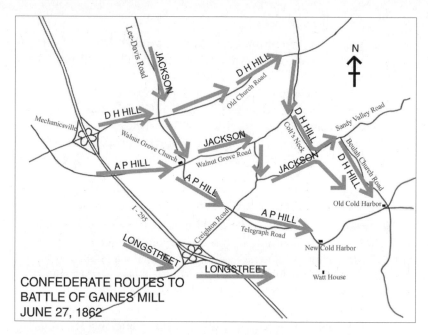

CONFEDERATE ROUTES TO
BATTLE OF GAINES MILL
JUNE 27, 1862

Report of Gen. *Robert E. Lee*, CSA, Commanding Army of Northern Virginia

After repairing the bridges over Beaver Dam the several columns resumed their march as nearly as possible as prescribed in the order; *Jackson*, with whom *D. H. Hill* had united, bore to the left, in order to cut off re-enforcements to the enemy or intercept his retreat in that direction. *Longstreet* and *A. P. Hill* moved nearer the Chickahominy. Many prisoners were taken in their progress, and the conflagration of wagons and stores marked the way of the retreating army. *Longstreet* and *Hill* reached the vicinity of New Bridge about noon. It was ascertained that the enemy had taken a position behind Powhite Creek [Boatswain's Creek], prepared to dispute our progress. He occupied a range of hills, with his right resting in the vicinity of McGehee's house and his left near that of Dr. Gaines [Watt House], on a wooded bluff, which rose abruptly from a deep ravine. The ravine was filled with sharpshooters, to whom its banks gave protection. A second line of infantry was stationed on the side of the hill behind a breastwork of trees above the first; a third occupied the crest, strengthened with rifle trenches and crowned with artillery. The approach to this position was over an open plain, about a quarter of a mile wide, commanded by this triple line of fire and swept by the heavy batteries south of the Chickahominy. In front of his center and right the ground was generally open, bounded on the side of our approach by a wood, with dense and tangled undergrowth, and traversed by a sluggish stream [Boatswain's Creek], which converted the soil into a deep morass. The woods on the farther side of the swamp were occupied by sharpshooters, and trees had been felled to increase the difficulty of its passage and detain our advancing columns under the fire of infantry massed on the slopes of the opposite hills and of the batteries on their crests. Pressing on toward the [Richmond and] York River Railroad, *A. P. Hill*, who was in advance, reached the vicinity of New Cold Harbor about 2 p.m., where he encountered the enemy. The arrival of *Jackson* on our left was momentarily expected, and it was supposed that his approach would cause the extension of the enemy's line in that direction. Under this impression *Longstreet* was held back until this movement should commence. The principal part of the Federal Army [actually the Fifth Corps] was now on the north side of the Chickahominy. *Hill*'s single division met this large force with the impetuous courage for which that officer and his troops are distinguished. They drove the enemy back and assailed him in his strong position on the ridge. The battle raged fiercely and with varying fortune more than two hours. Three regiments pierced the enemy's line and forced their way to the crest of the hill on his left, but were compelled to fall back before overwhelming numbers. The superior force of the enemy, assisted by the fire of his batteries south of the Chickahominy, which played incessantly on our columns as they pressed through the difficulties that obstructed their way, caused them to recoil. Though most of the men had never been under fire until the day before, they were rallied and in turn repelled the advance of the enemy. Some brigades were broken, others stubbornly maintained their positional but it became apparent that the enemy was gradually gaining ground.

The attack on our left being delayed by the length of *Jackson*'s march and the obstacles he encountered, *Longstreet* was ordered to make a diversion in *Hill*'s favor by a feint on the enemy's left. In making this demonstration the great strength of the position already described was discovered, and General *Longstreet* perceived that to render the diversion effectual the feint must be converted into an attack. He resolved with characteristic promptness to carry the heights by assault. His column was quickly formed near the open ground, and as his preparations were completed *Jackson* arrived, and his right division, that of *Whiting*, took position on the left of *Longstreet*. At the same time D. H. Hill formed on our extreme left, and after a short but bloody conflict forced his way through the morass and obstructions and drove the enemy from the woods on the opposite side. *Ewell* advanced on [*D. H. Hill*'s] right and engaged the enemy furiously. The First and Fourth Brigades of *Jackson*'s own division filled the interval between *Ewell* and *A. P. Hill*. The Second and Third were sent to the right. The arrival of these fresh troops enabled *A. P. Hill* to withdraw some of his brigades, wearied and reduced by their long and arduous conflict. The line being now complete, a general advance from right to left was ordered. On the right the troops moved forward with steadiness, unchecked by the terrible fire from the triple lines of infantry on the hill, and the cannon on both sides of the river, which burst upon them as they emerged upon the plain. The dead and wounded marked the way of their intrepid advance, the brave Texans leading, closely followed by their no less daring comrades. The enemy were driven from the ravine to the first line of breastworks, over which our impetuous column dashed up to the intrenchments on the crest. These were quickly stormed, fourteen pieces of artillery captured, and the enemy driven into the field beyond. Fresh troops came to his support and he endeavored repeatedly to rally, but in vain. He was forced back with great slaughter until he reached the woods on the banks of the Chickahominy, and night put an end to the pursuit. Long lines of dead and wounded marked each stand made by the enemy in his stubborn resistance, and the field over which he retreated was strewn with the slain.

On the left the attack was no less vigorous and successful. *D. H. Hill* charged across the open ground in his front, one of his regiments having first bravely carried a battery whose fire enfiladed his advance. Gallantly supported by the troops on his right, who pressed forward with unfaltering resolution, he reached the crest of the ridge, and after a sanguinary struggle broke the enemy's line, captured several of his batteries, and drove him in confusion toward the Chickahominy until darkness rendered farther pursuit impossible. [*OR* 11, pt. 2, pp. 491–93.]

The rebuilt Watt House.

It is apparent from the routes taken by *Jackson* and *D. H. Hill* and from the first part of his report that *Lee* still expected to cut off the Union army from its supply base. Unknown to him McClellan had already decided to abandon White House as a base and to open a new base on the James River on the other side of the Peninsula.

From this location proceed to the Watt House, where you will begin to take a close look at the fighting outlined in *Lee*'s report.

Drive south on the narrow road in front of you for 0.7 mile and turn right, into the parking lot at the Watt House. Get out of your car and walk east, across the road you just drove in on, for 60 yards to the cannon. When you reach the cannon, stop and face left, north. The Watt House will be behind you.

Stop 8, Position A—The Watt House

You are on the plateau where the Union Fifth Corps established its defensive position after retreating from Beaver Dam Creek. The northern and western edge of this plateau is traced by the course of Boatswain's Creek. The creek begins near the north-south section of Highway 156, which is 2,100 yards (1.2 miles) to your right. From its beginning the creek flows generally southwest for 2,700 yards (1.5 miles), where it makes a turn to the south and flows for another 2,200 yards (1.3 miles) and joins the Chickahominy River. The high ground just south of the swamp to your right, in front of you and to your left rear, was the location of the Union defensive line. You are in the left center of the Union defensive position. The tree line in front of you was not there in 1862. From here the road from New Cold Harbor to Old Cold Harbor and the road from New Cold Harbor that went southeast to Highway 156 near the McGehee House were intermittently visible.

To defend this position Brigadier General Fitz John Porter had his three divisions and fourteen batteries of artillery (eighty guns). In addition, heavy artillery on the south side of the Chickahominy River was able to fire into the flank of any Confederate force attacking Porter's left. Brigadier General George Sykes's Second Division defended the right of the Fifth Corps line. The division was composed of three brigades; two of them were U.S. Regulars. All three of Sykes's brigades were deployed on the battle line. Sykes's right was astride Highway 156, 0.6 mile after the road came south out of Old Cold Harbor. His division's left flank was six hundred yards to your right rear. This gave Sykes a defensive line of about sixteen hundred yards. Brigadier General George W. Morell's First Division defended the left of the position. The three brigades of this division were all deployed on the battle line. The right of Morell's division was five hundred yards to your right. From there the line went southwest past your location and continued on for another eleven hundred yards. After the line ran five hundred yards to your left, it swung back and went south to its end. Brigadier General George A. McCall's Third Division, which had borne the brunt of fighting at Beaver Dam Creek, was deployed in a reserve line behind Morell. As the battle progressed, Porter was reinforced with Brigadier General Henry W. Slocum's First Division from the Sixth Corps. This division was deployed in a reserve line behind Sykes and McCall. In addition, late in the day two more brigades were sent across the river to Porter. They arrived in time to help cover the Fifth Corps retreat. There was also a cavalry force under command of Brigadier General Philip St. George Cooke located behind the left of the defensive position. Porter's headquarters was located at the Watt House. All total, approximately thirty thousand Union troops defended this plateau.

The Chickahominy River ran three-quarters to one and one-quarter miles behind Porter's position. Normally a defensive position is not established with a river behind the defending line of troops. However, in this case Porter had the three bridges available for use. From west to east, they were Woodbury's Bridge, Alexander's Bridge, and Grapevine Bridge. These bridges allowed for the forward movement of supplies and reinforcements and, if necessary, for the retreat of the Fifth Corps.

Report of Brig. Gen. Fitz John Porter, USA, Commanding Fifth Corps, Army of the Potomac

I have the honor to report that on Friday, the 27th of June, after the successful withdrawal of the right wing of the army from Mechanicsville and its encampment on Gaines' and Curtis' farms, near New Bridge, it became necessary for the safety of the material to cover the bridges connecting with the main army across the Chickahominy. For this purpose the corps was disposed in a semicircle, having its extremities resting on the stream, while the intermediate portion occupied the ground designated by the major-general commanding, it being the best possible for defense under the circumstances. Part of the front was covered by the ravine of the Gaines' Mill stream [Boatswain's

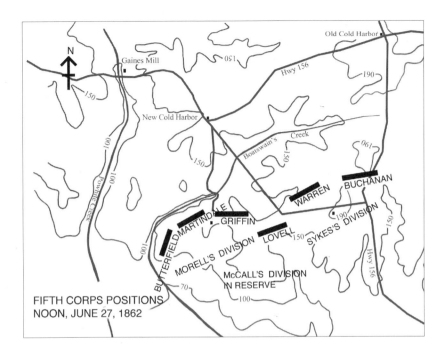

Creek], covered with trees and underbrush, which partially masked our force and screened the reserves from view.

By this disposition the roads from Cold Harbor and Mechanicsville, which converge at that point, were duly covered and defended. On the front thus formed were posted the divisions of Morell and Sykes, each brigade having in reserve two of its own regiments. Portions of the divisions of artillery of Morell and Sykes were posted to sweep the avenues of approach. The rest were held in reserve. McCall's division formed a second line in rear of the woods skirting the ravine, Reynolds' brigade being posted on the extreme right, to cover the approaches from Cold Harbor and Dispatch Station to Sumner's [Grapevine] Bridge. General Cooke, with his cavalry, was instructed to take a position under the hill in the valley of the Chickahominy to watch our left flank, and, should the opportunity occur, to strike the enemy on the plain. He was told that he would have nothing to do on the hill. The troops remained in position waiting the approach of the enemy's columns, known to be advancing in very great force. Believing my force too small to defend successfully this long line, I asked of General Barnard [Chief Engineer of the Army of the Potomac], who had selected and pointed out this position, to represent to the major-general commanding the necessity of re-enforcement, and he was to send me felling axes for defensive purposes.

Deserters from their ranks and loyal citizens of Virginia represented that General *Jackson* . . . had united his forces with those of *Longstreet, A. P.*

Hill, and *D. H. Hill*, from Richmond, and that they were advancing, with the determination to overwhelm and crush the Army of the Potomac. The dust from the immense columns of the enemy could be seen for miles, and soon our scouts and pickets warned us that they were extending over our whole front.

About 2 o'clock p.m. they began with their skirmishers to feel for the weakest point of our position, and soon large bodies of infantry, supported by a warm fire of artillery, engaged our whole line. Repulsed in every direction, a few hours of ominous silence ensued, indicating that their troops were being massed for an overwhelming attack. Our infantry and artillery were drawn in toward the center and posted to meet the avalanche. Re-enforcements were again asked for, and all available troops were sent forward by the major-general commanding. [*OR* 11, pt. 2, pp. 223–24.]

You are standing just behind the left rear of Morell's right brigade. This was Brigadier General Charles Griffin's Second Brigade. The brigade position ran from just forward of where you are to the east, your right, for five hundred yards. The first attack against this position was by Brigadier General *Maxcy Gregg*'s brigade of *A. P. Hill*'s Light Division. *Gregg*'s Brigade was the advance guard of *A. P. Hill*'s Division. *Gregg* marched along the same road you drove on from Beaver Dam Creek to New Cold Harbor. When he reached New Cold Harbor (Stop 7) he deployed his brigade on line facing to the southeast. From that location *Gregg*'s Brigade advanced against the Union position where you are and to your right. You will take a closer look at *Gregg*'s attack at Stop 9.

Several regiments of Brigadier General *Lawrence O'B Branch*'s brigade supported *Gregg*'s attack. These regiments were deployed on *Gregg*'s right. The center of *Branch*'s attack came directly toward where you are standing. However this attack was stopped by heavy rifle and artillery fire. When *Branch*'s regiments fell back, Brigadier General *William D. Pender*'s brigade took their place. Starting from just south of New Cold Harbor, *Pender* made numerous attacks against the Union regiments in front of you and to your right front. *Pender*'s regiments pressed their attacks close to the defensive position but were unable to break into the Union line. After several attacks by his brigade, *Pender*'s troops fell back toward New Cold Harbor.

Brigadier General *Joseph R. Anderson*'s brigade attacked on the right of *Pender*'s Brigade. *Anderson*'s attack struck the left of Griffin's line about where the park road to your left front is today.

Report of Brig. Gen. *Joseph R. Anderson,* CSA, Commanding *Anderson*'s Brigade, *A. P. Hill*'s Division, Army of Northern Virginia

After crossing the stream at Gaines' Mill I was ordered by you [*A. P. Hill*] to proceed up the right-hand road, and afterward I received an order from you, through one of your aides, to march with caution, as the enemy were said to be in force at Turkey Hill. I threw forward an advance guard and flankers on each side of the road in the woods until I arrived at the cross-roads where we observed the enemy's pickets, two of whom we captured in the woods on our right. I then filed to the right, marching through the woods by the right flank until my right reached the field in which General *Pender*'s battery was posted and playing on the enemy. Here I faced to the front and marched forward in line of battle, driving the enemy's skirmishers before us, while I was supported by General *Field*'s brigade, a few paces in rear.

On arriving near the edge of the woods we came under a brisk fire of the enemy, which increased as we emerged from it, and crossed the narrow slip of land to the crest of the hill. This hill was separated by a deep ravine and creek from the enemy's position. Here the brigade encountered a very hot fire, both of musketry and shell, which brought us to a halt from the double-quick in which I had commenced the charge. But it was only after a third charge, in which every effort was made by me to gain the enemy's lines beyond the ravine, that, in consequence of some wavering in the center, I concluded to order my men to lie down in the edge of the wood and hold the position. At the same time, it seeming to be totally impracticable at this point to effect a passage of the ravine, I ordered the Thirty-fifth and Forty-fifth Georgia, who, under their brave leaders (Cols. *E. L. Thomas* and *T. Hardeman,* the former on my right flank and the latter on my left), had proceeded a considerable distance in advance of the center, to fall back in line and lie on the ground, which position we maintained until by the general charge the day was won. [*OR* 11, pt. 2, pp. 878–79.]

To defend this part of the position, Griffin had three of his regiments deployed on line and one regiment in reserve. The Fourth Michigan was deployed just this side of the road. To your right front was the Fourteenth New York, and to that Regiment's right was the Ninth Massachusetts. In reserve was the Sixty-second Pennsylvania. On the other side of Boatswain's Creek a skirmish line of the First U.S. Sharpshooters was deployed.

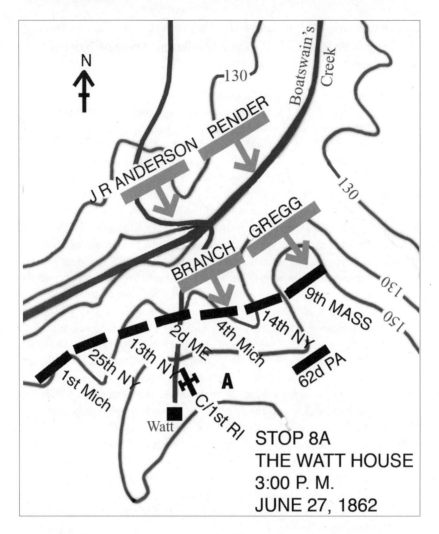

STOP 8A
THE WATT HOUSE
3:00 P. M.
JUNE 27, 1862

Report of Brig. Gen. Charles Griffin, USA, Commanding Second Brigade, First Division, Fifth Corps, Army of the Potomac

About 9 a.m. of the 27th the brigade received orders to fall back [from the vicinity of Beaver Dam Creek] and take position on the east side of [Boatswain's Creek], which point was reached about 10 o'clock. The urgency of the movement rendered the destruction of our commissary stores and camp and garrison equipage necessary in order to prevent them from falling into the hands of the enemy, a number of wagons belonging to the brigade train being at the White House. The Ninth Massachusetts, under command of Colonel

Cass, was ordered by General Morell [the division commander] to hold the enemy in check and prevent his crossing at Gaines' Mill, which duty was gallantly performed. The enemy crossing above the mill in force, Colonel Cass was ordered to fall back gradually to the line occupied by the other regiments of the brigade. [This is where you are.]

About 12 m. the enemy appeared in force in front of the Ninth Massachusetts, posted on the right, and made a fierce attack. The Ninth as a regiment received the onslaught with steadiness and repulsed it. The extreme left wavered for a moment, but soon recovered its place. The Fourteenth New York was in line of battle to the left of the Ninth and the Fourth Michigan some distance to the left of the Fourteenth. The right wing of the Fourteenth was exposed to a heavy fire of the enemy at this time, but nobly and repeatedly drove him back at the point of the bayonet. Lieutenant-Colonel Skillen, of the Fourteenth, was here mortally wounded. The Sixty-second Pennsylvania, which had been held in reserve, was moved up to support the Ninth Massachusetts, and after delivering a volley was pushed forward by its gallant colonel at a charge bayonet. Colonel Black was instantly killed at the head of his regiment during the charge. The right wing of the Fourteenth and the Ninth and the Sixty-second held their position in the wood, resisting repeated attacks by fresh troops of the enemy, until they were relieved by Newton's brigade and ordered to fall back. About 6 o'clock the Sixty-second, having received a fresh supply of ammunition, was gallantly led by Lieutenant-Colonel Sweitzer to support the troops on our left. In this advance Colonel Sweitzer was badly wounded and left on the field. The left wing of the brigade, consisting of the Fourth Michigan, and the left wing of the Fourteenth New York, under command of Colonel McQuade, held its position until late in the evening, but was forced to retire after the troops on the left of the line gave way.

It may be proper to mention here that the artillery, by order of General Porter and under my direction, opened fire upon the enemy advancing upon our left, but it was too late. Our infantry had already commenced to fall back, and nothing being left to give confidence to the artillerymen, it was impossible to make them stand to their work. The brigade was rallied and formed in its proper order near the hospital, where it remained until 2 o'clock the next morning, when it crossed the Chickahominy and encamped near general headquarters.

Our loss in the battle was as follows: Killed, 96; wounded, 354; missing, 136—an aggregate of 586. [*OR* 11, pt. 2, p. 313.]

Battery C, First Rhode Island Light Artillery was firing in support of Griffin's infantry.

Report of Capt. William B. Weeden, USA, Commanding Battery C, First Rhode Island Light Artillery, First Division, Fifth Corps, Army of the Potomac

During the night [of June 26–27 the battery] was ordered by the division general to fall back with General Griffin's column. Moved at daybreak, and was in position on the field at [Watt House] in rear of Griffin's brigade at about 11 a.m. By command of division general, before the enemy appeared in force I placed one section under Lieut. W. W. Buckley at the edge of the woods and on General Martindale's right. The enemy attacked General Martindale in force at about 3 p.m., and Lieutenant Buckley opened fire with shrapnel, bursting in the enemy's line as they appeared on the crest beyond the ravine. The practice with the guns was excellent, and the fire was continued until the enemy retired. He advanced and was repulsed three times, the section firing shell and shrapnel. At the fourth attack the infantry gave way; the pieces kept up their fire, using canister as the enemy came near. The cannoneers served the guns until the supporting infantry had all retired. There were then (including non-commissioned officers) 3 men at each piece. Three horses were killed at one limber, one horse was killed at the other, and the remaining ones stampeded under the tremendous musketry of the enemy, though the drivers made every effort to restrain them. The pieces were necessarily abandoned. The caissons retired in good order. I would respectfully submit that, from my own observation and the information of officers who saw the whole of the contest, Lieutenant Buckley made every effort to save his pieces, and that his section, as well as himself, should be commended for gallant conduct. The colors of one rebel regiment were struck to the ground by a case-shot. They were never raised again by the enemy. After he retired they were brought in by the Second Maine Regiment. In view of these facts I would respectfully ask that they be given to this battery.

The right and center sections, under command of Lieutenants Waterman and Clark, from their position in rear of Griffin's brigade, opened fire when our first line retired. After a few rounds they changed position 100 yards to rear and in line with the other artillery. After firing some 40 rounds we saw the enemy turning the left of the batteries. The smoke had filled the whole field to the woods, and it was impossible to direct the fire. The batteries were limbering to the rear in good order, to retire and renew the fire from the brow of the hill, when the cavalry, repulsed, retired in disorder through and in front of the batteries. The caissons were exchanging limbers with the pieces, and it was impossible to limber up and withdraw them. Men were ridden down and the horses stampeded by the rush of the cavalry. The whole line of artillery was thrown into confusion. Commands could be neither heard nor executed, and different batteries were mingled in disorder. One piece of my battery mired in the woods. Other caissons in front and rear of the same having been abandoned by the drivers, it was impossible to rescue the piece. [*OR* 11, pt. 2, p. 282.]

From here you will move and look at the action in the center of Morell's division.

Walk to your left (west), cross the road, cross the parking lot, and pick up the park foot trail that is next to a park map. Follow this trail for eighty yards, where it goes into the wood. Stay on the trail in

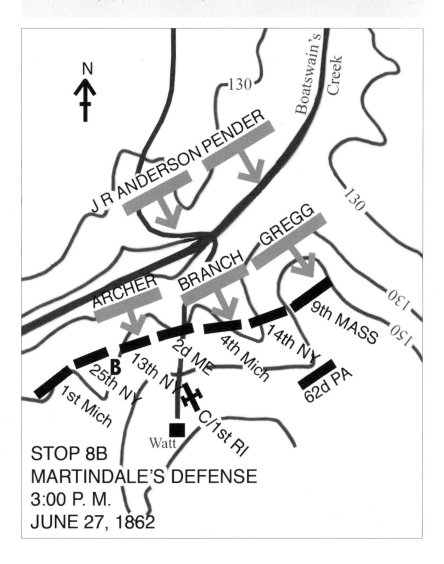

the woods for another thirty yards. At this point, turn right off the trail and walk for twenty yards. Stop and face left.

Position B—Martindale's Defense

You are in the center of Brigadier General John H. Martindale's First Brigade position. To defend this part of the line Martindale had five regiments. The Twenty-fifth New York was deployed where you are. To your right was the Thirteenth New York and farther right was the Second Maine. To your left was the First Michigan. The Twenty-second Massachusetts was located behind you in a supporting position. Fifteen yards behind you are what appears to be the remains of part of the Union defensive works. Boatswain's Creek is directly in front of you down the hill. The ground on the other side of the creek was more open in 1862 and provided for good fields of fire.

In conjunction with the attacks of *Gregg, Branch,* and *Pender* against the Union line across the road to your right (Position A), Brigadier General *James J. Archer*'s brigade attacked the right half of Martindale's position.

Report of Brig. Gen. *James J. Archer,* CSA, Commanding *Archer*'s Brigade, *A. P. Hill*'s Division, Army of Northern Virginia

On the 27th, at Cold Harbor, my brigade, reduced to less than 1,000 men, advanced alone and unsupported across an open field to attack the enemy, strongly posted and protected in the wood beyond by the works which a short time afterward it required seven brigades to carry. The troops under my command, except the Nineteenth Georgia, which was held in reserve, advanced at a double-quick to within 20 steps of the breastworks, when they fell back before the irresistible fire of artillery and rifles. The obvious impossibility of carrying the position without support prevented me from attempting to check the retreat. Had they not fallen back I would myself have ordered it. A half hour later my brigade, constituting the right of the Light Division, again moved forward to the attack of the same position and entered it in the front line of attack. Beyond this point my brigade, worn-out, exhausted, and intermingled with the regiments and brigades of the supporting line, did not advance as an organized body. With a few of my command, however (mostly Georgians, who, not having been engaged in the first charge, were fresher than the rest), and some soldiers of other brigades, I continued on from a quarter to half a mile farther under a heavy artillery fire from batteries which were taken [later in the day] by *Hood*'s brigade, while under the eminence on which they were posted I was forming for attack the few men, not more than 100, remaining with me. I remained on the field during the night, and the next morning was spent in burying the dead and attending the wounded.

My loss in this action was 49 killed and 271 wounded, making the total loss in the two battles 542, besides Corporal *Trezevant*, of the Hampton Legion, in command of my couriers, killed, and *James L. Crittenden*, volunteer aide, wounded. All the field officers of the Nineteenth Georgia, First and Seventh Tennessee Regiments, and the two senior captains successively in command of the Fifth Alabama Battalion were killed or wounded. [*OR* 11, pt. 2, pp. 897–98.]

> Although pushing the attack vigorously, *Archer*'s Brigade was not able to capture the Union position and remained pinned down by rifle and artillery fire for the rest of the afternoon. *Archer*'s attack struck the Thirteenth New York, to your right, and the right of the Twenty-fifth New York, where you are located.

Report of Maj. Francis A. Schoeffel, USA, Commanding Thirteenth New York Infantry, First Brigade, First Division, Fifth Corps, Army of the Potomac

... the regiment was deployed in line of battle in a ravine close to Gaines [Watts] house, on the right of the Twenty-fifth New York Volunteers. Here we lay, expecting the enemy, and were not disappointed, for about 1 or 2 o'clock p.m. the enemy came in sight, drove in our skirmishers and charged, but were repulsed with considerable loss, our regiment capturing 9 prisoners, with the battle-flag belonging to the First Tennessee Regiment. The prisoners belonged respectively to the First Tennessee, Seventh Tennessee, Fourteenth Tennessee, and Fifth Alabama Regiments.

Our regiment had built a barricade, which protected the men very much. We remained behind this barricade until 5 p.m. or later, when the enemy came on us again in stronger force than before. Our men stood their ground manfully, holding the enemy in check until all their ammunition was expended, when we fell back to the second line of defense. The enemy, seeing us fall back, pressed us hard. Here our loss was severe, but not as severe as some of the other regiments. The reported loss was 4 killed, 47 wounded, 29 missing.

The regiment in falling back rallied three different times, rallying the first time Colonel Marshall fell back, being taken sick. I took command [and] found I had but 160 men left. In looking around I found Colonel Marshall with the rest of the regiment at the general hospital. I then marched what men I had to this hospital. [*OR* 11, pt. 2, p. 309.]

Report of Capt. Shepard Gleason, USA, Commanding Twenty-fifth New York Infantry, First Brigade, First Division, Fifth Corps, Army of the Potomac

About 8 o'clock a.m., with the rest of the brigade, the regiment was formed in line in the woods in front at the bottom of the ravine, where we threw up a slight barricade and rested on our arms, awaiting the approach of the enemy. Four companies of skirmishers were thrown forward to the crest of the hill in front, with instructions to fire a volley upon the foe upon their approach and then retire behind the barricade. After some slight skirmishing the enemy advanced in line. The skirmishers fired upon them and then retired. The rebels came on in good style, but somewhat to our right, so that only the right wing of the regiment was engaged. They were soon compelled to retire. A small number of skirmishers were then sent forward by Major Gilbert to watch and report the movements of the enemy, which they from time to time did. The battle continued on the right and left of us, but not in our immediate front, until about 7 o'clock p.m., when the skirmishers again advised us of their approach and retired behind the barricades.

This time the enemy came on in deployed lines and columns by battalions closed in mass, one battalion immediately behind the other. The Twenty-fifth Regiment reserved fire until the enemy were half way down the hill, and then opened upon them. Each line of the enemy fired on descending the hill as soon as it was unmasked by the line in front. The firing was heavy and continuous. Our men behaved with great coolness, firing slowly and with precision. The enemy once wavered for a moment, and would have gone back, but for the impulsion of the mass behind. Major Gilbert stood just in rear of the colors, shooting the rebels as they advanced with his pistol. Captain Bates was wounded here, and Lieutenant Fairman, acting adjutant, twice, once in the leg and once in the hip. The break in the first line commenced to the left of our regiment, and ran like a wave through the whole line. I did not see Major Gilbert after he left the barricade, being considerably to the right of him, but I learn from two or three of the men that he fell, while going back up the hill, near the second line. Lieutenant Bishop and Assistant Surgeon Norris were among the missing officers in this engagement, and Captain Ferguson, of the provost guard, was also mortally wounded.

I had but few men with me on arriving at the top of the hill, and those of my own company. The plain beyond was filled with men scattered in every direction before we reached the second line, and as the artillery in rear was getting ready to fire we passed behind it. The confusion prevented me from rallying or even finding any more of the Twenty-fifth Regiment, though I spent the better part of the night in looking for them. [*OR* 11, pt. 2, p. 311.]

> Reverse your path and walk back to the trail. Turn right and follow the trail in a westerly direction for seventy yards, stop, then face right.

Position C—The First Michigan's Defense

You are just forward of the position occupied by the First Michigan. This unit was the left regiment in Martindale's line. The First Michigan's line was twenty yards behind you, where the ground rises up. If you wish, walk up the hill twenty yards to the actual position. In front of you is Boatswain's Creek. The initial attacks against the First Michigan were made by elements of *Pickett*'s Brigade, of *Longstreet*'s Division.

Report of Col. Horace S. Roberts, USA, Commanding First Michigan Infantry, First Brigade, First Division, Fifth Corps, Army of the Potomac

The men slept on their arms until 2 o'clock a.m., when, by order of [General Morell], the pickets were called in, and the regiment took up its march toward its camp. Arriving there, after a brief rest the command, with the rest of the brigade, moved forward across the bridge at the mill, then to the right, where it was placed in position for the battle of Gaines' Mill, on the left of the brigade, in a belt of woods, along a ravine, with the Twenty-fifth New York on its right and the Eighty-third Pennsylvania, of Butterfield's brigade [Third Brigade, First Division], on the left. In front of the position was the sloping side of Gaines' wheat field, up which and onto the field Companies E, Captain Pomeroy, and afterward A, Captain Alcott, were deployed as skirmishes. By direction of General Martindale a rude barricade was hastily thrown up along the line, and the men laid down awaiting the attack. It was not long before the skirmishers were actively engaged with those of the enemy. The firing was brisk, and we lost a number of men.

Meanwhile, about 12 o'clock, the enemy commenced firing shot and shell, which fell and burst among and near the men, costing us a few lives. Twice our skirmishers were driven in, but regained their position as soon as practicable, until I deemed it advisable to call them in permanently. About

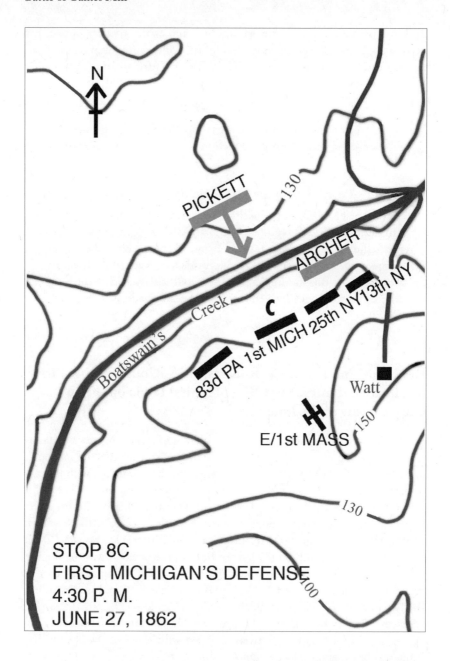

N

PICKETT

130

ARCHER

Creek

13th NY

25th NY

1st MICH

C

83d PA

Boatswain's

Watt

150

E/1st MASS

130

STOP 8C
FIRST MICHIGAN'S DEFENSE
4:30 P. M.
JUNE 27, 1862

100

3 o'clock the enemy's infantry appeared in force on our right on the brow of the hill, and were repulsed by a vigorous fire. An hour later they appeared in strength on our left, and were there handsomely repulsed and lost severely by our musketry. In both of these attacks the enemy must have lost great numbers. [*OR* 11, pt. 2, p. 307.]

Report of Col. *John B. Strange,* CSA, Commanding *Pickett's* Brigade, *Longstreet's* Division, Army of Northern Virginia

The brigade reached Gaines' Mill and was immediately led to the right in the direction of heavy firing. Passing through woods we soon reached a large, open, undulating field, with heavy timber on all sides, where we were formed in line of battle and awaited a few minutes the approach of the enemy, which was momentarily expected, as they were exactly in our front. Finding they would not advance, General *Pickett* ordered the brigade to advance, which it did in good order and at a double-quick until it reached the brow of a hill about 75 yards in front of the intrenched enemy. Here the firing became so fearful that the men threw themselves upon the ground and commenced returning the fire with spirit. Seeing the inequality of the contest a charge was ordered, which was obeyed with promptness.

Here our gallant General *Pickett* fell badly wounded while nobly urging on our boys. Colonel [*R. E.*] *Withers* also was badly wounded at the head of his regiment, and Colonel [*Eppa*] *Hunton* was sick, though he did not leave the field I understood afterward, the command of the brigade thus falling upon me even before I was aware of it.

The long lists of killed and wounded will show the determined manner with which the brigade conducted itself.

The brigade entered the battle with 1,481 men and officers, and lost in killed and wounded 426, including 41 officers. [*OR* 11, pt. 2, p. 767.]

Turn to your left and continue to follow the path for another 120 yards. Here you will find a trail intersection. This intersection is the center of the breakthrough made by the brigades of *Whiting's* Division late in the day. You will look at this breakthrough later from a position higher on the hill. At the intersection turn right and follow the trail toward the Alabama Monument (see sign) for 60 yards, stop, then face to the right, west.

Position D—Butterfield's Defense

You are in the area defended by Brigadier General Daniel Butterfield's Third Brigade. Butterfield deployed his brigade in two lines. The Forty-fourth New York and Eighty-third Pennsylvania were in the first line. The Sixteenth Michigan and the Twelfth New York were in the supporting second line. Although there was brush and trees in the bottom of the draw where the creek is, in 1862 the ground on the other side was a large open field where Butterfield had established a skirmish line. This field had to be crossed by the attackers and provide Union infantry and artillery excellent fields of fire.

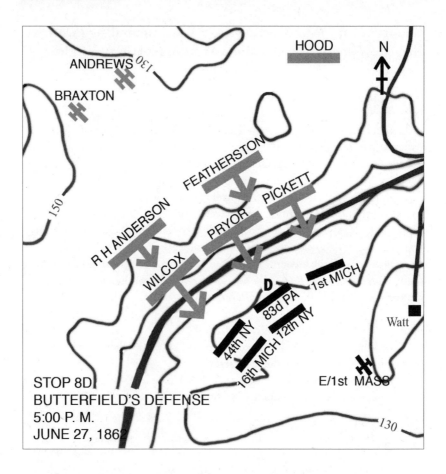

HOOD

N

ANDREWS

130

BRAXTON

150

FEATHERSTON

R H ANDERSON

PRYOR

PICKETT

WILCOX

D

1st MICH

83d PA

44th NY

16th MICH

12th NY

Watt

STOP 8D
BUTTERFIELD'S DEFENSE
5:00 P. M.
JUNE 27, 1862

E/1st MASS

130

Report of Brig. Gen. Daniel Butterfield, USA, Commanding Third Brigade, First Division, Fifth Corps, Army of the Potomac

The following was the disposition of my brigade: Eighty-third Pennsylvania Volunteers on the creek, with its right connecting with General Martindale's left (First Michigan Regiment); Forty-fourth New York to the left and on the same line of Eighty-third; Twelfth New York on the crest of the hill, in rear of and supporting the Eighty-third; Sixteenth Michigan back of crest of hill, in rear of and supporting the Forty-fourth; [Hyde's Battery E] Massachusetts [Artillery] to the right and rear of my position, so situated as to be used at any point of the line I might wish; skirmishers from the Eighty-third and Forty-fourth Regiments, together with the sharpshooters of the Sixteenth Michigan, were thrown well forward on the brow of the hill, com-

Boatswains Creek as it runs in front of Butterfield's defensive position today.

manding our entire lines. These skirmishers throughout the day performed their duties in a manner to merit my entire satisfaction, successfully holding the enemy in check and only retreating when attacked by two or three regiments of the enemy.

The first attack of the enemy in force on my brigade took place at about 2.30 o'clock p.m., it having been preceded by a like attack on the right and center of the general line. So soon as it began I ordered a section of [Hyde's] battery to take a position opposite to and fire through an interval in the woods commanding the hill in front of my center. Their fire proved very destructive to the assaulting column. Finding that my front line would successfully hold the enemy in check, I ordered the Twelfth New York and Sixteenth Michigan to the right in support of General Martindale's left; but as the result proved, their services were not needed there and they returned.

The second attack of the enemy, preceded as in the first one by an attack on the right and center, took place at about 5.30 o'clock p.m. and was more severe, but so far as the result is concerned met with a like reception and repulse. I brought forward my two reserves and had the whole of my force engaged. Constant information was brought me from the skirmishers of any change in the enemy's position. I was thus enabled to anticipate every assault. [OR 11, pt. 2, pp. 316–17.]

The initial units from *Longstreet*'s Division that came in contact with this portion of the Union defensive line were regiments of Brigadier General *Roger A. Pryor*'s brigade. *Pryor* deployed his brigade about 800 yards to the west of where you are standing. From that location his brigade proceeded forward in a reconnaissance to determine the location of the Union defensive position. His initial contact was made with the Union skirmish line located on the high ground west of Boatswain's Creek. From there he attacked this position as part of the general assault made by *Longstreet* late in the afternoon.

Report of Brig. Gen. *Roger A. Pryor*, CSA, Commanding *Pryor*'s Brigade, *Longstreet*'s Division, Army of Northern Virginia

Arriving at Hogan's house in pursuit of the enemy I was directed by Major-General *Longstreet* to conduct my brigade as an advance guard. I had not proceeded more than a mile when the enemy were observed in the woods on Dr. Gaines' farm. I detached a few companies to drive in his nearest skirmishers and to dislodge his sharpshooters from their cover. This was effected without much difficulty. A line of skirmishers extending along the entire front of the woods in rear of Dr. Gaines' house discovered to me the position in which the enemy had resolved to offer battle.

Of this position I attempted a reconnaissance. I deployed my entire brigade under a galling fire from the enemy's battery [south of the Chickahominy] river and advanced across the field a distance of half a mile to within range of the enemy's infantry. I found him in very great force.

A few hours afterward Captain *Meade,* of Major-General *Longstreet*'s staff, delivered me an order to engage the enemy. Immediately I moved from my position at Gaines' house straightforward to the wood in which the enemy was concealed. Ascending the hill in front of his position, my men were staggered by a terrific volley at the same time that, they suffered severely from the battery across the Chickahominy. [This is the Union artillery south of the Chickahominy River.] I was compelled to retire them to the cover of a ravine in my rear. After the lapse of a few moments I again moved them forward, and again they encountered a fire which it was impossible to endure. This time, however, they were not arrested before they had rushed down to the edge of the wood where the enemy lay.

In these assaults I sustained a very great loss—as much almost from the enemy's artillery as from his infantry fire. A single shell killed and disabled 11 of my men.

Meanwhile *Wilcox* had come to my assistance. Then *Featherston* and *Pickett* appeared. Forming line on the acclivity of the hill which screened us from the enemy we moved forward, but for several minutes of painful suspense we were held in check by the deadly volleys poured upon us. At last, with a terrific yell, our brave men rushed down the hill, leaped the ditch, and drove the enemy from his position at the point of the bayonet. Emerging from the woods, they encountered an awful fire of grape and canister from several batteries in the field before them. Nevertheless they pressed on, drove the enemy from his second line, and captured his artillery. So the field was won. [*OR* 11, pt. 2, p. 780.]

You are in the right part of Butterfield's defensive line. The regiment defending here was the Eighty-third Pennsylvania.

Report of Lieut. Col. Hugh S. Campbell, USA, Commanding Eighty-third Pennsylvania Infantry, Third Brigade, First Division, Fifth Corps, Army of the Potomac

At daylight next morning we were again on the march and partly retraced our route, halting for a short time near Gaines' Mill, and thence proceeded into the woods that skirt the wheat field from east to west, resting in the swamp, and distant about three-fourths of a mile from the mansion known by that name. Immediately in front of this wood and between it and the wheat field runs a ravine, through which winds an intricate, gorged rivulet, thickly overgrown with brier and brushwood, and in the rear of the same and through the forest we were ordered to form line of battle. This accomplished, the regiment stacked arms, unslung knapsacks, and for the better enabling of the defense by the river and the obstruction of the enemy, who were expectantly approaching down hill and through the wheat field in front, and threw up a temporary breastwork of all the felled timber and rubbish along their line.

For many hours in this position we waited the approach of the enemy, which was to be announced by the fire of the skirmishers, Companies B and A, who meanwhile lay extended in our front. When . . . he first showed himself in the expected direction our skirmishers fell back at once, capturing and bringing in 2 prisoners, who were sent to the rear. The Twelfth New York Volunteers [and Sixteenth Michigan], who were deployed in rear and on the heights in the woods above us, opening fire upon him, the fire was returned, and the right wing of the Eighty-third, being more on a level and in view of the enemy, commenced also a heavy fire. The enemy still approached in column of brigades, covered by his regiments in line of battle, but discovering when too late the position our regiment held, he precipitately fled back, with heavy loss of killed and wounded.

At this moment Brigadier-General Butterfield, amidst a galling fire from his lines of support in the rear and that of the enemy in front, came coolly down the knoll, and, sword in hand, seized our colors, waving them repeatedly aloft, and by all mortal means encouraged the valor of our regiment. His presence at once stimulated with new vigor our now thinned ranks, when the general loudly shouted out, "Your ammunition is never expended while you have your bayonets, my boys, and use them to the socket."

The battle at this juncture raged furiously. The fire was tremendous. The trees were lopped and branches and leaves fell as thick as snowflakes, whilst the balls flew like a hail-storm, the solid shot, grape, canister, and shrapnel unintermittingly scattering destruction in all directions, when it was intimated that the regiments on our right were repulsed and gave way under the destructive fire of the enemy, who also threatened our right flank and were at that moment gradually gaining on our rear. Placed in this situation, without a moment's respite to change our position, the regiment was ordered to face by the rear rank and wheel obliquely to quarter circle on the proper right, then become the left, a maneuver that was rapidly executed, and during its performance, I regret to state, its commander, Colonel McLane, was killed, and Major Naghel mortally wounded.

The command of the Eighty-third now devolved upon me. I found the enemy in vast numbers in front. The fire was terrific. The Eighty-third faced, as just stated, by the rear rank, mowed the assailants down in heaps, drove them back, and ultimately compelled them to abandon their object of advance. They accordingly retreated and rallied in contiguous lines of battle in another open field to the right and perpendicular to my proper left flank.

The enemy now being fairly driven from the woods, and as a last resort made his final stand on his own chosen ground. Major Von Vegesack came galloping along our lines, and, in a voice never to be forgotten, ordered the Eighty-third to face by the right flank, advance, half face to the left, thereby still keeping the rear rank in front, deep on the center, and again face the foe. This cool and determined move on the part of him, Major Von Vegesack, which shall never be too warmly appreciated on the part of the Eighty-third, so filled the enemy, who were drawn up in line at about 100 yards' distance, with consternation, that he remained perfectly motionless and evidently awe-stricken for many moments, and waved signals which we did not understand, and finally sent forward a flag of truce, the Eighty-third doing so likewise, to know their intentions, which were to the effect that they considered themselves so powerful we had better surrender; a proposition, I need hardly add, that caused indignant mirth among us; and ere the officer of the Eighty-third who bore the truce returned to our ranks they, contrary to the rules, I believe, of civilized warfare, poured a deadly volley into the partly incautious ranks of our regiment. At once we fell flat on the ground, raising on the knee and returning the fire, which was kept up in the bravest and most determined manner against overwhelming numbers, keeping the enemy at bay, until dark of the evening and the total expenditure of our cartridges caused us to retreat across the Chickahominy River. [*OR* 11, pt. 2, pp. 344–45.]

Face to the left and continue along the trail for another 250 yards to the Alabama Monument. Face to the right, west, so that you are looking across Boatswain's Creek.

Position E—The Fifth Corps Left Flank

You are directly in the center of the Forty-fourth New York's defensive position. This regiment was the left regiment in Butterfield's

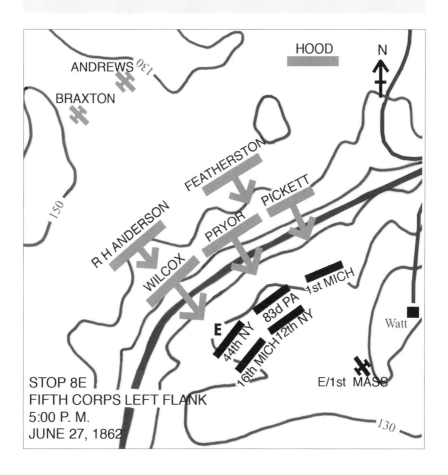

first line. In this position the Forty-fourth New York was not only the extreme left unit of Butterfield's brigade but of the entire Fifth Corps line. Directly behind you was the position of the Sixteenth Michigan, which was supporting the Forty-fourth New York. At this position you can see the advantage offered the defender by the rise in the ground on the Union side of the creek. Here, as all along the defensive position of the Third Brigade, the defenses were arranged with one regiment in front and a second regiment behind and higher up on the hill. This allowed the supporting regiments to fire over the heads of the regiments in the first line, doubling the firepower being brought to bear on the Confederate units as they crossed the open ground on the other side of Boatswain's Creek.

Report of Lieut. Col. James C. Rice, USA, Commanding Forty-fourth New York Infantry, Third Brigade, First Division, Fifth Corps, Army of the Potomac

The bridges having been destroyed between the rear guard and the enemy, I reported the fact to the general [Butterfield], who immediately ordered me to superintend the felling of the trees in front of his brigade as an abatis, and the construction of a dam on our extreme left across the stream, to more effectually obstruct the approach of the enemy. The Forty-fourth New York Volunteers, holding the extreme left of the line, had thrown up a temporary earthwork of considerable strength by order of the general, in addition to the other defenses he had ordered for the protection of the brigade. These speedily-thrown-up defenses eventually saved the left of the line from entire annihilation. Scarcely had these obstructions been thrown up before the line of skirmishers in front of the brigade gave evidence of the approach of the enemy. For nearly two hours, while the enemy was moving his troops into position on our center and right, the skirmishers and sharpshooters of the brigade held in check the right of the enemy's forces, and frequently compelled entire regiments to fall back under cover of the woods to escape their deadly fire. The effectiveness of this line of skirmishers and sharpshooters in front of our masked forces deserves especial notice. They not only constantly reported to the general the movements and disposition of the enemy's forces, but continually thinned his ranks by their unerring fire.

At thirty minutes past 12 o'clock in the afternoon the enemy commenced along our entire line a most determined attack. On the left of the line he was constantly repulsed till 6 o'clock in the afternoon, when an entire brigade of his forces charged upon our lines, broke through the left of the forces on our right, and vigorously attacked the right flank of our brigade. Thus severely pressed on the right and in front by a superior force, the Eighty-third Pennsylvania and the Twelfth New York, which supported it, were obliged to fall back. They were now quickly rallied by the general commanding, who ordered at once the Sixteenth Michigan to their support. Here, animated by the immediate presence and encouraging words of the general, these regiments sustained for a few moments a most murderous fire. Not far from this point of time Colonel McLane, of the Eighty-third Pennsylvania, gallantly fell at the head of his regiment . . . .

At this time the enemy had turned the right of our entire line of battle and the center was falling back, when the commanding officer of the Forty-fourth New York Volunteers with the left wing of the regiment commenced to retreat, and at length to fly toward the Chickahominy. I was in command of the right wing, and as soon as I saw the conduct of the left wing I was fired with indignation and anger, for not a moment before the entire regiment had assured the general, who had visited it under a terrible fire and animated it to deeds of valor by cheering words, that he might depend upon its constancy. With such feelings I at once ordered the right wing to stand firm, and overtook the left before it had reached the river. I halted the columns, seized the colors, rallied the battalion with the assistance of Captain Conner, and in line of battle led it back under a murderous fire to its original position. I regret to report the commanding officer of the regiment and Captain Walsh, of Company E, fled across the river at this time, and did not join their regiment till the next day at 11 o'clock a.m. Scarcely had the regiment been reformed and advanced to its original position before the enemy was closing fast upon our rear and right in overpowering numbers and pouring into our ranks a most deadly fire. The regiment was at once ordered to leap over the earthwork and pour its fire into the ranks of the enemy, now closing in upon us from the rear and right. At the same time the enemy had pushed forward a regiment not more than 100 yards to our front, now our rear. The Eighty-third Pennsylvania and Sixteenth Michigan had quickly changed front to meet the attack of this regiment.

Information was now brought to me by our skirmishers that this regiment desired to lay down its arms and surrender. This information as to the desire of this regiment to surrender, in addition to the fact that our skirmishers had already taken 20 prisoners and were just bringing in 10 others from this very regiment, induced me to send out Captain Conner, a trusty officer, to ascertain the facts. At the same time I was impressed with the apprehension that the reason why this regiment so long withheld its fire arose from the fact that it had mistaken us from the opposite direction of our fire for its friends. This apprehension soon proved true. In the mean time the Eighty-third

Pennsylvania and the Sixteenth Michigan, not being able to stand the deadly fire of the enemy from the right and rear, joined the Forty-fourth New York.

Now the enemy was drawing nearer and nearer around us, but still we poured into his advancing ranks a terrible fire. At this moment Major Von Vegesack, aide-de-camp, informed me that the general had ordered him to bring off from the field the remaining regiments of the brigade, but that he would be pleased to advise with me before he gave the order to retreat. I at once sorrowfully beheld the utter hopelessness of the unequal contest and ordered a retreat. The column had scarcely passed by the right flank from the rear of the earthworks and filed into the ravine running for a short distance in the direction of the river before the regiment of the enemy in our rear discovered its mistake and opened upon us a severe fire, while along the entire right upon the crest of the hill the enemy poured into our ranks from both musketry and artillery a sheet of iron and lead. Still the column pressed forward across the long meadow, its ranks becoming thinner and thinner, till at length through marsh and swamp and tangled underwood, dense and almost impassable, amid falling trees and bursting shells, it reached the [Chickahominy] river, and plunging in, waded to the opposite bank. In this retreat not less than 100 of this fragment of the brigade were either killed or wounded. Having crossed the river, I formed the fragments of the brigade in line and commenced the march toward the headquarters of General McClellan.

The Forty-fourth New York lost in this battle 5 killed, 22 wounded, and 29 missing. Most of the missing were killed or wounded in the retreat and remained in the hands of the enemy. [*OR* 11, pt. 2, pp. 338–41.]

Major General *James Longstreet*'s division was the Confederate force attacking the left of Martindale's brigade and Butterfield's brigade. *Longstreet*'s Division had begun the day in the vicinity of Mechanicsville. When *Lee* advanced his forces, *Longstreet*'s Division had marched on a parallel route south of the route traveled by *A. P. Hill*. This route brought *Longstreet* to a position about nine hundred yards to the west of where you are now.

Report of Maj. Gen. *James Longstreet*, CSA, Commanding *Longstreet*'s Division, Army of Northern Virginia

It was soon discovered that the enemy had fallen back rapidly from his right, burning and otherwise destroying most of the property that he could not remove. The pursuit was steadily continued until 1 o'clock, when the enemy was discovered strongly posted behind Powhite Creek [Boatswain's

Creek]. The three brigades under *Wilcox* were advanced to the edge of the creek to feel the enemy, and ascertain as far as practicable his strength. It was soon found that he was in full force. A message to this effect was received from Brig. Gen. *D. R. Jones* a few moments previous. The troops were halted in position to await the arrival of the other divisions.

Maj. Gen. *A. P. Hill* soon repaired the bridges at the mill, crossed the Powhite Creek, and took position for the attack.

The columns under General *Jackson*, having a longer march, were not in position for some time after. Finally these columns were reported in position, and the commanding general directed my brigades to be put in position on the right to co-operate. In front of me the enemy occupied the wooded slope of Turkey Hill, the crest of which is 50 or 60 feet higher than the plain over which my troops must pass to make an attack. The plain is about a quarter of a mile wide; the farther side of it was occupied by sharpshooters. [The plain Longstreet refers to is the open field west of Boatswain's Creek.] Above these and on the slope of the hill was a line of infantry behind trees, felled so as to form a good breastwork. The crest of the hill, some 40 feet above the last line, was strengthened by rifle trenches and occupied by infantry and artillery. In addition to this the plain was enfiladed by batteries on the other side of the Chickahominy. I was, in fact, in the position from which the enemy wished us to attack him.

The attack was begun by Maj. Gen. *A. P. Hill's* division. My troops were drawn up in lines, massed behind the crest of a hill, and behind a small wood, three brigades in each position, and held in readiness as the reserve. We had not been in position long, however, before I received an urgent message from the commanding general to make a diversion in favor of the attacking columns. The three brigades under *Wilcox* were at once ordered forward against the enemy's left flank with this view. *Pickett's* brigade, making a diversion on the left of these brigades, developed the strong position and force of the enemy in my front, and I found that I must drive him by direct assault or abandon the idea of making the diversion. From the urgent nature of the message from the commanding general and my own peculiar position I determined to change the feint into an attack, and orders for a general advance were issued. [*OR* 11, pt. 2, pp. 756–57.]

The Confederate force attacking at this point was *Wilcox's* Brigade of *Longstreet's* Division. This brigade had initially occupied a position near the Gaines house, about 1,100 yards to the west of where you are. From that location it then moved forward to the west side of the plain where the open field was and deployed with *Pryor's*

Brigade and *Featherston*'s Brigade for attack. Under cover of a skirmish line this force moved forward and joined in the attack against
the Union position. A monument to the Alabama units that fought
here is directly in front of you. Brigadier General *Cadmus Wilcox* is
predominately featured on the monument.

Report of Brig. Gen. *Cadmus Wilcox*, CSA, Commanding *Wilcox*'s Brigade, *Longstreet*'s Division, Army of Northern Virginia

I now made my preparations for an attack upon the enemy, intending
it to be made with the utmost vigor and with all the force at my command.
My brigade was advanced to the front, and two regiments (the Tenth and
Eleventh Alabama, the latter on the right) were formed in line of battle in
rear of the crest of the hill from which *Pryor*'s regiment was withdrawn from
the pursuit of the enemy's skirmishers. *Pryor*'s brigade, with the exception of
one regiment (Second Florida), formed in line on the left of mine. The two
remaining regiments of my brigade (the Eighth and Ninth Alabama, the former on the right) were formed in rear of the Tenth and Eleventh Alabama,
and *Featherston* in rear, to support both *Pryor*'s and my brigade.

It is proper that I should state that this placing of troops in position to
attack the enemy was made under a brisk enfilading fire of artillery from
the enemy's batteries of rifled cannon from the heights beyond the Chickahominy. [This was the Union heavy artillery on the south side of the Chickahominy River.] Our troops behaved admirably under this fire, no confusion
or disorder being perceptible in their ranks.

Every preparation being made for a vigorous attack, firing was now heard
on our left, which was the signal for our advance, and the order was immediately given. Our men moved forward in admirable order, preserving their
alignments perfectly. Ascending the crest of the hill they came in full view of
the enemy, and were instantly met by a heavy and destructive fire of infantry
within less than 100 yards. Our men now make a dash at the enemy, and the
conflict begins with an ardor and determination on our part that could not
fail to inspire the utmost confidence in those that witnessed it.

Nothing could surpass the valor and impetuosity of our men. They
encounter the enemy in large force directly in their front behind two lines of
breastworks, the second overlooking the first, and from behind this, as well as
the first, a close and terrible fire of musketry is poured in upon them. The bed
of the small stream at their feet and between them and the enemy is used as a
rifle pit, and from this a strong line of fire is also brought to bear on us. Thus

exposed to the three lines of fire, they bravely confront it all and press forward and close in upon the enemy. Now there is a slight halt and some wavering and a few men give way; but a second supporting line is near—the Eighth and Ninth Alabama press on in rear of the Tenth and Eleventh Alabama and *Featherston* in rear of *Pryor*. The first impulse is more than re-doubled. Other brigades come in on the left of *Pryor* and in rear of where we are so hotly engaged. Our men still press on with unabated fury. The enemy at length, with but a few yards between themselves and our men, are shaken and begin to yield. Our men, full of confidence, rush with irresistible force upon him, and he is driven from his rifle pit pell-mell over his first breastwork of logs, and here he vainly attempts to reform and show a bold front, but, closely followed by our men, he yields, and is driven over and beyond his second parapet of logs into the standing timber and finally into the open field. Now for the first time cheers are heard from our troops and the enemy is driven from his strong position. Our loss has been up to this time severe, but now the enemy is made to suffer. No longer screened by his breastworks or standing timber, his slaughter is terrible. Our men have no difficulty in chasing him before them in every and all direction. The precision of our fire is now demonstrated clearly. The numbers of the enemy's dead in regular lines mark in some places distinctly where the lines of battle of their different regiments were formed. The enemy, yielding in all directions, loses his battery of Napoleon guns. Many prisoners are taken. We pursue them far across the open field to the woods of the swamp of the Chickahominy, and the pursuit is only arrested by night. The victory is complete, the enemy is repulsed and pursued at every point, and those that escape falling into our hands do so under the cover of the darkness of the night.

Before closing this report I beg to say that the magnificent courage of our men as displayed in this action is worthy of all praise. To properly appreciate the gallantry of those that aided in the achievement of this brilliant victory we have only to examine the position occupied by the enemy's infantry and to recall the fact that the open field over which our men advanced was swept by a direct fire of artillery, shot, shell, grape, and canister from the rear of the enemy's infantry and from an enfilade fire from batteries of rifled cannon from beyond the Chickahominy. The enemy's infantry, as previously stated, occupied the bed of a small stream as a rifle pit, and on the ascending ground in rear of this were two lines of log breastworks, behind which were sheltered in comparative security heavy masses of their infantry. Their lines of infantry fire could thus be used against our men at the same time and within less than 100 yards. In driving the enemy from this strong position our loss was heavy, but we should be profoundly grateful that it was not more so.

The casualties among the officers of the brigade number in killed, 8; wounded, 35; officers and men killed, 117; wounded, 463; missing, 4; making an aggregate of 584 killed, wounded, and missing; this loss occurring in a force of about 1,850 men. [*OR* 11, pt. 2, pp. 773–74.]

Turn around and continue for another 10 yards along the trail as it goes up hill. Here you will find the remains of rifle pits. Continue on the trail for another 80 yards to a trail intersection. You will be returning to this intersection. But, for now follow the trail to the right for 175 yards. This will bring you to an overlook.

Position F—The Overlook

At this overlook there is a park photo mosaic that show items of interest to the southeast, south, and west of you. Of particular interest is Grapevine Bridge, which was located 2,666 yards (1.5 miles) to the southeast of you, or to your left front as you look at the park picture. This was the easternmost bridge used by the Fifth Corps when it retreated in the evening of June 27. You will be crossing the Chickahominy River on a modern version of this bridge when you drive to the Battle of Savage Station. Directly in front of you and south across the river on high ground at a distance of 2,100 yards (1.2 miles) was the Golding's Farm. At that location Union heavy artillery placed flanking fire into the right of the Confederate units attacking Butterfield's defensive line (Positions D and E). *Lee* commented on this artillery fire in his report, read at Stop 7. Major Elisha S. Kellogg, commanding the First Connecticut Artillery, reported, "Battery F having arrived at 9.30 a.m., by way of Woodbury's Bridge, it was ordered into position on Golding's Hill to the right of the redoubt erected in front of General Smith's division, and opened fire on the enemy at Gaines' house with extremely good effect, the shells from the battery constantly falling in and near their ranks, compelling them to disperse and retire to the woods." [*OR* 11, pt. 2, p. 970] To your right front and west of you at a distance of 700 yards (0.4 mile) is a tree line that marks the course of Boatswain's Creek as it flows toward the Chickahominy River. This tree line is the approximate location of where the right units of *Longstreet*'s Division crossed the creek in the attack on the left of the Union line.

Follow the park trail back 175 yards, to the trail intersection. Follow the trail to the right for 240 yards, to another trail intersection. Then take the trail to the right and walk for 10 yards. Here you will find a marker, "*Whiting*'s Advance," to the Confederate division of Brigadier General *William H. C. Whiting*. Position yourself so you can read the marker and look down the trail.

Position G—The Breakthrough

If you were to follow the trail behind you it would take you back to the Watts House. The trail in front of you goes between the left flank of Martindale's brigade and the right flank of Butterfield's brigade. If you were to walk down the trail for fifty yards you would come to the intersection with the trail that goes along the positions of the regiments of Martindale's and Butterfield's brigades. You were on this trail as you walked from Position C to Position E.

The Confederate breakthrough began where the trail you are now on intersects the other trail. The center of the leading Confederate unit in the breakthrough generally followed the trail as it comes up from the low ground to where you are. The breakthrough was initiated by part of Brigadier General *John B. Hood*'s brigade. *Hood*'s

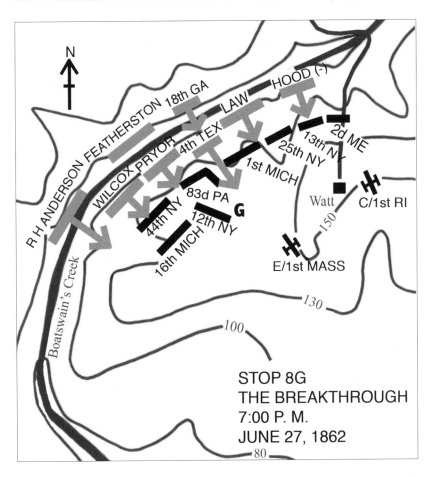

STOP 8G
THE BREAKTHROUGH
7:00 P. M.
JUNE 27, 1862

Brigade and the brigade of Colonel *Evander M. Law* formed the division commanded by Brigadier General *William H. C. Whiting*.

Report of Brig. Gen. *William H. C. Whiting*, CSA, Commanding *Whiting*'s Division, Army of Northern Virginia

Between 1 and 2 p.m. cannonading commenced in the direction of Cold Harbor. The march continued slowly, interrupted by frequent halts, until near 3 o'clock, when an aide of General *Jackson* directed me to form line of battle to my right and press through the woods to the firing, now become very heavy. This was at once done, the Texas Brigade [*Hood*'s] on the left and *Law*'s on the right, a regiment of each in reserve, the troops forcing their way in good order in line of battle through a dense forest and swamp. We came out on the Telegraph road in a heavy, but distant, fire of artillery about 4 p.m. At this point I met several aides from different generals, all desiring assistance, and informing me that the troops of both Generals *D. H.* [*Hill*] and *A. P. Hill* were hard pressed. Advancing, I shortly met the commander-in-chief, who indicated a direction a little to my right.

The field where we entered it was about the head of the ravine, which covered the enemy's left near the main road, a deep and steep chasm, dividing the bluffs of [Boatswain's Creek]. On the left side of this, as we fronted, General *Hood* put forward the First Texas and Hampton's Legion. Men were leaving the field in every direction and in great disorder; two regiments, one from South Carolina and one from Louisiana, were actually marching back from the fire. The First Texas was ordered to go over them or through them, which they did; the remaining Texas regiments were rapidly advanced, forming line on the right of the ravine, and [*Law*'s] brigade again on their right, and, pressing on, the whole line came under the enemy's fire. Here, from the nature of the ground and position of the enemy, [*Law*'s brigade] changed front obliquely to the left, bringing its front parallel to the ravine. The enemy, concealed in the woods and protected by the ravine, poured a destructive fire upon the advancing line for a quarter of a mile, and many brave officers and men fell. Near the crest in front of us and lying down appeared the fragments of a brigade's men were skulking from the front in a shameful manner; the woods on our left and rear were full of troops in safe cover, from which they never stirred; but on the right of [*Law*'s brigade] a brigade (*Pickett*'s) was moving gallantly up; still farther on the extreme right our troops appeared to be falling back.

The Texans had now come up and joined the line, led by General *Hood*, when the word was given to charge, and the whole line, consisting of the

Fourth and Fifth Texas, Eighteenth Georgia, Eleventh Mississippi, Fourth Alabama, and Sixth North Carolina, the Second Mississippi being held in partial reserve, but advancing with the line, charged the ravine with a yell, General *Hood* and Colonel *Law* gallantly heading their men. At the bottom ran a deep and difficult branch, [Boatswain's Creek] with scarped sides, answering admirably as a ditch. Over against this was a strong log breastwork, heavily manned; above this, near the crest, another breastwork, supported by well-served batteries and a heavy force of infantry, the steep slope, clad with an open growth of timber, concealing the enemy, but affording full view of our movements. Spite of these terrible obstacles, over ditch and breastwork, hill, batteries, and infantry, the division swept, routing the enemy from their stronghold. Many pieces of artillery were taken (fourteen in all) and nearly a whole regiment of the enemy. [*OR* 11, pt. 2, pp. 562–63.]

The units initiating the breakthrough were the Fourth Texas and Eighteenth Georgia of *Hood*'s Brigade. When *Whiting* began his attack *Hood* was on the left of his line while *Law* was on the right. This placed *Law*'s attack where it was striking the Union line to your right front, with *Hood* farther to your right. However, seeing an opportunity *Hood* crossed the Fourth Texas and Eighteenth Georgia behind *Law*'s Brigade. With *Hood* directing the charge these two regiments attacked on *Law*'s right. This brought the center of their advance along the trail to where you are.

Report of Brig. Gen. *John B. Hood*, CSA, Commanding *Hood*'s Brigade, *Whiting*'s Division, Army of Northern Virginia

Arriving on the field between 4 and 5 p.m., I was informed by Col. *J. M. Jones*, of General *Ewell*'s staff, that his troops were hard pressed and required assistance. Line of battle was formed at once with the Hampton Legion, Lieut. Col. *M. W. Gary* commanding, on the left, with orders to gain the crest of the hill in the woods and hold it, which they did, the Fifth Texas, Col. *J. B. Robertson* commanding, engaging the enemy on the right of the Legion, and the First Texas, Col. *A. T. Rainey* commanding, on the right of the Fifth Texas. The brigade moved gallantly forward, soon becoming engaged from left to right. The battle raged with great fury all along the line as these noble troops pressed steadily on, forcing the enemy to gradually give way.

Directing in person the Fourth Texas Regiment, Col. *John Marshall* commanding, on the right of my line: they were the first troops to pierce the strong line of breastworks occupied by the enemy, which caused great confusion in their ranks. Here the Eighteenth Georgia, Lieut. Col. *S. Z. Ruff* commanding, came to the support of the Fourth Texas, and these regiments pressed on over a hotly contested field, inclining from right to left, with the Fifth Texas on their left, taking a large number of prisoners and capturing fourteen pieces of artillery, when night came on and farther pursuit of the enemy ceased. The guns were captured by the Fourth Texas and Eighteenth Georgia and a regiment was taken prisoners by the Fifth Texas Regiment.

In this engagement I regret to report the loss of many gallant officers and men. Among those who fell, either killed or mortally wounded, were Col. *John Marshall*, Lieut. Col. *B. Warwick*, Capts. *E. D. Ryan*, *J. W. Hutcheson*, *P. P. Porter*, and *T. M. Owens*, acting commissary of subsistence, and Lieuts. *R. J. Lambert*, *C. Reich*, *D. L. Butts*, *L. P. Lyons*, and *T. H. Hollamon*, of the Fourth Texas; Lieuts. *J. E. Clute* and *W. G. Wallace*, of the Fifth Texas; Capt. *B. F. Benton*, First Texas; Lieuts. *L. A. McCulloch*, *T. J. Cohn*, and *Thomas Dowtin*, of the Eighteenth Georgia; also Major *Key*, of the Fourth Texas; Colonels *Rainey*, of the First Texas, and *Robertson*, of the Fifth Texas, received severe wounds while nobly discharging their duties.

All the field officers of the Fourth Texas being killed or wounded, the command of the regiment devolved upon Capt. (now Maj.) *W. P. Townsend*, who led it most gallantly. [*OR* 11, pt. 2, pp. 568–69.]

> In this attack the casualties of *Hood*'s Brigade were 89 killed and 477 wounded.
>
> Down the hill and to the right of the trail was the First Michigan. You looked at the defense of their position at Position C. The report of Colonel Roberts gives an example of the ferocity of the Confederate attack and breakthrough.

Report of Col. Horace S. Roberts, USA (Continued)

At about 6 o'clock he appeared in great force all along our line, with his troops massed and his columns heavier about our center. All along the lines fire was opened on him and maintained in a most vigorous manner. Nothing could have been better done; the effect upon his ranks was perceptible, and the slope of that hill must have borne testimony to the steadiness and accuracy of our fire. Yet he moved steadily along with a fire that cut down nearly one-fourth of my command until up and onto us, when, unable to resist the mass hurled at them, the line broke and the men commenced a retreat.

Hood leads his troop in the breakthrough of the Union defenses at Gaines Mill in vicinity of Stop 8G. Courtesy of Dale Gallon Historical Art.

The men were borne back by sheer force of numbers. Twice the enemy had been repulsed by our fire, but with fresh troops he moved in inestimable force against the line, and it had to give way. We fell back, reformed our line, and took position near to and in front of the hospital, ready for a renewal of the fight. We remained here until 3 o'clock a.m., when the regiment crossed the Chickahominy River. [*OR* 11, pt. 2, p. 307.]

Brigadier General Daniel Butterfield's brigade was deployed to the left of the trail. You looked at the defense conducted by several of his regiments at Positions D and E. You are now standing to the right rear of Butterfield's original defensive position. The line of the Twelfth New York, which was the right regiment in the second line, was thirty yards to your left front. Another thirty yards down the hill in front of the Twelfth New York was the Eighty-third Pennsylvania. Butterfield's report shows how confusing the fighting in this area became as the Confederates penetrated the Union defensive line. As the Confederate breakthrough developed, the right part of the Eighty-third Pennsylvania fell back so as to face the penetration. At the same time the Twelfth New York faced to the right.

Report of Brig. Gen. Daniel Butterfield, USA (Continued)

At the third and last assault, which took place shortly after 6 p.m., and which seemed simultaneous throughout the whole line, all four of my regiments were engaged, occupying the positions as first noted. Finding the pressure terribly severe upon General Martindale's line, I moved a portion of my command by the flank to his support, changing the front of the Eighty-third Pennsylvania partially to assist in resisting the attack on General Martindale's front, and moving the Twelfth by a flank, with the hope and endeavor to hold in check the enemy, who by their vastly superior strength and their overpowering re-enforcements of fresh troops had succeeded in breaking a portion of General Martindale's line without disgrace to any portion of his command; for no men could ever have fought better, braver, or more determinedly. In moving the Twelfth Regiment by the right flank a portion of the regimen gave way, the balance remaining firm, with the greater portion of my brigade, until surrounded and outflanked. At this time fell the gallant Colonel McLane, fighting at the head of his regiment; also Major Naghel.

Finding it useless to attempt longer to hold the ground, every effort was made to form a new line in the rear and gradually withdraw the brigade under cover of the batteries on our right. Twice did the greater portion of the command form and deliver a fire with a bravery and gallantry worthy of better success while the enemy pursued hotly in overpowering numbers. Finding from the position and condition of my command, their ammunition being exhausted, I ordered Major Vegesack to withdraw the left in as good order as possible and place it in condition of safety. The enemy had cut my line while I was endeavoring to rally those that had broken from my right and from the left of General Martindale. So emboldened were the enemy by their success in getting on all sides of my command, that a regiment sent a flag of truce to the Eighty-third, demanding their surrender. This was indignantly refused, and the regiment expended its last round of ammunition in fighting its way out. A large portion of these succeeded in forming in good order on the hill in rear of the batteries, and with other fragments of commands, aided by the Prince de Joinville, Captain Hoyt, and Major Webb, of the regular artillery, and Colonel Roberts, Second Maine, two good lines of troops were formed with some degree of precision. The firing of the artillery closed the scene and saved us all from destruction. [*OR* 11, pt. 2, p. 317.]

As the Confederate attack penetrated into this area and as it captured ground to the right of where you are, Butterfield's units were forced back. Several times the Twelfth New York attempted to reform, but it was pushed back each time.

Report of Lieut. Col. Robert M. Richardson, USA, Commanding Twelfth New York Infantry, Third Brigade, First Division, Fifth Corps, Army of the Potomac

. . . At 6 o'clock he renewed the attack, and for an hour and a half the battle raged fiercely along our entire line. The enemy was evidently in greatly superior numbers. Brigade after brigade of fresh troops poured down upon us from the opposite hills, but at about 7.30 o'clock the enemy gave way on our front and inclined to their left, bearing down in overwhelming numbers upon General Martindale. Our men were beginning to fire to the right oblique, when the right of my regiment was broken by the First Michigan Volunteers falling back through it. General Martindale's brigade having fallen back, the enemy occupied the hill on our right where General Martindale's brigade had been posted, and was evidently designing to cut us off. The Eighty-third had filed out of the ravine to our left and taken position out of the woods on our rear. Some of the companies on the right of my regiment were in disorder, owing to the First Michigan breaking through our lines, and I was rallying and aligning them at the time Major Barnum called my attention to the fact that our regiment was alone and that we were nearly surrounded. I gave the order to fall back. A portion of the regiment on the left formed on the right of the Eighty-third and Forty-fourth and returned again into the woods, under the direction of General Butterfield, and checked for a while the advance of the enemy, and afterward fell back under the command of Major Barnum, Captains Randall, Fowler, and Hoagland, and crossed the Chickahominy above Woodbury's Bridge. The other portion of the regiment gathered around the colors, Captains Wood and Huson rallying them, and until 1.30 o'clock served as a support to a battery at How's house, when by order they crossed the Chickahominy at Woodbury's Bridge. I was with this portion of the regiment.

Our loss in this engagement was 11 killed, 66 wounded, and 54 missing. There were many instances of real bravery exhibited by the non-commissioned officers and privates, but I cannot mention them by name now, but will do so when appointments are to be made.

Allow me here to mention with approbation the conduct of Quartermaster-Sergeant Hilton, who, after riding up and down the ranks encouraging the men, dismounted, took a musket, went into the ranks, and did good service as a soldier. It gave me great pleasure to notice the gallant conduct of

Major Welch, of the Sixteenth Michigan, who held his men steady under the hill in rear of the woods, and who afterward advanced them with some of my own men under Captain Randall against the enemy, covering the retreat of the brigade. [*OR* 11, pt. 2, pp. 327–28.]

At the *Whiting* marker turn around and follow the trail one hundred yards, to the top of the hill. Here you will find two artillery pieces. Stand next to the guns and look toward where you just came from.

Position H—Guns of E Battery, First Massachusetts Artillery

This is the position of Battery E, First Massachusetts Artillery. Initially a section of two guns had been positioned here. As the day wore

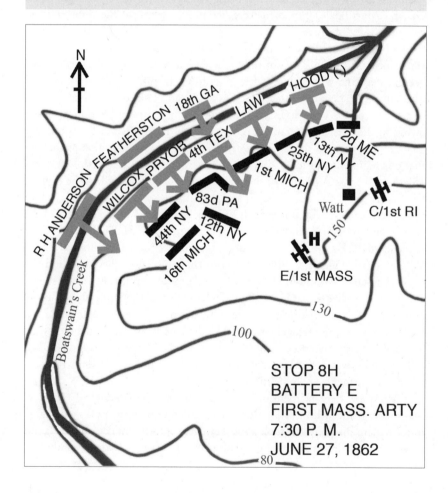

on and Confederate forces continued to arrive on the other side of Boatswain's Creek, the entire battery was positioned here. From this location they could provide support to the infantry of Martindale's and Butterfield's brigades by firing over the heads of the infantry at the Confederates on the other side of Boatswain's Creek. After the Confederate breakthrough this artillery became a point for the Union infantry to attempt a rally.

Report of Lieut. John B. Hyde, USA, Commanding Battery E, First Massachusetts Artillery, First Division, Fifth Corps, Army of the Potomac

[I] was ordered to take position near the edge of the woods by General Butterfield, and with the assistance of his brigade drove the enemy back several times in great disorder, after which we resumed our position on the hill and remained in readiness for the enemy to come out of the woods, then to give them double canister, which we did with great effect until, our support giving way, we were obliged to limber up and retire, which we did in good order, with all our pieces but one, the horses of which having been previously killed, I was obliged to leave. We had proceeded but a short distance when the fire of the enemy became so intense that the horses in three of the pieces were killed, thereby preventing their removal from the field. [*OR* 11, pt. 2, p. 285.]

Continue to follow the park path for 60 yards, where the trail meets a small road. Follow this road to the left, continue across the road circle, and walk 50 more yards to the cannons. Face left so that you are looking north. This is also Position A, where you started the tour of this part of the battle.

Position I—Center Artillery Line

You are at the left of an artillery line that was positioned here in mid-afternoon. It was the artillery of Brigadier General George A. McCall's Third Division, Fifth Corps. Along a line going 225 yards to your right, twenty-two pieces of artillery were deployed: Battery A, First Pennsylvania Artillery, four guns, Captain Hezekiah Easton commanding; Battery G, First Pennsylvania Artillery, six guns, Captain Mark Kerns commanding; Battery B, First Pennsylvania

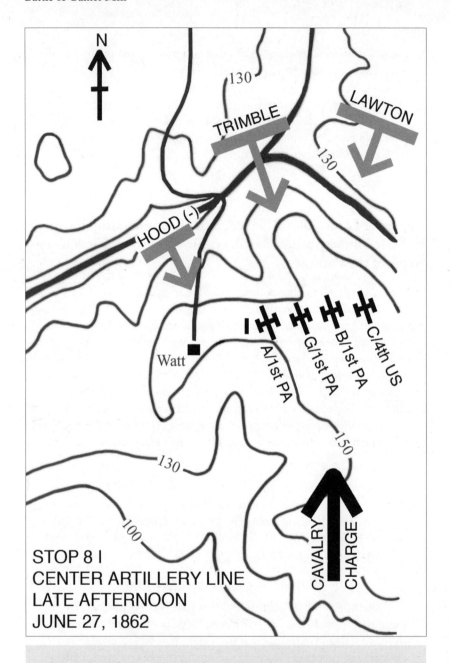

N

130

TRIMBLE

LAWTON

130

HOOD (-)

130

C/4th US

B/1st PA

G/1st PA

A/1st PA

Watt

150

130

100

CAVALRY

CHARGE

STOP 8 I
CENTER ARTILLERY LINE
LATE AFTERNOON
JUNE 27, 1862

Artillery, six guns, Captain James H. Cooper commanding; Battery C, Fourth U.S. Artillery, six guns, Captain Henry V. DeHart commanding. The fighting here was so fierce that of the four battery commanders only one would be standing at the end of the day. One was killed outright, one died of wounds, and another was wounded.

From this location this artillery fired against the numerous attacks made by *A. P. Hill*'s Division and did much damage to Captain *William G. Crenshaw*'s Virginia Battery, Captain *Marmaduke Johnson*'s Richmond Battery, and Captain *William J. Pegram*'s Purcell Battery. The report of Captain Cooper gives an account of this fighting from the perspective of the artillery.

Report of Capt. James H. Cooper, USA, Commanding Battery B, First Pennsylvania Artillery, Third Division, Fifth Corps, Army of the Potomac

. . . we formed in line of battle with General Reynolds' brigade in front of hospital buildings. Shortly afterward General Reynolds withdrew the infantry of his brigade, leaving for our support one regiment of New York troops. Remaining in this position until 5.30 p.m. the battery on our right retired, the enemy occupying their position, when we opened fire upon them and held them in check until 8 p.m., when, our support falling back, we retired in its rear to prevent the capture of our battery by a column of the enemy who were charging upon us. The effect of our shot on the enemy was destructive. [*OR* 11, pt. 2, p. 410.]

By late afternoon and early evening the Confederate forces were greatly increasing their combat power. This resulted in an attack against the entire Union line. You have already looked at the attack and breakthrough on the left. The preponderance of Confederate power at this point plus the breakthrough on the left caused the defense at this position to collapse.

Report of Lieut. John G. Simpson, USA, Commanding Battery A, First Pennsylvania Artillery, Third Division, Fifth Corps, Army of the Potomac

About 6 o'clock p.m. the enemy suddenly appeared in front and on our left flank, firing heavy volleys of musketry and charging up the hill on our battery, to which we replied with a brisk fire of shell and spherical case-shot, but without avail, as the dense masses of the enemy instantly closed the gap our fire made in their ranks and appeared to have little effect on them, although they were literally mowed down in heaps.

This continued for twenty minutes or a half hour, when they made a desperate charge, and we opened on them with double-shotted canister, which checked them for a time, but rallying again in overwhelming numbers they charged in on the battery, driving the cannoneers from their posts at the point of the bayonet, compelling them to leave their battery of four guns and two caissons in the enemy's hands.

A few minutes previous to this occurrence a body of cavalry were sent to support us, but after making a feeble charge were driven off by a volley of the enemy's musketry. Had the support consisted of infantry, the battery might probably have been saved.

It was at this period of the engagement that the brave Captain Easton was killed, receiving his death-wound from a musket-ball while gallantly cheering on his officers and men, who stood manfully and unflinchingly at their guns. [*OR* 11, pt. 2, p. 408.]

At this location occurred one of the few attacks made by mounted cavalry against infantry. Five companies of the Fifth U.S. Cavalry made this charge against the Confederate infantry as they attacked this location. The charge was designed to assist the artillery in withdrawing. It probably caused more harm than good, as the charge and retreat of the cavalry passed through this position and added to the confusion.

Report of Capt. Joseph H. McArthur, USA, Commanding Fifth U.S. Cavalry Regiment, First Cavalry Brigade, Cavalry Reserve, Army of the Potomac

During the first part of the engagement the regiment was kept out of fire, prepared to move wherever occasion demanded. Late in the action, and about 6 o'clock in the afternoon, the regiment was moved up and formed in line of battle to support [the artillery]. The regiment occupied this position until the battery on the right had ceased firing. The enemy advanced boldly on these batteries, which had opened a murderous fire upon them with the evident intention of carrying them. As soon as the battery on our right ceased firing Captain Whiting, who was at that time in command, gave the order to charge. The regiment charged the enemy's infantry under a most galling fire until 6 officers out of the 7 had been struck down. The column, being left without officers, wheeled to the right, and came off in as good order as could be expected.

I regret to state that Captains Whiting and Chambliss and Lieutenant Sweet have not been seen or heard of since the charge, and I am unable to state whether they are killed or merely wounded and taken prisoners. [*OR* 11, pt. 2, p. 46.]

Farther to the right Brigadier General George Sykes's Second Division had defended the Union position. As the Confederate attacks built up combat power two brigades from Brigadier General George A. McCall's Third Division reinforced him. The other brigade from McCall's division was sent into action where you are.

Report of Brig. Gen. George A. McCall, USA, Commanding Third Division, Fifth Corps, Army of the Potomac

At 3.30 p.m. the enemy advanced, and very soon after the action commenced. You [Porter] ordered me to move forward the Second Brigade

Charge of the Fifth Cavalry through the Union artillery at Stop 8I, Battle of Gaines Mill. U.S. Naval Academy Museum.

[commanded by Brigadier General George G. Meade to the vicinity of where you are] and Third Brigade [commanded by Brigadier General Truman Seymour to your right to reinforce Sykes's division] . . . . These two brigades soon were under fire, in some instances the regiments going immediately into line, while in others they halted directly in rear of the line already formed.

In a short time after this the First Brigade [commanded by Brigadier General John F. Reynolds] of my division also was ordered forward [and to your right to reinforce Sykes] and soon became engaged. In the mean time the batteries of my division . . . also advanced, and shelled the enemy over the heads of the men in line.

The action soon became general, and the fire in front of my division, which was near the center of the battle line, increased to a deafening roar of musketry, above which the artillery fire at times could scarcely be distinguished. The enemy was apparently drawn up in five lines, and one after another was thrown forward on my front as fast as the preceding one recoiled before the well-directed fire of the [Pennsylvania] Reserves, or with such short intervals that the thoroughly-heated muskets had not time to cool. In this way for upward of three hours my brave fellows were under fire, either relieving each other or some regiment of another division, when the men became exhausted. About this time, seeing some commotion on the left of my division, I rode rapidly to the ground, [where you are] and found that the Fourth had been driven in and was being rallied by General Meade. The line, however, was soon reformed, and I rode in front of the regiment, addressed the men briefly, and they soon resumed their place in line of battle.

Everything now on the left of the division was in successful and satisfactory operation. I therefore rode along the line, halting for short time in the center, and then proceeded to the right. Here I found General Reynolds coming from the woods with the First and Eighth Regiments of his brigade, he having relieved them and brought them out of action in consequence of their ammunition being exhausted. He reported to me that the Fifth Regiment had also nearly expended all its ammunition and ought to be relieved. I directed my assistant adjutant-general, Captain Biddle, to ride down the line and, if possible, bring up a regiment (of Morell's division, I think) that I had seen in reserve as I rode along the line. I had not proceeded far before I discovered a large number of men toward the left retiring. It soon became apparent that we had met with a reverse. I rode out in the direction of the retreating men and strove vigorously to rally them, placing a squadron of Indiana cavalry I happened to find on the ground in line, with orders to cut down any man who attempted to pass their line. My endeavor was partially successful, and I also stopped two batteries that were in retreat and brought them into battery against the enemy, who just then appeared on the opposite hill-side. This checked their advance on this point. [*OR* 11, pt. 2, pp. 387–88.]

The temporary rallying of troops by McCall and others like him was not sufficient to stop the Confederate assault, and the Union force in this area began a retreat that would take them back across the Chickahominy River. (At another location, you will see where *Gregg*'s Brigade attacked the center of the Union position and where *D. H. Hill*'s Division attacked the Union right flank and Sykes defended the Union right.)

Return to your car for the drive to Stop 9.

Follow the park road back north for 0.7 mile to the intersection with Highway 156. Turn right and drive on Highway 156 for 0.2 mile to a Park Visitors Center on the left. Park there and walk east, passing the Visitors Center and two cannons next to Highway 156. After the cannons follow the grass trail parallel to the road for fifty yards, stop, and then face right, south.

Stop 9—*Gregg*'s Attack

The Visitors Center and the two cannons you walked by are here to tell the story of the Battle of Cold Harbor, which was fought on June 3, 1864. In this battle the Union and Confederate lines were at right angles to the battle being fought on June 27, 1862. In 1864 the Confederate defensive position generally faced east and went north to south through where the Visitors Center is today. The Union position was farther east and faced west. We are still orienting on the battle fought here in 1862.

The Watt House (Stop 8) and the center of the Union Fifth Corps line are 1,275 yards (0.7 mile) south of you. As you face south, Highway 156 goes to your left and right. In 1862 it acted as a mark on the ground for Confederate artillery and infantry to deploy into combat formation. The ground in front of you was a mixture of open fields and woods. Boatswain's Creek is 500 yards ahead. Its steep bank on the Union side along with trees and scrub provided an obstacle to any attacker

Brigadier General *Maxcy Gregg*'s brigade and later the brigades of Brigadier Generals *Elzey* and *Trimble* passed through this area to attack the Union line at Stop 8, Position A and Position I, and the Union line east of Stop 8.

Gregg's Brigade had been the advance guard of *A. P. Hill*'s Division as it marched from Mechanicsville to New Cold Harbor. *Gregg* made his first contact with Union forces when he approached the bridge over Powhite Creek and was fired upon by the Union rear

guard. After securing the crossing and repairing the bridge he continued on and marched into the area where you are now. Here he
deployed into combat formation in preparation for a division attack
on the Union defenses at the Watt House. *Gregg* initially deployed
two regiments, the First South Carolina and Twelfth South Carolina, in the first line with the Thirteenth South Carolina and the
First South Carolina Rifles in the second and supporting line. The
Fourteenth South Carolina, which had been on detached duty and
had just rejoined the brigade, was placed in reserve.

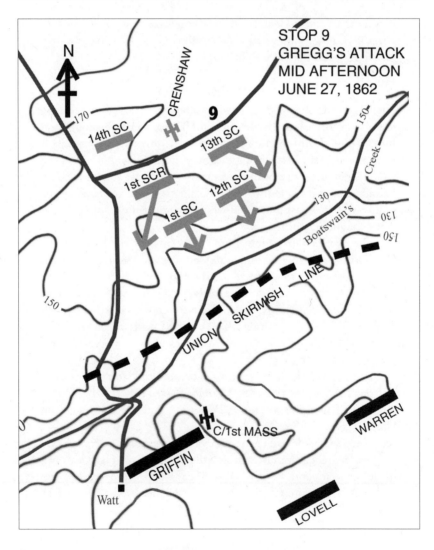

In mid-afternoon *A. P. Hill* began an attack with his division against the Union position. All six of his brigades were committed to the attack. *Gregg*'s Brigade, the left flank unit of the division, attacked the Union position on the high ground just to the east of Stop 8, Position A. In this attack his brigade took 815 casualties, the largest amount of any of *Lee*'s brigades that day. The First South Carolina lost 309, which was 57 percent of its strength. In his report *Gregg* gives a good account of the difficulties of command and control caused by the terrain, Union rifle and artillery fire, and a Union counterattack.

Report of Brig. Gen. *Maxcy Gregg*, CSA, Commanding *Gregg*'s Brigade, *A. P. Hill*'s Division, Army of Northern Virginia

When General *Hill* sent the order to make the attack I directed the First and Twelfth Regiments to advance up the hill-side. The ground, especially in front of the First, was covered by a dense thicket of young pines. As our troops ascended toward the open ground they were met by a continuous fire of small-arms from a much superior number of troops, and at the same time were exposed to a heavy fire of artillery, both direct and oblique. The fire was so destructive that they could not advance farther. Finding that great damage was done by an enfilading fire from a battery established a good way to our right, I directed Colonel *Marshall,* with his regiment, to charge and take it. [This was Battery C, First Massachusetts Artillery deployed on Griffin's right.] The two flank companies of Capts. *James M. Perrin* and *Joseph J. Norton* were thrown forward as skirmishers, under the command of Captain *Perrin.* The companies of Captains *Miller* and *Miles M. Norton* followed in support. The four leading companies were all under the command of Lieutenant-Colonel *Ledbetter.* The charge was made at the double quick, the column of six companies [the remainder of the regiment] being deployed into line after reaching the open ground. A most destructive fire of musketry and artillery in front and in flank did not check the charge, which was continued for several hundred yards across the open ground and into a wood where several regiments of the enemy were posted. The battery, which was the object of the charge, had been withdrawn. The regiment, on reaching the woods, commenced firing on the enemy's infantry and drove them on, many of the men engaging in hand-to-hand conflicts with the bayonet and with clubbed rifles. A strong body of New York Zouaves [Fifth New York] now made a hot attack on the left wing and flank of the regiment. They were repulsed and brought to a stand by a steady and well-directed fire from a party which, on the spur of the moment and with marked presence of mind and skill, Lieutenant *Higgins* formed to check them. Colonel *Marshall,* finding that no support was sent to him from the rest of the brigade, now, too, hard pressed on its own front, ordered his regiment to fall back, and reformed it in the wooded hollow some distance to the right of its original position, where a North Carolina regiment, which just then came up, and aided in holding the ground.

Of 537 men carried into action Colonel *Marshall's* regiment lost 81 killed and 234 wounded. Nearly all of this loss occurred in the charge just described.

While the First Rifles were thus engaged the First and Twelfth Regiments, although relieved from the enfilading fire of the battery on the right, had a hard struggle to maintain their ground against the superior forces in their front. The Twelfth was able at one time to gain some distance in advance in the open field, but Colonel *Barnes* found it necessary to withdraw and reform his line on or near his original ground in the hollow . . . . at this time, in consequence of the difficulty of the ground, the right of the Twelfth got in rear of the left of the First, and there was much danger in such a thicket of the First suffering from the fire of that portion of the Twelfth behind it, until Colonel *Hamilton* interposed and prevented it. The Twelfth advanced again abreast with the First, and the two regiments fought bravely to maintain the ground, but suffered great loss, and were compelled to fall back with some disorder.

In the First Regiment all the members of the color guard were shot down around Colonel *Hamilton,* who for a part of the time bore the colors himself.

Colonel *Barnes,* of the Twelfth, received a hurt, which, although he did not leave the field, in a great measure disabled him for the rest of the day.

The nature of the ground rendered it impracticable to preserve or reestablish regularity in the first line. I, therefore, ordered Colonel *Edwards* to hold the Thirteenth ready to receive the enemy with a steady fire at short range if they should descend the hill-side through the pine thicket. The Twelfth, not being at the time so heavily pressed as the First, I left to continue the struggle. The First I ordered to reform at some distance in rear of the Thirteenth. The Fourteenth Regiment, Colonel *McGowan's,* now arrived on the field at the moment it was so greatly needed.

Stopping the fire of *Crenshaw's* battery for a short time to allow a passage through the guns, I ordered the Fourteenth forward. Tired as they were, by two days and nights of outpost duty and by a rapid march under a burning sun, they recovered strength at once and advanced with a cheer and at the double-quick. Leading his regiment to the right of the Thirteenth and across the hollow, Colonel *McGowan* arrived just in time to repulse the advancing enemy and prevent them from establishing a battery at the edge of the open ground on the brow of the hill. The Fourteenth was formed along a fence up the hill, on the other side of the hollow, and maintained its position gallantly to the end of the battle. After it had held it some time alone other troops came up, and in concert with a North Carolina and Georgia regiment the Fourteenth made a charge across the open field for the purpose of taking a battery. In this charge Colonel *McGowan* was bruised by a grape-shot and for a short time disabled. The distance to the battery being too great, and the fire both direct and cross too heavy, our troops halted and lay down to shelter themselves, then retired, and the Fourteenth resumed its position near the brow of the hill, where after the close of the battle it lay on its arms.

Meanwhile Colonel *Edwards* held his position with the Thirteenth. The enemy did not venture to charge directly down the hill upon his position, but kept up a constant fire, which caused considerable loss. Colonel *Edwards* threw forward his right company, deployed as skirmishers, to dislodge the enemy from the pines in front and on the right, and then ordered the rest of the regiment to take a position a little in advance at the foot of the hill beyond the boggy stream. From the difficulty of crossing the bog and the incessant roar of cannon and musketry, his commands not being well heard, a separation of the regiment took place. A part of the left wing effected the movement intended by Colonel *Edwards*, and maintained the new position until the close of the battle. The right and center companies, supposing the order to be to move in a different direction, marched, under Maj. *T. S. Farrow*, a short distance to the rear. Desiring to form a reserve of this force and the First Regiment for further movements, I directed Major *Farrow* to march farther to the right and rear, and form near Colonel *Hamilton*. Two companies of the First, those of Capts. *W. T. Haskell* and *A. P. Butler*, not having heard the order to retire, remained engaged in the front, and on the advance of the other troops acted in concert with those nearest to them to the end of the battle. Before I made any other disposition the portions of the First and Thirteenth, under Colonel *Hamilton* and Major *Farrow*, were ordered by Major General *Hill* to take a position considerably to the right of my brigade, in support of the brigades of Generals *Anderson* and *Field*. At the close of the battle, being united with the First Rifles, the whole under the command of Colonel *Hamilton*, they bivouacked on their ground.

In the progress of the battle, after the wound received by Colonel *Barnes*, the Twelfth Regiment having suffered heavy loss and being in difficult grounds, became somewhat separated, but portions of the regiment, falling in with other commands, continued the fight to the end. Captain *Bookter*'s company thus joined and fought in company with Col. *James Cantey*'s [Fifteenth Alabama] regiment.

It was now toward sunset, and from this time until 8.30 o'clock, when the enemy were driven from the field under the repeated attacks of large bodies of fresh troops, the regiments of my brigade were engaged at different points, as I have stated above. [*OR* 11, pt. 2, pp. 854–58.]

Two artillery batteries from *A. P. Hill*'s Division were successively deployed about one hundred yards to your right. These batteries were firing in support of the attacks made by the left brigades of *A. P. Hill*'s Division against the Union position near the Watt House. The Union artillery near the Watt House, Stop 8, Position I, firing in a counter battery role, had a devastating effect on the Confederate artillery at this location. The first battery to deploy to your right was *Crenshaw*'s Virginia Battery.

Report of Capt. *William G. Crenshaw*, CSA, Commanding Virginia Battery, *A. P. Hill*'s Division, Army of Northern Virginia

On Friday morning, June 27, we started down the Chickahominy in rear of [*Gregg*'s] brigade, and my battery was the first to cross the bridge at Gaines' Mill, which was effected about 1 p.m.

Soon after crossing, in accordance with orders, we went into battery near New Cold Harbor house and commenced firing at the enemy's infantry, who were drawn up in line of battle across the hill above us. They were soon scattered and driven out of our sight, and we were opened upon by three batteries of the enemy on the same hill, who fired very rapidly, and against whom we then directed our fire. Unfortunately for us our position was such that we could not maneuver our battery 10 yards to the right or left, the opening in the woods through which we had to fire being very narrow. We continued under the incessant fire of the enemy's batteries for nearly two hours, ceasing our own fire more than once when the charge on the enemy's batteries was ordered to be made by our infantry.

During this engagement I received your [*Gregg*'s] message to maneuver the battery or remove it from under fire at my discretion. Finding that no infantry of the enemy were in sight, and that we had been so long under fire of their several batteries that they had been able to get our range very accurately and that we were being damaged by them, having lost in killed and seriously wounded 5 men and 11 horses, I, in the exercise of the discretion you [*Gregg*] gave me, withdrew my battery some 200 yards from the field. After resting about three-quarters of an hour, and finding the enemy's infantry had formed on the hill above us again, we returned with the battery to its original position, soon scattered them, and then continued firing upon their batteries. We continued in this second engagement about an hour, when, two of our brass pieces becoming disabled by the breaking of the axles and the other two brass pieces too hot to fire with safety, you ordered us to retire to make room for Captain *Johnson*, who had been ordered up to relieve us.

We had lost in it 4 men killed and seriously wounded and 11 horses, but succeeded in taking off the two disabled pieces by hand and the others by dismounting our chiefs and hitching three horses to most of the pieces. [*OR* 11, pt. 2, p. 903.]

> *Crenshaw*'s battery was replaced by *Johnson*'s Richmond Battery, which moved into position to your right to attempt to provide artillery support for the infantry attack. This battery also was a prime target for the Union artillery.

Report of Capt. *Marmaduke Johnson*, CSA, Commanding Richmond Battery, *A. P. Hill*'s Division, Army of Northern Virginia

Later in the day I marched to the scene of the bloody battle which took place on Friday, and quite late in the evening was ordered by General *Lee* to report with my battery to you [*Gregg*], which I immediately did with all possible dispatch. You yourself were a personal witness to the behavior of the men and officers. You saw the fearless courage with which they stood and fought through that deadly fire until 20 of them fell, 10 horses killed and wounded, and the battery entirely disabled—exposed to the fire not only of the batteries of the enemy, but of sharpshooters, who could not be seen. You saw them silence one of the batteries and manfully resist others until by your orders I withdrew them from the field. It is needless, therefore, for me to assure [you] of my gratification at their behavior. [*OR* 11, pt. 2, pp. 885–86.]

> The objective of *Gregg*'s attack was the ground east of Stop 8, Position A, that was defended by Warren's and Lovell's brigades. This position had been initially defended by Warren's small brigade, but as the Confederate force opposite him began to deploy, Lovell sent regiments forward to reinforce. When *Gregg*'s attack stalled, Warren and Lovell sent their regiments forward in a counterattack.

Report of Col. Gouverneur K. Warren, USA, Commanding Third Brigade, Second Division, Fifth Corps, Army of the Potomac

About 12.30 m. the enemy forced the passage of Gaines' Creek near the mill, and, cheering as they came, appeared in force at a distance in the open field beyond the wooded ravine in my front. About 1 o'clock p.m. they advanced in several lines, and at my request Captain Edwards brought up a section of his battery [Batteries L and M, Third U.S. Artillery] on my right and opened on them. Their artillery replied. Others of our batteries to the rear of my line also opened on them, and a fierce fire was carried on between them over our heads, in which we suffered considerably. Captain Edwards steadily kept up his fire, though opposed by several batteries, till, the enemy having driven in our line of skirmishers, I advised him to retire. The enemy now advanced sharpshooters to the edge of the woods to pick off our artillerymen posted behind us, but our rifle firing compelled them to retire.

I should think it was now nearly 3 o'clock p.m. Suddenly a regiment burst from the woods with loud yells, advancing at double-quick upon us. The Fifth New York Volunteers, which had been drawn back to be out of the fire of our own artillery, rapidly reformed to meet them on our first position. The enemy received a portion of the fire of the Tenth New York Volunteers as he came rapidly on, and when he neared the Fifth New York Volunteers we charged back, turning his charge into a flight, killing and wounding nearly all of those who fled. This charge of the enemy had also been accompanied by a vigorous attack on our position in the woods, and as we advanced we received a heavy fire from the enemy stationed in them. Our men, nothing daunted, continued to advance and drove them from it. The brigade was reformed (as well as the confusion produced by this charge would allow) in its first position, and again it successfully repulsed the advance of the enemy, driving him back to the woods in front, up to which point the colors of the Fifth New York were twice carried. During this part of the fight the artillery on both sides was silent. The enemy continued to throw forward fresh troops. The gallant Major Clitz [Twelfth U.S. Infantry] engaged them on the right.

The Sixth Regular Infantry came to re-enforce me and I placed them in position [to the left]. General Reynolds also came up now with his brigade, and I withdrew my shattered regiments. [*OR* 11, pt. 2, pp. 378–79.]

Although *Gregg*'s attack was thrown back with heavy loss, Confederate combat power in this area continued to increase as elements of *Jackson*'s command began to arrive and deploy. By late afternoon

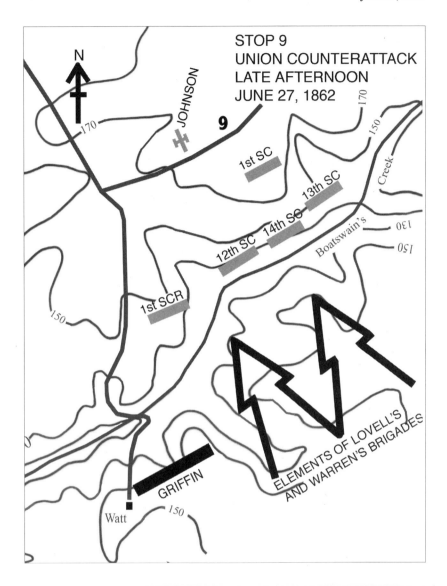

STOP 9
UNION COUNTERATTACK
LATE AFTERNOON
JUNE 27, 1862

there was sufficient Confederate strength in this area to attack as part of the general assault and capture the Union position.

Return to your car for the drive to Stop 10.

Drive back to Highway 156. Turn left and drive east 0.5 mile on Highway 156 to the Garthright House parking lot, on the right. Park, get out of your car, and face south.

Stop 10—*D. H. Hill* Deploys

At this stop and the next three stops you will be looking at the attack of *D. H. Hill*'s Division, which was the Confederate left, against the right of the Union Fifth Corps defensive line. The Union line was 1,100 yards (0.6 mile) south of where you are located. Brigadier General George Sykes's Second Division initially manned this part of the Union line. Colonel Joseph J. Bartlett's Second Brigade of Slocum's First Division of the Sixth Corps later reinforced him.

You are at the right flank of *D. H. Hill*'s Division after it deployed into attack formation in mid-afternoon. *D. H. Hill*'s Division was deployed into a battle line just to the south side of Highway 156. The division line extended east for 1,000 yards to the other side of Old Cold Harbor. *D. H. Hill*'s deployment from right to left were the brigades of Brigadier General *Roswell S. Ripley*, Colonel *Alfred H. Colquitt*, Brigadier Generals *Robert E. Rodes*, *George B. Anderson*, and *Samuel Garland*. Nine batteries of artillery were available to support *Hill*'s attack.

To the right of *D. H. Hill*'s Division were elements of Major General *Richard S. Ewell* and Brigadier General *Charles S. Winder*'s divisions of *Jackson*'s command. Units from these two divisions began deploying into that part of the Confederate battle line between *A. P. Hill*'s and *D. H. Hill*'s Divisions in mid-afternoon and participated in the final attack on the Union Fifth Corps. Twenty-four hours late, but *Jackson* was finally in the battle.

Report of Maj. Gen. *Daniel H. Hill*, CSA, Commanding *D. H. Hill*'s Division, Army of Northern Virginia

I received an order from General *Lee* to co-operate with Major-General *Jackson* on the Cold Harbor road, going by way of Bethesda Church. . . .

The shorter road, upon which Major-General *Jackson* marched, being obstructed, he was compelled to turn off and follow in my rear. We therefore reached [Old] Cold Harbor first, capturing a few wagons, ambulances, and prisoners. The division moved up cautiously to the edge of [Boatswain's Creek], where the Yankees were found to be strongly posted, with ten pieces of artillery commanding the only road upon which our guns could be moved. Captain *Bondurant*'s battery was brought into action, but in less than half an hour was withdrawn and badly crippled. By the order of Major-General *Jackson* the division was moved back to the edge of the woods parallel to the road to cut off the retreat of the enemy [if they retreated east] from the attack of Major-Generals *Longstreet* and *A. P. Hill.*

It soon became apparent, however, that the fire on our right was receding and that the Yankees were gaining ground. *Jackson*'s division and mine were then ordered forward to the support of *Longstreet* and *A. P. Hill,* who had been hotly engaged for several hours. My division occupied the extreme left of the whole Confederate line. The order of advance [left to right] of the division was, *Garland* on the left, next *Anderson,* next *Rodes,* next *Colquitt;*

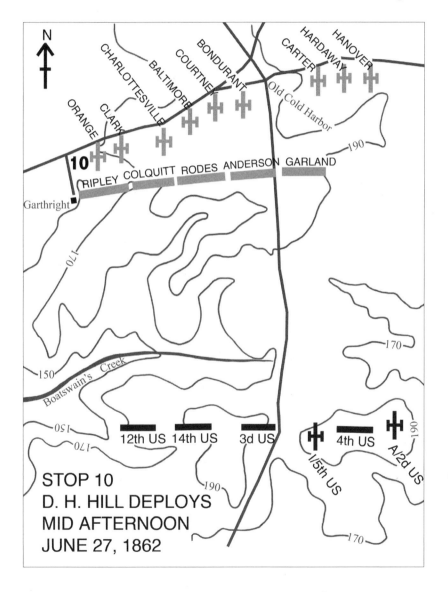

Ripley being on the extreme right. In advancing we had a dense swamp to cross, with tangled undergrowth, and the radius of the wheeling circle had to be shortened. These combined causes produced much confusion and a lapping of brigades and the separation of regiments from their proper places. [*OR* 11, pt. 2, p. 624.]

Return to your car for the drive to Stop 11.

Turn right on to Highway 156 and drive east for 0.4 mile to the intersection with Beulah Church Road, Highway 633. Highway 156 turns right at this intersection and goes south. Turn left and immediately turn left again into the grass and gravel parking area. You are parking on this private ground courtesy of Brian Deal; be careful how you park and depart so as not to cause any damage. Face south and walk a few yards to a position so that you can look past the intersection and along Highway 156 as it turns right from its easterly direction to a southerly direction. Be careful of traffic.

Stop 11—The Confederate Left Flank

This intersection is Old Cold Harbor. In 1862 the Burnett's Tavern was the only substantial building here. This is the area of the left flank of *D. H. Hill*'s Division. The division reached this area by marching along the Beulah Church Road. Beulah Church is 0.7 mile behind you on the east side of the road. When *Hill*'s Division reached a location behind you it began to deploy into battle formation. When deployed the left flank of the division was facing south and was on the other side of the intersection in front of you. Brigadier General *Samuel Garland*'s brigade was to the left of the highway and Brigadier General *George B. Anderson*'s brigade was to the right of the highway. To *Anderson*'s right were the brigades of *Rodes, Colquitt,* and *Ripley.* On the left side of the highway and 200 yards forward of your location was a line of three batteries of artillery. Directly in front of you and to the right of the highway was Captain *Bondurant*'s battery. To the right of this battery and spaced out back toward Stop 10 were the three batteries of Major *Hilary P. Jones*'s artillery battalion and two other batteries. Most of this artillery was firing in support of the attack. About 1,100 yards ahead, to the left of the highway, were two Union artillery batteries firing on the Confederate artillery with considerable accuracy.

Old Cold Harbor in the 1860s. *Century Magazine.*

The ground in front of you was a mixture of open land and woods. The road, Highway 156, going south from your location was there in 1862.

At about 5:00 p.m. the left flank of *Hill*'s Division in conjunction with the rest of the Confederate line moved forward to attack the Union position.

Report of Brig. Gen. *Samuel Garland*, CSA, Commanding *Garland*'s Brigade, *D. H. Hill*'s Division, Army of Northern Virginia

We moved to *Jackson*'s left, and taking a circuitous route by Beulah Church, proceeded to [Old] Cold Harbor, which point we reached early in the afternoon of Friday, the 27th. As we approached a road crossing the line of our route near [Old] Cold Harbor the enemy was discovered in line of battle with artillery to oppose our progress. Their position was quite a strong one and dispositions were made for an engagement. Captain *Bondurant*'s [*Jeff Davis* Alabama] battery, of this brigade, being brought up to the front, took position just to the right of the road, and *Anderson*'s brigade being in line of battle on the right, this brigade was placed in line of battle on the left of and perpendicular to the road by which we had advanced, the Fifth North Carolina, on the right, holding a little copse of timber just next the battery and the road, the rest of the line in the edge of a second growth of diminutive pines, which should be called a jungle—not a piece of timber—through which I threw forward a line of skirmishers to the farther side, next and near to the enemy. These skirmishers, found themselves on one side of a valley through the bottom of which ran a ditch, [this is about 500 yards in front of you] the ground rising to a crest on the other side, where on the edge of the woods the enemy's lines extended, being some 400 yards off. Their line of battle seemed oblique to our own, and in my view the advance of my own brigade in line of battle through the tangled growth in front seemed impracticable, and further liable to the objection that my right flank would be exposed to the fire of the enemy's line, posted obliquely to my own. These views were stated to the general of division and determined the direction of the subsequent movement of the brigade. An active artillery fight was now carried on for some time, in which Captain *Bondurant*'s battery was engaged. That fine officer, his men, and officers, behaved well and tendered an effective fire; but the enemy soon ascertaining the exact range and bringing up heavier metal, Captain *Bondurant* sustained a loss of 2 killed and 1 mortally wounded, since dead, making 3; 14 wounded and 28 horses killed and disabled. He was now relieved and sent to the rear, having fired nearly all his rounds.

Highway 156 today going south from Old Cold Harbor. *Garland*'s brigade was to the left of the road. *Anderson*'s brigade was to the right of the road. The Union's position was on the high ground where the far tree line is located.

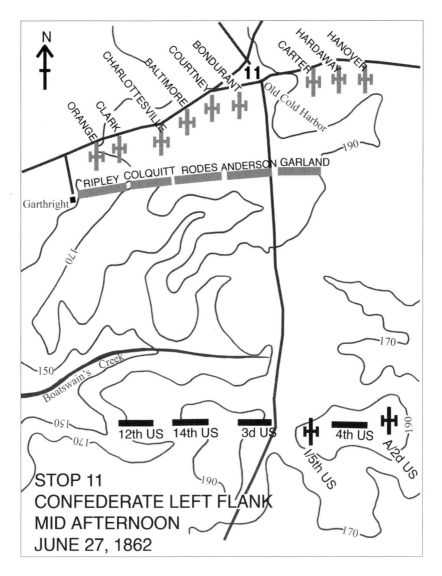

N

11

CHARLOTTESVILLE
BALTIMORE
COURTNEY
BONDURANT
CARTER
HARDAWAY
HANOVER
ORANGE
CLARK

Old Cold Harbor

190

RIPLEY COLQUITT RODES ANDERSON GARLAND

Garthright

170

150

Boatswain's Creek

170

150
170

12th US   14th US   3d US   4th US

1/5th US

A/2d US

190

190

170

STOP 11
CONFEDERATE LEFT FLANK
MID AFTERNOON
JUNE 27, 1862

The sounds of an active engagement were now heard going on immediately in front of the last position, and perceiving that the result was doubtful, brigade after brigade of our division was ordered to proceed toward the sound of the firing. To do this all had to cross an open field several hundred yards wide under a vigorous enfilading fire of artillery and gain a skirt of timber covering ravine some half mile in front. This brigade was ordered forward last to go to the support of the others, this being deemed more judicious on the whole than to charge the enemy's batteries and infantry supports already referred to.

Reaching the skirt of woods referred to, I there found the rest of the division lying unengaged under cover, the fight being still farther on in another woods, separated by an opening of 800 or 1,000 yards. General *Anderson*'s brigade, the first sent over, seems to have driven some of the enemy from the belt of woods in which I found the division. Owing to the necessity of prolonging lines to left or right as the brigades came up, I found that several regiments were detached from their brigades and that there were several lines of our troops in the belt of timber in reserve to each other.

Communicating with General *Anderson,* we ascended out of the ravine to commanding open ground, from whence we could see the engagement in front of us. We perceived a line of fresh troops brought up at right angles to our position to the edge of the woods in our front and pouring volley fires into a line screened from our view by the woods. We concluded, from our imperfect knowledge of localities, that the line we saw must be the enemy and that their flank was fairly exposed to us. In the absence of superior commanders we were consulting as to taking the responsibility of ordering a charge on this exposed flank of the enemy across the intervening open fields under the heavy fire of artillery when Major-General *Hill* joined us in person. We pointed out to him the situation and explained our proposed plan, which he at once adopted and ordered the charge to be made without delay, as the evening was already wearing late. Under the order of the general of division all the brigades were to advance, and accordingly no time was lost in sending back detached regiments to their brigades . . . .

The whole line now moved forward with rapidity and enthusiasm. So soon as it had well cleared the skirt of timber and emerged upon the open plateau the enemy's artillery played upon it. The effect of our appearance at this opportune juncture, cheering and charging, decided the fate of the day. The enemy broke and retreated, made a second brief stand, which induced my immediate command to halt under good cover of the bank on the road-side and return their fire, when, charging forward again, they broke and scattered in every direction, and following, I found that I had effected a junction with Major-General *Jackson*'s column, meeting with General *Lawton* in person and with the officers and troops of *Hood*'s and *Winder*'s brigades.

Thus ended the battle of Cold Harbor, in which this brigade bore an honorable part, sustaining a loss there of about 500 killed and wounded. That night, with the other troops, we bivouacked on the field. [*OR* 11, pt. 2, pp. 640–42.]

Return to your car for the drive to Stop 12. As you drive to the next stop you will see the ravine mentioned in the report. It will be to your right. Go south on Highway 156 for 0.6 mile, to the intersection with Dixie Ridge Lane. It is on your right. Pull off the road, get out of your car, and face back in the direction you just came from. Be careful of traffic.

Stop 12, Position A—The Union Right Flank

This is the location of the right of Sykes's Second Division and the right of the Union Fifth Corps's defensive line. Lieutenant Colonel Robert C. Buchanan's First Brigade of U.S. Regulars held this portion of the line. The Fourth U.S. Infantry was deployed on the other side of the highway in support of two artillery batteries. The Third U.S. Infantry was deployed where you are and to your left. Farther to the left were the Fourteenth and Twelfth U.S. Infantry. To the left of Buchanan's brigade were the brigades of Colonel Gouverner K. Warren and Major Charles S. Lovell. These brigades extend Sykes's line to the west, where it tied in with the right of Morell's First Division. This tie-in was just east of the Watt House. The ravine that *Garland* mentioned in his report as where many of the Confederate attacks came from is three hundred yards in front of you. This ravine was the beginning of Boatswain's Creek and had a growth of bushes and trees. In 1862 the ground here and along the Union position to this ravine was mostly open, with some woods, and had good fields of fire. Three of the five brigades of *D. H. Hill*'s Division were able to cross Boatswain's Creek and assault Buchanan's position.

Report of Lieut. Col. Robert C. Buchanan, USA, Commanding First Brigade, Second Division, Fifth Corps, Army of the Potomac

The brigade, consisting of the Third, Fourth, Twelfth, and Fourteenth Infantry . . . crossed the creek at Gaines' Mill to a position in front of McGehee's house, and covering the [Old] Cold Harbor cross roads, where it was disposed of in order to repel an attack of the enemy. I ordered the Fourth Infantry to support Weed's battery, posted on a knoll commanding the Cold Harbor road, whilst the Third was ordered to occupy a position along the head of the road and to the left of the battery, from which it could observe the road and a skirt of timber in front, through which the enemy might advance. The Twelfth and Fourteenth were drawn up in line in the corn field in front of McGehee's house. This disposition of my brigade was generally maintained throughout the battle, being only varied by the alternate successes of the opposing forces during the action, as the troops pressed back the enemy or were pressed back in turn. Our position was the extreme right of the line, and upon its being held very much depended.

About noon the enemy commenced by attacking our right flank with his artillery, to which Weed responded in a vigorous manner, soon silencing his battery and driving him from that part of the field. Tidball's battery was now advanced and took up a position on the right of Weed, and both retained their positions till the close of the battle. The action soon became lively, and the Fourteenth Infantry was first thrown into the edge of the woods fronting the house, through which the enemy's skirmishers soon attempted to advance, but without success, as the Fourteenth routed and drove them off handsomely. Meantime they came up in force through the woods and field to the left, and immediately Major Clitz changed the front of his battalion (the

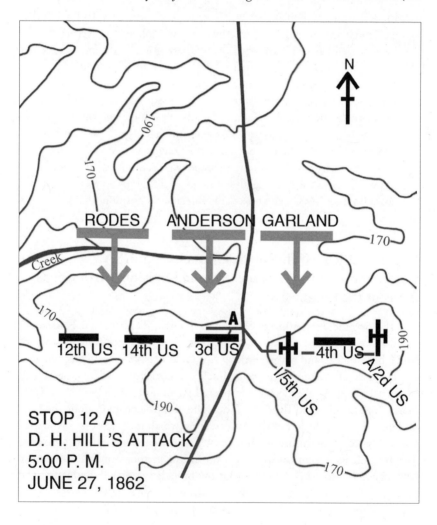

Twelfth) and repulsed them handsomely. Again the enemy brought up his artillery and engaged Weed and Tidball, but was repulsed, with the loss of several caissons blown up.

About 3.30 p.m. the enemy renewed his efforts, and the action soon became general throughout the entire extent of the lines. At this time the brigade was disposed as follows: The Fourth, still on the extreme right, was supporting Weed and Tidball; the Third in its position observing the road; the Twelfth along the fence running to the edge of the woods fronting the house, and the Fourteenth in the corn field facing toward this woods.

Seeing a considerable force of the enemy coming up from the ravine to the left, and moving up through the field to the left of that occupied by the Twelfth and Fourteenth, I directed the Fourteenth to change front to the rear, with the view of flanking him, and then to charge as he fell back. This was done, and the two battalions crossed the intervening fence and advanced in as handsome a line of battle as I ever saw on drill, driving the enemy from this field and killing many of them. I then advanced the Third into the field on the right and threw it into the edge of the wood in front, in order to repel any effort to turn my right. Having done this, I observed a company of pickets coming up from the Cold Harbor road without an officer, and upon inquiring whose, it was found that it was Captain Lay's Twelfth Infantry, who, the sergeant stated, had been taken sick and was then with the Fourth Infantry. This officer has since been arrested under charges for gross dereliction of duty on a subsequent occasion.

The battle now raged with varying success until night-fall, when all the troops were withdrawn from the field and the most of them were thrown across the Chickahominy. The conflict in this part of the field throughout the entire day was characterized by the most indomitable energy, perseverance, and gallantry of our troops. Every time that a regiment of the enemy was repulsed a fresh body came to take its place, whilst we occupied our original ground with the same forces that first went into action. Here it was that we met with the most of our loss, and yet my brigade maintained its ground against greatly superior odds for nearly eight hours.

During the entire action the Fourth Infantry, under command of Capt. J. B. Collins, covered the two batteries, and at its close formed in rear of them and marched there, when they were withdrawn, about 8 p.m. On the march to the rear, which was not commenced until the batteries were nearly out of ammunition, the Fourth on three several occasions formed, fronting the enemy and checking his advance, whilst the batteries were enabled to pass successfully obstacles that seriously impeded their progress and threatened their capture. [This was the late evening action referred to by Brigadier General *Samuel Garland* in his report, which you read at Stop 11.] This regiment did not cross the Chickahominy, but took up a position covering the

Grapevine Bridge on the north side, which it maintained that night. The next morning, after partially destroying that bridge, it crossed by the Woodbury Bridge to Camp Lincoln. [*OR* 11, pt. 2, pp. 358–59.]

Battery I, Fifth U.S. Artillery, and A Battery, Second U.S. Artillery, were located in a firing position on the high ground across the highway. These batteries and their supporting infantry, the Fourth U.S. Regulars, were the extreme right of the Union line.

Return to your car, turn left on Flaherty Drive, follow it for 0.2 mile, and then stop. As you drive notice how the ground to your left drops away.

Position B—Artillery on the Right

You are in the right part of the position occupied by the artillery and its supporting infantry. From this position the two batteries of Union artillery were able to bring effective counter battery fire on the Confederate artillery in the vicinity of the Old Cold Harbor intersection. When *D. H. Hill* sent his infantry forward in their attack, these two batteries placed devastating fire on the left of the Confederate battle line.

Report of Capt. Stephen H. Weed, USA, Commanding Battery I, Fifth U.S. Artillery, Second Division, Fifth Corps, Army of the Potomac

The position was a beautiful one for artillery and thoroughly commanded the road leading from [Old] Cold Harbor. There can, I think, be no doubt if that position had not been taken and strongly held by artillery our right would have been turned before 2 p.m. As it was, the enemy did not get possession of that ground until fully 7 in the evening. Immediately on my right was posted the Fourth Infantry; on my left the Third, covered by the neck of the woods on our left of the road. By this position the extreme right rested on ground inaccessible to the enemy.

Before 1 o'clock he appeared on the bluff about 1,000 yards or less in our front, first with cavalry drawn up to charge down the road. I opened fire at once, and almost immediately getting the range, the cavalry was broken in confusion and a fire of artillery was commenced in reply. About a half hour after the first firing Tidball's battery came into action immediately on my right. The enemy was soon silenced under our combined fire. [This was

Bondurant's, Jeff Davis Alabama Artillery Battery.] During the afternoon he several times changed position and reopened fire, but was in each case soon silenced.

Between 5 and 6 o'clock a line of infantry was seen crossing the road at double-quick to gain the wood on their right. At the same time their artillery opened fire to divert our attention from them. The artillery fire was, however, entirely disregarded, and a most destructive fire from our batteries was brought upon their infantry while passing and the woods they had gained were thoroughly shelled. Some of our infantry soon after became engaged with the enemy in the wood, but were forced to retire before greatly superior numbers. As soon as the wood was evacuated by our troops the guns of both batteries were turned obliquely upon it and a tremendous fire of canister from twelve guns poured in, with the effect of sensibly diminishing the fire of the

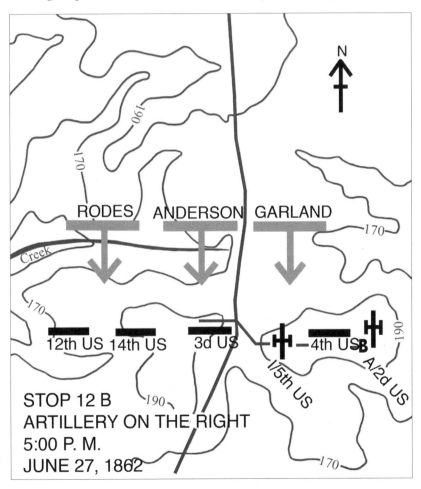

115

enemy on our immediate left and front and causing them to gain ground rapidly to their right. Their loss during this fire must have been very heavy.

About 6.30 p.m. they gained the open ground in their front of the wood, and opened a fire of musketry at close range upon the battery. No order had been received to retire, but it soon became very evident that the position was no longer tenable. A very few moments more would have lost my guns. Both batteries were limbered to the rear, and at about 7 p.m. I left the field, immediately after Captain Tidball. The enemy very soon occupied the ground. It was getting quite dark, and the battle closed. During the day there was fired from my battery something over 1,000 rounds of ammunition. [*OR* 11, pt. 2, p. 354.]

As the fighting in this area began to increase, Weed was reinforced with a battery of artillery from the artillery reserve.

Report of Capt. John C. Tidball, USA, Commanding Battery A, Second U.S. Artillery, Artillery Reserve, Army of the Potomac

General Sykes ordered me to place my battery on the extreme right of our position, there to assist Captain Weed, of the Fifth Artillery, who was then engaged with the enemy, then playing fiercely with his artillery from the ridge in front of his right flank. Hastening up at a trot and coming into battery, it required but a few minutes to silence the enemy at this point and cause him to change the position of his guns. The ground upon my left sloped off to a marshy slough, fringed with trees and bushes. Along this was posted a battalion of regular infantry (the Fourth), for my support; on my right and front came down to within 200 yards the point of a pine forest; directly in my front along the ridge, at about 1,000 yards distance, was a growth of young pines, and farther around to my left extended a thin strip of pine woods; upon my left was the open field where was posted the Third Regiment Regular Infantry. In about half an hour the enemy again returned with his guns, and placing them behind the small pines already mentioned opened a hot fire upon us. Sheltered as they were from our view it required an unusual amount of shelling to silence them. In this way at irregular intervals the enemy would return and as often be driven back by our fire.

In the mean while the battle raged upon the ridge extending around upon my left. About 4 o'clock p.m. our troops at this point for a time were forced back, and the enemy threatened to sweep down through the thin pine woods before mentioned as being upon my left and front. I at once changed front, so as to meet with canister this new danger. A few rounds were fired into the woods and shell into the open space beyond, which was now occupied by the enemy. Repeated charges of our infantry cleared this space, as far as I could see, of the enemy, and not knowing the position of our troops in this direction, I was fearful of continuing the fire. The ground in rear of my battery not admitting of my caissons in position, I left them near by in charge of my first sergeant, who supplied the exhausted limbers of the guns by constantly bringing up full ones from the caissons.

When the enemy took possession of the top of the hill the caissons were forced to retire by the falling back of our troops. I had received instructions from General Sykes that if forced to retire to take the main road leading to my rear. The ammunition of my limbers, with the exception of a few rounds which I wished to retain for an emergency, was exhausted, and being now exposed to a sharp fire of musketry as well as of artillery I thought it prudent to withdraw and seek a position where my few remaining rounds might be effective. I accordingly changed my position a few hundred yards and brought some of my pieces into battery, but it was now so dark that I could not see whether the troops in front were friends or foes, and perceiving it impossible in consequence of the woods to join our troops toward the center of the battlefield I again limbered up and retired slowly by the road prescribed by General Sykes. I fired during the day about 600 rounds. [*OR* 11, pt. 2, pp. 244–45.]

As the fighting raged on the right the Fifth Corps line was pushed back. It slowly fell back angling slightly to its left rear. Here the fight was continued with reinforcements that had been sent from the other side of the Chickahominy River.

Return to Highway 156, turn left, and drive south for 0.3 mile to Old Quaker Road; turn right and follow it for 0.1 mile, to a small knoll. Stop and get out of your car and face right, north. Note that Old Quaker Road is a private road that you are allowed to drive on courtesy Edwin Adams. Do not walk or drive off the road, as the fields are private land, and do not drive a bus or more than one car down it.

Stop 13—*D. H. Hill*'s Final Assault

You are at the location of the final defensive line of the Union Fifth Corps's right flank. The initial defensive position occupied by the right of Sykes's division was 600 yards in front of you. The Watt

House is 1500 yards (0.8 mile) to your left (west). In 1862 this road went from Highway 156 in a westerly direction for 880 yards (0.5 mile), where it made a half turn and went northwest for 1,400 yards (0.8 mile) to New Cold Harbor (Stop 7). The McGehee House was located to your left rear.

As the fighting continued to increase all along the Union defensive line Porter sent for reinforcement. Brigadier General Henry W. Slocum was ordered to march his division across the Chickahominy River and reinforce the Fifth Corps. Slocum's division crossed the Chickahominy River in mid-afternoon and marched to the Fifth Corps position. Two of Slocum's brigades were committed to the fighting to the right of the Watt House. The remaining brigade, Colonel Joseph J. Bartlett's Second Brigade, was held in a position to the rear of the battle line. This position was located three hundred yards to your left rear. From that location Bartlett deployed his brigade forward by regiments to where you are.

When Bartlett's brigade was fully deployed the Sixteenth New York was to your right front, the Ninety-sixth Pennsylvania was just in front of where you are, the Fifth Maine was to your left front, and the Twenty-seventh New York was farther to the left. Two batteries of artillery that had been engaging the Confederates were in position to support Bartlett. Battery D, Fifth U.S. Artillery, was located to your right next to the highway. Battery L/M, Third U.S. Artillery was in position toward the left of Bartlett's line.

Report of Col. Joseph J. Bartlett, USA, Commanding, Second Brigade, First Division, Sixth Corps, Army of the Potomac

I was ordered by an aide-de-camp of General Porter, commanding, to report with my command on the extreme right of the field to Brigadier-General Sykes, commanding the division of regular infantry, which I did at about 4.30 o'clock p.m., suffering a loss of 15 killed and wounded by round shot and shell while making the flank march across the whole length of the battle-field from left to right.

Immediately upon reporting to General Sykes I was permitted to cover my command in a ravine to his rear and right, and allow the men to rest, of which they were greatly in need.

At 5 o'clock p.m. I was ordered by General Sykes to bring forward my men to support . . . a portion of his own command, who were unable longer to withstand the fierce attacks and withering fire of the enemy, who were slowly but surely forcing back the right of the entire line of battle. At this juncture I ordered forward the Sixteenth New York Volunteers, Col. Joseph Howland commanding. From the position of the regiment it was necessary to change front forward on first company under the most terrific fire of musketry, with the shells and round shot of two batteries raking over the level plain, making it seemingly impossible for a line to withstand the fire a single instant. But with the calmness and precision of veteran soldiers the movement was executed, and the line, giving three cheers, long and loud, rushed on to relieve their now routed friends, led by their noble colonel and myself in person. The

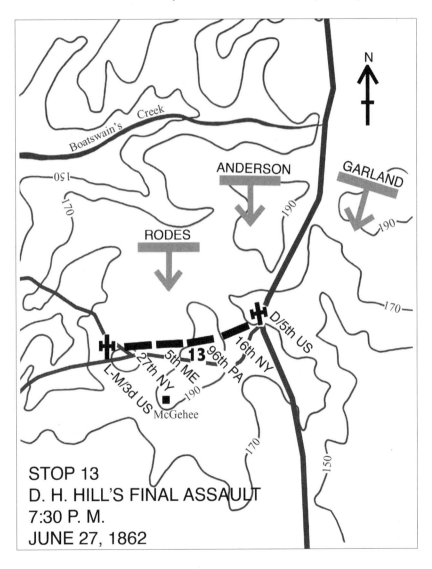

STOP 13
D. H. HILL'S FINAL ASSAULT
7:30 P. M.
JUNE 27, 1862

position was gained, and I then ordered up the Ninety-sixth Pennsylvania, Colonel Cake commanding, to continue my line to the left. The murderous fire across the plain rendered it almost impossible for their gallant colonel, aided by Lieutenant-Colonel Frick and Major Martin, to form his line of battle, and I am pained to state that their noble exertions were not in many instances seconded by some of the line officers, who lacked that impulsive enthusiasm and cool determination required of them under such trying circumstances, and I was forced to lead forward the third regiment in line, the Fifth Maine Volunteers, Col. N. J. Jackson. This regiment also changed its front in the most soldierly manner, and under the sweeping storm of iron and leaden hail sent up their battle-shout and rushed upon the enemy, forcing back his lines and holding the crest of the hill in our front, from which our troops had so recently been driven.

The Twenty-seventh New York Volunteers, Lieut. Col. A. D. Adams commanding, was now ordered to the front, and after executing the same maneuver of changing front under the same scathing fire charged bayonets, and giving three ringing cheers rushed at double-quick upon the enemy, who occupied the left crest of the hill, on which was a dwelling and numerous outhouses; nor did they stand to meet the impetuosity of their charge, but retreated so precipitately that they left as prisoners in our hands two of their officers, who were vainly endeavoring to make them stand their ground. Thus the left and right of my line of battle being retaken and established, and the Ninety-sixth Pennsylvania Volunteers being in line and eager for the fight, I ordered them to the front, and most nobly now did they respond to the command. No officer or man faltered, and their solid and unwavering line pressed forward to their position and completed the front.

The enemy now hurled his fresh troops in double numbers against my line, directing his heaviest fire upon my left, and the Twenty-seventh New York Volunteers and Fifth Maine staggered back under the fearful fire; but it was the recoil of the lion to gather new strength to support the undaunted resolution of every breast, and once more every man sprang to the front, where they nobly maintained the fight, without giving an inch of ground to the enemy, until long after darkness showed the flash of every musket, and revealed to the enemy how small a force was holding them in check.

To meet the fire which came from our left Colonel Howland, who held the right of my position, changed front forward on tenth company, and the line thus established held its position until all firing of musketry had ceased on the field except that from my own brigade, and not until nearly every cartridge had been expended was the order given to retire behind our batteries, which were posted about 600 yards in the rear.

In retiring I first withdrew my right regiment in line of battle, then the next from the right, holding the two left regiments to protect the movements, as I was completely flanked on the left by a brigade of the enemy which he had moved up in the darkness from the woods and had just opened a galling cross-fire upon my left and rear.

The withdrawal of my brigade was done under my immediate command, regiment by regiment, and in as good order as when they were taken into the field.

From the moment my troops were engaged up to 8.30 o'clock p.m. (at which hour it was too dark to distinguish an enemy at the distance of 50 paces) they nobly held the position assigned to them, and regretted the necessity which compelled them to retire from the field. I formed a new line of battle in front of the hospital on the second hill from the bridge, with the Twenty-seventh and Sixteenth New York and a part of the Fifth Maine, the Ninety-sixth Pennsylvania Volunteers.

With many painful regrets I have to report the loss of 500 officers and men. [*OR* 11, pt. 2, pp. 447–49.]

> The Confederate forces attacking this position were regiments from *Rodes's* and *G. B. Anderson's* brigades. These brigades had initially deployed along the road from Old Cold Harbor to New Cold Harbor. Much of each brigade's integrity had been lost in the attack, but sufficient regiments remained under control to strike this position hard.

Report of Brig. Gen. *Robert E. Rodes*, CSA, Commanding *Rodes's* Brigade, *D. H. Hill's* Division, Army of Northern Virginia

Then we were ordered forward by Major-General *Jackson* to attack the enemy in front of [Old] Cold Harbor, coming into the fight on the left of his troops. In crossing an almost impenetrable swamp [Boatswain's Creek] to get into action great confusion ensued, from the fact that at the same point several brigades were crossing at the same time, and upon emerging from the swamp and striking the field beyond three of my regiments, the Fifth, Twelfth, and Twenty-sixth, were found on the left and behind, and the Sixth and Third Alabama on the right of *Anderson's* brigade, which was in front of us. Before reaching the swamp I had received an order from or through Brigadier-General *Ripley* to charge through the swamp at double-quick time. This order was obeyed by my brigade with alacrity, but the three first-named regiments, finding *Anderson's* brigade at a halt and in front of them engaged in a heavy fire of musketry, were halted; the Third and Sixth Alabama went

From the center of Bartlett's brigade (Stop 13) looking north. The Confederate attacks against this position came from the wood line.

on, however. The Third encountered troops of our own in front of them across the swamp. The Sixth did not, but moved on at a rapid pace into the field in front of the enemy's battery and in the face of their infantry, encountering there an enfilading fire from the battery and a heavy fire of musketry in front; and finding themselves unsupported, the men were required by Colonel *Gordon* to lay down, and finally, no support arriving, they retired under cover in perfectly good order, and there awaited with the Third further orders.

Almost upon the return of the Sixth Alabama the brigades of Generals *Anderson* and *Garland* having in the mean time, with three of my regiments, been brought into some sort of alignment, were ordered to charge. The charge was intended to be general, and had been, I thought, extended throughout the line; but upon traversing the field before spoken of, and attaining the road beyond very nearly, I found upon examination of my line that two of my regiments had not moved with my brigade, and upon examining the line farther to the [left] found that they were not with General *Anderson* either, and that his right was at least the length of two or three regiments from the lower edge of the field and liable to be turned, while on the [left] of General *Anderson's* brigade, the whole line having a moment before paused and hesitated, nearly if not the whole of the left of the division, as far as one in my position could see, broke and retreated in apparent confusion. I thought the whole of the brigade on the left of mine as well as my three regiments were involved in it.

At that moment, though the whole of General *Anderson's* brigade seemed to be stanch at a halt, still his right, composed of regiments which joined him after his halt, wavered, and looking around for troops to sustain him I discovered some at the lower end of the field, to the rear, not engaged, but under artillery fire. I found them to be *Colquitt*'s brigade, and close to them on their left I found the Sixth and Third Alabama Regiments. Urging Colonel *Colquitt* to move up to *Anderson*'s right I ordered my two regiments directly forward to his support, and then moved up the original line to collect and return to the field, if possible, those who had fallen back from the left.

I arrived at the left in time to stop some fugitives, but was so utterly exhausted from weakness, proceeding from my wound (not yet by any means healed), that I could do no more. I found, however, that the confusion before spoken of on the left of the line had not been general; that my three first-named regiments had continued the charge, and had successfully and almost alone beaten back two large bodies of the enemy on the top of the hill, besides taking a battery of the enemy directly in our front. The Fifth Alabama Regiment, which took the battery, was sustained in this portion of the charge by the Twenty-sixth only, the Twelfth Alabama, in some confusion, having shifted to the left late in the evening and joined the troops which came up on the left of *Hill*'s division.

The total loss of the brigade in this battle was 31 men killed and 114 wounded. Of these the Fifth Alabama lost 21 killed and 45 wounded. [*OR* 11, pt. 2, pp. 631–32.]

The breakthrough at the Watt House and the steady attacks against this location caused the collapse of the Fifth Corps defensive line. This collapse occurred as darkness was falling. This prevented an effective Confederate pursuit and allowed the Union forces to retreat and cross to the other side of the Chickahominy River.

Throughout the day *Lee*'s force outnumbered the Union force on this side of the river. He had deployed six divisions totaling 57,000 troops. *Lee* had an opportunity to destroy or render combat ineffective the Fifth Corps. *Jackson*'s performance the previous day, June 26, had been poor and had prevented *Lee* from turning the flank of the Union position at Beaver Dam Creek. *Jackson* did not improve his performance on June 27, and his force arrived on the field late in the afternoon. Because of this *Lee* was not able to coordinate his attacks until late in the day, and by the time he had captured the high ground it was too dark for pursuit.

Lee had begun the day thinking that McClellan was still tied to his supply base at White House. He had made his troop dispositions and plans to attack this line of supply to draw the Army of the

Potomac out from defensive work for a fight in the open. The morning after the Battle of Gaines Mill *Lee* realized that McClellan had abandoned his base at White House and was preparing to retreat. What he did not know was in what direction McClellan would go: southeast down the Peninsula or directly south to the James River.

Report of Gen. *Robert E. Lee*, CSA, Commanding Army of Northern Virginia

Our troops remained in undisturbed possession of the field, covered with the Federal dead and wounded, and their broken forces fled to the river or wandered through the woods.

Owing to the nature of the country the cavalry was unable to participate in the general engagement. It rendered valuable service in guarding *Jackson*'s flank and took a large number of prisoners.

On the morning of the 28th it was ascertained that none of the enemy remained in our front north of the Chickahominy. As he might yet intend to give battle to preserve his communications, the Ninth Cavalry, supported by *Ewell*'s division, was ordered to seize the York River Railroad, and General *Stuart*, with his main body, to co-operate. When the cavalry reached Dispatch Station the enemy retreated to the south bank of the river and burned the railroad bridge. *Ewell*, coming up shortly afterward, destroyed a portion of the track.

During the forenoon columns of dust south of the Chickahominy showed that the Federal Army was in motion. The abandonment of the railroad and destruction of the bridge proved that no further attempt would be made to hold that line; but from the position it occupied the roads which led toward James River would also enable it to reach the lower bridges over the Chickahominy and retreat down the peninsula. In the latter event it was necessary that our troops should continue on the north bank of the river, and until the intention of General McClellan was discovered it was deemed injudicious to change their disposition. *Ewell* was therefore ordered to proceed to Bottom's Bridge to guard that point, and the cavalry to watch the bridges below. No certain indications of a retreat to James River were discovered by our forces on the south side of the Chickahominy, and late in the afternoon the enemy's works were reported to be fully manned. The strength of these fortifications prevented Generals *Huger* and *Magruder* from discovering what was passing in their front. Below the enemy's works the country was densely wooded and intersected by impassable swamps, at once concealing his movements and precluding reconnaissance except by the regular roads, all of which were strongly guarded. The bridges over the Chickahominy in rear of the enemy were destroyed, and their reconstruction impracticable in the presence of his whole army and powerful batteries. We were therefore compelled to wait until his purpose should be developed.

Generals *Huger* and *Magruder* were again directed to use the utmost vigilance and pursue the enemy vigorously should they discover that he was retreating. During the afternoon and night of the 28th the signs of a general movement were apparent, and no indications of his approach to the lower bridges of the Chickahominy having been discovered by the pickets in observation at those points, it became manifest that General McClellan was retreating to the James River. [*OR* 11, pt. 2, pp. 493–94.]

General *Lee* wasn't the only commander to miss an opportunity. McClellan also had the potential to inflict damage and maybe defeat on the Army of Northern Virginia during the Battle of Gaines Mill. When Porter established his defensive line on June 27 he had it facing to the north and west, thus correctly anticipating the directions from which the Confederate attacks came. McClellan for his part refused to study the possible course of actions available to him and, other than sending one division and two brigades from another as reinforcements, eventually did nothing to assist Porter. While the fighting ranged all along Porter's line north of the Chickahominy River, McClellan sat on the south side of the river with six divisions.

The left flank of the Confederate attack against Porter's position was located initially at Old Cold Harbor and generally moved south along the road that went from there to the river. East of this flank was a cavalry screen. There were sufficient bridges and roads east of the Confederate and Union flanks that would have allowed a substantial Union force to cross the river and deploy on Porter's right and then attack the Confederate left. Such a maneuver and attack would have hit the left flank of the Confederate line as it moved forward against Porter's position in the late afternoon. With all of his forces north of the river committed to the attack and now outflanked and forced to fight in two directions, *Lee*'s attack would have stalled. The damage done to his left flank may have caused him to pull back from Gaines Mill and redeploy his force.

However, McClellan chose not to consider this opportunity and lost the Gaines Mill position. With all Union corps south of the Chickahominy River he now began a retreat to the James River. During this retreat he was given another opportunity to strike *Lee* a hard blow. But for the next three days his primary concern was to prevent his routes of retreat from being cut.

Chapter 4

Battle of Savage Station and White Oak Swamp Bridge
Sunday, June 29, 1862, and Monday, June 30, 1862

Drive forward for 50 yards to the driveway on your left. Use it to turn around. Drive back to Highway 156. Turn right on Highway 156 and drive south. In 2.2 miles you will cross the modern-day Grapevine Bridge. The original bridge was built by the Union army to cross the Chickahominy River and was one of three available for Porter's use. The other two bridges no longer exist. In 0.3 mile after crossing the bridge, turn left on to Old Hanover Road, and in another 0.1 mile turn left on Grapevine Road. After driving 0.2 mile on the Grapevine Road you will come to the Trent House, on your right (west). Pull off to the side of the road where the marker is.

The house was built around 1825. In 1862 it was the home of Doctor *Peterfield Trent*. The road you are on was not here in 1862. The original road ran parallel to the present road but was on the other side of the house. The Trent House was McClellan's headquarters from June 12 to June 28. McClellan's headquarters tents were in a field to your left, on the east side of the road. Here on the night of June 27 McClellan announced his decision to abandon the supply base at White House and retreat south across the Peninsula to the James River. The next day McClellan moved his headquarters to Savage Station. The route you have been following was taken by part of *Jackson*'s command after it crossed the Chickahominy River in the early morning hours of June 30

Resume driving on the Grapevine Road for 1.0 mile. At the T-intersection with Meadow Road, turn left and drive for 100 yards. Pull into the small parking area to the right of the road, at the historical markers. Get out of your car and face south looking across the field. Meadow Road will be behind you.

The Trent House. McClellan's headquarters for part of the Seven Days. The photo was taken from north side of house where the old road was in 1862. *Century Magazine.*

The Trent House today. The road today is on the opposite side of the house from where it was in 1862.

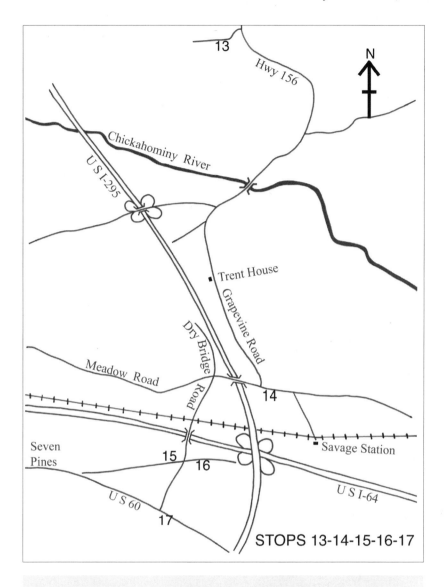

The Richmond and York River Railroad ran from your right to left 0.5 mile in front of you. Directly in front of you on the railroad was Savage Station. The area around the station was Savage Farm. On the morning of June 29, 1862, the Union army had a supply depot and a field hospital in this area. In addition, when McClellan moved his headquarters from the Trent House it came here for a short period of time. On the afternoon of June 29 the Union units here were the army's rear guard and were preparing to follow the main body in the retreat south to the James River. Yet, because of the next plan of maneuver decided on by *Lee,* Savage Station was the next battle to be fought in the Seven Days. From your vantage point, the Union forces were deployed in a reverse L-shaped position. The long part of the L was to your right and went south from the railroad to Williamsburg Road. The short part of the L comprised the units deployed generally along the ground where you are and facing to the north toward the Chickahominy River, which is two miles behind you.

Stop 14—General *Lee*'s Second Plan

On the morning of June 28 *Lee* was not sure exactly what McClellan's intentions were. As *Lee* saw it, McClellan had three possible courses of action. First, McClellan could defend the Richmond and York River Railroad and protect his supply base at White House. Second, he could retreat down the Peninsula toward Williamsburg or even as far as Yorktown. Third, he could abandon his base at White House and retreat south across the Peninsula to the James River, where he could be supported and supplied by the navy. McClellan chose the third course of action. By mid-afternoon *Lee* had received enough

Savage Station and the Union hospital in 1862 as seen from Stop 14. *Century Magazine.*

information to suspect that McClellan was headed for the James River.

On June 29 *Lee* sent a letter to *Jefferson Davis.* In this letter he gave is appraisal of the situation and his future course of action.

Headquarters
Williamsburg Road
June 29, 1862

Mr. President:

I have the honor to report for your information that after the enemy had been driven from the left bank of the Chickahominy on the 27th instant, he seemed to have determined to abandon his position on the right bank and commenced promptly and quietly his arrangements for its evacuation. His intention was discovered but his proposed route could not be ascertained, though efforts were made all day yesterday with that in view. Having however discovered that no movements were made on his part to maintain or recover his communications with York River, which were entirely severed by our occupation of the [Richmond and] York River Railroad and the Williamsburg Road; his only course seemed to me was to make for James River

Savage Station and Farm as seen from Stop 14 today.

and thus open communications with his gunboats and fleet. Though not yet certain of his route, the whole army has been put in motion upon this supposition. It is certain that he is south of the Chickahominy and can only cross it at or below Long Bridge. General *Stuart* is on the left bank watching his movements in that direction. General *Jackson* will cross to the right bank at Grapevine Bridge. General *Magruder* is pursuing down the Williamsburg road. General *Huger* is on the Charles City [Road] and General *Longstreet* on the Darbytown [Road]. The cavalry on the several roads south of the Chickahominy have not yet reported his forces in their front.

> I am with high respect,
> your obedient servant,
> *R. E. Lee*

[Lee-Davis Correspondence, Virginia State Library]

The Long Bridge that *Lee* mentions in his letter to *Davis* is fourteen miles down the Chickahominy River from where you crossed it at Grapevine Bridge. This is the first place that McClellan could begin to recross the river. Any signs that he was doing this would indicate he was retreating back down the Peninsula and not toward the James River. Conversely, lack of movement toward Long Bridge would further confirm *Lee*'s analysis that McClellan was probably retreating toward the James River.

McClellan's primary concern when he began his retreat was to move his entire force fourteen miles south to the James River. Once there, the gunboats and supply vessels of the Union Navy could support him. The task facing McClellan was imposing. He had to march almost 100,000 men with their supporting artillery, approximately 280 field guns, over very few roads. In addition, marching within this force was an artillery siege train of 26 heavy guns, more than 3,800 wagons and ambulances, and a herd of 2,518 cattle.

When McClellan ordered his army to retreat across the Peninsula the immediate threat of capturing Richmond was lifted. Having reduced the threat to Richmond, *Lee* now decided he would maneuver so as to attack and destroy the Union army. *Lee* developed a plan that was designed to attack and maintain pressure on the rear of McClellan's army as it retreated. At the same time four divisions were to march southeast and position themselves so as to attack the head of the Union army. These multiple attacks if successful would break McClellan's army into fragments and cut off the routes of retreat. To accomplish his intentions *Lee* gave a series of orders that

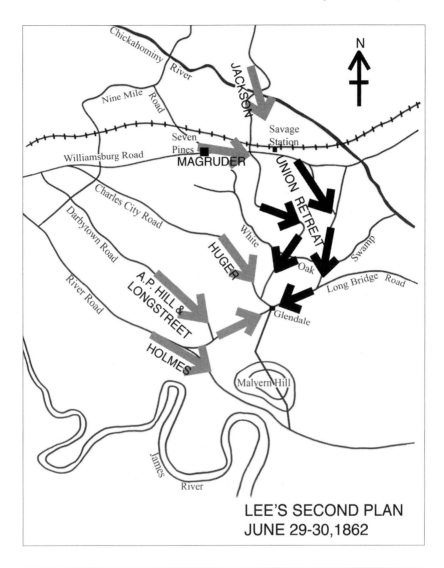

LEE'S SECOND PLAN
JUNE 29-30,1862

moved his army east and southeast on the roads that radiated out from Richmond.

Major General *John B. Magruder*'s command, which consisted of his division and the divisions of Major General *Lafayette McLaws* and Brigadier General *David R. Jones,* had been occupying the defensive works south of the Chickahominy River while *Lee* attacked the Union force north of the river. This force, along with Major General *Benjamin Huger*'s division, had deceived McClellan into believing that the Confederate defenses were fully manned and too strong for him to attack. *Magruder* was ordered to move his force east, parallel with the Williamsburg Road and the Richmond and York River Railroad, and attack the rear of the Union army. His attack would be supported by *Jackson*'s command, which had marched south from the Gaines Mill battle to the north side of the Chickahominy River. *Jackson* was ordered to rebuild bridges, cross the river, and attack the rear of the Union army. These attacks were designed to cause the rear of the Union column to halt and fight. This in turn would slow down the retreat and give the rest of *Lee*'s army a chance to intercept the head of the column.

Huger's Division was ordered to march southeast on the Charles City Road to the vicinity of Glendale. *Huger* was expected to strike the front part of the Union column.

The divisions of *Longstreet* and *A. P. Hill* had the longest distance to march. These two divisions recrossed to the south side of the Chickahominy River and, passing behind *Magruder*'s command, marched south to the Darbytown Road. Once on Darbytown Road they marched southeast to the intersection with the Long Bridge Road, where they turned left and marched northeast toward Glendale. Their orders were to come up on the right of *Huger*'s Division and attack the head of the retreating Union column. The division of Major General *Theophilus Holmes* was ordered to march parallel to *Longstreet* and *A. P. Hill* along the River Road to New Market and then to Malvern Hill. The marches of *Longstreet*'s, *A. P. Hill*'s, and *Holmes*'s Divisions were to cut off the Union route of retreat.

Return to your car for the drive to Stop 15. Make a U-turn and drive west on Meadow Road for 0.4 mile to the intersection with Dry Bridge Road. You will go by the intersection with Meadow Road and Grapevine Road and then you will cross over Interstate 295. Turn left, south, on Dry Bridge Road and drive for 0.6 mile to Old Williamsburg Road. This road is not the modern road to Williamsburg, which is farther on. Turn right, west, on Old Williamsburg Road and drive for 0.2 mile to the Allen Farm. Make a U-turn and park. Get out of you car and look east down the Old Williamsburg Road.

Stop 15—*Magruder* Deploys

Major General *John B. Magruder* was responsible for holding the defenses south of the Chickahominy River while the remainder of

Lee's army attacked north of the river. When McClellan began his retreat *Magruder* was ordered to maintain pressure on the rear of the Union army. His report shows the situation just south of the Chickahominy River from June 26 to June 29.

Report of Maj. Gen. *John B. Magruder,* CSA, Commanding *Magruder*'s Command, Army of Northern Virginia

About June 25 I received from Lieut. Col. *R. H. Chilton,* assistant adjutant-general, on the staff of General *Lee,* commanding the Army of Northern Virginia, an order giving a general plan of operations about to be undertaken against the enemy, whose troops occupied the right and left banks of the Chickahominy, the greater number being immediately in front of the lines occupied by me and the division of Major-General *Huger* on my right.

This directed me in general terms to hold my position in front of the enemy against attack and at all hazards; to make such demonstrations as to discover his operations, and in case of the abandonment of his intrenchments to pursue him closely.

I was in command of three divisions, those of Major-General *McLaws,* Brig. Gen. *D. R. Jones,* and my own, each consisting of two brigades, the numerical strength being about 13,000 men.

In obedience to these instructions I caused the pickets and skirmishers to observe the utmost vigilance; attacked the enemy's pickets from time to time, and opened a frequent fire of artillery on his works to insure a full knowledge of his position, strength, and movements as far as it was possible, moving my own headquarters to the line occupied by the troops, and sleeping near them in order to observe more closely.

After the battle of Friday, June 27, [Gaines Mill] on the opposite bank of the Chickahominy, it was ascertained that the enemy had withdrawn his troops to the right bank, and therefore the whole of his forces were massed in front of our lines, and that he had destroyed the bridges over this river, thereby separating our army and concentrating his own. I immediately ordered, without awaiting instructions, the bridge known as the New Bridge to be rebuilt, which was done by the troops under Brigadier-General *Jones,* in order to establish at least one line of communication between the two portions of our army. This was completed on Saturday, 28th.

From the time at which the enemy withdrew his forces to this side of the Chickahominy and destroyed the bridges to the moment of his evacuation—that is, from Friday night until Sunday morning—I considered the situation of our army as extremely critical and perilous. The larger portion of it was on the opposite side of the Chickahominy, the bridges had been all destroyed, but one was rebuilt, the New Bridge, which was commanded fully by the enemy's guns from Golding's [Farm], and there were but 25,000 men between his army of 100,000 and Richmond.

I received repeated instructions during Saturday night from General *Lee*'s headquarters enjoining upon my command the utmost vigilance, directing the men to sleep on their arms, and to be prepared for whatever might occur. These orders were promptly communicated by me to the different commanders of my forces and were also transmitted to General *Huger*, on my right. I passed the night without sleep and in the superintendence of their execution.

Had McClellan massed his whole force in column and advanced it against any point of our line of battle, as was done at Austerlitz [December 2, 1805] under similar circumstances by the greatest captain of any age [Napoleon], though the head of his column would have suffered greatly; its momentum would have insured him success, and the occupation of our works about Richmond, and consequently of the city, might have been his reward.

His failure to do so is the best evidence that our wise commander fully understood the character of his opponent. Our relief was therefore great when intelligence reached us almost simultaneously from Colonel *Chilton* and one of my staff that the enemy, whose presence had been ascertained as late as 3.30 a.m., had evacuated his works and was retreating.

Colonel *Chilton*, who rode into my camp on Sunday morning, hurried me off to see General *Lee*, on the Nine-mile road, and I gave, while riding with him, the necessary orders to put in motion my whole command, which extended over a distance of some miles, directing Brigadier-General *Griffith*'s brigade, which was nearest to the road, to advance at once from the center, and ordering Brigadier-General *Jones'* division in advancing to incline toward Fair Oaks Station, as I had been informed that Major-General *Jackson* had crossed or was crossing the Grapevine Bridge, and would operate down the Chickahominy.

Having overtaken General *Lee*, we rode together down the Nine-mile road, and the general informed me of the plans which he had adopted for the pursuit of the enemy.

On our arrival at Fair Oaks Station we found the enemy's lines in that vicinity, which had been evacuated, in possession of a part of Brigadier-General *Kershaw*'s brigade, the remainder of my command being then on the march. Here General *Lee*, having repeated his instructions, left the ground.

I directed Major-General *McLaws* to consolidate *Kershaw*'s brigade and place it on the right of the railroad, and as the other brigade of General *McLaws* did not arrive for some time, I ordered two regiments of an advance brigade (*Griffith*'s) of my own division to take post in reserve also on the right of the railroad, so as to support *Kershaw*'s brigade . . . . I then formed the other two regiments of *Griffith*'s brigade on the left of General *Kershaw*'s, their right resting on the railroad. Brigadier-General *Cobb*'s, which marched in rear of General *Griffith*'s, was, as soon as it arrived, formed on the left of these two regiments, two of his own being kept in reserve. I then dispatched a staff officer to ascertain the position of General *Jones'* division, which had crossed the swamp at Golding's house, and directed it to be formed on the left of General *Cobb*, with the proper interval. While these dispositions were being made I ordered skirmishers to be thrown out in front of General *Kershaw*'s brigade, and my own division to find the enemy and ascertain his position. The enemy having thrown up a heavy obstruction across the railroad track, I caused men to be detailed for the purpose of removing it for the passage down the road of a heavy rifled gun, mounted on a railway carriage, and protected by an inclined plane of iron. I also dispatched a staff officer toward Grapevine Bridge, some 3 miles off, to ascertain the position of Major-General *Jackson*'s troops, which I had supposed from the statements above given had already crossed.

These orders given and disposition made I received information from Brigadier-General *Jones* that the enemy was in force in his front and fortified. This, it was reported to me, was derived from a prisoner, who had been just captured, and the presence of the enemy in front was verified by the skirmishers of General *Jones* being engaged with those of the enemy.

I received about the same time a communication from General *McLaws* stating that the enemy was in front of *Kershaw*'s brigade and in works well manned. Desiring to ascertain the extent of his front, I directed Brigadier-General *Cobb* to detail a trusty officer and some of his best skirmishers to feel the enemy, if to be found in front of my division, and to report the result.

In the mean time Major *Bryan*, the staff officer who had been sent to Major-General *Jackson*, returned with his engineer, Lieutenant *Boswell*, who reported that Major-General *Jackson* was compelled to rebuild the bridge, which would be completed in about two hours, Major *Bryan* reporting that Major-General *Jackson* had crossed but a small portion of his infantry, not more than three companies, over the broken bridge. About the same time I received a message from Major-General *Huger*, stating that a large portion of his command had been sent elsewhere . . . .

The enemy, having ascertained the general disposition of our troops opened a brisk artillery fire upon the railroad and our center, unfortunately mortally wounding the gallant General *Griffith*, commander of the Mississippi Brigade, who was borne from the field and died the next morning. [Colonel *William Barksdale* took command of *Griffith*'s Brigade.] The enemy's fire was responded to with effect by the railroad battery, as well as by *Carlton*'s battery, which that practiced artillerist Lieut. Col. *Stephen D. Lee* had placed in advance in a commanding position in front of our center.

I received information from Major-General *Huger* that his two brigades would be withdrawn, as I understood, for other service, and subsequently a note reached me from General *Jones* stating that Major-General *Jackson* regretted that he could not co-operate with him, as he had been ordered on other important duty.

Thus, the forces which General *Lee* had left to operate against the enemy being reduced from some 35,000 or 40,000 to some 13,000 men, I was compelled to abandon the plan of capturing any large portion of the enemy's forces, and directed that *Semmes'* brigade (*McLaws'* division) should be placed on the Williamsburg road, and *Cobb's* on the left of the railroad in line with *Kershaw's*; *Jones'* division being on the extreme left, and *Barksdale's* [*Griffith's*] brigade marching in reserve behind the center. I ordered the whole to move to the front and each commander to attack the enemy in whatever force or works he might be found. This was executed promptly and in beautiful order, though the ground was difficult and the wood dense. [*OR* 11, pt. 2, pp. 661–64.]

You are located on the road that went from Richmond to Williamsburg in 1862. In reports it is referred to as Williamsburg Road; today it is Old Williamsburg Road. The modern Williamsburg Road is Highway U.S. 60, 525 yards (0.3 mile) to your right. The land on either side of the road belonged to the Allen Farm. Notice the farmhouse and sign to your right. The Richmond and York River Railroad was located 700 (0.4 mile) yards to you left, and 2,300 yards (1.3 mile) in front of you was Savage Station, a stop on the Richmond and York River Railroad. It had become a collecting point for the Union wounded from the Battle of Gaines Mill. Directly behind you the road in 1862 went to Seven Pines. Today the road is blocked just before it intersects with U.S. 60. Seven Pines and the intersection of Williamsburg Road and Nine Mile Road are 1,760 yards (1 mile) behind you.

Following the orders he received from *Magruder*, *McLaws* began deploying the two brigades of his division and advanced along the railroad and Williamsburg Road toward the Union defenses now at Savage Station.

Report of Maj. Gen. *Lafayette McLaws*, CSA, Commanding *McLaws's* Division, Army of Northern Virginia

On the 29th two regiments of General *Kershaw's* brigade, South Carolina Volunteers, [were] ordered forward at an early hour. One regiment (*Kennedy's*) being in reserve, supporting the pickets, had sent out companies

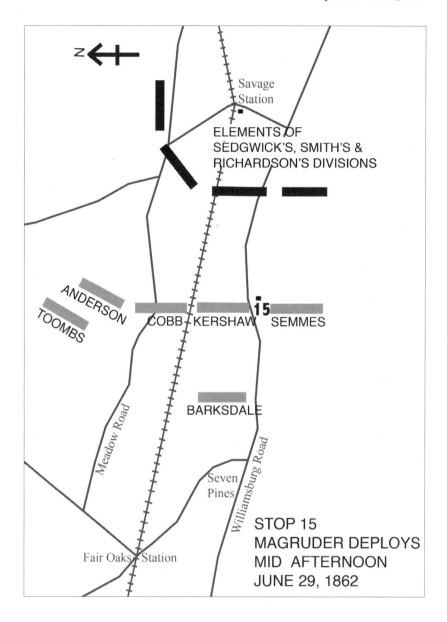

STOP 15
MAGRUDER DEPLOYS
MID AFTERNOON
JUNE 29, 1862

to reconnoiter, and finding the enemy's works deserted, the whole regiment occupied the lines most advanced toward ours. The remaining regiments of the brigade, being ordered onward, joined that of Colonel *Kennedy*, and the whole brigade, under General *Kershaw*, went forward and took position beyond Fair Oaks Station in the woods to the right of the railroad, keeping their skirmishers well to the front. This brigade was in advance of all other troops and waited their arrival.

The enemy were seen crossing the railroad about a mile or less in front, coming from the woods on our left, but it being understood that General *Jackson's* forces were crossing at Grapevine Bridge, every one was very much concerned, fearing that we would become engaged with them. So much was General *Kershaw* impressed with that idea that he withheld the fire of his troops and sent a regimental flag down the railroad, waving it, in order to give notice of the presence of Confederate forces.

General *Semmes'* brigade in the mean while came up along the railroad and was halted behind the works about Fair Oaks Station. The enemy had opened a scattering fire from several pieces, which, however, did no harm to my command.

General *Magruder,* having arranged his forces on the left, ordered that General *Semmes'* brigade should move to *Kershaw's* position and *Kershaw* to advance.

General *Huger's* forces, or a portion of them, were seen at this time coming toward my right flank. They soon, however, retired, going in the direction of the Charles City road. Their purpose I did not understand.

This was about 3 p.m. General *Kershaw* now advanced his brigade, leaving his left on the railroad, supported by that of General *Semmes. Kemper's* battery, as it came down the Nine-mile road, was ordered forward, supported by the Tenth Georgia, Colonel *Cumming.* The brigades advanced in two lines, *Semmes* receiving orders to cross the Williamsburg road with his right. Not long after passing the junction of the Nine-mile and Williamsburg roads the enemy opened fire from a battery on our right, which was replied to with such effect by *Kemper's* battery that the enemy retired without engaging with their infantry. *Kershaw,* continuing the march, relieving the Tenth Georgia from the support of his battery, engaged the enemy with his whole force, *Semmes'* brigade resting immediately behind and extending well to the right. *Kemper's* battery, taking position on the right of the Williamsburg road upon elevated ground, opened fire with extraordinary rapidity and great effect. Finding that *Kershaw's* right was being outflanked by the enemy, I ordered in two regiments from *Semmes'* brigade, and afterward the whole remaining force, which effectually prevented the design. Our troops and those of the enemy were in very close proximity—so much so that at one time the order was given by some commanders to cease firing, they being fearful that we were engaged with our own men. [*OR* 11, pt. 2, pp. 716–17.]

Return to your car for the drive to Stop 16. Drive east on the Old Williamsburg Road for 0.5 mile. You will pass through the intersection with Dry Bridge Road. After 0.5 mile, pull over to the side of the road. Get out of your car and face east, your direction of travel.

Stop 16—*Kershaw*'s Attack

You are located in the vicinity of where *Kershaw*'s Brigade was fully deployed and began its attack against the Union position at Savage Station. *Kershaw*'s right flank regiment was the Eighth South Carolina. This regiment was located to your right. *Kemper*'s Battery was deployed astride the road where you are now. To your left was the Seventh South Carolina, on that regiment's left was the Third South Carolina and farther left and touching upon the railroad tracks was the Second South Carolina. Directly to your front at a distance of 400 yards was the Union defensive position, with six infantry regiments on line and two more in reserve and an additional stronger force farther back that could be called upon if required.

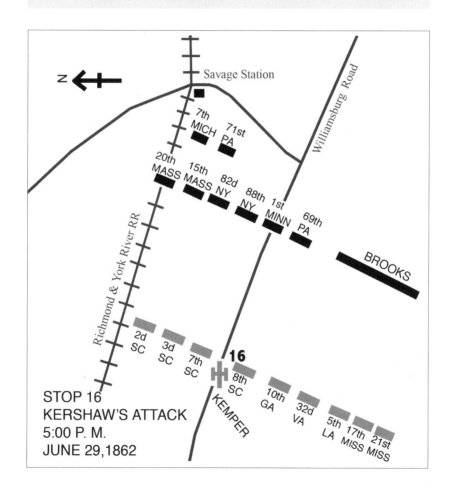

Report of Brig. Gen. *Joseph B. Kershaw,* CSA, Commanding *Kershaw*'s Brigade, *McLaws*'s Division, Army of Northern Virginia

I received orders from Major-General *Magruder* to continue my advance and attack any position I might meet the enemy in. I ordered my command forward, preceded as before by skirmishers commanded by Major *Gaillard,* to whose assistance I sent Maj. *W. D. Rutherford,* of the Third Regiment. I signified to Major *Brent,* who brought me the order, that in my opinion there should be troops to my right, which only extended to the Williamsburg road, though my skirmishers were extended beyond to cover that flank. In a few minutes I heard that Major-General *McLaws* had ordered forward General *Semmes'* brigade to that position. Continuing the advance through the abandoned works and camps of the enemy, taking some prisoners on the way, we arrived at the edge of the wood, which skirts Savage's farm. Sending forward the line of skirmishers to brush the wood, they soon encountered the enemy in heavy force and a formidable artillery fire. *Kemper*'s battery was placed in position on the road, Colonel *Henagan*'s Eighth South Carolina regiment was thrown to his right across the road, and the whole command became engaged. I ordered the Second and Third Regiments to charge, which they did in gallant style, and immediately after the Seventh Regiment, Colonel *Aiken.* These regiments steadily and rapidly advanced, driving the enemy before them through the wood and well into the field beyond, throwing them into confusion and strewing the ground with dead. In the mean time the Seventh Regiment, which was next to the Williamsburg road, found itself flanked by the enemy, who had advanced along that road, in the direction of Kemper's battery and the Eighth Regiment, to a position some 200 yards in our rear. Matters were in this position when General *Semmes* attacked on my right. The line of his fire upon the enemy rendered the position of my advanced regiments on the left of the road extremely hazardous, and Colonel *Aiken* very properly fell back to the general line of battle, followed by Colonels *Nance* and *Kennedy.* In the mean time *Kemper*'s battery, flanked by the Eighth Regiment, had inflicted terrible havoc upon the enemy, whose dead lay in heaps along the road scarcely 200 yards from the battery.

The conduct of both officers and men in this engagement was most commendable. Nothing could exceed the gallantry, self-possession, and efficiency of the regimental commanders, Colonels *Henagan, Kennedy, Nance,* and *Aiken,* to whom my thanks are especially due. Though my loss was heavy, it is with pride and satisfaction that we turn to 500 dead of the enemy left on the field as attesting the bravery and efficiency of the troops engaged at Savage's, and that our loss was fearfully avenged. [*OR* 11, pt. 2, pp. 726–27.]

The report of the commander of the Seventh South Carolina, which was deployed just to the left of where you are, gives a typical account of the fighting done by all of *Kershaw*'s regiments.

Report of Col. *D. Wyatt Aiken*, CSA, Commanding Seventh South Carolina Infantry, *Kershaw*'s Brigade, *McLaws*'s Division Army of Northern Virginia

We advanced until the skirmishers announced the enemy in line of battle. This line of the enemy being dispersed by a battery of artillery we were again ordered forward, and about 4.30 or 5 p.m. were halted in a valley in the woods beyond [Allen] farm. In my rear a battery was again drawn up, and, firing directly over the right of my regiment, subjected us to a very severe cannonading, from which there was no escape. This duel resulted in my losing 1 man and having 2 slightly wounded.

At about 5.30 p.m. I was ordered by some one I did not see to move my regiment forward after a couple of volleys of musketry had been heard on my left. I moved forward, and immediately upon emerging from the oak grove and entering the pine thicket I encountered the enemy. Cautioning the men to reserve their fires, I ordered a charge. The charge was made, some few firing, and the enemy gave back. Another forward was given, and onward we went, firing generally as we advanced. I next ordered, "Load advancing and fire at will." This command, heard by but a few was intuitively obeyed by all. After the enemy had been pressed back about 150 yards a heavy firing began on my right and considerably in the rear. Fearing this might be from our friends, I sent the sergeant-major to inquire of the lieutenant-colonel how the right was progressing, for it was impossible in the thicket to see half the length of the regiment. He returned almost immediately with the word that the lieutenant-colonel was taken from the field wounded, two companies on my right were cut off, and the enemy were in our rear. I forthwith issued the order to retire in line, which was heard by but two companies. I withdrew these to an old cross-road and in a few minutes collected the others. Cautioning this portion of the regiment to lie down and be on the watch, I started to look for the two right companies, which soon reported and were attached to the regiment. I then formed line of battle, but the firing on my left having ceased, I faced by the rear rank and retired about 50 yards into the oak grove, halting and fronting again. No enemy advancing, I faced about again and marched out of the woods, where I found the two left regiments and formed upon them. The battle over, we were permitted to lie in line of battle in the valley whence we first started, and there we remained until Monday, 7 a.m.

The casualties of my command were: Two sergeants, 2 corporals, and 9 privates killed; 1 lieutenant-colonel, 4 lieutenants, 9 sergeants, 8 corporals and 46 privates wounded. Total killed, 13; total wounded, 68. Two of the wounded privates have since died. [*OR* 11, pt. 2, p. 741.]

As *Kershaw* deployed and moved forward to attack the Union line, *McLaws* ordered Brigadier General *Paul Semmes* to deploy part of his brigade to the right of *Kershaw*'s and provide support. *Semmes*'s left was to the right of the Eighth South Carolina. His line extended south from that location so that his right was in the vicinity of where Highway U.S. 60 is today. Colonel *William Barksdale* deployed the Seventeenth Mississippi and Twenty-first Mississippi of his brigade in a supporting role to the right of *Semmes*'s line. These two regiments were on the other side of where Highway U.S. 60 is today.

Report of Brig. Gen. *Paul J. Semmes*, CSA, Commanding *Semmes*'s Brigade, *McLaws*'s Division, Army of Northern Virginia

. . . Having received orders from Major-General *McLaws* to send forward two regiments to the support of Brigadier-General *Kershaw*'s brigade, then engaged with the enemy, the Tenth Georgia, Colonel *Cumming*, and the Thirty-second Virginia Lieutenant-Colonel *Willis* commanding, were ordered to advance. Very soon after, perceiving that the firing bore to our right, without waiting to communicate with the major-general I moved in that direction with the Fifth Louisiana, Colonel *Hunt*. These three regiments found themselves confronting the enemy in the following order from right to left: Fifth Louisiana, Thirty-second Virginia, and Tenth Georgia Volunteers. Having halted the Fifth Louisiana and reformed it in the thick wood through which the advance had been made, and discovering troops not more than 40 yards in front, and being necessarily uncertain as to whether they belonged to our army or that of the enemy, I directed Private *Maddox*, Company K, Fifth Louisiana, to advance and challenge, "Who are you?", to which the reply was, "Friends." Hearing the reply, I demanded, "What regiment?" and was answered, "Third Vermont." Thereupon the order was given to commence firing. After the firing had continued for some time with spirit, hearing firing immediately in our front at a distance of some hundreds of yards, and apprehending that our troops might become engaged with each other, it being then quite dark, I gave the order to cease firing, to reform the line, and for the men to rest on their arms.

After thus resting for half an hour, and the battle having terminated by the cessation of all firing, I, at about 8.30 o'clock, conducted the Fifth Louisiana and the Thirty-second Virginia back to camp, whither the Tenth Georgia had just repaired.

Much of the time the enemy were engaged at a distance of not above 40 yards. Their heavy comparative loss doubtless resulted mainly from the greater efficiency of our smooth-bore muskets with buck and ball at short range, the superior steadiness of our men, and the precision of their fire.

Cumming's regiment, being longer and more severely engaged, suffered incomparably more than the two others and inflicted heavier loss on the enemy. [*OR* 11, p. 2, pp. 720–21.]

The Union position was 400 yards in front of you. Directly in front of you and deployed astride the road was the First Minnesota. To that regiment's left, right as you see it, was the Sixty-ninth Pennsylvania. To the right, left as you see it, of the First Minnesota was the Eighty-eight New York. Manning the line to the right of the Eighty-eight New York in order of sequence was the Eighty-second New York, Fifteenth Massachusetts, and Twentieth Massachusetts. The last regiment was astride the railroad tracks. The Seventh Michigan and Seventy-first Pennsylvania were held in reserve. These regiments were from Brigadier General John Sedgwick's Second Division, of the Second Corps. The remainder of Sedgwick's regiments were deployed in a reserve position. The three brigades of Brigadier General Israel B. Richardson's First Division of the Second Corps were located behind and in a supporting position. Caldwell's and Meagher's brigades were in position behind the defensive line and French's brigade was deployed to the right of the Union line so that it covered the road from Grapevine Bridge. Two brigades, Brigadier Generals William Brooks's and Winfield S. Hancock's, from W. F. Smith's division were deployed on both flanks of the defensive position. Brooks's brigade was deployed on the south flank of the Sixty-ninth Pennsylvania. Regiments from that brigade engaged *Semmes*'s and *Barksdale*'s regiments. Hancock's brigade was in position on the right near Meadow Road. Much of this force had already begun to march south and away from Savage Station, but were called back when the fighting began.

Although the Union regiments in the defensive line to your front were drawn from the three different brigade of Sedgwick's division and one from Richardson's division, the commander of the Second Brigade, Brigadier General William W. Burns, was in charge of the defense.

Report of Brig. Gen. William W. Burns, USA, Commanding Second Brigade, Second Division, Second Corps, Army of the Potomac

About 12 o'clock we received orders to fall back upon Savage's [Station], passing through the lines of General Heintzelman, when lying at Savage's, expecting an attack in the direction of Bottom's Bridge. About 4.30 o'clock the enemy appeared in the corner of the field to our left rear, having evidently followed us, and, avoiding Heintzelman's work, passed to the left of the railroad. General Sumner ordered me to take two regiments and move promptly back across the field about half a mile, and hold the woods between the Williamsburg road and the railroad. Before I reached the position a scout informed me that the enemy were in large force on the Williamsburg road. Seeing that both of my flanks would be exposed, I sent to General Sumner for another regiment. Fortunately the enemy did not attack until Lieutenant-Colonel Miller, First Minnesota Regiment, reported, and I had time to throw it to the left, across the Williamsburg road, with the left flank retired. I found I still had not sufficient length of line to cover the ground, and was obliged to move Colonel Baxter [Seventy-second Pennsylvania] to the right and throw back his right flank to cover the railroad, leaving a gap in the center of my line.

These dispositions were in progress when the enemy attacked most furiously with infantry, he having been playing with artillery upon me during the whole movement across the field, which was answered by General Sumner's batteries. The battle raged along the whole line, but concentrated gradually toward my two weak points, the center and the Williamsburg road. I urged more regiments, which were promptly sent me. Before these arrived, however, the enemy made a rush on the center, wounded me and killed the captain of the left company of Baxter's [regiment], Captain McGonigle, forced through to the fence, and flaunted their flag across the rails, broke the line for a moment, but the brave men rallied and drove them back.

The fight then moved toward the Williamsburg road, when most opportunely the Eighty-eighth New York, [Major James Quinlan], came across the field double-quick and cheering. I threw them into the gap on the road, when the enemy opened artillery and infantry upon them, but they never faltered—not only went up to my line but beyond it, and drove secesh before them. The Eighty-second New York, Colonel Hudson, then came over the field, and I advanced it to the gap of the center. It too advanced beyond the original line. The Fifteenth Massachusetts coming up, I relieved Colonel Morehead [One hundred and sixth Pennsylvania] with it, and Colonel Baxter with the Twentieth Massachusetts, Colonel Lee. The Seventy-first Pennsylvania [also called the First California Regiment, commanded by Lieutenant Colonel

William G. Jones] and Seventh Michigan [Colonel Norman J. Hall] coming up, I held them in reserve, looking to the flanks. Colonel Owen, of the Sixty-ninth Pennsylvania Volunteers, was led to the left of the [First] Minnesota by my aide, and still farther to the left General Brooks' brigade was thrown by General Sumner, on learning the enemy was moving in large force in that direction. The fight closed, however, with the fire of the Eighty-eighth New York, Eighty-second New York, and Fifteenth Massachusetts.

The battle ceased at 7 o'clock. About 11 o'clock I received orders from General Sumner to withdraw my brigade and march to White Oak Bridge. [*OR* 11, pt. 2, pp. 91–92.]

Return to your car for the drive to Stop 17. Make a U-turn and drive 0.3 mile on Old Williamsburg Road to the intersection with Dry Bridge Road. Turn left on Dry Bridge Road and drive for 0.4 mile to the intersection with U.S. Highway 60, the modern Williamsburg Road. Turn left on to the eastbound lanes and immediately pull off to the right of the road.

Stop 17—*Barksdale* Supports the Attack

You are in the vicinity of *Semmes*'s right flank and *Barksdale*'s left flank as regiments from both brigades supported *Kershaw*'s attack. *Semmes*'s right regiment was the Fifth Louisiana, and *Barksdale*'s left regiment was the Seventeenth Mississippi. To that regiment's right was the Twenty-first Mississippi. The rest of *Barksdale*'s regiments were deployed to your left rear near the railroad tracks.

Report of Col. *William Barksdale*, CSA, Commanding *Griffith*'s Brigade, *Magruder*'s Division, Army of Northern Virginia

On Sunday morning we were ordered to pursue the enemy, who had abandoned his fortifications on the Nine-mile road and was understood to be retreating down the York River Railroad. On reaching these fortifications a fire was opened upon us by the enemy's rear guard. The brigade was at once ordered in line of battle, and while gallantly executing this order General *Griffith* fell mortally wounded. The command devolved upon me. Continuing the pursuit, I was ordered to support General *Cobb*, who was in the advance, should he become engaged with the enemy. The brigade advanced in line of battle on the left of the railroad, through the thick woods and over a marshy country, until we reached [a position west of] Savage Station, when an attack

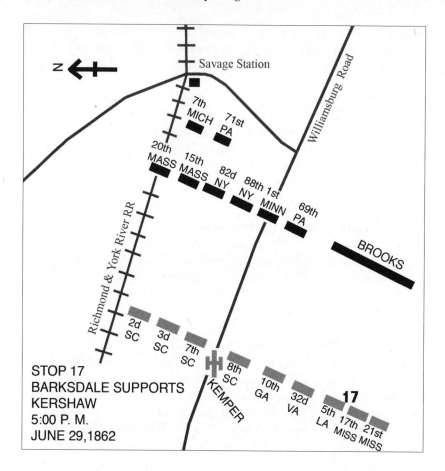

N

Savage Station

Williamsburg Road

7th MICH   71st PA

20th MASS   15th MASS   82d NY   88th NY   1st MINN   69th PA

Richmond & York River RR

BROOKS

2d SC   3d SC   7th SC

STOP 17
BARKSDALE SUPPORTS
KERSHAW
5:00 P. M.
JUNE 29,1862

KEMPER

8th SC   10th GA   32d VA   5th LA   17th MISS   21st MISS

17

was made on the right side of the road upon the enemy by General *McLaws'* division. The Seventeenth Regiment, Colonel *Holder,* and the Twenty-first, Colonel *Humphreys,* were ordered to that side of the road, and to support *Kershaw*'s brigade if it should become necessary to do so.

About sundown these regiments advanced gallantly and promptly when the order was given under a severe fire across an open field to the support of a battery and engaged the enemy, then strongly posted in the woods beyond the field, and poured several destructive volleys into his ranks, when messengers arrived and requested that the firing should cease, as danger would result from it to our friends, who were maneuvering between them and the enemy. The men were ordered to lay down, and night coming on and the firing having ceased, they retired in good order to the woods in rear of the battle-field. [*OR* 11, pt. 2, p. 750.]

The Confederate force at this location was engaged with Brigadier General William Brooks's brigade. This brigade was the left of
the Union line and was located approximately four hundred yards in
front of you.

Report of Brig. Gen. William T. H. Brooks, USA, Commanding Second Brigade, Second Division, Sixth Corps, Army of the Potomac

On the 29th the brigade left its camp near Golding's farm, as part of the
division, to make the change of base. After passing Savage Station en route
for the White Oak [Swamp] the division was ordered to return to that point,
on account of an attack being made by the enemy. The brigade was formed
in this order: The Fifth Vermont, Lieutenant-Colonel Grant, in line on the
right; the Sixth Vermont, Colonel Lord, deployed to the left; the Second
Vermont, Colonel Whiting, in column of division in support of the Fifth;
the Third Vermont, Lieutenant-Colonel Veazey, in column in support of the
Sixth. In this manner the brigade entered the woods that bound the plain to
the left and south of the station.

After advancing through a dense wood, preceded by two companies
of the Second Vermont, under Major Walbridge, about 1½ miles, we came
upon the enemy, and a brisk fire of musketry was opened on both sides, and
kept up until darkness seemed to terminate the action. The Fifth Vermont,
Lieutenant-Colonel Grant, debouched from the woods into an open field,
where they found a large regiment of the enemy posted, which they routed
in gallant style. As soon as the firing commenced the Second and Third,
that were in column, soon deployed, and got hotly engaged with the enemy,
as well as the two regiments that were originally in line. The conduct of the
troops in this action was generally very commendable.

After the engagement the brigade retired across the White Oak Swamp.
[OR 11, pt. 2, pp. 476–77.]

The Battle of Savage Station had the potential to be much
larger than it was. Initially, the Union rear guard consisted of the
three brigades of Sedgwick's division. Once the fighting began, five
brigades, which had begun to march south, were returned to reinforce Sedgwick. This brought the Union strength at Savage Station

to nine brigades. *Magruder* began his move toward Savage Station with eight brigades. However, two that belonged to *Huger* were sent down Charles City Road to rejoin their division in the march toward Glendale. The six brigades left to *Magruder,* although only four were committed to the fight, were insufficient strength to successfully attack the Union position. By not pressing his attack against a superior force and ordering his units to fall back out of rifle and artillery range, *Magruder* saved his command from taking an unacceptable amount of casualties. The combat power necessary for Confederate success was with *Jackson's* command north of the Chickahominy River. *Jackson's* failure, for whatever reason, to cross a large force to the south side of the Chickahominy River played a major role in the attacks on the rear of the Union column not accomplishing what *Lee* intended.

From here you will drive to White Oak Bridge. You will be following the route of Smith's and Richardson's divisions as they retreated from Savage Station during the night of June 29–30. When you turn off Williamsburg Road you will also be following the route taken by the advance units of *Jackson's* command as it followed the Union rear guard.

Continue to drive east on U.S. Highway 60 for 2.6 miles to the intersection with Elko Road, Highway 156. Turn right on to Old Elko Road and drive for 3.3 miles to Elko, where you will cross a set of railroad tracks. After you have driven for 2.5 miles from the intersection of U.S. Highway 60 and Elko Road, White Oak Road will intersect from the left. The retreating Union units and the advancing Confederates used both of these roads. After crossing the railroad tracks at Elko, continue on for 0.2 mile, where you will come to a parking area with a marker. This is just before a bridge. Pull off to the right side of the road, near the marker, and get out of your car. Face in the direction you were driving. Be careful of traffic.

Stop 18—White Oak Bridge

Directly in front of you is White Oak Swamp and White Oak Swamp Creek. The swamp extends three and one-half miles to your right (west), with the creek extending even farther. To your left the swamp and creek go for two miles, where it flows into the Chickahominy River. This low swampy ground was a natural barrier that had to be crossed by the retreating Union army and the Confederate forces in direct pursuit. In 1862, as today, this area had limited visibility because of the trees and undergrowth.

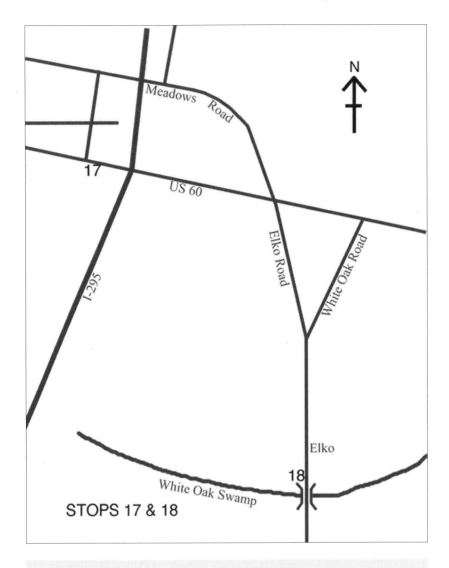

STOPS 17 & 18

In 1862 there were limited places where the swamp could be crossed by a large body of troops. One of the best crossing areas was where you are now. Another good area was located two miles to your right. Between these two bridged crossing points there were three fords. All of the corps of the Army of the Potomac crossed at these locations. Roads from the two bridged crossing sites funnel into the road junction at Glendale, where one road then goes south over Malvern Hill to the James River. It was this choke point at Glendale that the divisions of *Huger, Longstreet,* and *A. P. Hill* were marching to cut off the Union retreat. These divisions had by passed the swamp to the west. *Lee* was counting on the direct pursuing force, now under *Jackson,* to maintain pressure on the Union rear guard and slow down the retreat.

On the night of June 29 the Union divisions of W. F. Smith and Israel Richardson marched along the roads you drove over and at dawn crossed the creek in front of you. These two divisions, under the command of the Sixth Corps commander, Brigadier General William B. Franklin, occupied defensive positions on the high ground across the creek from where you are now. Richardson's division was to the west of the road, and Smith's division was to the east. The last Union unit to cross over destroyed the bridge.

Report of Brig. Gen. Israel B. Richardson, USA, Commanding First Division, Second Corps, Army of the Potomac

Late at night [June 29] I received an order to act as a rear guard with my division in covering the movement of the army across the White Oak Swamp, and also to take charge personally of the breaking up of the bridge across the creek, so as to make it impracticable for the passage of artillery. My march commenced about 1 o'clock on the 30th of June, and after marching until nearly daybreak in the morning, on coming up to the bridge I found the mass of stragglers from other parts of the army wedged in so as to be unable to move. I impressed them with the necessity of crossing as rapidly as possible or the enemy would be upon us and the rear of the army cut off. By the greatest exertions of myself and staff, I succeeded in getting this mass over by sunrise and my own division, and the bridge was broken up and burned by about 10 o'clock a.m.

I was now directed by General Sumner to remain here until further orders, the division of General Smith being on my right. Early in the afternoon, while our troops were resting, a heavy cannonade was opened by the enemy on the other side of the creek from a hill partly covered by timber. It appeared to be some three batteries, and they all opened at once. My division stood firmly. The battery of Hazzard's exhausting its ammunition, the captain being wounded and many men and horses disabled, it was replaced by the battery of Captain Pettit [Battery B, First New York Artillery], which kept up continuous fire until night. After firing away all their ammunition these were now replaced by a battery of [W. F. Smith's] division, which kept up a

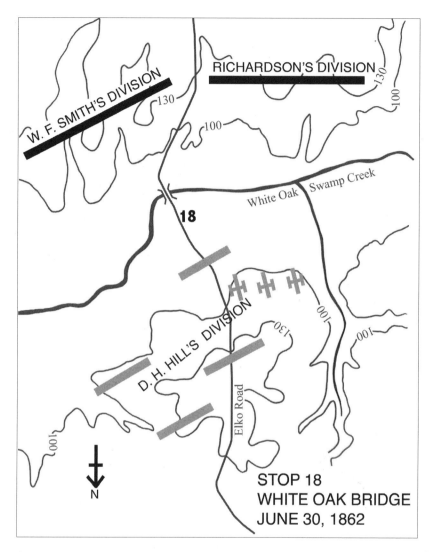

RICHARDSON'S DIVISION

W. F. SMITH'S DIVISION

130

100

130

100

White Oak Swamp Creek

18

D. H. HILL'S DIVISION

130

100

100

100

Elko Road

N

STOP 18
WHITE OAK BRIDGE
JUNE 30, 1862

fire with two pieces until 12 o'clock at night, when I was ordered again to fall back to form the rear guard. Two of my brigades had been detached during the day, and I had only that of General French to cover the movement. [*OR* 11, pt. 2, p. 55.]

Jackson's command crossed the Chickahominy River in the early morning hours of June 30. The unit leading the pursuit was *D. H. Hill*'s Division. *Hill* marched through Savage Station to the vicinity of White Oak Bridge generally along the same route that you drove. Upon arriving on the high ground north of White Oak Swamp he discovered the bridge had been destroyed and Union infantry and artillery were in defensive positions south of the swamp.

Report of Maj. Gen. *Daniel H. Hill*, CSA, Commanding *Hill*'s Division, Army of Northern Virginia

Jackson's command, my division leading, passed Savage Station early in the morning of the 30th instant, and followed the line of the Yankee retreat toward White Oak Creek. We picked up about 1,000 prisoners and so many arms, that I detached the Fourth and Fifth North Carolina Regiments to take charge of both.

At White Oak Creek we found the bridge destroyed and the Yankee forces drawn up on the other side. Twenty-six guns from my division and five from *Whiting*'s division opened a sudden and unexpected fire upon the Yankee batteries and infantry. A feeble response was attempted, but silenced in a few minutes. *Munford*'s cavalry and my skirmishers crossed over, but the Yankees got some guns under cover of a wood which commanded the bridge, and the cavalry was compelled to turn back. The skirmishers staid over all day and night. We attempted no further crossing that day. [*OR* 11, pt. 2, p. 627.]

The artillery that *Hill* makes reference to was located on the higher ground 700 yards to your right rear. This artillery was under the command of *Jackson*'s chief of artillery.

Report of Col. *Stapleton Crutchfield*, CSA, Chief of Artillery, *Jackson*'s Command, Army of Northern Virginia

On Monday, June 30, we crossed the Chickahominy at Grapevine Bridge and moved toward White Oak Swamp. At this point the swamp was crossed by a trestle bridge, which the enemy had just fired, while it was commanded by their guns from the opposite hill, and all approach to it prevented by their sharpshooters, who were concealed in a thick woods near by. After examining the ground, I found it possible with a little work to open a way through the woods to the right of the road on which we advanced, by which our guns could be brought, unseen by the enemy, into position behind the crest of the hill on this side, about 1,000 yards from the enemy's batteries and some 1,200 yards from their infantry. Seven batteries, in all twenty-three guns, were accordingly ordered up from Maj. Gen. *D. H. Hill*'s division. Having met their officers for the first time on that day I do not now readily recall their names, and can only mention the batteries of Capts. *T. H. Carter, R. A. Hardaway, G. W. Nelson, A. B. Rhett, James Reilly,* and *W. L. Baithis,* the last two belonging to Brigadier-General *Whiting*'s division, as being of the number.

About 1:45 p.m. we opened suddenly upon the enemy, who had no previous intimation of our position and intention. He only fired four shots in reply and then abandoned the position in extreme haste and confusion. A house near by was first either fired by themselves or by our shell and burned down. Captain *Wooding*'s battery was immediately ordered down nearer to the burned bridge to shell out the sharpshooters from the woods, which was soon accomplished, and our cavalry crossed the swamp.

It was then found that the enemy was bringing up a considerable artillery force to take position on the opposite side of the road to his former place and directly opposed to our guns, from which he would be concealed by a thick intervening wood. Capt. *G. W. Wooding*'s battery was therefore withdrawn and our batteries turned in the new direction. The enemy soon opened on us with about eighteen guns, I think and we replied, though it was extremely difficult to estimate the distance, as the enemy's guns were entirely concealed from view and our only guide was the sound, while our exact position was of course known to him. His fire was rapid and generally accurate, though the nature of the ground afforded us such shelter as to protect us from much loss. The effect of our own fire could not be estimated until we crossed the swamp next day, when there were palpable evidences of its having been much more destructive than that to which we were subjected. This engagement lasted till dusk without intermission. [*OR* 11, pt. 2, p. 561.]

The artillery fire forced the Union infantry and artillery to fall back about three hundred yards to positions along a wood line. From here they were able to maintain control of the bridge site. The Union defenders retreated during the night and *Jackson*'s command crossed White Oak Swamp the next day.

Through out Monday, June 30, while *Jackson* was stalled at White Oak Bridge, the remainder of the Confederate army and five divisions of the Army of the Potomac were locked in a desperate battle around the Glendale crossroads.

Return to your car for the drive to Stop 19.

Chapter 5

Battle of Glendale
Monday, June 30, 1862

Continue driving south for 1.2 miles to the intersection with Charles City Road, turn right, and drive west for 1.1 miles to the intersection with Willis Church Road, Darbytown Road, and Charles City Road. Turn to the right and immediately pull off to the right and stop.

Stop 19—Glendale Intersection

You are at the intersection of the roads that the majority of the Army of the Potomac had to pass through during its retreat south to the James River. It is this intersection that *Lee* also had his army pointed toward in an attempt to attack, cut off, and break up the Union army.

The road in front of you is the Charles City Road. It goes in a northeasterly direction and in two and one-half miles crosses the western end of White Oak Swamp. *Lee* ordered *Huger* to march his division down this road and attack the Union forces passing through or in the vicinity of this intersection.

The road to your left is Darbytown Road. This road has been redirected since 1862. At that time it did not come to the Glendale crossroads but intersected with the Long Bridge Road about two miles southwest of here. It was the Long Bridge Road that came into this intersection from the southwest. *Lee* had ordered *Longstreet* and *A. P. Hill* to march around White Oak Swamp, march southeast on the Darbytown Road to its intersection with the Long Bridge Road, and then march northeast on the Long Bridge Road, which would place them on the right flank of *Huger*'s attack, where they were to also attack that part of the Union army in this area.

The road behind you is the Willis Church Road. In 1862 it was also called Quaker Road and was sometimes confused with another road southwest of here also called Quaker Road. Willis Church Road was vital to the Army of the Potomac. It goes south from this intersection for two and three-quarter miles to Malvern Hill, a major defensive position, and only one mile from the James River. The capture of Willis Church Road or the Glendale intersection by Confederate forces would be a disaster for McClellan's army. There was also an old overgrown farm road that started just east of Glendale at the 1862 Long Bridge Road and went south toward Malvern Hill. Union soldiers cleared this road of growth and it was used by part of McClellan's army as it retreated.

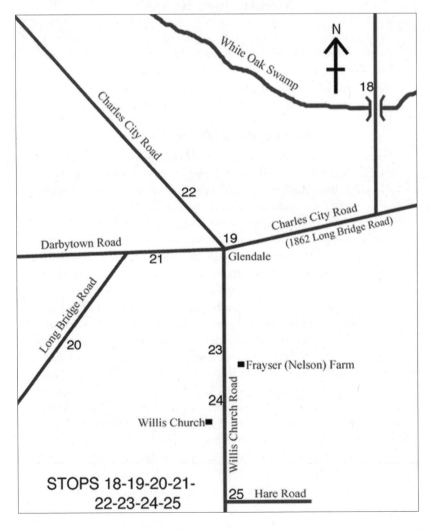

By the morning of June 30 only the two divisions of Brigadier General Erasmus D. Keyes's Fourth Corps and two of the three divisions of Porter's Fifth Corps had marched down Willis Church Road and on to Malvern Hill. The remaining seven divisions of McClellan's army were still deployed to hold open the route of retreat while the supply trains continued to move toward James River on Willis Church Road and the overgrown parallel farm road.

Seven Union divisions were involved in the fighting on June 30. Two divisions were located at White Oak Bridge, where you just came from. Slocum's division was deployed across the Charles City Road, facing northwest, about one mile from where you are now. Kearny's division was parallel to and just west of Charles City Road. This division faced southwest and was loosely tied in with the left flank of Slocum's division. West of this location and stretching south was McCall's division. Behind McCall and along Willis Church Road was Sedgwick's division. Farther south and just west of Willis Church road was Hooker's division. These seven divisions were from the Second, Third, Fifth, and Sixth Corps of the Army of the Potomac. After McClellan had a meeting with his corps commander at this crossroads at midmorning, he left and went on to the James River. Not one corps commander had been placed in overall command of the defenses.

Lee had accomplished part of his objective. He now had two-thirds of the divisions of the Army of the Potomac stopped so that he could attack them, cut their route of retreat, and render them combat ineffective.

Return to the intersection and turn right on Darbytown Road. Drive west for 0.5 mile to the intersection with Long Bridge Road. Turn left on Long Bridge Road and drive for another 0.3 mile to where there is a low historical marker on your left. Pull off to the left and park. Be careful; you are stopping on a curve in the road. Get out of your car and face east, with the road behind you. Notice the power lines going east. They will be a point of reference later on.

Stop 20—*Longstreet's* Attack

Report of Gen. *Robert E. Lee,* CSA, Commanding Army of Northern Virginia

Jackson reached Savage Station early on the 30th. He was directed to pursue the enemy on the road he had taken and *Magruder* to follow *Longstreet* by the Darbytown road. As *Jackson* advanced he captured such numbers of prisoners and collected so many arms that two regiments had to be detached for their security. His progress was arrested at White Oak Swamp [Stop 18]. The enemy occupied the opposite side and obstinately resisted the reconstruction of the bridge.

Longstreet and *A. P. Hill*, continuing their advance on the 30th, soon came upon the enemy strongly posted across the Long Bridge road, about 1 mile from its intersection with the Charles City road. *Huger*'s route led to the right of this [Union] position, *Jackson*'s to the rear, and the arrival of their commands was awaited to begin the attack.

On the 29th General *Holmes* had crossed from the south side of James River with part of his division.

On the 30th, re-enforced by General *Wise* with a detachment of his brigade, he moved down the river road and came upon the line of the retreating army near Malvern Hill. Perceiving indications of confusion, General *Holmes* was ordered to open upon the column with artillery. He soon discovered that a number of batteries, advantageously posted, supported by an infantry force superior to his own and assisted by the fire of the gunboats in the James River, guarded this part of the line.

Magruder, who had reached the Darbytown road, was ordered to re-enforce *Holmes*, but being at a greater distance than had been supposed, he did not reach the position of the latter in time for an attack.

Huger reported that his progress was obstructed, but about 4 p.m. firing was heard in the direction of the Charles City road, which was supposed to indicate his approach. *Longstreet* immediately opened with one of his batteries to give notice of his presence. This brought on the engagement, but *Huger* not coming up, and *Jackson* having been unable to force the passage of White Oak Swamp, *Longstreet* and *Hill* were without the expected support. [*OR* 11, pt. 2, p. 495.]

Lee's report of the Battle of Glendale gives a description of how his army was deployed on June 29 and 30 as it maneuvered into positions that centered on the Glendale intersection. *Lee* also presented his plan to trap the Union army. This plan called for *Longstreet* and *A. P. Hill* to attack the head or the center of the retreating Union column, with *Holmes* on the right, *Huger* on the left, and *Jackson* attacking from the rear. However, as *Lee* reports, *Jackson* failed to cross White Oak Swamp as scheduled and *Holmes* and *Huger* did not attack as planned. The only Confederate divisions attacking were those of *Longstreet* and *A. P. Hill*. This attack was placed under the direction of *Longstreet*. *Longstreet* had a total of twelve brigades from both divisions to use in the attack.

You are in the left center of the Confederate attack, in the location of Brigadier General *Richard H. Anderson*'s brigade, commanded by *Colonel Micah Jenkins*. *Anderson* commanded *Longstreet*'s Division, while *Longstreet* had control of both divisions. To this brigade's left was the brigade of Brigadier General *Cadmus M. Wilcox*. To *Wilcox*'s left was Brigadier General *Roger A. Pryor*'s brigade. To the right of *Anderson*'s Brigade was Brigadier General *James L. Kemper*'s brigade. All of these brigades were from *Longstreet*'s Division. Deployed to *Kemper*'s right was Brigadier General *Lawrence Branch*'s brigade of *A. P. Hill*'s Division.

A second line was formed with Brigadier General *Winfield S. Featherston*'s brigade [*Longstreet*'s Division] behind *Pryor*'s Brigade; Brigadier General *Charles W. Field*'s brigade [*A. P. Hill*'s Division] behind *Wilcox*'s Brigade; and *Pickett*'s Brigade [*Longstreet*'s Division], commanded by Colonel *Eppa Hunton,* behind *Anderson*'s and *Kemper*'s Brigades.

A third line was formed with the remainder of *A. P. Hill*'s brigades with Brigadier General *Maxcy Gregg*'s brigade behind *Featherston*'s brigade; Brigadier General *Dorsey Pender*'s brigade behind *Field*'s Brigade; and Brigadier General *James J. Archer*'s brigade behind *Pickett*'s Brigade. Brigadier General *Joseph R. Anderson*'s brigade was held farther back as a reserve. *Longstreet* committed eleven of these twelve brigades to the attack.

Report of Maj. Gen. *James Longstreet,* CSA, Commanding *Longstreet*'s Division, Army of Northern Virginia

The march was resumed on Monday morning [June 30]. Soon after taking up the line of march I was joined by the commanding general. Our forces came upon the enemy at Frayser's farm about noon, when the enemy's skirmishers were reported as advancing. Colonel *Jenkins,* commanding [*Anderson*'s] Brigade, was directed to ascertain the condition of the enemy. After driving in his pickets it was found that he was in force and position, ready for battle. My own division was put in position for attack or defense at once, and one of Maj. Gen. *A. P. Hill*'s brigades [*Branch*'s] ordered forward to support my right flank, the rest of *Hill*'s division being left for the time on the road to secure the right or to move up to support the front.

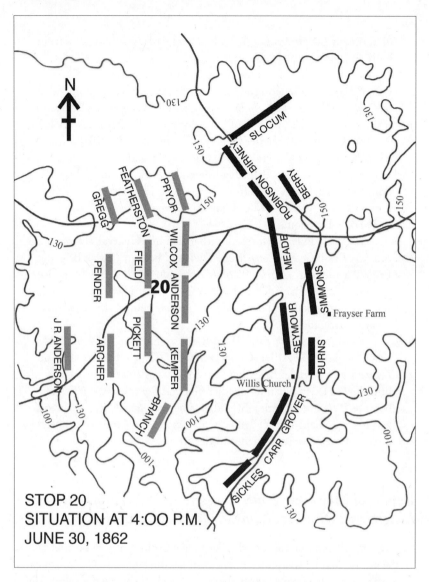

STOP 20
SITUATION AT 4:OO P.M.
JUNE 30, 1862

About this time information was received that Major-General *Magruder* was in rear in easy supporting distance; but as information was also received that the enemy was in force in front of Major-General *Holmes*, it was deemed advisable to order *Magruder*'s forces to join *Holmes*, about 3 miles off to our right.

After getting into position artillery fire was opened about 3 p.m. upon the enemy, apparently from the Charles City road. Taking this for *Huger*'s attack, and thinking that his troops would expect early co-operation, I ordered several batteries forward hurriedly in order to assure those troops that we were in position. The enemy's batteries returned the fire immediately and with great rapidity. One battery was found to be so near our front line that I ordered Colonel *Jenkins* to silence it. The enemy was found to be in such force there, however, that the engagement was brought on at once (4 o'clock). Troops were thrown forward as rapidly as possible to the support of the attacking columns. Owing to the nature of the ground that concert of action so essential to complete success could not be obtained, particularly attacking such odds against us and in position. The enemy, however, was driven back slowly and steadily, contesting the ground inch by inch. He succeeded in getting some of his batteries off the field, and, by holding his last position until dark, in withdrawing his forces under cover of night. [*OR* 11, pt. 2, p. 759.]

Elements of four Union divisions were in position to oppose the Confederate attack. About 1,300 yards (0.7 mile) directly in front of you was Brigadier General George A. McCall's Third Division of the Fifth Corps. To McCall's left, your right, was Brigadier General Joseph Hooker's Second Division of the Third Corps. To McCall's right, your left, was Brigadier General Philip Kearny's Third Division of the Third Corps. In a reserve position behind McCall was Brigadier General John Sedgwick's Second Division of the Second Corps. McClellan left no one in overall command of the units deployed to defend the crossroad and the vital road south to Malvern Hill and the James River. Brigadier General Samuel P. Heintzelman, the commander of the Third Corps, and Brigadier General Edwin V. Sumner, commander of the Second Corps, took it upon themselves to provide what overall direction there was of the defenses.

Return to your car for the drive to Stop 21. Retrace your route north on the Long Bridge Road for 0.3 mile to its intersection with Darbytown Road. Turn right on Darbytown Road and drive for 0.2 mile. Pull off to the right of the road. Get out of your car and face west, toward the intersection of the Long Bridge Road. Be careful of traffic.

Stop 21—Meade's Defense

You are standing in the center of the defensive position of Brigadier General George G. Meade's Second Brigade of McCall's division. To Meade's left was Brigadier General Truman Seymour's Third

Brigade. McCall had placed Reynolds's First Brigade in a reserve position behind Meade and Seymour. Reynolds had been captured during the retreat from Gaines Mill and Colonel Seneca G. Simmons now commanded his brigade. To Meade's right was the left flank brigade of Kearny's division. This was Brigadier General John C. Robinson's brigade. Lieutenant Alanson M. Randol's Battery E, First U.S. Artillery, deployed to the right of the road, supported Meade. In addition, Captain James Thompson's Battery G, Second U.S. Artillery, which was located farther to the right, was able to fire in support of Meade. To Meade's left Lieutenant Frank P. Amsden's Battery G, First Pennsylvania Artillery, could also assist Meade's defense.

McCall's initial outpost line was the Fourth Pennsylvania Cavalry. When the cavalry reported Confederate infantry moving toward the Glendale crossroads, McCall deployed the First and Third Pennsylvania Infantry Regiments as a picket line across the division front. The Third Pennsylvania was covering the right half of the division front and made initial contacts with the Confederate attack against this position. This regiment engaged the Confederate force then fell back and assumed a position on the battle line just to the left of the road, where you are.

Report of Col. Horatio G. Sickel, USA, Commanding Third Pennsylvania Reserves, Second Brigade, Third Division, Fifth Corps, Army of the Potomac

June 30, at 11 o'clock a.m., the Third Regiment was posted on picket duty in front of the camp of McCall's division, the right resting on the Long Bridge road, extending southward about one mile. It was soon reported to me by the outpost pickets and by me to the rear that the enemy was rapidly covering our front with heavy columns of infantry. Their advance soon drove in our outposts, when we received orders to retire on our camp, which was done in good order to the skirt of the woods, when we again took up position in line of battle. Here we remained until the enemy approached to within 50 paces, when the entire line delivered a well-directed fire upon the enemy's front, utterly cutting to pieces the Ninth [Alabama] Regiment. Their column was momentarily checked, when we delivered the second fire with the same good results.

At this time our artillery had opened fire upon them, and we were obliged to retire to get out of range of our own guns. Immediately after a regiment in

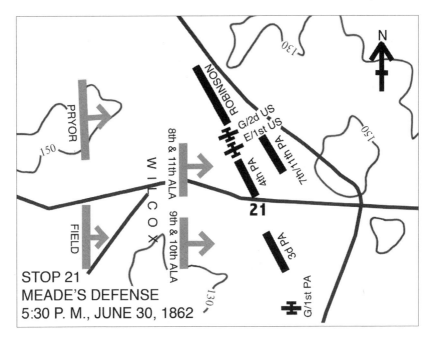

STOP 21
MEADE'S DEFENSE
5:30 P. M., JUNE 30, 1862

our rear commenced to fire upon my men, which caused them to break and run in great confusion, and it was not until very late in the day that I could rally them together in any great force. I would here state that in our retirement we captured and took in with us 7 prisoners—one a Lieutenant. In this part of the engagement our loss was very considerable, including several officers. [*OR* 11, pt. 2, p. 420.]

The Fourth Pennsylvania was deployed just to the right of the road where you are and was in a position to support Lieutenant Randol's battery.

Report of Col. Albert L. Magilton, USA, Commanding, Fourth Pennsylvania Reserves, Second Brigade, Third Division, Fifth Corps, Army of the Potomac

June 30 we were in position as given to the Second Brigade by General Meade. The Fourth Regiment Pennsylvania Reserve Volunteer Corps was to the left and slightly to the front of Randol's battery. Here we laid concealed in the grass until the enemy came within 60 feet of my regiment, when I ordered my men to rise and fire, when the enemy broke to the rear. We kept up the firing, but the enemy being re-enforced, we were obliged to retire; but shortly we faced to the front and drove them again, but being hotly pressed and losing many of my men, we were obliged to retire. A third attempt was made to rally, which was very weak, and finally my regiment broke and scattered in the woods. The next morning I collected about 200 men. [*OR* 11, pt. 2, p. 421.]

To the right of the Fourth Pennsylvania, Lieutenant Randol's battery was placing punishing fire upon the Confederate attack. Around this battery, attack and counterattack swirled in the late afternoon hours.

Report of Lieut. Alanson M. Randol, USA, Commanding Battery E, First U.S. Artillery, Second Artillery Brigade, Artillery Reserve, Army of the Potomac

About 2 p.m. our advance pickets on the [Long Bridge] road were driven in and measures immediately taken for forming our line of battle. I was ordered by Brigadier-General Meade to place my battery on a field on the right of the [Long Bridge] road and on the left of Captain Thompson's Battery G, of the Second Artillery. Not having room for the whole battery, I placed four pieces in position, leaving the left section, Lieutenant Olcott, movable. Soon after General Kearny appeared on the field and changed the front of Captain Thompson's battery to right angles with mine. I then placed one piece of Lieutenant Olcott's section in position in the road on my left [where you are], near the woods, to command it.

Shortly after the enemy appeared in some force on our left and drove a regiment of our skirmishers. Immediately after the enemy opened fire on the batteries on my left, which was at once replied to, and a fierce cannonading ensued, which lasted about thirty minutes. As the enemy was beyond the range of my guns and their movements hidden by the woods I did not open on them, lest I should unnecessarily expose the battery to a fire which we could not return with any effect. After the firing of the enemy had ceased, and while they were supposed to be forming for a charge, at the suggestion of General Meade I fired four rounds of spherical case into the woods in front of me, but receiving no reply, a regiment of Pennsylvania Reserves was sent into the woods on my left to ascertain their position. They met them, fired one volley, broke and ran, closely pursued by the enemy. As soon as our flying troops had unmasked Lieutenant Olcott's gun he opened on the enemy with canister, making a terrible slaughter in their ranks. After this first attack of the enemy on the batteries on my left having been repulsed, I ordered Lieutenant Olcott to limber up and come in battery with his section on my right. Soon the enemy made a second attack on the batteries on my left, [Lieutenant Amsden's Battery G, First Pennsylvania Artillery] when I changed front forward on my left piece, so as to take them in flank. Again they were forced to retire, but not until they had driven the cannoneers away from all of the batteries on the left and killed many of their horses. They next appeared on my present right flank, my former front, when I immediately changed front to the rear on my left piece. [Randol's battery was now back in its first position.] Captain Thompson also changed front to a line parallel to mine, his pieces being in line with my caissons. The rebels approached under cover to within 300 yards, when I opened on them with canister. They came boldly on, notwithstanding the frightful havoc made among them, to within 100 yards of the battery, when they broke and ran, but were rallied behind a second regiment, advancing to the attack, who approached to about 50 yards, but they too were driven back in confusion with great slaughter. My infantry supports, who during the attack were lying down between the lines of my limbers and caissons firing at the enemy, arising for a charge on the disordered mass, I ceased firing.

Early in the engagement I had cautioned both officers and men of my supports [Fourth Pennsylvania] that if they charged in front of the battery and were obliged to fall back, they should at once unmask my fire by returning by the flanks of the battery. They rushed boldly to the charge, confident of an easy victory, but being met by a fresh regiment, the third of the column of attack, they fired once, were seized by unaccountable panic and fled, threw away their arms, and rushed directly for the battery. I in vain endeavored to make them unmask my fire. On they came, the foe close behind them, till when within 30 yards I gave the command to fire; but it was too late. They rushed through the battery, followed by nearly 50 of the enemy. When our troops broke I ordered the pieces to be limbered to the rear, but 38 of my horses lay dead on the field and many were badly wounded. Captain Thompson's battery had opened fire also, and being on the same line with our caissons it was impossible to-move up the limbers of the caissons, so I ordered them to leave the field.

When the enemy entered the battery they drove the cannoneers, who had up to this time kept up the fire, from their posts at the point of the bayonet, and took Lieutenant [Edward B.] Hill, who was badly wounded, a prisoner. It was impossible to stop all our frightened, flying supports, but I rallied a few companies, and with them charged the battery and retook it, one of their officers recapturing Lieutenant Hill: but we could not hold our advantage. The enemy were within 50 yards, charging again, and I was obliged to leave the field. [OR 11, pt. 2, pp. 255–56.]

Confederate attack on Randol's Battery E, First U.S. Artillery. *Century Magazine.*

The collapse of much of McCall's defensive line opened the way for Confederate forces to cut the road to the James River. However, counterattacks by Brigadier General John Sedgwick's division, which had been placed in a reserve position east of the Willis Church Road, and regiments from other divisions were instrumental in holding the Union position. The actions of Sedgwick's division will be covered at Stop 24.

The Confederates attacking the Union line at this location were *Wilcox*'s Brigade. *Wilcox* deployed his brigade on both sides of the Long Bridge Road and made multiple attacks.

Report of Brig. Gen. *Cadmus M. Wilcox,* CSA, Commanding *Wilcox*'s Brigade, *Longstreet*'s Division, Army of Northern Virginia

It was now near 5 p.m., and the enemy's artillery began to fire. Shot and shell passed over and fell beyond us, some exploding near us. One of our batteries was placed in position on the road in front, and, replying to the fire of the enemy, continued for nearly an hour, but as a heavy forest intervened little effect was produced on either side.

The order was now given to forward, and the brigade was marched in line across the field to the woods. Finding this so thick with undergrowth that a forward movement in line of battle was impracticable, the order was given for the regiments to move by the right of companies to the front. Marching in this manner they made their way slowly for 100 or 200 yards until the woods became more open. At this place I met General *Anderson,* and was ordered by him to press on directly to the front. I was aware that the enemy was in my front, but as to the distance, his strength, the position of his batteries and their supports I knew nothing. I had no knowledge as to the character or topography of the ground over which I had to march in the execution of my orders. Marching directly to the front as ordered, and being guided alone by the artillery fire of the enemy, the shot and shell from which passed over and often very near, without, however, causing any casualties, I had not advanced more than 200 yards when I found that two of my regiments were on the right and two on the left of the road (Long Bridge road) which ran in the direction of my line of march. The woods on either side were so thick as to prevent my seeing well the extreme right and left regiments. The road, now descending slightly for some distance, at length crossed a small stream, in the bed of which rails had been thrown to fill it up, so as to allow wagons and artillery to pass. This stream on the right of the road was boggy, and with a dense growth of trees in it, rendering it difficult for the regiments on this side to make their way through it. We were now under a close fire of artillery, the grape shot coming thick and fast through the trees.

Having crossed the little stream above referred to, on the left the woods were less dense, being small and scattered pine, and ascending slightly for some distance, we came to a field on the left of the road, and the enemy's infantry, in the woods on the left of this field, opened a brisk and close fire upon the left regiment of my line. This regiment, the Eighth Alabama, halted and engaged the enemy at this point. In this field, about 300 yards to the front and 100 yards to the left of the road, was a house, and beyond the house about 200 yards more was a six-gun battery of the enemy. This battery had an open field of fire, the ground in front being perfectly level.

The Eighth Alabama being engaged with the enemy, the Eleventh Alabama, the next regiment to it, continued to advance, and entering upon the open field, came within full view of the six-gun battery on this side, the left, of the road. [This was Lieutenant Randol's Battery E, First U.S. Artillery.] This battery began at once a rapid discharge of grape and canister upon this regiment. It did not halt an instant, but continued to advance steadily and rapidly and without firing until it approached within 200 yards of the battery, when it gave loud cheers and made a rush for the guns. Halting for an instant in front of it, they fire upon the battery and infantry immediately in rear of it and then make a successful charge upon and take the battery. The enemy's infantry are in the woods in heavy force beyond and 200 yards distant and in the woods skirting the field to the left of the battery and not so far, and here in like manner in strong force. The enemy having a direct and flank fire upon this regiment, now at the battery.

The two regiments on the right of the road continued steadily to advance through the woods which extended along the road-side to within 100 yards of a second six-gun battery, this battery being nearly opposite to the one on the left of the road and some 200 yards distant from it. [This was Captain Cooper's Battery B, First Pennsylvania Artillery. By this time, Lieutenant Amsden's Battery G, First Pennsylvania Artillery, which had been between Cooper's and Randol's batteries, had been withdrawn because of a lack of ammunition.] Halting for a few minutes in the woods fronting this battery to deliver their fire, these regiments—the Ninth and Tenth Alabama—charge upon and take this also, the enemy's infantry supports being driven back.

Both these batteries were now in our possession, having been carried in the most gallant manner, the men and officers behaving with the most determined courage and irresistible impetuosity. The taking of the battery on the right of the road was not attended by such a bloody strife as followed the assault and capture of the one on the left, for here the enemy had not the heavy pine forests so close in rear and on one flank in which he could retire, reform, and then renew the conflict with increased numbers. The battery on the left of the road was the first taken. The Eleventh Alabama had experienced severe loss in crossing the open field while advancing against this battery. Here the enemy, at first repulsed and driven from the battery, retire to the woods both on our left and in rear of the battery, and from there, under shelter of the woods and with superior numbers, deliver a terrible and destructive fire upon this regiment. With its ranks sadly thinned it heroically stands its ground and returns the enemy's fire with telling effect. The latter, under cover of trees on our left flank and directly in our front, confident and bold from their superior strength, and seeing this regiment isolated and unsupported, now advance from their cover against it. Our men do not flee from their prize so bravely and dearly won overwhelmed by superior numbers, but, with a determination and courage unsurpassed, they stubbornly hold their ground, men and officers alike engaging in the most desperate personal conflicts with the enemy. The sword and bayonet are freely used. Having assaulted and carried this battery and driven the infantry into the woods to the left and beyond they hold it until the enemy reform and return in superior force, and now they resist in a hand to hand conflict with the utmost pertinacity. There are no supports for them—no re-enforcements come, and they are at length forced to yield and retire to the pine woods on the right of the road and in rear some 150 or 200 yards, the enemy not pursuing, having left dead upon this field, in the battery and its vicinity, in front and rear beyond it.

The Eleventh Alabama retired, as above stated, to the right of the road into the pine woods, and there, together with the Ninth and Tenth Alabama, remained. From this position the battery on the right of the road was in full view and not more than 100 yards distant. The enemy made no effort to retake this battery, though their infantry continued to fire at long range upon our men then in the pine woods.

The Eighth Alabama, as explained previously, became engaged with the enemy's infantry before reaching the batteries, and contending against superior forces maintained its ground until regiments from General *Pryor*'s brigade, and afterward *Featherston*'s, arrived on this part of the field. The severity of the fight at this point of the field is evident from the loss sustained by this regiment.

Of my four regimental commanders all were wounded. It gives me pleasure to bring to your particular notice the conduct of them all as deserving high praise. Lieutenant-Colonel *Royston*, commanding Eighth Alabama, received a severe wound from a fragment of a shell. Major [*John*] *Caldwell*, commanding the Tenth Alabama, was also wounded by a piece of shell striking him over the eye. Captain [*J. H.*] *King*, commanding the Ninth Alabama, is deserving of especial praise for his coolness and bravery, and he also received a severe wound in the leg.

A list of the killed and wounded in this battle has been forwarded before this. It will suffice in this report that I should state that the total loss in killed, wounded, and missing was 471, of which 16 are missing and since ascertained to have been taken prisoners—a loss proportionately greater than in the engagement [at Gaines Mill] of the 27th ultimo. [*OR* 11, pt. 2, pp. 775–79.]

As *Wilcox*'s Brigade fell back Brigadier General *Charles W. Field*'s brigade replaced it and continued the attack.

Report of Brig. Gen. *Charles W. Field*, CSA, Commanding *Field*'s Brigade, *A. P. Hill*'s Division, Army of Northern Virginia

Forming in line of battle, the Fifty-fifth and Sixtieth Virginia on the right of the road and the Forty-seventh Virginia and the Second Virginia Battalion on the left, the command was given to cheer heartily and charge. About 300 yards directly in our front were two of the enemy's batteries, posted in an open field and on the right and left of the road we were advancing on. I had heard that these batteries had been several times during the day taken and retaken, a constant struggle being maintained for their possession. At this time they were held by the enemy, but the horses being killed or wounded, he was unable to remove the guns. The whole line now rushed forward under heavy fire, beat the enemy back from the guns into the woods beyond, and pushing him on the right of the road back half a mile. The two regiments on this side [of] the road, the Fifty-fifth and Sixtieth Virginia, were at this time in the enemy's rear, having penetrated through his center in the eagerness of pursuit, but were withdrawn before he could profit by the circumstance.

Lieutenant-Colonel [*William S.*] *Christian* was wounded and Major [*Thomas M.*] *Burke* was killed, both of the Fifty-fifth Virginia.

The charge was impetuously made, and was an instance where bayonets were really crossed, several of the enemy being killed with that weapon and several of the Sixtieth now being in [the] hospital bearing bayonet wounds upon their persons. It is proper to state that the Fortieth Virginia, Colonel [*J. M.*] *Brockenbrough*, forming my extreme left, became detached on account of the inequalities of the ground and was not under my eye. The colonel reports, however, meeting with an overwhelming force and his loss heavy. My brigade held that part of the battle-field until relieved late at night by some fresh troops, I having in the mean while sent to the rear for horses and removed all the captured guns and equipments to a place of safety.

I omitted to mention that the Forty-seventh Virginia, Colonel [*Robert M.*] *Mayo*, after getting possession of the guns on the left of the road, manned two of them and used them against the enemy. This regiment also captured [Brigadier] General McCall, commanding the Federal forces on the field. [*OR* 11, pt. 2, pp. 842–43.]

As soon as *Field*'s Brigade was committed to the attack, Brigadier General *William D. Pender*'s brigade was ordered forward to support *Field*'s right flank.

Report of Brig. Gen *William D. Pender,* CSA, Commanding *Pender*'s Brigade, *A. P. Hill*'s Division, Army of Northern Virginia

Meeting the enemy again on Monday evening, my brigade, after being in direct range of the enemy's shell for some time, was ordered forward, and went in rear of [*Wilcox*'s] brigade—at least his men were coming out from my front as we went in. Reaching the farther side of the field, on the right, at the junction of the Long Bridge and Darbytown roads, we came in contact with the enemy once more. Here, just as my brigade was getting under fire, a regiment of the enemy bore down at double-quick in our front, passing from right to left, apparently not seeing us. When in our front, about 75 yards off, our men fired a volley into them and scattered them in every direction. In our front was a fine battery of rifle pieces [Cooper's battery] that had been abandoned, but they were apparently trying to regain it, as we had quite a skirmish near it. They continued to make efforts here to flank us. They had quite a force upon my right, which was several times pushed forward.

General *Field*, I have since learned, was a long way in front, but the enemy were in considerable force between us, if I am to judge from the stand they made. At this position I left a few men to hold the flank and pushed forward the rest well into the woods, and but for the untimely failure of ammunition would have captured many prisoners. They were in considerable disorder, but were still too strong to be attacked with what few men I had, most of whom were without ammunition. We here soon forced a battery, [Captain Knieriem's Battery C, First New York Artillery] which had opened upon our right, to limber up and leave. They evidently, from what I saw and from what I heard from prisoners, had a strong force within a few hundred yards of these batteries.

Dark coming on, I withdrew my men to the edge of the woods, holding our ground and the batteries taken. I had but a handful of men, but succeeded in getting two other regiments I found near, of General *Field*'s brigade, which he had withdrawn, posting them so as to hold the front, while I held the right flank. I subsequently led forward one of these regiments, and ordered it to move in such a direction as to flank a force which seemed to be hotly engaging a part of our troops on the left of the road.

After making these arrangements I found that General *Archer* was on the right flank and on my right. [*OR* 11, pt. 2, p. 901.]

Return to your car for the drive to Stop 22. Continue driving east for 0.3 mile to the intersection with Chares City Road and Willis Church Road. Turn left at the intersection and drive northwest on Charles City Road for 0.3 mile. Pull off to the side of the road in the vicinity of a low stone marker (about three feet high) on the left side of the road. This is just before Parker Creek Road. Stand next to the marker and face southwest, with Charles City Road behind you. Respect private property and be careful of traffic.

Stop 22—Kearny's Defensive Position

If you had continued to drive northwest on Charles City Road, you would have crossed the western edge of White Oak Swamp. Charles City Road was the route *Huger*'s Division was to follow as he marched toward Glendale. *Huger* was to attack in a southeasterly direction along this road to assist in stopping the Union retreat.

The Union division of Brigadier General Henry W. Slocum was positioned one-half mile to your right. This division faced to the northwest, with its left flank units across the Charles City Road. In this position it was a block to the advance of *Huger*'s Division. When *Huger* made contact with Slocum's division he halted his movement and never developed a strong attack against Slocum's position or the right of Kearny's division.

The Union division positioned where you are was a three-brigade division command by Brigadier General Philip Kearny. Kearny deployed two brigades on the west side of the road, facing southwest. Brigadier General John C. Robinson's First Brigade was on the left, and Brigadier General David B. Birney's Second Brigade was on the right. Birney's brigade loosely tied in with the left of Slocum's division. Kearny positioned Brigadier General Hiram G. Berry's Third Brigade as a reserve behind you across Charles City Road. You are located behind the left of Kearny's defensive line, which was defended by Robinson's brigade.

Report of Brig. Gen. Philip Kearny, USA, Commanding Third Division, Third Corps, Army of the Potomac

In taking up my line of battle, General Robinson, with the First Brigade, was posted on the left supporting Thompson's battery [Battery G, Second U.S. Artillery]. General Birney divided the distance with him to the Charles City road. General Berry was in reserve. General Slocum was to the right of my line of battle, General McCall to its left. The enemy's attack commenced on General McCall at about 2 p.m. At about 3 p.m. it seemed to be fully developed.

At 4 p.m. the attack commenced on my line with a determination and vigor and in such masses as I had never witnessed. Thompson's battery, directed with great skill, literally swept the slightly-falling open space with the completest execution, and mowing them down by ranks would cause the survivors to momentarily halt; but almost instantly after increased masses came up and the wave bore on. These masses coming up with a rapid run, covering the entire breadth of the open ground some 200 paces, would alone be checked in their career by the gaps of the fallen. Still no retreat, and again a fresh mass would carry on the approaching line still nearer. Their loss by artillery, although borne with such fortitude, must have been unusual. It was by scores. With the irrepressibility of numbers on they persisted. The artillery, destructive as it was, ceased to be a calculation. It was then that Colonel [Alexander] Hays, with the Sixty-third Pennsylvania and half the Thirty-seventh New York Volunteers, was moved forward to the line of the guns.

I have here to call to the attention of my superior chiefs this most heroic action on the part of Colonel Hays and his regiment. That which grape and canister failed in effecting was now accomplished by the determined charge and rapid volleys of this foot. The enemy at the muzzles of our guns for the first time sulkily retired, fighting. Subsequently, ground having been gained, the Sixty-third Pennsylvania was ordered to "Lie low," and the battery once more reopened its ceaseless work of destruction.

This battle saw renewed three onsets as above with similar vicissitudes, when finally the enemy betokened his efforts as past by converting his charges into an ordinary line fight of musketry, embracing the whole front of the brigade; for by this period he was enabled to do so from Thompson's pieces having left the field after expending their grape and becoming tired of the futility of round shot.

It may have been then about 7.30 p.m.; full daylight remained, and anticipating that the enemy, foiled in the attempt to carry the [Long Bridge] road and adjacent open ground, would next hazard an attack toward the Charles City road or intermediate woods, my attention was called there. I therefore left everything progressing steadily in the left and visited the entire line to the right. The cheerful manner and solid look of Birney's brigade gave assurance of their readiness to be measured with the foe, and they met my warning of the coming storm with loud cheers of exultation. Half an hour or forty minutes may have been thus passed. I then returned to the extreme left of my line. Arriving there, I found that Colonel Hays had been relieved by Colonel [Francis C.] Barlow, of the Sixty-first New York Volunteers, General Caldwell's brigade [of Richardson's division], sent to me from Sumner's corps, and which had reported to General Robinson.

The Sixty-first New York Volunteers, under its most intrepid leader. Colonel Barlow, had vied with the brave regiment he had relieved, and charging the enemy bore off as a trophy one of his colors. It had subsequently taken up its position to the left of the One hundred and fifth Pennsylvania and itself been subsequently retired, but none appointed to take its place, that breastwork being unoccupied. It was at this conjuncture that I arrived from my right. I found McCall's position abandoned, although not occupied by the enemy. I placed in it the First New Jersey Brigade, General [George W.] Taylor [of Slocum's division]. I then knew it to be in true hands. I observed that whilst the enemy were amusing my entire front with an ordinary musketry fire strong parties of rebel skirmishers in the gloom of the evening, rendered denser by the murky fogs of the smoke, were feeling their way slowly and distrustfully to the unoccupied parapet. Galloping back to find the nearest troops I met General Caldwell, who, under General McCall's supervision, was putting two or more of his regiments into line to the right of the road, a quarter of a mile in rear of the breastworks, to move up in order. Circumstances denied this delay. Accordingly I directed General Caldwell to lead a wing of a regiment at double-quick up the road to open on these rebel skirmishers. This was done promptly, but from their being foreigners not with a full comprehension, and darkness embarrassing them, they fired at the rebels, but in the direction of others of my line; and thus whilst the enemy were swept off the arena it left for some little time our troops firing at each other. To increase this confusion the residue of the brigade who had not filed into the woods and formed on the road opened on us all who were in the front. It is my impression that General McCall must have been killed by this fire. [McCall was actually captured by the Forty-seventh Virginia of Field's brigade.]

The errors of cross-firing having at last subsided my Fifth Michigan gallantly crossed the parapets and pursued the retiring enemy. The Eighty-first Pennsylvania, then nobly responding to my orders, gallantly led by Lieutenant-Colonel [Eli T.] Conner and Captain [Nelson A.] Miles, of General Caldwell's staff, dashed over the parapet, pursued, charged, and with a few vigorous volleys finished the battle at 9.30 at night. I remained much longer on the field, and then reported in person to General Heintzelman at his quarters. [This was under a tree at the junction of the Long Bridge and Charles City roads.] [*OR* 11, pt. 2, pp. 162–64.]

Brigadier General John C. Robinson's brigade was deployed directly in front of where you are. This brigade was the left of Kearny's defensive line. Robinson had four of his five regiments available for defense of this area. He placed three regiments on the battle line and held one in reserve. The battle line consisted from right to left of the Twentieth Indiana, Fifty-seventh Pennsylvania, and the Sixty-third Pennsylvania. The One hundred and fifth Pennsylvania was held in reserve. Two companies of the Twentieth Indiana were deployed in front of the position as skirmishers.

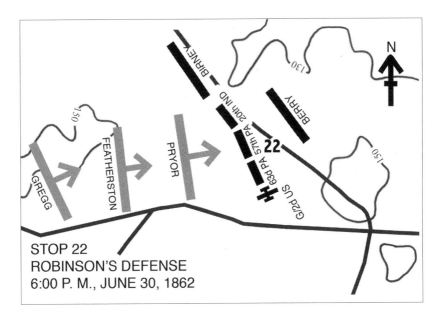

STOP 22
ROBINSON'S DEFENSE
6:00 P. M., JUNE 30, 1862

Report of Brig. Gen. John C. Robinson, USA, Commanding First Brigade, Third Division, Third Corps, Army of the Potomac

On the morning of the 30th ultimo my brigade left the edge of White Oak Swamp and took the position assigned it on the right of the [Long Bridge Road], McCall's division being on the left. About 2:30 o'clock p.m. the enemy commenced a furious attack upon McCall's position. While he was there engaged I employed a portion of my brigade in constructing a slight barricade of rails on the right of my line. Before this was completed the enemy relinquished his attack on McCall, and at 4 o'clock turned his whole force against my front. I had two companies of the Twentieth Indiana deployed as skirmishers in the woods in front of the clearing, who held their position as long as possible and fought their way back to the brigade. The remainder of the Indiana regiment was in line behind the barricade. In the center was the Fifty-seventh Pennsylvania, and on the left the Sixty-third Pennsylvania, while the One hundred and fifth Pennsylvania was formed in column and held in reserve. Against this line the enemy brought his whole force, constantly sending in fresh regiments to relieve those already engaged.

For five hours my brigade sustained these assaults under a terrific fire, and frequently repulsed the enemy and drove him to seek shelter in the woods. I was supported during the afternoon and evening by regiments from Birney's,

Berry's, and Caldwell's brigades, but many of the regimental commanders having failed to report to me, I leave it for those brigade commanders to report their operations. The enemy was twice driven back by our troops charging upon him.

The Sixty-third Pennsylvania, in addition to guarding the left of our line, was charged with protecting Thompson's battery, which duty was most gallantly performed. The regiment, although few in numbers, made a brilliant charge upon the enemy, contended with him hand to hand, and drove him from the field. [*OR* 11, pt. 2, p. 175.]

> The use of the time before the attack to strengthen the position by building a breastwork made for a strong defensive position. Colonel William L. Brown, defending the right of Robinson's line in his report, credits it with saving many of his soldiers' lives.

Report of Col. William L. Brown, USA, Commanding Twentieth Indiana Infantry, First Brigade, Third Division, Third Corps, Army of the Potomac

In the action this afternoon the left wing of my regiment was engaged from 5 to the close of the battle, about 9 o'clock, suffering a loss of 1 captain and 1 lieutenant killed, 28 enlisted men wounded, and 22 missing; in all a loss of 52. During the few hours in which we were in position before the commencement of the engagement the command constructed a breastwork—precious hours well employed, saving many valuable lives. Behind this work but 1, the lamented Lieutenant [John W.] Andrew, fell, pierced in the head by a ball, and 1 man wounded, nigh all our loss occurring from the pickets in retiring becoming engaged with the masses of the rebels on their left. Here Capt. Alfred Reed, Company K, fell, with his son, quartermaster sergeant, fighting with more than heroic bravery. In the death of Lieutenant Andrew and Captain Reed we mourn the loss of two most excellent and valuable officers.

The regiment behaved with the greatest coolness, the wing engaged jesting, cracking jokes, loading and firing deliberately as if at a target. The enemy's force assailing, vastly our superiors in numbers, suffered terribly from our rifles. Time and again their officers were seen and heard rallying and endeavoring to bring them to a charge, but of no avail. When the contest ceased the moans of their wounded, the large number of searchers with torches, continued through the night, tell unmistakably a fearful loss to the rebels; and, saving our line to my left being flanked, the number of wounded and missing will probably be reduced by returns to our ranks of some who were on picket, and who, being suddenly assailed, were unable at the time to rejoin us. . . . [*OR* 11, pt. 2, pp. 176–77.]

In the center, Lieutenant Colonel Elhanon W. Woods, commanding the Fifth-seventh Pennsylvania reported that his 14 officers and 174 soldiers fought for five hours from behind a fence and fired from 80 to 130 rounds of ammunition per man. [*OR* 11, pt. 2, pp. 177.]

Captain James Thompson's Battery G, Second U.S. Artillery, was deployed just forward and to the left of where you are. This battery provided an anchor for the left portion of Robinson's defensive line. It was located with the Sixty-third Pennsylvania Infantry.

Report of Capt. James Thompson, USA, Commanding, Battery G, Second U.S. Artillery, Third Division, Third Corps, Army of the Potomac

The enemy appeared by the [Long Bridge] road, and as soon as they began to show themselves in front the battery opened on them with spherical case-shot just in the edge of the woods about 400 yards. They advanced in line, stooping down and firing, and we continued firing spherical case-shot until they reached the torn-down fence, brush, &c., about 150 yards in front, where they appeared to falter. They soon, however, rallied for a charge, and canister was poured upon them, and as they advanced double canister was used and served without sponging, which with the terrible infantry volley poured into them by Colonel Hays' Sixty-third Pennsylvania Volunteers, gallantly supporting the battery, drove them back. They retired to about 150 yards at the fence, when spherical case was again used with half-second fuses. Three successive charges were made by overwhelmingly large forces, but they were each time hurled back with terrible slaughter. The battle continued in this manner when, at about 7.30 o'clock p.m., the canister and spherical case-shot having become exhausted, and after firing round shot, it became apparent that the battery was being risked without doing the enemy injury, and it was therefore retired. [*OR* 11, pt. 2, p. 171.]

The report of Colonel Alexander Hays gives a vivid account of the fighting as Confederate attacks came forward in this area.

Report of Col. Alexander Hays, USA, Commanding Sixty-third Pennsylvania Infantry, First Brigade, Third Division, Third Corps, Army of the Potomac

Early in the day the regiment, of 300 men, was detailed to protect the battery commanded by Captain Thompson, Second U.S. Artillery.

About 3 o'clock p.m. the enemy opened fire upon one advanced section, in command of Lieutenant Butler, which was soon withdrawn, and with the regiment retired to the rear to join the battery. The battery was placed in position to sweep an extended field, over which it was necessary that the enemy should advance to the attack.

In about an hour's time the enemy opened upon us with shot, shell, and other missiles, to which Captain Thompson replied most gallantly. For the space of an hour the firing was unremitting. In the obscurity of the smoke it was communicated to me that the battery was endangered. I at once gave the order to charge, which was responded to by my men leaping the fence and moving forward at double-quick in better order than at an ordinary drill. The alarm was false, and I withdrew to my original position.

Very soon afterward General Kearny, as also Captain Thompson, announced danger to the battery. Again the order was given to charge, and again the regiment moved forward, passing the battery, and were halted 50 feet in front, the enemy retiring to the woods and houses beyond. The order was given to lie down and open spaces for the artillery. Within good range of our "Austrians" and the continued fire of the artillery we hurled into the enemy a perfect storm of shot. The enemy, however, replied vigorously and presented an obstinate resistance. The contest was thus carried on for an hour, when Captain Thompson announced to me that his ammunition was exhausted and the necessity of withdrawing his battery. To cover his withdrawal, as the enemy had been made emboldened by heavy reenforcements, I ordered again a charge. At once the men sprang to their feet, and with leveled bayonets dashed upon the enemy. The conflict was short, but most desperate, especially around the buildings. It was muzzle to muzzle, and the powder actually burned the faces of the opposing men as they contended through the paling fences. The enemy fled, and I withdrew my force back to the position occupied by the battery—one piece of which still remained upon the field. I was here informed that another force was relieving us, and retired to our original position at the fence. Night was coming on. We had been under fire for five hours, in action half the time, and our loss very heavy.

We are indebted to a detachment from the Thirty-seventh New York Volunteers for assistance during our last charge, and I would be pleased if I could name the officers in command. [The regimental commander was Colonel Samuel B. Hayman.]

The following list of killed and wounded speaks for those enumerated: Killed—enlisted men, 10; wounded, 85; missing, 23. Killed—commissioned officers, 1; wounded, 6. Aggregate—killed, wounded, and missing, 125. [*OR* 11, pt. 2, pp. 177–78.]

> During the fighting at this location several regiments from other brigades were committed to reinforce the defenses. The actions of the Sixty-first New York Infantry were typical of this reinforcement.

Report of Col. Francis C. Barlow, USA, Commanding Sixty-first New York Infantry, First Brigade, First Division, Second Corps, Army of the Potomac

On the morning of June 30, 1862, the regiment under my command was placed in line with Meagher's brigade at White Oak Swamp as a support to [Capt. George W.] Hazzard's and [Capt. Rufus D.] Pettit's batteries, which were hotly engaged with the enemy. We remained in this position nearly all day, exposed at times to a severe artillery fire, which killed 2 and wounded several of the men. During the afternoon a heavy musketry fire commenced on our left, at some distance from us, and about 6 p.m. this regiment, together with the others of this brigade, was moved in the direction of the firing. After a march of some 1½ miles we arrived at the scene of the engagement, and my regiment became separated from the remainder of the brigade in the confusion arising from some of our troops firing upon each other. I at once reported to the first general officer I could find (Brigadier-General Robinson, of Kearny's division) for orders. By his directions the regiment was formed in line on the border of an open field into which our men were firing from two sides. We were formed behind a fence which our men were occupying as a parapet and from which they were then firing.

After stopping the firing of these other regiments General Robinson directed this regiment to go over the parapet into the open field, which was done with bayonets at a charge. We advanced quickly, and without firing, into the field. It was quite dark and the atmosphere was thick with smoke, for which reason I am unable to state what was the position or number of the enemy in the open field. They broke and fell back at our approach, and a flag with the inscriptions "Williamsburg" and "Seven Pines" was abandoned by them. I took possession of this, and have forwarded it to brigade headquarters. Upon approaching the woods at the opposite side of the field the enemy shouted from the woods, "What regiment is that?" Upon being answered by the men that it was the Sixty-first New York, the enemy shouted, "Throw down your arms, or you are all dead men." We at once opened fire, which was vigorously continued on both sides. I requested Lieutenant [Jabez B.] Greenhalgh, of the staff of Brigadier-General Berry, who came into position with us, to procure us re-enforcements, as we were the only regiment in the field or in sight. He returned, and informed me that he could bring none.

After we had continued firing for some time Captain Miles, of the staff of General Caldwell, brought in to our assistance the Eighty-first Regiment Pennsylvania Volunteers, Colonel [Charles F.] Johnson, of this brigade. This regiment took position in our front, and opened and sustained a vigorous and determined fire. I directed my men to lie down and rest for a time. They came again into line and recommenced fire before we left the position. I am unable to state how long we remained in this position. Both regiments exhausted nearly all their ammunition, and we once changed position to avoid a threatened attack on our left flank. [OR 11, pt. 2, pp. 66–67.]

Brigadier General Kearny had placed Berry's brigade in a reserve position. As the battle progressed, regiments of Berry's brigade were called forward to reinforce the defensive position.

Report of Brig. Gen. Hiram G. Berry, USA, Commanding Third Brigade, Third Division, Third Corps, Army of the Potomac

We took up a position to the rear and reserve to the two brigades. At 4 p.m. I received orders to place my brigade on the right of the central road, in the skirt of the woods, directly in the front of division headquarters.

At 5 p.m. the action in front of Robinson's brigade and Thompson's battery opened severely. It was evident that the troops on the left of the road (McCall's division) were giving way. At this time I placed the First New York, Colonel [Garrett] Dyckman, in support of Thompson's battery. General Robinson called on me for a regiment to sustain his line, and I sent him the Second Michigan, Major [Louis] Dillman. Captain [W. G.] Sturges, acting assistant adjutant-general, took the Third Michigan Volunteers, Major Pierce, to support General Birney [on the right of the division line]. Thompson's battery was severely assailed, and by the use that gallant officer made of canister, and the support rendered by General Robinson's brigade, together with that rendered by the First New York and afterward by the Thirty-seventh New York and Fifth Michigan, Major [John D.] Fairbanks, of my own, prevented them from advancing their lines toward us. This regiment operated in front of General McCall's line and the road. The enemy were pressing in that direction very hard, and I thought it my duty to check them to save our left flank.

At 7.30 p.m. it was evident that the enemy was preparing a column to make a strong effort to pierce our lines. I made known the fact to General Burns [commanding the Second Brigade of Sedgwick's division], who was forming a second line to McCall's. That officer gave me the Twenty-fourth Regiment New York Volunteers. I marched up to the road and placed the Fifth Michigan, of less than 200 men, and they, the remaining one, on its right; filed by the right across our front and in rear of Thompson's battery, and ordered to charge the enemy, who had appeared in a strong column. Lieutenant Greenhalgh, one of my aides, gallantly led the regiment, drove back the enemy, and captured a stand of colors. Other re-enforcements arrived, and we held our line without falling back an inch. [*OR* 11, pt. 2, p. 186.]

The Confederate forces attacking this part of the Union line were brigades from *A. P. Hill*'s and *Longstreet*'s Divisions. These two divisions had marched around the western end of White Oak Swamp then turned east and approached Glendale from the southwest. As they marched along the Long Bridge Road they deployed for attack against the Union forces around and south of the crossroads. The first to deploy was *Longstreet*'s Division. His left flank unit was the brigade of Brigadier General *Roger A. Pryor*. This brigade's attack was the first of three attacks against Robinson's position.

Report of Brig. Gen. *Roger A. Pryor,* CSA Commanding *Prior*'s Brigade, *Longstreet*'s Division, Army of Northern Virginia

About 4 o'clock I received an order from Major-General *Longstreet* to go into the fight. At once I moved in line toward the field, but the wood and other obstructions forced me to form column and to send my regiments in successively. Arriving on the field, I discovered that the brigade on my right had been repulsed and that my command was exposed to a destructive fire on the flank as well as in front. Nevertheless they stood their ground and sustained the unequal combat until re-enforced by the brigade of General [*Featherston*]. We did not return to our original position until the enemy had abandoned the field and surrendered his artillery into our possession.

In this engagement my loss was uncommonly heavy in officers as well as men. The Fourteenth Alabama, bearing the brunt of the struggle, was nearly annihilated. I crossed the Chickahominy on the 26th with 1,400 men. In the fights that followed I suffered a loss of 849 killed and wounded and 11 missing. [*OR* 11, pt. 2, p. 781.]

As the battle progressed, Brigadier General *Winfield S. Featherston*'s brigade reinforced *Pryor*.

Report of Brig. Gen. *Winfield S. Featherston*, CSA, Commanding *Featherston*'s Brigade, *Longstreet*'s Division, Army of Northern Virginia

My brigade was held in reserve at the beginning of the fight, but about 5 o'clock in the evening was ordered to attack the enemy on the left of General *Longstreet*'s division. As I passed up to the place designated I found the contest was becoming very hot on the left, and I thought the enemy advancing. On reaching General *Pryor*'s brigade, which was then on the extreme left of General *Longstreet*'s division, I was requested by General *Pryor* to bring my brigade to the support of his. I immediately saw the necessity of doing so, threw my men into line of battle, and marched them in. On looking to our extreme left I saw that an attempt would be made by the enemy to flank us, probably with a very heavy force, and immediately sent back one of my aides (Lieutenant [*W. G.*] *Sykes*) to General *Longstreet,* requesting him to hurry up the re-enforcements. General *Longstreet* had informed me on our march to the field of action that re-enforcements would be sent forward.

My brigade was advanced to the front lines to or near a fence at the edge of the field. Here they opened a steady fire on the enemy's lines, and the enemy pouring a well-directed fire into our ranks, and seemed not to be giving way, but inclined to advance. My first determination after giving them a few fires was to order a charge, but believing the force in front to be vastly superior to ours, and seeing that a flank movement was contemplated by the enemy, I declined to do so, for the reason that it might have resulted in having my small command surrounded and cut off before the re-enforcements sent for could come up to our support. At this time I received a painful wound in the shoulder and was compelled to retire from the field. When I left the field General *Gregg*'s brigade had reached it and was but a short distance in rear of mine, forming in line. [*OR* 11, pt. 2, pp. 785–86.]

The fence and the field *Featherston* mentions in his report are the same ones mentioned in Thompson's and Hay's reports.

The next Confederate brigade to be committed to action on this part of the field was the brigade commanded by Brigadier General *Maxcy Gregg. Gregg*'s Brigade was part of *A. P. Hill*'s Division and joined the battle as a general reinforcement of *Longstreet*'s attacks by *A. P. Hill*'s Division. Not all of *Gregg*'s five regiments joined in the fight. Three regiments were positioned so as to protect the left flank. The Thirteenth and Fourteenth South Carolina Infantry Regiments participated in the attack against the Union position where *Prior* and *Featherston* had conducted their attacks. *Gregg* was mortally wounded at Fredericksburg in December of 1862 and did not complete his report. Therefore, we have nothing from him about the actions of his brigade on June 30. However, the report of one of his regimental commander gives a good description of the attack of one of the regiments. The attack of this regiment went toward the position of the Twentieth Indiana of Robinson's brigade.

Report of Col. *Samuel McGowan*, CSA, Commanding Fourteenth South Carolina Infantry, *Gregg*'s Brigade, *A. P. Hill*'s Division, Army of Northern Virginia

We had marched all day until late in the evening, and soon after we arrived in the neighborhood of the fight it was represented to us that the enemy was turning the left of our lines. I was directed to form the Fourteenth, which was the leading regiment, in line of battle immediately, and send forward through the thick undergrowth, skirmishers, to feel the enemy and ascertain his position. I accordingly sent forward Captain [*A. P.*] *West,* who threw out his men as skirmishers and gallantly advanced some 300 yards toward our left and front. In a few moments he returned, stating that he had found General *Featherston* in the undergrowth wounded. As soon as Captain *West* made this report my regiment was ordered forward through a perfect jungle of vines and bushes. We took the direction indicated by the skirmishers, and as soon as we approached the open ground in which the enemy had hastily thrown up a breastwork we fell upon his skirmishers, who upon our approach scattered and fled in every direction. The regiment was halted at the edge of the cleared ground and volley after volley thrown into the ranks of the enemy, who returned upon us a very hot and fatal fire. In this musketry fight some of my men, having obtained patent cartridges, shot seventy times. At one time, just after dark, the belief seemed to take possession of the enemy, as it did of ourselves, that we were mutually fighting our friends, and the firing ceased for a time entirely. During the cessation of fire an officer came over to us and inquired who we were. I demanded to know to what regiment he belonged; to which he replied the Twentieth Indiana, which was in the woods to our left and front. Thereupon he was politely informed that he was in the midst of the Fourteenth Regiment South Carolina Volunteers, and at the same time ordered to the rear for safe-keeping. A few moments after this interview an officer of the enemy was distinctly heard to give the command, "Commence firing," and in a moment the whole ridge in our front was a sheet of flame. They poured into the regiment for a short time the most destructive fire. We, however, held our ground and returned the fire until the enemy fled. We remained on the ground until all the firing had ceased, and then joined the other regiments of the brigade. Once during the evening the enemy endeavored to turn our left flank, but Lieutenant-Colonel [*W. D.*] *Simpson* directed upon them the fire of the left companies, and with distinguished gallantry drove them back. If we could have had a regiment on our left we certainly would have captured the Twentieth Indiana Regiment. [*OR* 11, pt. 2, p. 870.]

Return to your car for the drive to Stop 23. Retrace your route on Charles City Road for 0.3 mile to the intersection with Darbytown Road. Go straight through the intersection, where the road now becomes Willis Church Road. Continue driving south for another 0.4 mile, to where the power lines cross the road, and pull over to the right and park. Get out of your car and face west, to your right as you were driving.

Stop 23—The Union Center

The Frayser farm was located behind you and across the road. Although the Nelsons owned the farm after the Frayser family, it continued to be known as the Frayser farm. The Battle of Frayser Farm is also another name for the Battle of Glendale. The power lines go west and are the same ones you stood under at Stop 20.

You are directly behind the defensive position of Brigadier General Truman Seymour's Third Brigade. This was the left brigade in McCall's defensive line. Seymour deployed all three of his regiments on the battle line. To your right front was the Ninth Pennsylvania and Captain James H. Cooper's, Battery B First Pennsylvania Artillery. Farther right was Lieutenant Frank P. Amsden's Battery G, First Pennsylvania Artillery. In front of you was the Tenth Pennsylvania, and to your left front was the Twelfth Pennsylvania and Captain

John Knieriem's Battery C, First New York Artillery, and Captain Otto Diederichs's Battery A, First New York Artillery. Behind you, deployed along the edge of the road in a reserve position was Colonel Seneca G. Simmons's First Brigade. Also in a reserve position was part of Brigadier General John Sedgwick's division.

As on the right of McCall's division, the regiments on the left of the line would be subjected to multiple Confederate attacks. Much of the fighting was centered on the artillery batteries.

The first attacks against this position were by *Anderson*'s and *Kemper*'s brigades of *Longstreet*'s Division.

Report of Col. C. Feger Jackson, USA, Commanding Ninth Pennsylvania Reserves, Third Brigade, Third Division, Fifth Corps, Army of the Potomac

I have the honor to report that before the attack of the enemy the Ninth Regiment was posted on the edge of the wood, the line extending northeast and southwest. In an open field on an elevated ridge, and parallel to the line

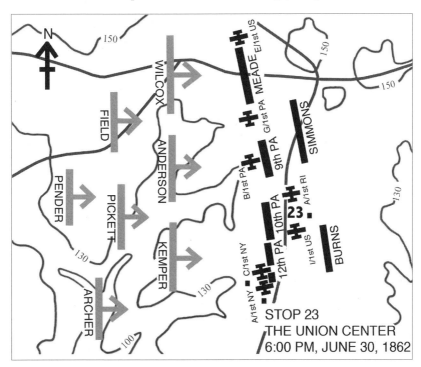

of my regiment, was posted Cooper's battery. After the attack, and when the battery had opened, I was ordered to advance to its support, and took my position a few yards in its rear, being covered by the ridge occupied by the battery. While in this position I was informed that the enemy was advancing on our left flank, and was directed to change front to oppose any force from that direction. Having occupied the position as directed some time and no enemy appearing, I was ordered to take my original position on the edge of the woods. While in the act of making this change Cooper's battery was captured, which fact was told me by the captain himself.

Finding that the men deeply sympathized with the captain in his loss, I at once determined to recapture the guns. A successful charge was made. The enemy was driven from the guns diagonally to the right and into the woods. I immediately commenced reforming my regiment on the road. At this time a heavy firing was opened upon us from the right. We advanced into the woods, where skirmishing commenced and continued until after dark. In this second charge I became separated from the regiment. We rallied near the hospital in rear of the battle-field. This was the most disastrous day of the three, having a number of my most efficient line officers killed or wounded. With the exception of a small percentage of skulkers, officers and men conducted themselves admirably. Casualties—17 killed, 84 wounded, 36 missing. [*OR* 11, pt. 2, p. 423.]

> The fighting centered on Cooper's battery, which the Ninth Pennsylvania was supporting. In this Confederate attack and the one that followed, Cooper's guns were overrun, recaptured, and then overrun a second time.

Report of Capt. James H. Cooper, USA, Commanding Battery B, First Pennsylvania Artillery, Third Division, Fifth Corps, Army of the Potomac

The battery having been ordered by General McCall to take position in line of battle at 2 o'clock p.m., where we remained until 4:30 p.m., when one of the enemy's batteries, concealed in the woods to our front, opened fire upon us, to which we replied with marked effect, [and] soon but one gun replied to us. During the engagement parties of infantry attempted to cross the field in our front, but with the assistance of Battery G, First Pennsylvania Artillery, we compelled them to retire in disorder and confusion. This continued about one and a half hours, when Battery G was compelled to retire for want of ammunition, and our infantry support, with the exception of three companies, retired. The enemy, availing themselves of this opportunity, advanced a regiment from a point of woods in our front, which our canister failed to check, although it did marked execution.

The remaining infantry falling back, we were compelled to retire from our guns. The charge being so sudden and over powering; it was impossible to remove them, many of the horses being killed by the enemy's fire. [*OR* 11, pt. 2, p. 410.]

> The fighting to your left front centered on Knieriem's battery and Diederichs's battery which were supported by the Twelfth Pennsylvania. Part of the Twelfth Pennsylvania had constructed a strong point in and around the Whitlock farm buildings. *Kemper's* Brigade conducted the initial attack against this position.

Report of Col. John H. Taggart, USA, Commanding Twelfth Pennsylvania Reserves, Third Brigade, Third Division, Fifth Corps, Army of the Potomac

On Monday afternoon, June 30, the regiment was formed in line of battle on the left of the Third Brigade, Pennsylvania Reserve Corps, awaiting the approach of the enemy and in support of a battery on our right. By direction of Brigadier-General Seymour the position of two of the guns in the battery was changed by moving them to a hill in the rear of my regiment, and six companies were detached and posted in two log huts and a breastwork of rails temporarily thrown up about 200 yards in advance to the left, commanding the approach of the enemy, while four companies were posted in rear of the two pieces of artillery. I had just succeeded in posting the companies in the log huts and breastwork when a heavy fire was opened upon us from the enemy's artillery and his forces advanced in heavy columns from the direction of the road in front. One column of the enemy attempted to surround the men in the breastwork and log huts by advancing in the rear toward a ravine. The officers and men maintained their position and fired three volleys at the advancing foe, which failed to check his progress. Seeing that they were about to be surrounded the men retired from the log huts, but not until after losing several of their number. Captain [Franklin] Dannells, of Company A, was wounded in the side at this time. The position was untenable from the concentrated fire of artillery which the enemy poured upon it. As a number of men in these works have been missing since the battle there is no doubt that they were here killed, wounded, or taken prisoners.

The enemy now advanced in force upon the two-gun battery, pouring a continuous fire of artillery and musketry upon the position, which compelled its evacuation. Here Lieut. William W. Arnold, commanding Company G, was killed while gallantly cheering on his men. Capt. Thomas D. Horn, of Company D, was also wounded here. Captain Horn was taken to the rear, but we were unable to carry away the body of Lieutenant Arnold. A portion of the regiment was rallied after this by myself and Major [Peter] Baldy, and a number of the men joined other regiments near the front and did good service while the action lasted. [*OR* 11, pt. 2, pp. 428–29.]

The two artillery batteries were also hit hard by *Kemper*'s attack.

Report of Maj. Albert Arndt, USA, Commanding Third Brigade, Artillery Reserve, Army of the Potomac

On the 30th, at 4 o'clock p.m., they [Diederichs's and Knieriem's batteries] were put in position by General McCall himself on a field about 600 or 700 yards square, and surrounded on all sides by woods. On the left wing they commenced shelling the woods. At 4.30 o'clock Knieriem, whose position was about 100 yards in advance of Diederichs', was attacked by infantry on his left flank at a distance of no more than 60 yards, wounding 4 men and killing 22 horses. Two men were missing. In consequence of the loss of horses he had to abandon two caissons. He lost in this action also two pieces, but saved the limbers.

The moment Knieriem had left his position Diederichs fired at the attacking infantry as long as he had canister and shrapnel, used with very short fuses. Then he also was obliged to withdraw. When entering the road the traces of the wheel horses of a caisson broke, and caused the loss of the hind part of that caisson. Diederichs lost in this action 1 man killed, 1 wounded, 1 missing, and 12 horses killed. [*OR* 11, pt. 2, p. 265.]

In an attempt to restore this part of the defensive line the Tenth Pennsylvania conducted a counterattack.

Report of Col. James T. Kirk, USA, Commanding Tenth Pennsylvania Reserves, Third Brigade, Third Division, Fifth Corps, Army of the Potomac

My command was then posted, by order of General McCall, in the edge of a wood, the right resting near upon the left of the Ninth Regiment. Companies B and G were thrown forward to support a battery situated immediately on our left. At about 4 o'clock p.m. the left of the regiment was exposed to a raking fire from the enemy's batteries, which opened on the batteries immediately on our left and front. I was ordered to move forward by General McCall in person, which I did, halting for several minutes behind one of our batteries. Here the horses of the batteries on our left came in wild confusion on my men. The enemy were charging boldly upon the breastworks occupied by the Twelfth Regiment Pennsylvania Reserve Corps, when I charged most successfully upon their flank, completely routing the enemy, killing large numbers, and capturing about 60 prisoners. A stand of American colors, said to be that of the Fifth Regiment Pennsylvania Reserve Volunteer Corps, was rescued and brought off by E. E. Douglass, Company I, Tenth Regiment.

A considerable number belonging to the Tenth Regiment were at this time posted at the breastworks near the house on our line of battle, and were the last to leave this post. The enemy came up to close range without receiving our fire under protection of Union colors. Our loss in killed and wounded amounted to about 70. Several were also taken prisoners, who soon after made their escape while a panic raged among the rebels. About 300 were again rallied behind the first woods with the colors, who, with others of the reserve rallied by Major [Roy] Stone and other officers, were moved up by Lieutenant-Colonel [A. J.] Warner in line of battle to within about 100 yards of where the right of the regiment rested when the battle began. The fire of the enemy here was very hot, but was not returned, for fear of firing upon parties of our own men. [*OR* 11, pt. 2, p. 425.]

R. H. *Anderson*'s and *Kemper*'s brigades were attacking this part of the Union position. *Anderson* was commanding *Longstreet*'s Division, while *Longstreet* commanded the combination of his and *A. P. Hill*'s Divisions. Colonel *Micah Jenkins* commanded *Anderson*'s Brigade in this attack. *Jenkins* did not write a report, but *Kemper*'s report gives a good account of how the attack appeared from the Confederate side of the field.

Report of Brig. Gen. *James L. Kemper*, CSA, Commanding *Kemper*'s Brigade, *Longstreet*'s Division, Army of Northern Virginia

My command constituted the extreme right of our general line of battle and was posted upon the rear edge of a dense body of timber, the Seventeenth Virginia Regiment, Col. *M. D. Corse*, occupying the right; the Twenty-fourth Virginia Regiment, Lieutenant-Colonel [*Peter*] *Hairston* commanding, the left; the First Virginia, Capt. *G. F. Norton* commanding, the center; the

Eleventh Virginia, Capt. *K. Otey* commanding, the right center, and the Seventh Virginia, Col. *W. Tazwell Patton,* the left center. [Colonel *Patton* was the great uncle of George S. Patton Jr. of World War II fame.]

Soon after getting into position I received orders from Major-General *Longstreet* to use the utmost care in guarding against any movement of the enemy upon my right, and I at once caused Colonel *Corse,* of the right regiment, to change front to rear on his left company, so that his regiment formed an obtuse angle with the line of the brigade and fronted obliquely to the right. I also caused two companies of this regiment to move forward from *Corse's* new front as skirmishers, under command of Captain *[Robert H.] Simpson.* After advancing several hundred yards these skirmishers were halted upon the rear edge of an open field, a good view of which was commanded from their position. I also posted *Rogers'* battery of four pieces upon an open eminence near the right of my line and in supporting distance of *Corse's* regiment, the position being such as to command an extensive field upon my right.

About 5 p.m. an order being received from Major-General *Longstreet* to advance my line, I immediately in person ordered Colonel *Corse* to change his front forward, so as to bring the right of his regiment up to the brigade line, and sent my staff along the line toward the left, so as to insure the simultaneous advance of the entire line. The brigade advanced in line of battle steadily and in good order, notwithstanding the unevenness of the ground, which in places was almost precipitous, the entangled undergrowth which filled the woods, and the firing of one of the enemy's batteries located directly in front, which rapidly threw shell and round shot over and almost in the midst of my command.

The advance continued to be conducted in good order until, very soon coming upon the pickets of the enemy and driving them in, the men seemed to be possessed of the idea that they were upon the enemy's main line, and in an instant the whole brigade charged forward in double-quick time and with loud cheers. Nothing could have been more chivalrously done and nothing could have been more unfortunate, as the cheering of the men only served to direct the fire of the enemy's batteries, and the movement in double-quick time through dense woods, over rough ground, encumbered with matted under-growth and crossed by a swamp, had the effect of producing more or less confusion and breaking the continuity of the line, which, however, was preserved as well as it possibly could have been under the circumstances. But a single idea seemed to control the minds of the men, which was to reach the enemy's line by the directed route and in the shortest time; and no earthly power could have availed to arrest or restrain the impetuosity with which they rushed toward the foe, for my orders, previously given with great care and emphasis to the assembled field officers of the brigade, forbade any movement in double-quick time over such ground when the enemy were not in view. The obstructions were such as to make it impossible for any officer to more than a few files of his men at one view, and it was apparent that any effort to halt and reform the entire brigade would be futile, and would only serve to produce increased confusion. But whatever the error of the men in advancing to rapidly in disregard of previous orders to the contrary, it was an error upon the side of bravery.

After advancing in this way probably 1,000 or 1,200 yards, crossing two bodies of woods and a small intermediate field, the lines suddenly emerged into another field, facing a battery of the enemy [Diederichs's and Knieriem's batteries], consisting of not less than eight pieces, distant but a few hundred yards, while the enemy's infantry were found protected by an imperfect and hastily constructed breastwork and a house near by. At the same time it became apparent that another battery [Cooper's battery] of the enemy was posted a considerable distance to our left. These two batteries and the enemy's infantry poured an incessant fire of shell, grape, canister, and lead upon my line, and did much execution; still there was no perceptible faltering in the advance of these brave men who rushed across the open field, pouring a well-directed fire into the enemy, driving him from his breastworks and the battery in our front. The guns of the battery were abandoned to us for the time being, and my command was in virtual possession of the chosen position of the enemy. A more impetuous and desperate charge was never made than that of my small command against the sheltered and greatly superior forces of the enemy.

It is proper to be stated here that the left of my line was entirely unsupported, and greatly to my surprise and disappointment, for I had supposed that the movement of my brigade was part of a general advance of our entire lines. Up to this time no firing was heard upon my left except the firing of the enemy, which was directed upon my line with telling effect.

It now became evident that the position sought to be held by my command was wholly untenable by them unless largely and immediately re-enforced. The inferior numbers which had alarmed the enemy and driven him from his breastworks and batteries soon became apparent to him, and he at once proceeded to make use of his advantage. While greatly superior numbers hung upon our front considerable bodies of the enemy were thrown upon both flanks of my command, which was now in imminent danger of being wholly captured or destroyed. Already they were capturing officers and men at different points of my line, principally upon the right. No re-enforcements appeared, and the dire alternative of withdrawing from the position, although of obvious and inevitable necessity, was reluctantly submitted to. [OR 11, pt. 2, pp. 763–65.]

In this attack *Kemper*'s Brigade took severe casualties, losing 414 officers and men: 44 killed, 205 wounded, and 165 missing.

Colonel Seneca G. Simmons's brigade was the reserve for McCall's division. This brigade's position was used as a rallying line for the regiments driven back by the Confederate attack.

McCall ordered the units in the reserve line forward to strengthen the defensive position. During this movement McCall rode into the Confederate advance line and was captured, and Brigadier General Truman Seymour assumed command of the division. Seymour's report presents a good overview of McCall's division at Glendale.

Report of Brig. Gen. Truman Seymour, USA, Commanding Third Division, Fifth Corps, Army of the Potomac

The division was scarcely formed before the attack commenced by a distant fire of shot and shell upon the ground occupied by the left, and attracted, doubtless, by a few discharges from the 20 pounder Parrotts. The advanced pickets of the First and Third were rapidly driven back by a force of skirmishers upon the main body, which at short range delivered a deliberate fire upon the advancing foe, cutting to pieces a regiment supposed to be the Ninth Virginia, and taking from it a number of prisoners. The position of the Third [Pennsylvania] interfering with the range of our artillery, which now began to open, it fell back, and being unfortunately fired upon by our own men, retired in some confusion, and reformed only late in the day.

On the extreme left a small log farm-house, Whitlock's, had hastily been prepared for defense by piling rails and logs so as to shelter a part of the Twelfth Regiment, and from which, supported as it was by other troops, it should never have been driven. A fire from skirmishers, added to that of the distant artillery, drove these men, however, early in the action, and with very weak resistance, from their posts, and lost to us a very important point. The Fifth and a part of the Tenth and the small remnant of the First Rifles gallantly and successfully for a time stemmed the overwhelming tide. The Tenth, driving the enemy back by a brilliant charge, took some 60 prisoners from the Alabama and Georgia Regiments; but the success was only momentary. The force thrown upon us was too great to be long withstood.

Immediately upon the enemy presenting himself the batteries opened along the entire line, but at a great disadvantage, so close could the enemy advance under cover. On the left, no sooner were the Parrott guns subjected to the fire of musketry than they were limbered up and withdrawn, causing much confusion. The cavalry, crowded into a narrow ravine and shaken by the disorder, soon followed. It formed farther to the rear, but found no good opportunity to be of service on the field. Cooper's guns were finally taken from him after many of his officers and men had been disabled. Lieutenants [Henry T.] Danforth and [Thomas] Cadwallader both died at their posts. Veterans could have done no more. The Ninth, Colonel Jackson, retook these pieces by a successful charge, and drove the enemy well back, but in so doing drew a heavy fire from his right that compelled his return. Amsden stood fast, doing excellent service until his ammunition was exhausted, then withdrew.

On the right General Meade met a severe attack, but the capacity of Randol's and Thompson's batteries, all light 12-pounders, for canister gave another aspect to the fight. The enemy was repeatedly driven back with great loss, yet from the woods in front of Randol a fire was sustained that first weakened, then destroyed his effect. A force came down to take his guns, but Colonel [Albert L.] Magilton, Fourth, keeping his men well to the ground until close at hand, met it with perfect success; followed with the bayonet; gave and received many wounds recaptured Lieut. E. B. Hill, of the battery, who, after much gallantry, was already a prisoner, wounded, and returned gloriously to his position with three secession flags in proof of the obstinate courage of both parties. The Seventh, by similar conduct, added to the success of the resistance. It also charged gallantly with the bayonet. All its color guard being killed or wounded, Capt. R. M. Henderson seized the standard and bore it off the field, when by main strength the enemy compelled the regiment to withdraw. The chief credit of the stand here made may, however, be ascribed to the tenacious skill with which Captain Thompson handled his pieces.

About this time General Meade was severely wounded and compelled to retire, and the services of an able officer were lost to the command. But along the line generally the sturdiest efforts of officers and men could not have resisted unaided the impulse and force of this attack, and although but little ground was lost, it was evident that the enemy was gaining. Happily a part of Richardson's division came to our relief, and when night fell and the battle ceased but trifling, if any, advantage had been conquered.

The parts of regiments that had most suffered and had fallen to the rear were reformed successfully by the exertions of several field and staff officers: Lieutenant Collamer, Major Roy Stone, Captain Chandler Hall, Captain Henderson, and Lieutenant [Charles B.] Lamborn, with others and moved to the front in support of those still on the field. While passing forward by the main road, led by General McCall in person and somewhat in advance and in company of Major Stone, they came suddenly upon the head of a body of rebels who demanded their surrender. Major Stone escaped with a slight hurt from a volley fired upon him, but General McCall fell into their hands. The presence of our men staid the enemy's farther advance.

The object of the enemy was doubtless to divide our forces by a strong attack upon the center of our line and to seize the roads by which the army was changing its base. [*OR* 11, pt. 2, pp. 403–4.]

Brigadier General John Sedgwick's division was in a reserve position to the east of the Willis Church Road. Earlier in the day two of his brigades had been ordered toward White Oak Bridge, Stop 18, to assist Richardson's and W. F. Smith's divisions against a possible crossing by *Jackson's* force. This initially left Sedgwick with only one brigade to reinforce McCall's division. However, because *Jackson's* weak attempt to capture the crossing site at White Oak Bridge, these two brigades were returned to Sedgwick in time to support the defensive line west of the Willis Church and Charles City Roads. *Jackson's* continued inactivity along White Oak Swamp also allowed regiments from Richardson's division to be sent to assist in the defense of the Glendale crossroads. You will see part of this reinforcing action at the next stop.

The night of June 30 found McCall's Division wrecked. It had fought three battles in five days, the most severe being at Glendale.

Center of the Union line at the Battle of Glendale. Willis Church is in the center of the picture. The Frayser (Nelson) Farmhouse is on the left side of the picture. Stop 24 is on the road between them. *Century Magazine.*

During those three battles it had sustained 3,067 killed, wounded, and missing. This was a casualty rate of 30 percent. In addition to this high number of casualties, the command structure had been decimated. The division commander was captured, one brigade commander had been captured and his replacement killed, and one brigade commander had been wounded. The surviving brigade commander commanded the division, and the senior regimental commander in each brigade commanded his brigade. Losses among regimental and company grade officers had been high. The five batteries of artillery supporting the division went into the battle at Glendale with a total of twenty-four cannon. Fourteen of these guns were capture by the attacking Confederates, thereby rendering the artillery minimally effective in future action. As the division limped south toward Malvern Hill, the survivors could say they had given everything they had.

Return to your car for the drive to Stop 24. Continue to drive south on Willis Church Road for 0.2 mile. Pull off to the right and park at Historical Marker PA 180. Get out of your car and face to the west, the right of your direction of travel, so you can look across the field to the west of the road.

Stop 24—Sedgwick's Counterattack

To your left at a distance of 0.2 mile is the modern-day Willis Church building. Its predecessor was here in 1862 and gave its name to the road you are on.

You are standing in the area of the left flank of McCall's defensive position. The right of *Kemper*'s Brigade initially attacked this area. As *Kemper*'s regiments were repulsed, the attack was taken up by *Pickett*'s Brigade, which was initially commanded by Colonel *Eppa Hunton* and then Colonel *John B. Strange*. Brigadier General *James J. Archer*'s brigade of *A. P. Hill*'s Division supported this brigade's attack.

Report of Col. *John B. Strange*, CSA, Commanding *Pickett*'s Brigade, *Longstreet*'s Division, Army of Northern Virginia

About 5 o'clock Colonel *Hunton* gave the order to charge, to which the respective regiments responded with alacrity; but after proceeding across an open field, exposed to grape and shell, we entered a skirt of woods, where we were halted and then ordered to march by the right flank, which was done until the brigade had crossed to the right of the Darbytown road, when we changed direction to the front, but over such broken ground and through an almost impassable marsh, as well as encountering a brigade in full retreat, which forced its way through our ranks, that the command was thrown into confusion. After passing through the marsh the line was again formed, but before starting forward a column of the enemy posted in the woods on our right flank opened fire upon us, while the batteries threw a shower of grape into us through the open field in front, to avoid which and gain cover we marched by the left flank . . . at this point [I] took command by request of General *Pickett*'s aide, as Colonel *Hunton* had become separated from the command, not being able to keep up on account of exhaustion. I then ordered the brigade forward in line of battle under cover of this wood, and on emerging from it discovered a large force approaching one of the batteries, which seemed deserted. Thinking our forces were in the woods in front engaging the enemy, as there was hot firing there, I assumed that those in their rear were friends, until convinced to the contrary by the open, honest display of the old flag, whereupon I ordered a fire, and a charge drove them from the battery back to their line in the woods beyond. I regret, though, that in this fire we had to kill nearly all the fine horses attached to the battery.

Upon capturing this battery, Adjutant *McCulloch,* of the Eighteenth Regiment Virginia Volunteers, asked my permission to turn the guns on the retreating enemy; but being satisfied that we had friends in front, and not knowing the exact position, I prohibited it, for fear of doing more damage to our own troops than to the enemy. I gave permission afterward, just before dark, to turn the guns upon the foe, which was done, and a continuous fire kept up until about 8:30 p.m., when night closed the conflict. [*OR* 11, pt. 2, p. 769.]

The Confederate attacks on this part of the field drove back McCall's left and part of his center. This defensive line was saved by the commitment of Sedgwick's division to restore the defenses.

Earlier in the day two of Sedgwick's brigades had been sent back to White Oak Bridge to support the defenders there. Left in position just to the east of Willis Church Road was Brigadier General William Burns's brigade. As the powerful Confederate attacks began to develop all along McCall's line, Sedgwick recalled his two brigades from White Oak Bridge. However, the Confederate attacks developed with such speed that Sedgwick could not wait, but was forced to send in Burns's brigade and committed the other regiments hurrying back from White Oak Bridge as they arrived.

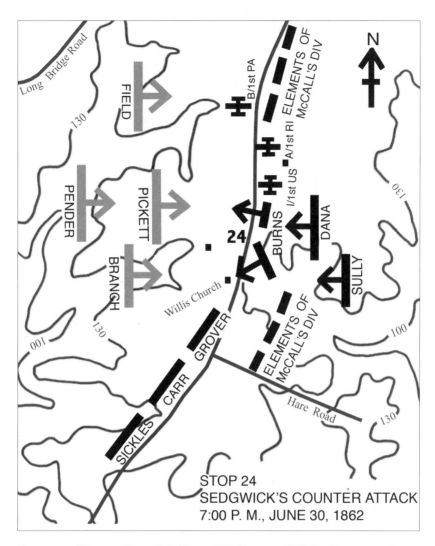

STOP 24
SEDGWICK'S COUNTER ATTACK
7:00 P. M., JUNE 30, 1862

Report of Brig. Gen. William W. Burns, USA, Commanding Second Brigade, Second Division, Second Corps, Army of the Potomac

About 11 o'clock the enemy attacked the troops of General Franklin at the [White Oak] bridge. General Sumner sent two of General Sedgwick's brigades back to his support, leaving but mine at Glendale. About 3:30 o'clock an attack was made on General McCall's division in front of Nelson's [Frayser] house. Soon his left gave way and broke toward us in confusion. General Sumner made the disposition of my brigade, placing Colonel Baxter

[Seventy-second Pennsylvania] on the right, Colonel Owen [Sixty-ninth Pennsylvania] in center, and Colonel Turner Morehead [One hundred and sixth Pennsylvania] left, the Seventy-first Pennsylvania, Colonel Jones, in rear of Lieutenant Edmund Kirby's battery [Battery I, First U.S. Artillery], in support. At the request of General Hooker, General Sumner forwarded Colonel Owen to the right of Hooker's first line [seven hundred yards to your left] and sent Colonel Morehead in reserve of General Hooker's right. I was then directed to lead Baxter to the wood on the right of the field, through which McCall's left retreated, as the enemy seemed to be moving that way to rid themselves of the terrible fire of Kirby's battery, which swept this field. Soon after General Dana's [Third] brigade came back from the bridge and went forward, filling the space between Colonel Owen's right and Colonel Baxter's left.

Another heavy attack broke McCall's center and sent the fugitives shamefully through our ranks. Our line was advanced, and Colonel Owen, Sixty-ninth Pennsylvania Volunteers, unsupported, pursued the victorious rebels back over the ground through which they were passing and crowned the crest of the hill where McCall had lost his artillery. The line followed this noble example, and McCall's position was held and the enemy discomfited. By direction of General Sedgwick I placed the Seventy-first Pennsylvania Volunteers and Nineteenth Massachusetts [of Dana's Brigade] in support of the first line, in connection with Baxter's Seventy-second, Colonel Hudson's Eighty-second New York [of Sully's Brigade], Colonel Suiter's Thirty-fourth New York [of Sully's Brigade]. While perfecting this line another attack was made on the left center, and I found that the Seventh Michigan [of Dana's Brigade] and Forty-second New York [of Dana's Brigade] had broken from the front line, the enemy rapidly advancing through the gap. I threw the Seventy-first Pennsylvania, Colonel Jones, and Nineteenth Massachusetts, Colonel Hinks, into the breach, and nobly did they redeem the faults of their comrades. These two noble regiments met the enemy face to face, and for nearly one hour poured into them such tremendous volleys that no further attack was had at that vital point.

On going to the right I received a message from General McCall that he was wounded and hard pressed on his right. By authority of General Sumner I immediately forwarded the Thirty-fourth New York, Colonel Suiter, to the left of General Berry [brigade of Kearny's Division], at his request, and advanced our right, then in reserve, to relieve McCall, but before reaching him three staff officers came back, and informed me that the enemy had been taken in flank on the right and was in a fair way of being captured. I halted, our line, as it was growing late and I was fearful of firing upon friends coming from the right flank. [OR 11, pt. 2, pp. 92–93.]

The first of Sedgwick's brigades to arrive back from White Oak Bridge was Brigadier General Dana's Third Brigade. This brigade was committed to reinforce Burn's brigade.

Report of Brig. Gen. Napoleon J. T. Dana, USA, Commanding Third Brigade, Second Division, Second Corps, Army of the Potomac

After remaining in this position [at White Oak Bridge] about two hours a very heavy fire of artillery and musketry was heard in the position we had left two hours ago. Messengers came to me almost every moment from General Sumner to hurry up my command by regiments in double-quick time and to make all possible haste. Very many men broke down on the road, and those who arrived at Nelson's [Frayser] farm, although in excellent spirits, showed the marks of great fatigue. The regiments were formed and marched into the woods as rapidly as they arrived. The first three which arrived were under command of Colonel Lee. The last one which arrived was the First Minnesota, which I formed myself and marched forward to the woods. The first line, under Colonel Lee, advanced beyond support and was subjected to a tremendous fire. One of the regiments broke, but was afterward rallied, which compelled the Twentieth Massachusetts, which had advanced farther than any, to fall back, which they did in order.

Soon after dark orders were given to withdraw the regiments and continue the retreat. [*OR* 11, pt. 2, pp. 94–95.]

One of the regiments in Dana's Brigade was the Twentieth Massachusetts. A company commander in this regiment was the future U.S. Supreme Court Justice Oliver Wendell Holmes Jr. In a speech given on Memorial Day 1884 Holmes reminded all of the cost of war when he spoke of a friend and fellow company commander. "I see another youthful lieutenant [James J. Lowell] as I saw him in the Seven Days, when I looked down the line at Glendale. The officers were at the head of their companies. The advance was beginning. We caught each other's eye and saluted. When next I looked, he was gone." [O. W. Holmes speech, May 30, 1884, at Keene, New Hampshire, to the John Sedgwick Post #4, Grand Army of the Republic.]

During this counterattack two batteries of artillery, located to your right, had supported Sedgwick's division, Captain John A. Tompkins's Battery A, First Rhode Island Artillery, and Lieutenant Edmund Kirby's Battery I, First U.S. Artillery.

Report of Col. Charles H. Tompkins, Chief of Artillery, Second Division, Second Corps, Army of the Potomac

Shortly after the action commenced large bodies of infantry and some artillery of McCall's division broke through the woods in our front, retreating within our lines in the utmost confusion and disorder. They were closely followed by the enemy, who advanced some 200 yards from the woods, where they were checked and soon driven back by a terrific fire from Tompkins' and Kirby's batteries and Burns' brigade.

From this time till after dark, when the enemy were repulsed and the action ceased, both batteries kept up an almost continuous fire, doing, I have every reason to believe, excellent execution. [*OR* 11, pt. 2, p. 83.]

Return to your car for the drive to Stop 25. Continue driving south on Willis Church Road for 0.5 mile to the intersection with Hare Road. Turn left on to Hare Road, make a U-turn, drive back toward the intersection of Hare Road with Willis Church Road. Just before the intersection pull off to the right, stop, and get out of your car.

Stop 25—The Union Left

You are in the position of the right flank brigade of Brigadier General Joseph Hooker's division. This three-brigade division formed the left of the Union defensive line. The right brigade of the division was Brigadier General Cuvier Grover's First Brigade. The other two brigades of the division formed the defensive line as it stretched to the left of where you are.

Report of Brig. Gen. Joseph Hooker, USA, Commanding Second Division, Third Corps, Army of the Potomac

About 9 o'clock my line of battle was established, Grover on the right, [Colonel Joseph B.] Carr [Third Brigade] in the center, and [Brigadier General

Willis Church in 1862. *Century Magazine.*

Willis Church today.

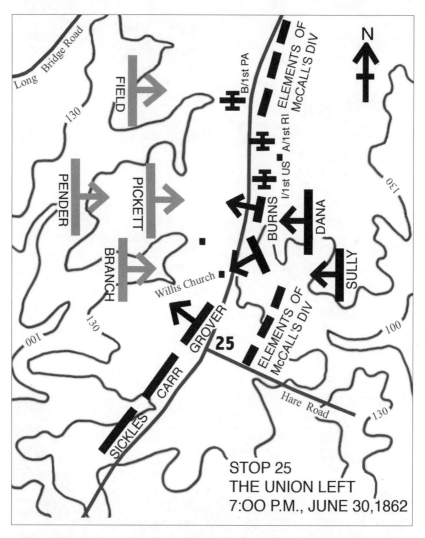

STOP 25
THE UNION LEFT
7:OO P.M., JUNE 30,1862

Daniel E.] Sickles [Second Brigade] on the left. In the mean time directions were given for all of my batteries to continue on their march to our proposed camp on James River, in order that they might be put in position there.

About 3 o'clock the enemy commenced a vigorous attack on McCall, and in such force that General Sumner voluntarily tendered me the services of a regiment, which was posted in an open field on my extreme right and under shelter from the enemy's artillery. This was the Sixty-ninth Regiment Pennsylvania Volunteers, under Colonel Owen.

Meanwhile the enemy's attack had grown in force and violence, and after an ineffectual effort to resist it, the whole of McCall's division was completely routed, and many of the fugitives rushed down the road on which my right was resting, while others took to the cleared fields and broke through my lines from one end of them to the other. At first I was apprehensive that the effect would be disastrous on my command and was no little relieved when they had passed my lines. Following closely upon the footsteps of these demoralized people were the broken masses of the enemy, furiously pressing them on to me under cover of the woods until they were checked by a front fire of the Sixteenth Massachusetts Volunteers and afterward by a diagonal fire on their right and left flanks from the Sixty-ninth Pennsylvania Volunteers and the left of the Sixteenth Massachusetts Volunteers; also, whenever the enemy ventured to uncover himself from the forest, a destructive fire was poured into him along my right wing.

After great loss the enemy gave way, and were instantly followed with great gallantry by Grover, at the head of the First Massachusetts Regiment, while the Sixty-ninth Pennsylvania Regiment, heroically led by Owen, advanced in the open field on their flank with almost reckless daring.

Grover was re-enforced by the Second New Hampshire and the Twenty-sixth Pennsylvania Regiments, but not until after he had suffered severely from the enemy's reserves.

During all this time several of Sumner's batteries had been doing splendid execution in the rebel ranks and greatly contributed to our success. The troops under Grover were withdrawn from the pursuit at dark and restored to their places in our line of battle.

The loss of the rebels in this battle was very severe. The field on which it was fought was one of unusual extent for the numbers engaged, and was almost covered with their dead and dying.

From their torches we could see that the enemy was busy all night long in searching for his wounded, but up to daylight the following morning there had been no apparent diminution in the heart-rending cries and groans of his wounded. The unbroken, mournful wail of human suffering was all that we heard from Glendale during that long, dismal night.

I was instructed to hold my position until Sumner and Kearny had retired over the Quaker [Willis Church] road, and soon after daylight my command was withdrawn and followed them. [*OR* 11, pt. 2, pp. 111–12.]

Hooker's right brigade, Grover's brigade, was engaged with the right half of Brigadier General *Lawrence Branch*'s brigade of *A. P. Hill*'s Division. *Branch*'s Brigade was the right flank brigade of the multibrigade attack against the Union position. As such the left of *Branch*'s Brigade engaged the left of McCall's division and part of the Union counterattack by Sedgwick's division. The right of *Branch's Brigade* engaged the right brigade of Hooker's division.

Report of Brig. Gen. *Lawrence O'B. Branch*, CSA, Commanding *Branch*'s Brigade, *A. P. Hill*'s Division, Army of Northern Virginia

Forming my line of battle in a cleared field and advancing, we soon encountered the enemy. This was done under the fire of two batteries, one of which we silenced and the other of which enfiladed the left of my line. After proceeding about this distance, the enemy's force rapidly accumulating as they fell back and finding that the enemy extended much beyond my right flank, no farther advance was attempted. At dark I placed my brigade in bivouac on the edge of the battle-field, and having reported to Major-General *Hill* through a member of my staff, was ordered to remain there until daylight and then return to the point from which I had started into battle the previous afternoon. [*OR* 11, pt. 2, p. 883.]

During the night of June 30 and the early morning hours of July 1, the seven divisions of the Army of the Potomac that had been involved in the Battle of Glendale retreated south to positions on or beyond Malvern Hill.

The Battle of Glendale had seen some spectacular and some poor performances by senior leaders in both armies. The worst example of leadership was the commander of the Army of the Potomac, Major General George McClellan. His absence from the battle on June 30 was a dereliction of duty on his part. By late Monday morning, June 30, only four of his eleven divisions and part of the supply train had passed through the choke point at Glendale and marched south to Malvern Hill or the James River. With the majority of his army, seven divisions, deployed to hold open the route of retreat McClellan's place was clearly with those forces. However, after holding a meeting with some of his commanders at about 10:00 A.M., he turned his back on his command responsibilities, departed Glendale, and rode south over Malvern Hill to the James River. Then, as today, in any military or civilian organization, when the senior leader shirks his responsibilities, one of two things happen. One, without direction the organization will falter and eventually collapse, or, two, strong subordinates will rise to the occasion and will cooperate among themselves to ensure the organization survives. The latter happened on June 30 at Glendale and helped ensure the Army of the Potomac would survive to fight another day.

After the Battle of Savage Station *Lee* had conceived an excellent plan of maneuver to trap and destroy a large part of the Union army. His plan was designed to bring eight of his eleven divisions against the Union line of retreat with another three held in a position to reinforce success. However, when it came to the execution of his plan many of his subordinates did not perform as they should have.

At White Oak Bridge, on the left of the Confederate line, *Jackson*'s failure to press the attack kept four Confederate divisions out of the fight. This inactivity allowed Richardson to send two of his brigades to reinforce the Glendale defenses. In addition, two brigades of Sedgwick's division at Glendale that had been sent to White Oak Bridge were recalled and committed to action to reform McCall's line.

On *Jackson*'s right *Huger* failed to vigorously push his attack down Charles City Road. His lack of aggressiveness allowed Slocum to send one of his brigades to assist Kearny's division.

On the Confederate far right Major General *Theopilus Holmes*, advancing on River Road toward the western edge of Malvern Hill failed to deploy his division so as to use its full combat power against the Union defenses. As a result *Holmes* added nothing to the accomplishment of *Lee*'s plan.

Within the Army of Northern Virginia, *Longstreet* and *A. P. Hill* gave the two most promising performances. Their two divisions were the only ones that actually conducted a full attack against the Union defenses. And though they tried mightily, they were unable to generate the combat power necessary to break a portion of the Union position that was being continually reinforced.

As night fell on Monday, June 30, Lee's most promising opportunity to inflict major damage on the Army of the Potomac, or maybe even render it combat ineffective, slipped away.

Return to your car for the drive to Stop 26.

Chapter 6

Battle of Malvern Hill
Tuesday, July 1, 1862

Turn left on Willis Church Road and drive south for 1.0 mile to the National Park Service grass and gravel parking lot, located on your left. Turn left into the parking lot, park, and get out of your car.

Stop 26, Position A—Lee Deploys for Attack

Willis Church Road is the route a majority of Union forces at the Battle of Glendale used in their retreat on the night of June 30, 1862. They passed by this location and then continued to follow the road for an additional 0.3 mile to Malvern Hill. Some of the units were deployed in positions to enlarge the defensive position on Malvern Hill that had been established by the commander of the Fifth Corps, Brigadier General Fitz John Porter.

On Tuesday morning *Jackson* and *Lee* met at the Glendale crossroads where *Lee* issued orders to continue the pursuit of the retreating Union army. *Lee* sensed that this would be his last chance to inflict major damage on McClellan's army before it reached the James River and the protection of the Union navy gunboats.

Report of Gen. *Robert E. Lee*, CSA, Commanding Army of Northern Virginia

Early on July 1 *Jackson* reached the battle-field of the previous day [Glendale], having succeeded in crossing White Oak Swamp, where he captured a part of the enemy's artillery and a number of prisoners. He was directed to continue the pursuit down the Willis Church road, and soon found the enemy

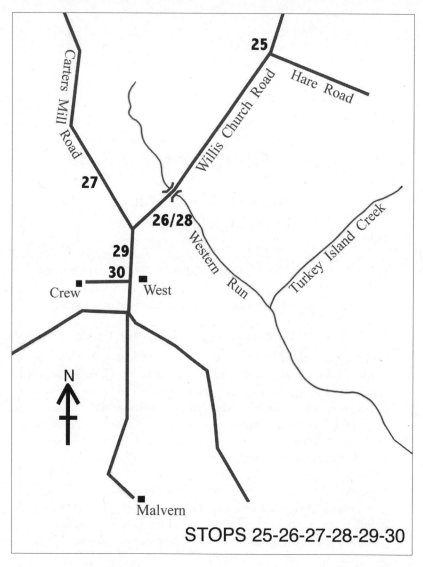

Carters Mill Road

25

Willis Church Road

Hare Road

27

26/28

Western Run

Turkey Island Creek

29

30

Crew

West

N

Malvern

STOPS 25-26-27-28-29-30

occupying a high range, extending obliquely across the road, in front of Malvern Hill. On this position of great natural strength he had concentrated his powerful artillery, supported by masses of infantry, partially protected by earthworks. His left rested near Crew's house and his right near Binford's. Immediately in his front the ground was open, varying in width from a quarter to half a mile, and, sloping gradually from the crest, was completely swept by the fire of his infantry and artillery. To reach this open ground our troops had to advance through a broken and thickly-wooded country, traversed nearly throughout its whole extent by a swamp passable at but few places and difficult at those. The whole was within range of the batteries on the heights and the gunboats in the river, under whose incessant fire our movements had to be executed.

Jackson formed his line with *Whiting*'s division on his left and *D. H. Hill*'s on his right, one of *Ewell*'s brigades occupying the interval. The rest of *Ewell*'s and *Jackson*'s [*Winder*'s] own divisions were held in reserve. *Magruder* was directed to take position on *Jackson*'s right, but before his arrival two of *Huger*'s brigades [*Armistead*'s and *Wright*'s] came up and were placed next to *Hill*. *Magruder* subsequently formed on the right of [*D. H. Hill*] which, with a third

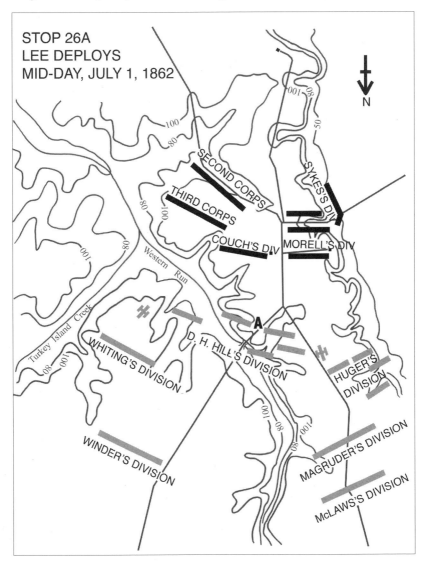

[*Mahone*'s brigade] of *Huger*'s, were placed under his command. *Longstreet* and *A. P. Hill* were held in reserve and took no part in the engagement. Owing to ignorance of the country, the dense forests impeding necessary communication, and the extreme difficulty of the ground, the whole line was not formed until a late hour in the afternoon. [*OR* 11, pt. 2, pp. 495–96.]

Major General *Jackson*'s command rebuilt the White Oak Bridge, Stop 18, and crossed White Oak Swamp Tuesday morning. It then marched to the Glendale crossroads, turned south, and marched on Willis Church Road. *Jackson*'s lead division was *Whiting*'s division, which turned left off the road about 0.5 mile back from where you are and began deploying on the Poindexter farm. The farmhouse was 1,300 yards (0.7 mile) east of your present location. The center of *Whiting*'s Division, as it faced southwest, was 900 yards (0.5 mile) northeast. Following *Whiting, Winder*'s Division turned off the road and deployed behind *Whiting*. *D. H. Hill*'s Division continued on down the road and began deploying on both sides of the road, which put it on *Whiting*'s right front. As they were in the open and were being subjected to Union artillery fire from Malvern Hill, most of *Hill*'s brigades moved forward and took cover in the wood that followed Western Run. You crossed this creek just before entering the

The Parsonage in 1862. The road in the picture is the Willis Church Road. Parking area and stop 26A is to the left of the photo. *Century Magazine*.

parking lot. It flows in a southeasterly direction and will be on your left for part of the walk to the next position. *Ewell*'s Division, the last in *Jackson*'s march column, stopped and went into a reserve position near Willis Church.

Deployed to the right of *D. H. Hill*'s Division were the brigades of Brigadier Generals *Lewis A. Armistead, Ambrose R. Wright, William Mahone,* and *Robert Ransom Jr.* These four brigades belonged to *Huger*'s Division. Because *Huger* had not arrived with his brigades they were placed under the command of Major General *Magruder,* who had arrived in advance of his command.

Within two miles of the Union position on Malvern Hill, *Lee* had eleven divisions with a total of forty brigades. However, due to traffic jams on the roads and poor command and control, only fourteen brigades would be ordered to attack the Union position. Some of these brigades would attack together, but many of them would not participate in coordinated attacks. In several instances only parts of a brigade would make it into the fight.

With your back to Willis Church Road find the walking trail on the other side of the parking area that goes away from the road. This trail goes south, with a tree line to your left and an open field to your right. Walk for 150 yards on this trail, stop, then face right.

The ruins of the Parsonage.

Position B, The Confederate Left

The house to your left front is the rebuilt West House. The original was there in 1862. It is just east of the road that goes over Malvern Hill. This road is a continuation of the Carter's Mill Road. On the high ground to your left front was the right of the Union defensive position. When the attacking Confederate troops came out of the woods along Western Run, they saw a line of Union infantry and three batteries of artillery with sixteen guns directly in front of them. As they progressed up the slope of the hill they saw more infantry and artillery to the right and left.

Several brigades would pass through this location in multiple attacks against the Union defenses. However, before the infantry attacks began, an attempt was made to neutralize the Union artillery.

Lee and *Longstreet* had developed a plan whereby a large amount of Confederate artillery would be positioned on two flat and open areas on the Confederate left and right. From these locations, two "grand batteries" of up to fifty or more guns each would bring a crossfire on the Union line, destroying and damaging the artillery and disrupting the defending infantry regiments. The "grand battery" on the left was to be deployed in the Poindexter Farm's wheat

The right and center part of the Union position on Malvern Hill as seen from Stop 26B. The West House and Union right is in the left of the photograph. The Union center is in the right of the photograph.

field, which is 800 yards, east-northeast, behind you. The range from the Confederate artillery to their targets was from 1,000 to 1,300 yards.

However, *Lee*'s artillery organization was not up to carrying out the concept. *D. H. Hill*'s artillery was not present on the field, having been sent to the rear to rearm and refit. Because of the number of units trying to use the same road, *Jackson* was able to bring up only five of the ten batteries available to him.

The first artillery into position was Captain *James Riley*'s Rown (N.C.) Battery of *Whiting*'s Division. *Riley*'s battery was soon joined by Captain *W. L. Balthis*'s Staunton (Va.) Battery. *Riley*'s battery initially received the full weight of the Union counter battery fire and was soon forced to retire with heavy loss. Soon thereafter three batteries from *Jackson*'s (*Winder*'s) division were committed to the fight. The reports of these battery commanders gives a good account of the intensity of the artillery duel.

Report of Capt. *William T. Poague*, CSA, Commanding Rockbridge (Va.) Battery, *Winder*'s Division, *Jackson*'s Command, Army of Northern Virginia

About 10 o'clock on the morning of July 1, while following the brigade on the march near Frazier's farm, I received an order from Major-General *Jackson* to hurry on to the front and report to Major-General *Whiting*. Not being able to find the latter officer, by direction of General *Jackson* I took position in a wheat field on the left of *Balthis*' battery, Staunton Artillery, which had just preceded us. My guns were posted behind the crest of a ridge, by which they were to some extent protected from the enemy's fire.

Shortly after opening fire the impression got out by some means that all the batteries were ordered to leave the field. Not being able to trace it to an authoritative source, I ordered my pieces to continue firing. One or two batteries in the mean time left the field. Captain *Balthis* soon exhausted his ammunition, and shortly afterward left the field. By this time Lieutenant *Carpenter* had gotten two pieces in position and opened fire.

The fire of the enemy's batteries was most terrific, and in the main very accurate. That the loss on our side was not much heavier is owing to the protection afforded by our position.

The detachment of the 6-pounder was now so much reduced as not to be able to work the gun; it was sent off the field, and the remainder of the detachment distributed among the other pieces. Finding that the contest was a very unequal one, having the fire of several batteries concentrated upon five guns on our side, my pieces were ordered to cease firing. The gun of Lieutenant *Carpenter*, next to us, also ceased at my suggestion. My object was to induce the enemy to hold up until we could get other batteries to our assistance.

Soon thereafter I was ordered to report with my battery to Major-General *Hill*, but was not called on to go into action again. About 5 o'clock I obtained permission to go to the rear for ammunition.

The following are the casualties which occurred during this artillery engagement: Killed—privates, 2. Wounded—non-commissioned officers, 1; privates, 9. One horse was killed and several disabled. [*OR* 11, pt. 2, pp. 573–74.]

> Advancing into the Poindexter field *Carpenter*'s battery took position next to *Poague*'s.

Report of Lieut. *John C. Carpenter*, CSA, Commanding Alleghany (Va.) Battery, *Winder*'s Division, *Jackson*'s Command, Army of Northern Virginia

. . . we were ordered to the front, to report to General *Whiting*, who ordered us to take position in the field near Poindexter's residence. Some three batteries being in advance, all took immediate positions. Sending Lieutenant *McKendree* back to report the fact, halted the battery, and started to look out a position, when I met a battery coming off, and directly another. Learning from them there was no suitable place in that direction, returned, and found my battery gone with the others. Overtaking them as soon as possible, immediately ordered them back, in the mean time inquiring by whose orders they left. They could not tell me who he was; said he rode up and told them to move back in the woods.

General *Whiting* hurried us back, and we took position on the right of Capt. *W. T. Poague* under the most severe fire I think I ever experienced, where we were engaged for about an hour and a half, when we were ordered to cease firing and wait further orders, having lost 1 man killed and 5 wounded.

Commenced firing again about 2.30 o'clock, continuing until about 5 o'clock. Our ammunition being nearly exhausted, was ordered to the rear, losing 1 man killed, 2 wheels broken, and 2 horses wounded. [*OR* 11, pt. 2, p. 574.]

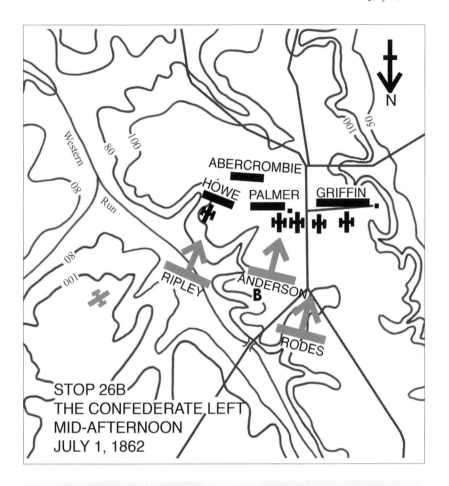

STOP 26B
THE CONFEDERATE LEFT
MID-AFTERNOON
JULY 1, 1862

Captain *George W. Wooding,* Danville Artillery, was able to get two of his guns in position to the left of *Poague.* From there his guns joined in the artillery duel.

The artillery in the Poindexter field, being unable to suppress the Union batteries, was withdrawn. The "grand battery" on the right was also unable to bring sufficient fire to bear on the Union guns. You will look at this artillery action later.

Through a series of communication mishaps, which will be covered when you are on the Confederate right flank, *Lee*'s infantry now moved forward to the attack.

The first brigade on the Confederate left to attack was commanded by Brigadier General *George B. Anderson*, who was wounded, and command fell upon Colonel *C. C. Tew*. This brigade crossed Western Run and passed through the location where you are now. *Anderson*'s Brigade advanced part way across the field when the Union fire and a counterattack stopped it. It then fell back to this general location. Here it waited to participate in a larger attack late in the afternoon.

To *Anderson*'s left rear the next unit to come into action was *Ripley*'s Brigade.

Report of Brig. Gen. *Roswell S. Ripley*, CSA, Commanding *Ripley*'s Brigade, *D. H. Hill*'s Division, *Jackson*'s Command, Army of Northern Virginia

Taking different positions during the morning, in the afternoon the brigade advanced, under orders from the major-general commanding division, through a heavy fire of artillery, to a dense wood in close proximity of the enemy's position, where it lay for a time in reserve.

At about 5 o'clock it was ordered to take position in a jungle [the woods along Western Run] near the hill upon which the enemy was established and to the left of General *Anderson*'s brigade, which it did in the following order: The Forty-eighth Georgia was on the right, the Third North Carolina, the Forty-fourth Georgia, about 170 men of which had rallied and been brought by Captain *Beck* and other officers, and the First North Carolina on the left, under Lieutenant-Colonel [*William P.*] *Bynum*.

In obedience to the orders of General *Hill*, I made a reconnaissance of the enemy's position, and found him immediately in our front in strong force, with a battery well advanced toward us and supported by strong lines of infantry. The number of his guns could only be judged of by the rapidity of his fire, owing to the nature of the country.

At about 6:30 or 7 o'clock an attack was made by the troops on our right, and we were, with the other brigades in advance, ordered by General *Hill* to move forward at once and attack the enemy. [*Rodes*'s brigade, commanded by *Gordon*] and *Anderson*'s brigade were on my right, and the troops of the three mounted the hill in a gallant manner. At its brow our troops were met with a furious fire of shot, shell, and musketry; officers and men fell fast, but they maintained their ground, opening and keeping up a severe fire upon the enemy in return, before which his advanced battery fell back and his troops wavered. He pressed hard upon our left, however, and while moving his regiment to its support the gallant and accomplished Col. *Gaston Meares*, of the Third North Carolina Regiment fell. Meanwhile *Garland*'s and *Colquitt*'s brigades had been advanced . . . on the right.

Fresh troops were ordered forward, and the troops of the brigade were collected in parties by such officers as they fell in with. A portion remained in the vicinity of the field during the night, and the remainder, with portions of other brigades of the division having been collected, were retired a short distance on the [Willis Church] road. During the night the enemy fell away from the hardly contested field. [*OR* 11, pt. 2, p. 650.]

The fresh troops *Ripley* referred to were units from *Winder*'s Division that arrived too late to have any influence on the attack.

Retrace your path and return to your car for the drive to Stop 27. Turn left on Willis Church Road. Continue to drive for 0.1 mile to the intersection with Carter's Mill Road. Willis Church Road ends at this intersection. Turn right on Carter's Mill Road and drive for 0.5 mile to where a dirt road intersects from the left. This is just past a small woods. Turn around here and drive back 0.3 mile to the pedestrian crossing. Park on the side of the road, leave your car, and walk 160 yards along the path to your right, which leads to some artillery in an open field. When you reach the guns, stop, face left, and look in the direction they are pointed.

Stop 27, Position A—The Right Flank Artillery

Had you not turned around but continued driving on Carter's Mill Road, in 1.2 mile you would have intersected with the Long Bridge Road. The Long Bridge Road goes to the intersection at Glendale, where it connects with Charles City Road and Willis Church Road. The latter road is how you initially drove south to the Confederate position in front of Malvern Hill. Confederate forces moving through the Glendale intersection now had two routes that would lead them to the battlefield—Willis Church Road, incorrectly marked on their maps as Quaker Road, and Long Bridge Road to Carter's Mill Road.

Directly in front of you is the center of the Union position. The right of the Union position, which you could see from Stop 26, Position B, was to the left of the road that goes over the hill. Along the line of artillery in the Union center the defensive position went to your right, to the vicinity of the Crew House. The woods in front of you were smaller in 1862. Today they prevent you from seeing the Crew House. You are in the location of the planned right "grand battery" that, with the one on the left, was to neutralize the Union artillery prior to the attack by *Lee*'s infantry. The range from this position to the center of the Union line is one thousand yards. To the left of the Union line the range is eight hundred yards.

The best description of how the ground in front of you looked in 1862 is in Brigadier General *Wright*'s report.

Report of Brig. Gen. *Ambrose R. Wright*, CSA, Commanding *Wright*'s Brigade, *Huger*'s Division, Army of Northern Virginia

Having reached this position, we were enabled to get a very complete view of McClellan's army. Immediately in our front and extending 1 mile stretched a field, at the farther extremity of which was situated the dwelling and farm buildings of Mr. Crew, formerly Dr. Mettert. In front and to our left the land rose gently from the edge of the woods to the farmyard, when it became high and rolling. Upon the right the field was broken by a series of ridges and valleys, which ran out at right angles to a line drawn from our posi-

The Union line on Malvern Hill as seen from the Confederate right (Stop 27A and B). The West House is to the left. The Crew House is behind the trees to the right.

tion to that of the enemy, and all of which terminated upon our extreme right in a precipitous bluff, which dropped suddenly down upon a low, flat meadow, covered with wheat and intersected with a number of ditches, which ran from the bluff across the meadow to a swamp or dense woods about 500 yards farther to our right. This low, flat meadow stretched up to, and swinging around, Crew's house, extended as far as Turkey Bend, on James River. The enemy had drawn up his artillery, as well as could be ascertained about fifty pieces, in a crescent-shaped line, the convex line being next to our position, with its right, on our left, resting upon a road [Carter's Mill Road] which passed 300 yards to the left of Crew's house, the left of their advanced line of batteries resting upon the high bluff which overlooked the meadow to the right, our right, and rear of Crew's house. Their infantry, a little in rear of the artillery and protected by the crest of the ridge upon which the batteries were placed, extended from the woods on our left along the crest of the hill and through a lane in the meadow on our right to the dense woods there. In rear of this and beyond a narrow ravine, the sides of which were covered with timber and which ran parallel to their line of battle and but a few rods in the rear of Crew's house, was another line of infantry, its right resting upon a heavy, dense woods, which covered the Malvern Hill farm on the east. The left of this line rested upon the precipitous bluff which overhung the low meadow on the west of the farm. At this point the high bluff stretched out to the west for 200 yards in a long ridge or ledge, nearly separating the meadow from the low lands of the river, upon the extreme western terminus of which was planted a battery of heavy guns. This latter battery commanded the whole meadow in front of it, and by a direct fire was able to dispute the maneuvering of troops over any portion of the meadow. Just behind the ravine which ran in rear of Crew's house and under cover of the timber was planted a heavy battery in a small redoubt, whose fire swept across the meadow. These two batteries completely controlled the meadow from one extremity of it to the other and effectually prevented the movement of troops in large masses upon it. The infantry force of the enemy I estimated at least 25,000 or 30,000 from what I saw. Large numbers, as I ascertained afterward, were posted in the woods on our extreme right and left, and the line of ditches across the meadow were lined with sharpshooters. [*OR* 11, pt. 2, pp. 811–12.]

Where you are the Confederates deployed four artillery batteries, at the maximum twenty guns. They were Captain *Carey F. Grimes*'s Portsmouth (Va.) Battery, Captain *M. N. Moorman*'s Lynchburg (Va.) Battery, Captain *William J. Pegram*'s Purcell (Va.) Battery, and Captain *Greenlee Davidson*'s Letcher (Va.) Battery. The first two batteries were from *Huger*'s Division, and the last two came from

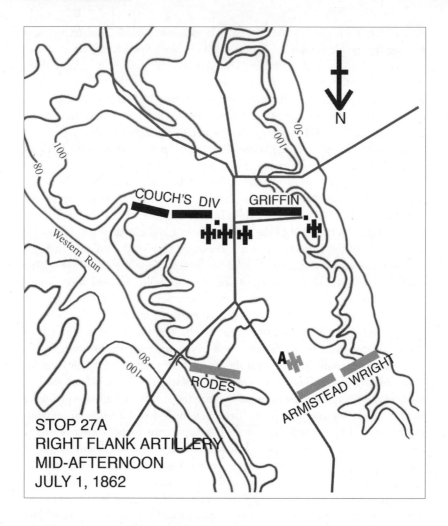

STOP 27A
RIGHT FLANK ARTILLERY
MID-AFTERNOON
JULY 1, 1862

A. P. Hill's Division. This deployment, just as on the left flank, was far short of the number of guns envisioned in the plan. Additional batteries, to include fourteen batteries of the artillery reserve, were potentially available for commitment to the fight. Again the problem of command and control and overcrowded roads prevented the guns from being ordered forward. The report of Captain *Grimes* illustrated the fight as seen at the battery level.

Report of Capt. *Carey F. Grimes*, CSA, Commanding Portsmouth (Va.) Battery, *Huger*'s Division, Army of Northern Virginia

On [July 1] I was on the Charles City road with General *Mahone*'s brigade, and was ordered back to Darbytown road to report to Brigadier-General *Armistead*, which I immediately did. When I arrived at the position and reported General *Armistead* told me that a captain had just reported his battery to him for duty, and directed me report to the first general I saw, and General *Wright* being the first, I reported to him, and while talking with General *Wright* General *Armistead*'s aide came up, stating that General *Armistead* had become disgusted with the captain that had reported his battery to him and had driven him with his battery from the field, and that he wished to see General *Wright*. General *Wright* asked me to ride with him, which I did. When we found General *Armistead* he told General *Wright* that the captain alluded to above had formed so many excuses about getting his battery on the field that he had driven him from the field, and that he wanted General *Wright* to send a battery that was willing to go in and engage the enemy. General *Wright* told him he had one, naming mine. General *Armistead* asked me if I could carry my battery on the hill. I told him if any battery in the world could go mine could. He directed General *Wright* to show me the position to take, which he did. I found the enemy with their batteries planted and their infantry drawn up in line of battle at about 1,200 yards distant. I then went to the rear for my battery and carried it on the field. As soon as the battery entered the field the enemy opened fire on it, killing 1 man and wounding 3 and killing 1 horse and wounding 2 before I fired a gun. I unlimbered and commenced firing as soon as possible and with telling effect on the enemy.

I remained on the field about two hours. Lost 3 men killed outright and 8 wounded; 2 of them have since died. I lost 10 public horses killed and 7 wounded; 1 of them has since died. My own private horse was killed; also my first lieutenant's horse.

My officers behaved very well, but feel it to be my duty to speak more particularly of First Lieut. *John H. Thompson*, who remained on the field with me until the last gun was taken off. I had so many horses killed and wounded that it took three trips to get my guns all off. [*OR* 11, pt. 2, p. 802.]

Captain *Grimes*'s battery was the first one to occupy this position. The best overall description of the artillery action here is again from Brigadier General *Wright*.

Report of Brig. Gen. *Ambrose R. Wright*, CSA (Continued)

. . . General *Armistead*, being the senior officer present, directed me to bring up *Grimes'* battery and place it in position on the crest of the ridge in front of our position. *Grimes'* battery was moved up, but the distance being so great only two pieces of his battery (rifles) were put in battery. As soon as *Grimes'* guns opened the enemy began a fierce cannonading along their whole line, concentrating their fire upon *Grimes'* two pieces.

Returning down the hill after conducting *Grimes* to his position I met General *Armistead*'s and my own brigade advancing toward the open field, in the far edge of which the enemy was posted. Having received no order for this advance of my brigade, and being convinced the movement was not a judicious one, I ordered my brigade to halt just before emerging from the woods and fall upon the ground, as the enemy's shells were falling in a pitiless storm all around us. Just as I got my men quiet I was officially notified that General *Armistead* had ordered the advance, and I moved my brigade on. Emerging from the woods we passed into the open field, set at this point with clover, and continuing the ascent some 50 or 60 yards we reached the summit of the hill, where we found the fire from the enemy's guns so incessant and well directed that I deemed it prudent to halt and make my men lie down in the high clover. Meanwhile *Grimes'* guns had been silenced by the loss of his horses and men and he was forced to retire, leaving one of his pieces.

I immediately ordered my brigade to fall back and seek cover under the woods in the ravine and reported to General *Armistead* what I had done. In this ill-timed advance my loss was very severe. Part of my brigade—the Fourth Georgia and a small portion of the Twenty-second Georgia, under Major [*Joseph*] *Wasden*, and a few of the Third Georgia, under Capt. (Acting Lieut. Col.) *R. B. Nisbet*—had advanced on the extreme right so far as to pass over the crest of the ridge and were lying in a hollow about 200 yards in advance of the line of woods. These were permitted to remain, as they were comparatively secure from the effects of the enemy's shell.

General *Armistead* directing, I ordered up another battery [*Moorman's*] and got it in position a little under the crest of the hill in the clover field and opened upon the enemy. The superior number and metal of the enemy's guns, in addition to his strong position, gave him the decided advantage of us, and very soon this battery was forced to retire.

Meanwhile Captain *Pegram's* battery was ordered up, and, taking position 200 yards to the left of *Moorman*, opened a well-directed fire upon the enemy, which told with fearful effect upon them. But this chivalric commander, by the retiring of *Moorman's* battery, was left alone to contend with the whole force of the enemy's artillery. Manfully these gallant men maintained the unequal conflict until their severe losses disabled them from using but a single piece; even then, with one single piece, they firmly held their ground and continued to pour a deadly fire upon the enemy's line until, seeing the utter hopelessness of the contest, I ordered them to cease firing until I could get more guns in action.

It was now 3 p.m. We had been fighting since 11.30 a.m., and still the enemy continued to pour volley after volley upon us from their whole line. Another battery [*Davidson*'s] was soon ordered up, and again the gallant *Pegram* opened with his single gun, himself assisting to work it. Still the superior number and caliber of the enemy's guns enabled him to pour a continuous and galling fire upon our artillerists and keep the skirt of woods in which my men lay wrapt in a sheet of flame and hail from their immense shells. [*OR* 11, pt. 2, p. 812–13.]

An excellent account of the intensity of the fighting by Captain *Pegram*'s Purcell Battery appears in the 1893 *Southern Historical Society Papers*, published in Richmond, Virginia:

At three o'clock on Tuesday, our forces having come up with the enemy, the Purcell battery was ordered to engage a battery of the enemy half a mile distant across a field. This proved, by all odds, the fiercest fight our men had been engaged in. Two [Union] batteries opened on them at once, and one of them was so near that our men could see the Yankees loading their pieces. In the course of half an hour we silenced one of enemy's batteries, but with fearful loss on our side. Two men had been killed at the guns. Lieutenant *Fitzhugh*, who had been wounded at Mechanicsville, had his leg so mangled early in the engagement that it had to be amputated on the spot. Lieutenant *McGraw* had two of his ribs broken, and fifteen privates were wounded, some of them severely, and many of them several times. Several of the men who had been [hit] three times stuck to their post and served their gun to the last. Captain *Pegram*'s courage and gallantry showed pre-eminent where all were brave. He went from gun to gun as long as they could be fired, cheered the remnants of his men, and assisted them in loading . . . . every gun of the battery but one had been disabled, twenty men had been cut down and twenty horses killed, when an order was received for the battery to retire. [*Southern Historical Society Papers* 21 (Jan.–Dec. 1893): 365]

Continue walking along the path for twenty yards, then stop. You should be looking toward the Union position on Malvern Hill.

Position B—The Confederate Right Flank

Prior to the emplacement of the artillery on the right and left flank *Lee*'s chief of staff, Colonel *Robert H. Chilton*, sent an order to various commanders. The order stated:

Batteries have been established to rake the enemy's lines. If it is broken, as is probable, *Armistead*, who can witness the effect of the fire, has been ordered to charge with a yell. Do the same.

By order of General *Lee:*

R. H. Chilton,
Assistant Adjutant-General

[*OR* 11, pt. 2, p. 677.]

This poorly worded order had two basic flaws. First it was sent even before the attempt was made to establish the two large battery positions on the left and right of the Confederate line. Second, the order was written at 1:00 P.M. but the time was not indicated. Therefore, a commander receiving the order late in the afternoon would not know that it might have been overcome by events. This order and a series of circumstances would eventually lead the Confederate infantry to conduct a frontal attack against the Union defenses. Once this series of events began, *Lee* lost the ability to decide when and where to attack.

There was a skirmish line that ran in front of and across the Union defensive position. This skirmish line was the highly trained and very accurate First U.S. Sharpshooters, commanded by Colonel Hiram Berdan. On this side of the field the Sharpshooters had aggressively pushed forward their line and were firing upon the Confederate cannoneers. To protect the artillery *Armistead*, whose brigade was in position three hundred yards behind you, sent forward units to drive back the Sharpshooters.

Report of Brig. Gen. *Lewis A. Armistead*, CSA, Commanding *Armistead*'s Brigade, *Huger*'s Division, Army of Northern Virginia

. . . the enemy approached with a heavy body of skirmishers. I ordered the Thirty-eighth, Fourteenth, and Fifty-third Virginia Regiments, of my

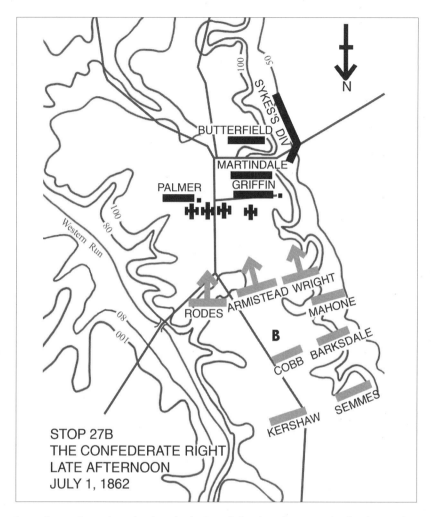

STOP 27B
THE CONFEDERATE RIGHT
LATE AFTERNOON
JULY 1, 1862

brigade, to drive them back, which they did in handsome style. In their ardor they went too far, but fortunately gained some protection by a wave of the ground between our position and that of the enemy. I was thinking of the best way to withdraw them and of the practicability of charging the enemy's battery, but another view of the ground and the distance, three-fourths of a mile, determined me in the opinion that it was folly to attempt it, unless there could be a simultaneous charge made on the right and left.

About this time, somewhere between 4 and 5 p.m., General *Magruder* came to where I was, assumed command, and gave orders for a charge, my three regiments being still in advance of Generals *Mahone*'s and *Wright*'s brigades, which came up immediately, upon my right; following my three regiments came General *Cobbs*' brigade, and soon after the Ninth and Fifty-seventh Virginia, of my brigade. [*OR* 11, pt. 2, p. 819.]

Magruder's arrival on the field had been delayed by the march of his command on the wrong road. Earlier in the day he had been ordered to march down Quaker Road. The intent was for him to march on Willis Church Road, which was mislabeled as Quaker Road on maps. Using local guides who knew of Willis Church Road, but also of another road called Quaker Road, *Magruder* initially march his command at an angle away from the battlefield. Discovering his mistake he turned his column around, retraced his movement, and, picking up Carter's Mill Road, had his forces approach the battlefield on this road. After directing his units to the correct road, *Magruder* rode ahead and found *Armistead* and other brigades of *Huger*'s Division. As *Huger* was not present *Magruder* assumed command of all units on the Confederate right.

At this point events began to spiral out of control. Upon arriving on the field, *Magruder* sent a member of his staff to *Lee* to report his arrival and location and the successful forward move of *Armistead*'s regiments. At about the same time *Lee* received an erroneous report that part of the Union line was falling back. *Lee* then sent word to *Magruder* to attack. At about the same time *Magruder* also received the earlier written order signed by *Chilton*. Not realizing that *Lee*'s verbal order was probably discretionary, and believing he had been ordered twice to attack, *Magruder* sent the Confederate brigades on the right toward the Union defenses. Before it was over, nine attacking brigades would pass through and to the left and right of where you are.

Armistead's, *Wright*'s, and *Mahone*'s Brigades made the first attack on the right. *Armistead*'s Brigade passed through the location where you are. To his right was *Wright*'s Brigade and farther to the right was *Mahone*'s Brigade. *Wright*'s report typifies the action of all three of these attacking brigades.

Report of Brig. Gen. *Ambrose R. Wright*, CSA (Continued)

Major-General *Magruder* came on the field about 4 o'clock, and, assuming command, directed the future movements of my brigade. I was ordered by him to advance, supported by Brigadier-General *Mahone*'s brigade, upon the enemy's [left], and charge upon the enemy's batteries. This movement was to be simultaneous with an advance upon the enemy's [right] and center. I immediately took my brigade around by a flank movement to the right, and by filing to the left under the edge of the bluff got it in line in the hollow already occupied by the Fourth Georgia and portions of the Twenty-second and Third Georgia. Here I formed my line, the Fourth Georgia upon the right, the First Louisiana and a few of the Twenty-second Georgia, under Major *Wasden*, in the center, and the Third Georgia on the left. I had lost a few men wounded getting into this position, and the enemy, detecting the movement, opened a furious fire upon us, but my gallant soldiers lay quietly upon their faces, ready and eager for the order to advance.

At 4.45 o'clock I received an order from General *Magruder*, through [Major] *Henry Bryan*, one of his staff, to advance immediately and charge the enemy's batteries. No other troops had yet come upon the field. I ordered my men forward, and springing before them led my brigade, less than 1,000 men, against a force I knew to be superior. Onward we pressed, warmly and strongly supported by General *Mahone*'s brigade, under a murderous fire of shot, shell, canister, and musketry. At every step my brave men fell around me, but the survivors pressed on until we had reached a hollow about 300 yards from the enemy's batteries on the right. Here I perceived that a strong force of infantry had been sent forward on our left by the enemy with a view of flanking and cutting us off from our support, now more than 1,000 yards in our rear. I immediately threw the left of the Third Georgia Regiment a little back along the upper margin of the hollow, and suddenly changing [the] front of this regiment, poured a galling fire upon the enemy, which he returned with spirit, aided by a fearful direct and cross-fire from his batteries. Here the contest raged with varying success for more than three-quarters of an hour; finally the line of the enemy was broken and he gave way in great disorder.

In the mean time my front, supported by General *Mahone*, had been subjected to a heavy fire of artillery and musketry and had begun to waver, and I feared would be compelled to fall back. Just at this moment firing was heard far away on our left, and soon we saw our columns advancing upon the enemy's center. This diverted a portion of the enemy's fire from us, and I succeeded in keeping my men steady. We had now approached to within a few hundred yards of the enemy's advanced batteries, and again I gave the order to charge, which was obeyed with promptness and alacrity. We rushed forward up the side of the hill, under the brow of which we had been for some time halted, and dashing over the hill reached another hollow or ravine immediately in front of and, as it were, under the enemy's guns. This ravine was occupied by a line of Yankee infantry, posted there to protect their batteries. Upon this we rushed with such impetuosity that the enemy broke in great disorder and fled.

During this little engagement the enemy's batteries in front of us, and to which we had approached within a few rods, were moved off around and behind the barn and stables which stood [on] the side of the hill, and were again put in position upon the crest of the hill just in front of Crew's house. But for our encountering the infantry of the enemy in the ravine we should have certainly captured this battery, but the delay occasioned by the fight there enabled them to move off their guns to a safer and better position. The firing had now become general along the left and center of our line, and night setting in, it was difficult to distinguish friend from foe.

Several of my command were killed by our own friends [elements of *Armistead*'s or *Cobb*'s brigades], who had come up on our immediate left, and who commenced firing long before they came within range of the enemy. This firing upon us from our friends, together with the increasing darkness, made our position peculiarly hazardous; but I determined to maintain it at all hazards as long as a man should be left to fire a gun. The fire was terrific now beyond anything I had ever witnessed—indeed, the hideous shrieking of shells through the dusky gloom of closing night, the whizzing of bullets, the loud and incessant roll of artillery and small-arms, were enough to make the stoutest heart quail. Still my shattered little command, now reduced to less than 300, with about an equal number of General *Mahone*'s brigade, held our position under the very muzzles of the enemy's guns, and poured volley after volley with murderous precision into their serried ranks.

Night had now thrown her black pall over the entire field, and the firing ceased except from a few of the enemy's guns, which continued at intervals to throw shell and grape around the entire circuit of the field. Our forces had all retired and left us, *Mahone* and myself, alone with our little band to dispute the possession of the field. Upon consultation we determined to remain where we were, now within 100 yards of the enemy's batteries, and if any of the foe should be left when morning dawned to give him battle again. We had lost too many valuable lives to give up the decided advantage, which we had won from the enemy.

Just at this time a portion of Colonel *Ramseur*'s North Carolina regiment, having got lost upon the field, was hailed by me and ordered to fall in with my brigade. A strong picket was advanced all around our isolated position, and the wearied, hungry soldiers threw themselves upon the earth to snatch a few hours rest. Detachments were ordered to search for water and administer to our poor wounded men, whose piercing cries rent the air in every direction. Soon the enemy were seen with lanterns busily engaged in moving their killed and wounded, and friend and foe freely mingled on that gloomy night in administering to the wants of wounded and dying comrades.

My loss in this engagement was very severe, amounting to 55 killed, 243 wounded, and 64 missing. [*OR* 11, pt. 2, pp. 814–15.]

The next brigade to pass through this location was Brigadier General *Howell Cobb*'s. *Cobb* was responding to a call from *Armistead* for support. *Cobb* reported that he moved forward with 1,500 soldiers, of which 500 became casualties. [*OR* 11, pt. 2, p. 750.] Colonel *William Barksdale* reported that his brigade, attacking to the right of *Cobb*'s also, lost one-third of his force. [*OR* 11, pt. 2, p. 751.]

As the late afternoon moved on to early evening Major General *Lafayette McLaws*'s two brigade division approached the battle along the Carpenter's Mill Road. *McLaws* was ordered to move into a position 0.5 mile behind you and await orders.

Report of Maj. Gen. *Lafayette McLaws*, CSA, Commanding *McLaws*'s Division, Army of Northern Virginia

About 6 [P.M. *Kershaw* and *Semmes*] were ordered to the front, advancing one [brigade] on the right flank of the field and the other [brigade] on the left, separated 400 or 500 yards, and entirely out of sight of each other. They were carried to the front, from which they were to advance, by a staff officer of General *Magruder*, and General *Kershaw*'s brigade was assisted as much as possible after their arrival by Major *McIntosh*, of my staff, in taking position.

Brigadier-General *Semmes*, advancing on the right, owing to various causes—viz: the thickness of the woods, miscarriage or misconception of orders, and the fatigue his command had undergone—carried into action but 557 men. The dead of his command, however, found in advance evidenced the gallantry of those few. His loss was: Killed, 17; wounded, 56; missing, 63. Aggregate, 136.

General *Kershaw*, going forward on the left, lost in killed, 22; wounded, 113; missing, 29. Aggregate, 164. Carried into action, 956 men. [*OR* 11, pt. 2, p. 719.]

Semmes's Brigade passed four hundred yards to the right of your location and went into the attack to support the right of the Confederate line. *Kershaw*'s Brigade passed by just on the other side of the road and actually went into the attack as part of the center part of the Confederate line.

Report of Brig. Gen. *Joseph B. Kershaw,* CSA Commanding *Kershaw's* Brigade, *McLaws's* Division, Army of Northern Virginia

I was directed by an officer of Major-General *Magruder's* staff to advance and attack the enemy's battery. Having no specific instructions and no knowledge of the ground or position of the enemy: I led the brigade in line of battle through a wood for half a mile toward the right of the enemy's line of fire, exposed all the while to a front and flank fire of artillery, which could not be avoided. During this march I passed three lines of troops who had preceded me in the attack. Arriving immediately in front of that portion of the enemy where I determined to assail him, I was indebted to [Captain *Clemons* assistance in] finding my way to a ravine which led immediately up to the plateau upon which the enemy was formed. Availing myself of this shelter, I led my command up to the Willis Church road [and Carter's Mill Road intersection]. Here the enemy occupied the open field in two lines in force in my front, forming an obtuse angle, facing toward the road in such a manner as to flank any force which might ascend the brow of the hill in my front. Between these two lines of the enemy at the point of intersection a battery of artillery was placed, pouring over our heads a crushing shower of grape and canister, while the infantry lines blazed with a constant stream of fire. Still farther to my right the artillery on the hill near the orchard enfiladed my line, and their infantry, in Crew's farm, were engaged with some of our forces.

In the position we occupied a fence and thick hedge in front of the road formed a considerable obstacle to an advance along the center of my line, while the rising ground in front screened the enemy from view, except on my extreme right and left. The Second Regiment, which extended to near the parsonage, having open ground in front, engaged the left line of the enemy with some effect; but the rest of the command were powerless to accomplish anything in their then position, and I was satisfied that any farther advance at that point would insure the destruction of my command unless some change was made in the enemy's position. The nature of the ground affording considerable protection to the men, I determined to hold them there, in the hope that some diversion by an attack either on the right or left might be created in our favor.

After some time a galling fire was opened from our rear, killing and wounding the men and producing a general feeling of uneasiness in the whole command. Captain *Holmes,* assistant adjutant-general, and Lieutenant *Dwight,* acting assistant inspector-general, of my staff, went back in person to arrest the fire. Major *Rutherford,* of the Third Regiment, attempted to do the same, and Corpl. *T. Whither Blakely* is especially commended by Colonel *Nance* for having volunteered for the same dangerous duty. Finding that the fire still continued for some time, doing us more damage than that of the enemy, I ordered the command to retire by the route we came to the next road in our rear.

At this point I found Major *Galliard*, commanding, reforming the Second Regiment. With this regiment I retired to the next road in our rear, where I again halted, supposing that the other regiments would be found there, but owing to the intricacies of the wood and the approaching darkness the commanding officers conducted their regiments severally to the field whence we entered the fight.

While collecting on the flag of the Second Regiment all the men of the brigade who came by, General *Ewell* rode up and desired me to advance my command to support a brigade he was about to lead into action in Crew's field. Calling attention to the small number of men with me and my desire to collect the remainder of the brigade, I indicated my unwillingness to do so on account of the inefficiency of any support I could render, but as he became very urgent I yielded, and led the Second Regiment, under command of Major *Galliard*, to the point indicated. Soon General *Ewell*'s forces appeared, and he led two regiments in beautiful order to the attack under a terrible fire of artillery and infantry. While we were at this point, Sergeant *Harley*, color-bearer of the Second Regiment, exposed himself with gallantry worthy of especial mention in his efforts to encourage and animate the men around him, and was wounded by a shell while thus engaged.

Several regiments having arrived and taken position in our rear in support of General *Ewell*'s advance, and the infantry fire having materially diminished, I brought off the Second Regiment about 9 p.m., and reformed the brigade in the field from which we had advanced. [*OR* 11, pt. 2, pp. 728–29.]

Return to your car for the drive to Stop 28. Drive 0.2 mile to the intersection with Willis Church Road and turn left. Drive 0.1 mile to the Parsonage parking lot. This is the grass and gravel parking lot where you parked for Stops 26A and 26B. Park, get out of your car, and look across the open field toward the Union defensive position on Malvern Hill.

Stop 28—The Confederate Center

As the road to your right continues on in a southerly direction it goes through the Union position. The house to the left of the road is the West house, which you saw from Stop 26, Position B. The Crew house is located in the trees in front of you. Those trees were not so numerous in 1862 and the house could be seen from here. Stop 26,

Position B, is located 150 yards to your left. Directly south and 700 yards in front of you is artillery marking some of the Union battery positions. In 1862, from this location, you would have seen aimed in your direction a line of artillery that began at the Crew house and went to the left, past where the guns are today, to a position across the road to this side of the West house. This artillery line was 800 yards long and consisted initially of twenty-five guns from six batteries. A solid line of infantry regiments supported the artillery batteries. A skirmish line was in place halfway from where you are to the defensive line.

D. H. Hill's Division was initially deployed about 0.5 mile behind you. Hill had also received the 1:00 P.M. order from Chilton. When he heard the firing and the rebel yell, not from Armistead's Brigade but Wright's, he ordered his division forward.

Report of Maj. Gen. *Daniel H. Hill*, CSA, Commanding *Hill's* Division, *Jackson's* Command, Army of Northern Virginia

By the order of Major-General *Jackson* the division was halted in the woods and an examination made of the ground. The Yankees were found to be strongly posted on a commanding hill, all the approaches to which could be swept by his artillery, and were guarded by swarms of infantry securely sheltered by fences, ditches, and ravines. Tier after tier of batteries were grimly visible on the plateau, rising in the form of an amphitheater. One flank was protected by [Western Run] and the other by gunboats. We could only reach the first line of batteries by traversing an open space of from 300 to 400 yards, exposed to a murderous fire of grape and canister from the artillery and musketry from the infantry. If that first line were carried, another and another still more difficult remained in the rear. I had expressed my disapprobation of a farther pursuit of the Yankees to the commanding general and to Major-Generals *Jackson* and *Longstreet* even before I knew of the strength of their position. An examination now satisfied me that an attack could not but be hazardous to our arms.

About 2 o'clock, I think, I received a note from General *Jackson*, inclosing one from Col. *R. H. Chilton*: chief of General *Lee's* staff, saying that positions were selected from which our artillery could silence the Yankee artillery, and as soon as that was done Brigadier-General *Armistead* would advance with a shout and carry the battery immediately in his front. This shout was to be the signal for a general advance, and all the troops were then to rush forward with fixed bayonets. I sent for all my brigade commanders and showed them the note. Brigadier-General *Rodes* being absent sick, the gallant *Gordon* was put in command of his brigade. That accomplished gentleman and soldier Col. *C. C. Tew*, Second North Carolina Regiment, took command of *Anderson*'s brigade. *Garland, Ripley,* and *Colquitt,* and these two colonels were present at the interview. I wrote to General *Jackson* that the firing from our batteries was of the most farcical character. He repeated the order for a general advance at the signal of the shouting from General *Armistead.* As well as I could learn the position of our troops the division of Brigadier-General *Whiting* was on my left: Major-Generals *Magruder* and *Huger* on my right, and Major-General *Holmes* [on the road along the James River and on the west flank of the Union position].

While conversing with my brigade commanders shouting was heard on our right, followed by the roar of musketry. We all agreed that this was the signal agreed upon, and I ordered my division to advance. This, as near as I could judge, was about an hour and a half before sundown. The division fought heroically and well, but fought in vain. *Garland,* in my immediate front, showed all his wonted courage and enthusiasm, but he needed and asked for re-enforcements. I sent Lieutenant-Colonel *Newton,* Sixth Georgia, to his support, and observing a brigade by a fence in our rear, I galloped back to it and found it to be that of Brigadier-General *Toombs.* I ordered it forward to support *Garland* and accompanied it. The brigade advanced handsomely to the brow of the hill, but soon retreated in disorder. *Gordon,* commanding *Rodes'* brigade, pushed gallantly forward and gained considerable ground, but was forced back. The gallant and accomplished *Meares,* Third North Carolina Regiment, *Ripley*'s brigade, had fallen at the head of his regiment, and that brigade was streaming to the rear. *Colquitt*'s and *Anderson*'s brigades had also fallen back. *Ransom*'s brigade had come up to my support from Major-General *Huger.* A portion of it came, but without it's Brigadier. It moved too far to the left and became mixed up with the mass of troops near the parsonage on the [Willis Church Road], suffering heavily and effecting little. Brigadier-General *Winder* was sent up by Major-General *Jackson,* but he came too late, and also went to the same belt of woods near the parsonage, already overcrowded with troops. Finally Major-General *Ewell* came up, but it was after dark and nothing could be accomplished. I advised him to hold the ground he had gained and not to attempt a forward movement.

The battle of Malvern Hill might have been a complete and glorious success had not our artillery and infantry been fought in detail. My division batteries, having been three times engaged, had exhausted all their ammunition and had been sent back for a fresh supply. If I had had them with me with a good supply of ammunition I feel confident that we could have beaten the force immediately in front of us. Again, the want of concert with the infantry divisions was most painful. [*OR* 11, pt. 2, pp. 627–29.]

When *Hill*'s Division advanced he had three brigades in the first line with two brigades in the supporting second line. *Rodes*'s Brigade was on the right, *G. B. Anderson*'s Brigade was in the center, and *Ripley*'s Brigade was on the left. *Garland*'s and *Colquitt*'s Brigades were in the supporting line. During the attack *Garland* would eventually place his brigade to the right of *Rodes*'s Brigade. When you were at Stop 26, Position B, you were in the location through which the left of *G. B. Anderson*'s Brigade and the right of *Ripley*'s Brigade attacked. You are now in the location through which *Rodes*'s Brigade, commanded by Colonel *John B. Gordon*, and the right of *Anderson*'s Brigade attacked.

Report of Col. *John B. Gordon*, CSA, Commanding *Rodes*'s Brigade, *D. H. Hill*'s Division, *Jackson*'s Command, Army of Northern Virginia

I formed the brigade in line of battle on the right of the division, and threw out a portion of the Third Alabama as skirmishers, covering my right flank. Remaining in this position for two hours, I received an order to move immediately forward. Ordering the Third Alabama to call in its skirmishers, and by a rapid forward movement to join the brigade, I moved on. The enemy's batteries were distant about 1 mile and the ground intervening exceedingly rough. Passing across an open meadow and up a precipitous hill through dense woods, one of the regiments of General *Anderson*'s brigade [Colonel *Tew* now commanding] reported to me as having lost its brigade. Forming it upon the left of this brigade, I moved forward, halting when near the open field in which the enemy had stationed his batteries. I here sent forward Capt. *H. A. Whiting*, assistant adjutant-general, to ascertain the respective positions of the Confederate and Federal batteries. Upon his report I half-wheeled the brigade to the left, and moving forward placed it under cover of a low hill, in sight of the enemy's batteries, to await orders. The Twenty-sixth Alabama and the right wing of the Fifth [on the brigade right] were suffering from the enemy's artillery fire directed at our batteries. I therefore at once moved these portions of the brigade by the left flank in rear of the Third Alabama, which I had previously brought into line. This was my position when Major-General *Hill* gave me the order to charge the batteries in our front, distant 700 or 800 yards across an open field. I ordered Capt. *H. A. Whiting* to bring the

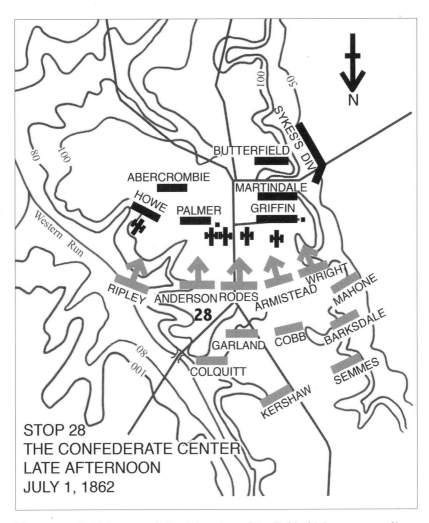

STOP 28
THE CONFEDERATE CENTER
LATE AFTERNOON
JULY 1, 1862

Twenty-sixth Alabama and the right wing of the Fifth Alabama as rapidly as possible into line. The whole ground in front of the Twenty-sixth, Fifth, and Third Alabama Regiments was swept by the fire of the artillery, which had, in rapid succession, silenced two Confederate batteries. As there was no artillery to attract the enemy's attention, his batteries from the beginning, and his infantry finally, poured a most destructive fire upon my ranks.

Never was the courage of troops more severely tried and heroically exhibited than in this charge. They moved on under this terrible fire, breaking and driving off the first line of infantry, [this is the Union skirmish line] until within a little over 200 yards of the batteries. Here the canister and musketry mowed down my already thinned ranks so rapidly that it became impossible to advance without support; and had it been possible to reach the batteries,

I have high authority to back my own judgment that it would have been at the sacrifice of the entire command. I therefore ordered the men to lie down and open fire, and immediately sent back to notify Major-General *Hill* of my position and to ask him to send up support. A brigade was sent forward, but failed to reach my line. The troops sent up from another division on the right had already fallen back, and refused to rally under the efforts made by Captain *Whiting*, assistant adjutant-general, and myself.

Nearly one-half of the brigade had been killed or wounded, leaving me about 600 men able to load and fire. With the enemy's batteries and heavy lines of infantry concentrating their fire on my ranks it was folly, without immediate and steady support, to hold the brigade longer in this position. I therefore ordered it to fall back. [*OR* 11, pt. 2, p. 634.]

The report of Major *Sands*, who commanded a regiment in the attack, gives an excellent account of the attack from the regimental level.

Report of Maj. *Robert M. Sands*, CSA, Commanding Third Alabama Infantry, *Rodes*'s Brigade, *D. H. Hill*'s Division, *Jackson*'s Command, Army of Northern Virginia

About noon on July 1, when in the neighborhood of Malvern Hill, I was ordered to take my regiment to the extreme right of our line, deploy it as skirmishers, and send out a few scouts to find out the position of the enemy in front; also to look out for the approach of friends from that direction. We remained in this position for about two hours, the enemy's shell occasionally falling in close proximity to my men. At one time a shell of very heavy caliber, evidently from the enemy's gun-boats in James River, fell and buried itself, without exploding, about 20 feet from the left of my line.

From this point I was ordered to march left obliquely until I came up to the brigade. In doing this I got under a very hot fire from a battery of the enemy in my immediate front. Here I halted, and sending forward a courier I found that if I followed the instructions I had received I would march directly on the battery, and that the brigade was near a quarter of a mile to my left. I immediately went by the left flank and joined the brigade under a heavy fire, having 2 men wounded.

After joining the brigade I was ordered to send out 50 men as sharp-shooters to annoy the enemy at a battery of field pieces about 400 yards in our front. This was done and brought us to the notice of the battery, which, opening on us with grape, canister, and shell, subjected us to a most terrific fire for some time, when the sharpshooters were called in and the command was given to charge. My regiment advanced with the brigade until it was brought to a halt and made to lie down for a few moments to protect the men from the murderous fire of the enemy. It was at this time the fighting became general, and that each man behaved and fought as though the issue of the battle depended on his own individual efforts. Men never fought more gallantly.

There were 6 men shot down while carrying the colors forward, the seventh bringing off the field after the fight a portion of the staff, the colors being literally cut to pieces, and portions of them picked up on that part of the field where the regiment fought.

My loss in this day's fight was 37 killed and 163 wounded—a total of 200 out of 354 taken into the fight. [*OR* 11, pt. 2, pp. 636–37.]

Return to your car for the drive to Stop 29. Turn left on Willis Church Road and drive for 0.1 mile to the intersection with Carter's Mill Road. Veer left and follow Carter's Mill Road for 0.1 mile, toward the higher part of the plateau. At 0.1 mile pull over to the side of the road and stop. Get out of your car and face back in the direction you just came from. There is a marker here for Berdan's Sharpshooters. Be careful of traffic.

Stop 29—The Union Skirmish Line

You are in the center of the Union skirmish line as it was deployed in mid-afternoon on Tuesday July 1, 1862. A skirmish or outpost line was normally deployed in front of a defending position to give early warning of an attack. This would slow down the attack by bringing it under fire and causing the columns to deploy, if they weren't already, and by inflicting early casualties and driving back the skirmish line of the attackers, thus minimizing the attackers' ability to gain information about the defense. Usually several companies of a regiment or regiments would be detailed to establish the skirmish line.

A special unit, the First U.S. Sharpshooters, also known as Berdan's Sharpshooters, established the skirmish line passing east to west through this position.

Colonel Hiram Berdan, a pre–Civil War inventor and well-known marksman, had recruited this regiment. To join the regiment a candidate had to pass a marksmanship test that consisted of firing ten rounds into a target ten inches in diameter at a range of two hundred yards. All ten rounds had to hit the target with an average distance of no more than five inches from the center.

Berdan's Sharpshooters were armed with the Sharps .52 caliber, breech-loading rifle. Highly trained, each sharpshooter could fire from five to seven rounds per minute, with a high percentage of hits out to a range of four hundred yards. Dressed in green uniforms, these soldiers deployed in pairs and in an extended order, with five yards interval between pairs. On the northern slope of Malvern Hill these marksmen used the concealment offered by the stacks of wheat sheaves. As you have seen, their aggressive tactics and very accurate fire caused *Armistead* to send several of his regiments forward to protect the Confederate artillery. This action helped set up the situation, in part, that caused the Confederate attack.

Berdan's Sharpshooters in action in front of the Union defenses on Malvern Hill. *Century Magazine.*

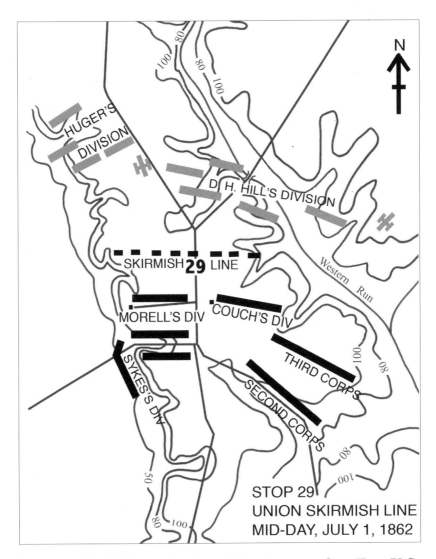

STOP 29
UNION SKIRMISH LINE
MID-DAY, JULY 1, 1862

Report of Col. Hiram Berdan, USA, Commanding First U.S. Sharpshooters, Fifth Corps, Army of the Potomac

On Tuesday morning [July 1], being unable to find General Morell, and learning that the enemy was approaching, I marched my command to the front and was about to deploy them as skirmishers, when General Porter came along, and he approving my suggestion, I posted them in front of the batteries, where they remained all day, receiving and repelling the enemy's skirmishers, and received the rebel infantry in the afternoon standing firm and firing with great rapidity and coolness until the enemy's line was within grape-range of our artillery, when they fell back [and joined] the Fourth Michigan, firing constantly. [*OR* 11, pt. 2, p. 279.]

Continue driving south on Carter's Mill Road for 0.1 mile, to the intersection with a small road to the right. Turn right on this road and drive into the parking lot. Park, get out of your car, and find a position where you can look north across the field toward the intersection of Willis Church and Carter's Mill roads.

Stop 30, Position A—The Union Defense

You are in the center of the Union defensive position. As you face north you are looking at the line of Confederate brigades that attacked this position in the afternoon of July 1. Five hundred yards directly in front of you is the intersection of Willis Church and Carter's Mill roads. This was the center of the Confederate attack. One thousand yards to your left front is the right Confederate artillery position at Stop 27 and the right of the infantry attack. Six hundred yards to your right front is Stop 26, Position B, where the left of the Confederate attack came out of the woods. Just to the right of that, one thousand yards from you, was the left Confederate artillery position.

To your left is the rebuilt Crew House. The woods north of the Crew House were not so large in 1862, and artillery and infantry near the house had a clear field of fire at the attackers. To your right and across the road is the rebuilt West House. This is the house you saw from Stop 26, Position B. The width of the defensive position facing north was 1,200 yards. Carter's Mill Road, to your right, continues on south for 0.1 mile to an intersection, where it veers to the southeast and in 1.3 miles descends from the plateau and continues on to join River Road, which parallels the James River. At the intersection where the Carter's Mill Road veers southeast, another road goes west for 0.3 mile, then descends the plateau for 0.8 mile, where it joins the River Road. Reports by Union commanders called the section of road going west from Carter's Mill Road the Richmond Road. At the intersection of Carter's Mill and Richmond Roads, a small road goes directly south for 1.0 mile to the Malvern House, which was used as a hospital during and immediately after the battle. Malvern Hill is actually two hills on a plateau. In previous times it was called Malvern Hills, but by 1862 the area was called Malvern Hill. Several of the reports by Union commanders make a distinction in the two higher points. Malvern Hill was the area behind you. The area around the Crew House was called Crew Hill. We have used the more common "Malvern Hill" to mean the plateau and both of the high points on it.

Malvern Hill was an ideal defensive position for the Union army. Western Run, whose course from northwest to southeast took it across the right front and then right flank of the position, protected the right flank of the defense to some degree. This creek and the marsh ground along its course made a flanking maneuver against the right difficult. On the left flank of the position, the plateau came to an abrupt end and fell away fifty vertical feet to an open plain. This cliff formed a natural barrier to a flanking movement on the left. On the north side of the position, where the defense was, the ground was an even slope down that provided excellent fields of fire and observation. Many of the approach roads that the Confederates used to move into position were observable by the defenders and were within artillery range. Behind the defensive line there were sufficient roads and trails to allow the lateral movement of troops and artillery and the bringing forward of reserves. It was a formidable position that presented *Lee* only two options: frontal attack or a movement far to the east to maneuver the defenders out of their position.

The Malvern House in the 1880s. *Century Magazine.*

The defense position was established on June 30 by two divisions of Brigadier General Fitz John Porter's Fifth Corps. On that day Porter's third division, McCall's, was involved in the Battle of Glendale. The defense was initially established as a right angle line with the apex at the Crew House. The left of the line ran north to south and faced the open plain west of the hill. Supporting artillery was placed on the cliff top so as to be able to fire over the heads of the defenders. The right of the line ran east from the Crew House, through the location where you are, to just on the other side of the road. Porter would initially have nine infantry brigades on the defensive line or supporting it.

In the early morning hours of July 1 Brigadier General Darius Couch's First Division from the Fourth Corps reinforced Porter and went into position on his right. In addition, by late morning the Third and Second Corps moved into position to Porter's right rear to add more protection to that flank. Before the fighting was over on July 1, Porter was reinforced with three brigades, two brigades from the Second Corps and one brigade from the Third Corps. Initially, Porter deployed eight batteries of artillery. Six batteries were in the area where you are and two batteries supported the defense facing west. Supporting this artillery were nine batteries from Hunt's artillery reserve, sixteen heavy guns from the siege train—which included 4.5-inch Rodmans and 32-pound howitzers—and Union navy gunboats on the James River.

Brigadier General Porter's report presents an overall situation and an overview of the Battle of Malvern Hill.

Report of Brig. Gen Fitz John Porter, USA, Commanding Fifth Corps, Army of the Potomac

On the 29th of June, the major-general commanding having decided to move on the following day the whole of the material of the army to a position on the James River near Turkey Island, I was directed, with Morell's and Sykes' divisions and a portion of the reserve artillery, to proceed to the vicinity of Turkey Bridge, and there select and hold a position behind which the army could be withdrawn in safety. I moved the command at sundown that evening . . . from White Oak Swamp, but, ignorant of the country, having but one guide, we were misled that night and did not succeed in reaching our destination until the following morning at 9 o'clock, where I had two hours earlier selected a position on Malvern Hill west of Turkey Bridge. This

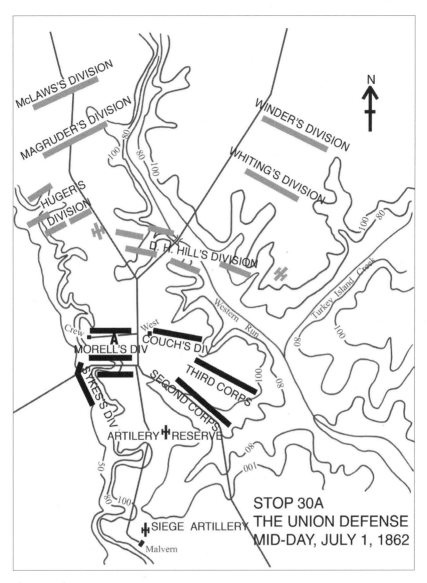

McLAWS'S DIVISION

MAGRUDER'S DIVISION

WINDER'S DIVISION

WHITING'S DIVISION

HUGER'S DIVISION

D. H. HILL'S DIVISION

Turkey Island Creek

Western Run

Crew

West

MORELL'S DIV

COUCH'S DIV

THIRD CORPS

SYKES'S DIV

SECOND CORPS

ARTILERY RESERVE

STOP 30A
THE UNION DEFENSE
MID-DAY, JULY 1, 1862

SIEGE ARTILLERY

Malvern

N

hill commanded all the roads leading from Richmond and Chickahominy
Swamp to James River, which converge at Turkey Bridge. Here as soon as
possible were posted the two divisions, thoroughly covering the River road
and the *débouchés* from the New Market, Charles City, and Williamsburg
roads. Warren's brigade, of Sykes' division, was posted in the valley of the
creek, across the River road, to prevent the left flank from being turned by an
advance from Richmond along the road. Through the command thus posted
passed in safety the supply trains of many of the divisions and the reserve

artillery of the army, the current only ceasing to flow at about 4 o'clock p.m. 30th of June.

At about this hour [4:00 P.M., June 30] the enemy began to appear and to feel our front, and about 5 o'clock showed themselves in large force, advancing upon our left flank. [This was *Holmes*'s division.] Under the cover of the woods skirting the River road the enemy planted his artillery to engage our main force on Malvern Hill, while his infantry, with some artillery, moved direct upon Colonel Warren, with whom he was soon engaged.

The enemy's demonstration soon brought upon him the concentrated fire of some thirty guns, together with the infantry fire of Colonel Warren's troops. Under these influences the force which had advanced against that part of our line incontinently retreated, leaving two guns in the hands of Colonel Warren and numerous evidences of the destructiveness of the artillery which crowned the crest of Malvern Hill.

In this connection should be mentioned with due acknowledgment the help of the gunboats, whose well-directed fire of heavy shells gave the very greatest support, moral and physical . . . . This is known as the battle of Turkey Bridge. [*OR* 11, pt. 2, pp. 227–28.]

This engagement on June 30 was a poorly executed attack carried out by part of Major General *Theophilus Holmes*'s division. *Holmes*'s division was a continuation of the right flank of *Longstreet*'s and *A. P. Hill*'s Divisions that were involved in the Battle of Glendale on June 30. *Lee* had ordered *Holmes* to make an attack toward Malvern Hill to cut the Union route of retreat. During the July 1 attacks against Malvern Hill *Lee* did not use *Holmes*'s Division. The repulse of *Holmes*'s Division on June 30 created the opportunity for a Union counterattack by the two divisions of the Fourth Corps. Supported by the long-range artillery on the western edge of Malvern Hill, these two divisions could have inflicted severe damage on *Holmes*. However, McClellan was not present on the battlefield on this day and another opportunity slipped away.

Report of Brig. Gen. Fitz John Porter, USA (Continued)

While the battle [of Turkey Bridge] was taking place, McCall's division posted [at Glendale] to cover the withdrawal of our trains, was attacked by the enemy in immense force. He maintained his place till night-fall, when the surviving portion of his command rejoined the corps, coming in under the command of Brigadier-General Seymour, the only remaining general officer on duty. I have here to regret the loss of Brigadier-General McCall, commanding division, taken prisoner, and of the services of Brigadier-General Meade, severely wounded, and of many other valuable field and line officers, as well as many brave men.

This action [the Battle of Glendale on June 30] lasted from about 4 p.m. till after dark, during which period the remainder of the trains of the whole army had successfully passed the contested point and reached a place of safety within the interior lines of the army.

While the battle of Turkey Bridge was taking place the necessary arrangements were being made to resist the enemy coming from the direction of [Glendale], who, as a natural consequence of previous operations, might be expected to launch on the following day his whole power against this force, with the hope of annihilating it and destroying the Army of the Potomac.

The position in which we were thrown had certain elements of great strength, and was the best adapted for a battle-field of any with which we have so far been favored. All elevated plateau covered the converging roads and was fronted to a certain extent with defensible ravines and low grounds, over which our artillery had excellent play. On the night of the battle of Turkey Bridge the division of General Morell was placed on the right of the line [facing north between the Crew House and the road to your right], with a portion of his division artillery and of Hunt's reserve artillery; the division of General Sykes on the left, [from the Crew House south and facing west] with the same support, and the reserve artillery, under Colonel Hunt, advantageously posted for general efficiency, crowning the crest of Malvern Hill. In this position the corps lay on its arms during the night and waited the attack, which took place at about 4 in the afternoon of the 1st of July.

Couch's division, which had been sent [to Malvern Hill] on the night of the 30th of June remained in support of our immediate right, and, like our own force, lay on its arms through the intermediate time.

On the following morning, July 1, the lines were visited and rectified by the major-general commanding, and Generals Heintzelman and Sumner, who had retired from White Oak Swamp within our lines during the night, took position on the right of Couch, prepared to resist attack or give support to the left and center, as circumstances should require. Our position was strengthened by the arrival of heavy artillery under Colonel Tyler, whose siege guns were posted so as to control the River road and sweep our left flank, and by firing over the heads of our own men to reach the enemy, advancing on the [Carter's Mill Road].

At about 1 o'clock p.m. the enemy commenced with his artillery and skirmishers, feeling along our whole front, and kept up a desultory firing till about 4 with but little effect.

The same ominous silence which had preceded the attack in force at Gaines' Mill now intervened, lasting till about 6 o'clock, at which time the enemy opened upon as suddenly with the full force of his artillery, and at once began to push forward his columns of infantry to the attack of our positions. Regiment after regiment, and sometimes whole brigades, were thrown against our batteries, but our infantry withheld their fire till they were within short distance, artillery mowing them down with canister, dispersed the columns in every case, and in some instances followed the retiring mass, driving them with the bayonet, capturing prisoners, and also flags and other trophies, some of which have been forwarded to your headquarters.

This contest was maintained by Morell's and Couch's divisions, the former supported by Sykes, who had thrown some of his regiments to the front and dispersed a large column attempting to take us in flank. A portion of the reserve artillery was also here in action. While the battle was proceeding, seeing that the enemy was pressing our men and accumulating his masses to pour fresh troops upon them, I called for aid from General Sumner, which call was promptly responded to by the arrival of General Meagher, with his brigade, followed by that of Sickles, which General Heintzelman voluntarily and generously sent to complete the contest. These brigades I posted—Sickles on the right of Couch and Meagher on the left of Morell and in their support with instructions to push their regiments forward in echelon of about 100 paces, extending to the rear from the right or left of Couch's division, to relieve those in advance whose ammunition had been expended and to drive the enemy. These directions were promptly and successfully executed. McCall's, now Seymour's, division was held in reserve.

In the mean time Colonel Hunt hastened and brought up artillery to relieve the batteries whose ammunition had been exhausted and who had successfully borne the brunt of the engagement throughout the day. [*OR* 11, pt. 2, pp. 228–30.]

As you face north walk forward seventy yards to the artillery in front of you.

Position B—The Union Left

The infantry unit defending this side of the road was Brigadier General George Morell's First Division, Fifth Corps. You studied this division's actions at the Battle of Gaines Mill. Morell had three brigades in his division, which he placed in position so as to have an in-depth defensive position.

You are in the vicinity of the right flank of the first line. Brigadier General Charles Griffin's Second Brigade initially occupied this
line with his four regiments. In a supporting line 100 yards behind
you was Brigadier General John Martindale's First Brigade. Another
150 yards back in a reserve position just south of the Richmond Road
was Brigadier General Daniel Butterfield's Third Brigade. Before
the day was over, all three of Morell's brigades would be involved in
the fighting.

Report of Brig. Gen. George W. Morell, USA, Commanding First Division, Fifth Corps, Army of the Potomac

Near a mile north from Malvern house is a large cultivated field [in front
of you], stretching about three-fourths of a mile from south to north and
one-fourth from east to west. It lies on the west side of the [Carter's Mill]
road and north side of one known to us as the Richmond road. On the west is
a valley some 800 or 1,000 yards wide, which, sweeping around the westerly
base of Malvern Hill, extends to the river. For 100 yards [north] from the
Richmond road the ground rises gradually to the height of about 40 feet, and
then gently descends [500 yards] to the woods, which bound the field on the
north and for some distance on the east. These woods extend also westerly
across the valley and along its west side. On the west edge of the field, not
far from the Richmond road and overlooking the field and valley, is a large
white house, Dr. J. H. Mellert's [this is the Crew House], at which were my
headquarters. My division occupied the extreme left of the line [that was facing north], and in this field bore its part in the battle of Malvern.

The Second Brigade, General Griffin, was ordered to the front. The artillery advanced toward the woods, and was supported on the left by the Ninth
Massachusetts, Colonel Cass, and Sixty-second Pennsylvania, Captain Hull,
and on the right by part of Couch's division. While getting into position a
few casualties were caused by shot thrown from a battery on our left and rear
and on the opposite side of the valley, which, however, was soon silenced by
guns near Malvern house. At evening the Eighty-third Pennsylvania, [Lieu-
tenant Colonel] Campbell, Third Brigade, was sent forward to the left of the
batteries, and in this position we passed the night [of June 30] on our arms.
Early in the morning of July 1, Tuesday, the Eighty-third was relieved by the
Fourth Michigan, Colonel Woodbury, Second Brigade, and retired to its brigade. The Fourteenth New York Volunteers, Colonel McQuade, Second Brigade, with a section of Weeden's battery, was placed in the edge of the field,

between the Richmond road and Dr. J. H. Mellert's house, facing to the west, to watch the road and valley and protect our left. The First and Third Brigades were under cover of a narrow strip of woods, which skirts the [Carter's Mill] road after it turns to the east. The artillery in front was placed under command of General Griffin. Berdan's Sharpshooters were thrown forward as skirmishers, under Lieutenant-Colonel Ripley. Shells were thrown into the woods where the enemy were supposed to be approaching and forming, to which they replied on my right front, but on my left front and left maintained an ominous silence.

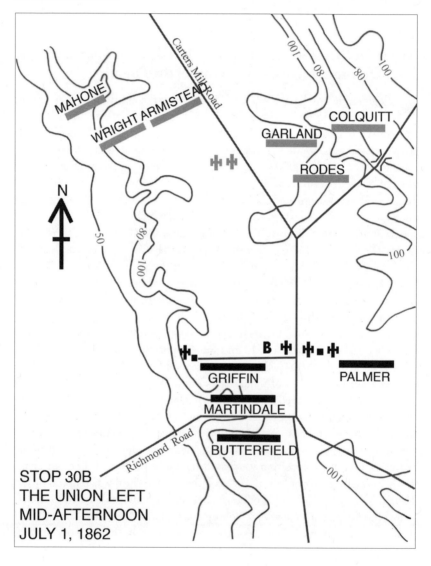

STOP 30B
THE UNION LEFT
MID-AFTERNOON
JULY 1, 1862

An attack was made upon General Couch's right by a moderate force, which was repelled by his batteries and those in my front. Satisfied that a heavy attack was impending, and my First and Third Brigades being too far to the right and rear to render prompt assistance I moved the First, General Martindale, into Mellert's field, immediately north of the Richmond road, and the Third, General Butterfield, in its rear on the south side, both in close order, making the men lie down, in which position, while sheltered by the rise of the ground in front from all except vertical fire, they were near at hand to support Griffin's brigade, directly in front, Couch's division on the right, or to meet an attack on the left. Further, to guard against accident, I directed Generals Martindale and Butterfield to support General Griffin, if he called for assistance, and each other, without waiting for further orders, if the emergency required it. Sykes' division and the Pennsylvania Reserve Corps, under General Seymour, were in reserve. General Couch was on my right, on the east side of the [Carter's Mill] road.

The batteries first in position were Captains Edwards' and Livingston's, Third U.S. Artillery; Lieutenant Kingsbury's (D) and Lieutenant Ames' (A), Fifth U.S. Artillery; part of Captain Weeden's (C), First Rhode Island [Lieutenant Waterman commanding], part of Captain Allen's (E), Massachusetts, Lieutenant Hyde commanding, and Captain [Grimm's] New York, which were relieved by others whose designation I am unable to give.

About 12 o'clock the enemy advanced against my left front and some two hours later against my right, but were driven off by the fire of the artillery, the infantry not being engaged. Neither of these attacks was vigorously pressed, and I considered them demonstrations made to feel our position prior to the commencement of more serious work. [*OR* 11, pt. 2, pp. 274–75.]

The initial attacks Morell wrote of were the attempt by Confederate artillery to suppress the Union artillery and the movement forward by part of *Armistead*'s Brigade in response to Berdan's Sharpshooters.

In early afternoon the batteries in position along the defensive line were: Captain Livingston's Battery F and K, Third U.S. Artillery deployed where you are, 250 yards to your left Lieutenant Waterman's Battery C, First Rhode Island, Half way between Livingston and Waterman's batteries and slightly rearward was a section (2 guns) of Lieutenant Hyde's Battery E, First Massachusetts Artillery. Just on the other side of the Carter's Mill Road, 150 yards to your right, was Lieutenant Ames's Battery A, Fifth U.S. Artillery. To Ames's right was Lieutenant Kingsbury's Battery D,

Fifth U.S. Artillery and farther right was Captain Grimm's Battery D, First Battalion, New York Artillery. On either side of the Carter's Mill Road and 150 yards behind the line of guns were more artillery—Captain Edwards's Battery L and M, Third U.S. Artillery and Captain Snow's Battery B, Maryland Artillery. Several of these batteries had the longer range and more accurate rifled guns, which was to their advantage when engaging the Confederate artillery. This artillery line was not a static position as guns were shifted as the situation required and batteries were replaced when they used up their ammunition.

Captain Livingston, in command of the battery where you are gives a description of the initial artillery action.

Report of Capt. La Rhett L. Livingston, USA, Commanding Batteries F and K (Combined), Third U.S. Artillery, Fifth Brigade, Artillery Reserve, Army of the Potomac

My firing first commenced on the enemy's infantry, who debouched from the woods on my right and front. They soon retired, however. An hour later

Union artillery in action on Malvern Hill. *Century Magazine.*

the enemy opened fire from some guns directly in front of us, and very soon after his infantry advanced from that point. They were soon driven back. About this time they made another attempt on the right, advancing in line in fine style. Here I had an enfilading fire on them with two of my guns, assisting in driving them back, and in such haste and disorder that they left their colors on the field. While this was going on they advanced again in front, but did not succeed in getting nearer the battery than 400 yards. About 4.30 p.m. my battery was relieved by Captain Edwards' battery [L and M], Third Artillery, and I went to the rear for a supply of ammunition, my case-shot and shell being almost exhausted. [*OR* 11, pt. 2, pp. 270–71.]

Report of Capt. John Edwards, USA, Commanding Batteries L and M (Combined), Third U.S. Artillery, Second Division, Fifth Corps, Army of the Potomac

On the 1st of July, in the afternoon, I was ordered to the front. General Griffin directed me to a position near a small house, about 900 yards from the woods in front, where the enemy had their forces concealed. Their artillery, hidden by the woods, played upon us, but their fire was bad. The battery returned their fire with effect. The enemy's sharpshooters crept along a

The center and right of the Confederate position as seen from the Union center.

wooded ravine to the right and on to the left some 250 yards off, from which points they annoyed us a good deal by attempts to pick off the cannoneers. Our own sharpshooters would not advance sufficiently to drive them off, and I was forced to fire canister at them.

After some time a regiment of rebels emerged from the woods waving their flag. The battery plied them with case-shot, and as they approached nearer with double rounds of canister. I continued the fire of canister, and under its effects the rebel ranks were broken and many men ran to the rear. I then urged [a] regiment forward. They advanced a short distance beyond my guns. I ordered the latter to be limbered up and to withdraw. The rebels had approached so near one of my guns that Corporal Himmer shot one with his revolver. In this engagement Lieutenant Brownson was wounded in the head by a fragment of a shell. I directed him to retire to the rear. One private was killed, 1 corporal and 5 privates wounded, and 1 private wounded and missing; 5 horses were shot. [*OR* 11, pt. 2, p. 357.]

Face left and walk west for forty yards. Now face right so that you are again looking north.

Position C—Griffin's Defense

You are in the center of the infantry defensive line on this side of Carter's Mill Road. The first unit to defend this part of the line was Brigadier General Griffin's brigade. Griffin had four regiments. The Ninth Massachusetts was deployed to your left, the Sixty-second Pennsylvania to your right. To the right of the Sixty-second Pennsylvania was Captain Livingston's Battery F and K, Third U.S. Artillery, until it was relieved by Captain Edwards's Battery L and M, Third U.S. Artillery. The Fourth Michigan, initially in reserve, was deployed to the left of the Ninth Massachusetts. The Fourteen New York was placed to the left rear to protect the flank. Battery C, First Rhode Island Artillery, was positioned between the Fourth Michigan and Fourteenth New York. All of the artillery along this part of the position was placed under Griffin's command. He was an experienced artillery officer and had commanded Battery D, Fifth U.S. Artillery, at the first Battle of Bull Run in August 1861. Placing the divisional and attached artillery under his control resulted in a coordinated artillery action and used the batteries to their greatest effect.

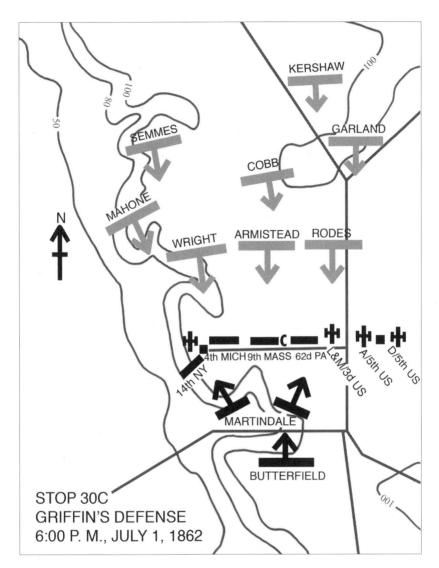

STOP 30C
GRIFFIN'S DEFENSE
6:00 P. M., JULY 1, 1862

Report of Brig. Gen. Charles Griffin, USA, Commanding Second Brigade, First Division, Fifth Corps, Army of the Potomac

About 8 o'clock General Porter placed the artillery under my command. It was supported on the right by Couch's division. The enemy advanced two brigades in front of Couch's right, approaching so close as to throw their musket balls into our batteries, but by a quick concentration of the fire of the four batteries on the field they were soon repulsed. About two hours afterward the enemy attempted an advance upon our extreme left with what appeared to be two brigades, forming in the open field, but the same artillery fire caused him to break and retreat in the greatest disorder. An hour, perhaps, after this the enemy attempted the same maneuver near our right and along the road by which the troops came up, but was again handsomely repulsed by our artillery fire, leaving a stand of colors on the field, which fell into our hands. Here Couch's right wing advanced and drove the enemy far through the wood. The batteries engaged were Captains Edwards' and Livingston's Third U.S. Artillery, four Parrott guns each; Battery D, Fifth U.S. Artillery, under command of Lieutenant Kingsbury, six Parrott guns; Battery A, Fifth U.S. Artillery, Lieutenant Ames, six light 12-pounders, and three guns of Weeden's Rhode Island and two of Fifth Massachusetts, under command of Lieutenants Waterman and Hyde. The batteries were excellently served. The greatest coolness and bravery were displayed by officers and men, and my only regret is my inability to mention the officers by name.

After this a sharp fire was kept up by skirmishers and artillery until 5.30 o'clock, when the enemy made his final and fiercest attack on our left. The artillery continued its effective fire until the enemy arrived within a few yards of our batteries, when the supporting regiments—Fourth Michigan, Colonel Woodbury; Ninth Massachusetts, Colonel Cass, and Sixty-second Pennsylvania, Captain Hull—gallantly moved forward and repulsed him. But a fresh force making its appearance both on left and right, the regiments were compelled to fall back, being relieved by the Twelfth New York, Forty-fourth New York, and Eighty-third Pennsylvania. [The relieving regiments were from Butterfield's brigade.] Five times were the colors of the Sixty-second cut down and as often determinedly raised and rescued, the last time being picked up by an officer of the Forty-fourth New York, who delivered them to Captain Hull upon the demand of a sergeant of Company D of his regiment. The Sixty-second Pennsylvania left the field with its colors flying. The handsome manner in which the Fourth Michigan stood its ground and the good order in which it retired from the field was the subject of comment among all who witnessed it. The gallant Colonel Woodbury fell dead urging his men on to victory. The Ninth Massachusetts well maintained the reputation it has ever borne, the colonel being dangerously wounded. The Fourteenth New York was moved from its first position to resist an attack of the enemy, who was endeavoring to turn our left flank, and exposed to a most deadly fire, which it withstood without flinching during the entire engagement, repulsing the enemy three times. The Fourteenth was not relieved, but held its position on the field of battle until 2 o'clock the next morning, when the entire army was ordered to fall back.

The casualties were as follows: Killed, 79; wounded, 414; missing, 38; an aggregate of 531 [*OR* 11, pt. 2, pp. 314–15.]

> The first units to be called forward to reinforce Griffin's position were the regiments of Martindale's brigade. This brigade had been positioned one hundred yards behind you, in a covered position to protect it from Confederate fire.

Report of Brig. Gen. John H. Martindale, USA, Commanding First Brigade, First Division, Fifth Corps, Army of the Potomac

Under orders from General Morell I moved my brigade forward and formed in line of battle by battalions at half distance. They were slightly covered by ground rising in front. I directed them to lie down. Griffin's brigade was in front. Butterfield's brigade was immediately in my rear.

The battle was now an affair of artillery, and none of Porter's corps had yet engaged the infantry. Couch, however, was pressed severely on the right, but held his ground. I had encountered artillery before, but now it opened as I had never yet seen it. I went along the line of my regiments and told them my dispositions for battle, and reminded them that a retreat would be annihilation. It would be better to face the enemy to the last than to retire—that there was no Washington to fall back upon, as at Bull Run; no Chickahominy to cross, as at Gaines' Mill. We must be victorious or perish. That statement of the case was true, and the men knew it and appreciated it.

During the progress of the cannonading my men were held inactive. I saw repeatedly the wounded rise from their places and retire to the shelter of a bank to our left and rear, which place was selected for a hospital, and those that could not go without aid borne by comrades, who deposited them with the surgeon, and promptly and quietly returned to their places. In this position a number of men were killed and were borne away in like manner, and the places thus made vacant were immediately closed again. At length the enemy ceased their cannonading. There was a calm, but the storm burst again speedily. I had directed the Second Maine to the right, to be in readiness to support Couch. I formed the Twenty-second Massachusetts with the Twenty-fifth New York, which was reduced to a fragment, and advanced it to the support of Griffin's brigade. I reformed the Second Maine in rear of the Twenty-second Massachusetts and ordered it forward.

At this time the enemy was attempting to move around under cover of a bank and turn our left flank. Griffin had one regiment, the Fourteenth New

York, in that direction. I received orders from General Morell to use my own judgment in repelling that attack. Deeming the emergency imminent, I went in person to form and lead the Thirteenth New York in that direction. Major Schoeffel, who was in command, Colonel Marshall and Lieutenant-Colonel Stephan both being absent sick, under my direction formed line to the left and moved to the support of the Fourteenth New York. I returned to the First Michigan Regiment, and deploying it, ordered it forward. At nearly the same time Butterfield's brigade came forward and one of the regiments, the Twelfth New York, reported to me. Other re-enforcements appeared on the ground not belonging to Morell's division. There was danger of confusion. I placed the Twelfth New York in position to protect the extreme left, and I think also another of the regiments which moved up from the rear. As I made these dispositions General Porter himself appeared on the ground, and I explained to him how the commands were situated.

At this time a considerable body of wounded men and stragglers were retiring from the lines. General Porter directed me to form a line to prevent straggling and collect the wounded. I proceeded to execute his orders, and took the Twenty-fifth New York and stretched it across the field for that purpose. The enemy had been driven back at all points. I was directed by General Porter to send out pickets to the front, and did so. My brigade, except the Twenty-fifth New York, bivouacked in line of battle. [*OR* 11, pt. 2, pp. 293–94.]

> The Twenty-second Massachusetts Infantry, with the Second Company, Massachusetts Sharpshooters, attached, moved forward to this location to reinforce.

Report of Capt. Walter S. Sampson, USA, Commanding Twenty-second Massachusetts Infantry, First Brigade, First Division, Fifth Corps, Army of the Potomac

Tuesday, July 1, about 11 o'clock a.m., a forward movement was made. Here they were subject to a very heavy and severe cross-fire from the enemy's artillery. Here we lost some 8 men. Captain Wardwell moved the regiment forward about 400 yards and deployed in line of battle for shelter and protection. Soon they moved forward to support a battery, which they did firmly and steadily. Orders soon came for the regiment to move forward to support the first line of battle, which was being pressed very hard by the enemy. The regiment moved to its position and opened fire by file, using up their 60 rounds of ammunition. The Second Company of Sharpshooters, under Lieutenant Stiles, fired upward of 40 rounds with their target rifles. The regiment advanced so close to the enemy that they took 32 prisoners, who were sent to the rear. The regiment maintained its position with out ammunition until properly relieved, then retired in the best order.

Among the casualties of this day was the loss of Capt. S. J. Thompson, who was severely wounded and left in hospital. The loss of rank and file was about 60. In this day's action Companies G, E, and I were led into action by sergeants, and Company K was commanded by Corp. Andrew Wilson. [*OR* 11, pt. 2, pp. 305–6.]

> The next brigade committed to action in this location was Butterfield's brigade. This brigade was composed of four regiments and had been initially placed in a covered position just south of Richmond Road. When the Confederate artillery opened fire, any rounds that went over the first line of defense landed in the vicinity of the reserve brigades.

Report of Brig. Gen. Daniel Butterfield, USA, Commanding Third Brigade, First Division, Fifth Corps, Army of the Potomac

About noon, apprehending an attack from the enemy in large force upon the position held by General Griffin, near [Crew] house and the junction of the road and private road, my brigade was formed, by General Morell's order, in close column in two lines in the rear of General Martindale's, and lay for a long time, suffering a severe artillery fire by the enemy, which killed and wounded several of my command. Shortly after this disposition the enemy opened a severe fire of shell, canister, grape, and round shot from different batteries on his right and left, which, for the most part, converged in the vicinity of this open space. The brigade for a long time and with great patience endured this artillery fire.

I at once endeavored to thoroughly acquaint myself with the nature of the ground in front, and, if possible, the threatening disposition which the enemy was continually making of his own forces. For this purpose I rode to the front frequently and personally gained the knowledge required, and often communicated the same to the general commanding the corps by orderlies furnished me for that purpose.

It soon became evident that General Couch's left would require support. I visited General Couch and consulted with him. His opinion corresponding with mine, I informed him that I would assist him in case of necessity. I also advised the general commanding the corps to that effect. On receipt of this dispatch General Porter ordered Colonel Caldwell's brigade to report to me for such disposition as I might deem necessary. I ordered this brigade to remain in reserve on General Couch's left and rear and report to him for orders. The enemy now attacked our line with renewed vigor, and advanced with the design of capturing our batteries on the crest of the hill. General Couch sent an orderly to me for further support. I immediately ordered the Eighty-third Pennsylvania and Sixteenth Michigan to the point of junction of the Fifth Corps with General Couch's left.

It soon became evident that the enemy was throwing large forces on our front and left with a resolution to flank us, and thus decide the fortunes of the day. The struggle became along the front and left desperate on both sides. Sensible of the importance of the moment, advising the general commanding the corps of my actions in the premises, the brigade stationed in front of mine not moving, I determined to and did order the Forty-fourth New York to advance in line of battle, cross the field in front, and relieve a portion of General Griffin's command, whose ammunition seemed to be exhausted, and to charge the enemy with the Eighty-third Regiment. At the same time I directed the Twelfth New York Volunteers to advance to the left and check the approach of the enemy and relieve the Fourth Michigan. The gallantry with which these two regiments, joined by the Eighty-third on their right, obeyed this order under the galling fire of the enemy is faithfully set forth in the respective reports of their commanding officers. The Forty-fourth New York and Eighty-third Pennsylvania were under the immediate eye of the general commanding the corps, who witnessed their heroic conduct.

[When] the ammunition of my command was exhausted, we were relieved by the Irish Brigade and some troops of General Sykes. [*OR* 11, pt. 2, pp. 319–20.]

Butterfield committed the Eighty-third Pennsylvania and the Sixteenth Michigan to reinforcing the defensive line from your right to the road. The Eighty-third Pennsylvania was to your immediate right and the Sixteenth Michigan was to the right of the Eighty-third.

Report of Lieut. Col. Hugh S. Campbell, USA, Commanding Eighty-third Pennsylvania, Third Brigade, First Division, Fifth Corps, Army of the Potomac

Shortly after 4 p.m. the regiment, being in line, counter-marched and fronted in the supposed direction of the adversaries, and then deployed into column of division, right in front, and lay down, distance nearly one-third of a mile in rear of our batteries, which were directly in front and hotly engaged with the enemy. A terrific cannonading was now kept up between the contending artillerists. The shot and shell plowed up and tore the earth and trees in all directions. Many of our men were becoming wounded and carried to the rear . . . .

About 6 p.m. the order to advance was given. A wild yell rang from our ranks. Onward we went, passing through the ranks of General Martindale's brigade, gaining our position only just in time to save our guns, as most assuredly if we had been a moment later the enemy would have captured them. Here, confronted with the enemy, both lines steadily advanced toward each other, and when within about 200 yards of the foe we halted, delivered a volley, and dropped on our knees. Our opponents, although shaken by this fire, still approached, and evidently intended to charge. Our regiment opened fire again, pouring in volley after volley until, when within 150 yards, he was completely brought to a stand-still.

All this time the enemy delivered his fire whilst advancing, but now finding the fire of the Eighty-third so very sharp, he was unable to proceed farther. The battle was now very hot. It became evident we were exposed to a cross-fire. Another regiment, whose number or name I cannot learn, came to our assistance and formed on our left, and, I regret to say, who, after only receiving a few rounds of the enemy's fire, gave way and fled. Numbers of the Eighty-third saw this and indignantly hooted; but their temper and bravery was presently calmed and aroused by the timely and unexpected appearance of their old friends, the Forty-fourth New York Volunteers, who rapidly formed line on our left . . . .

It was now nearly 8 p.m. The battle raged with all the horrors of war. Repeatedly the enemy advanced, and was as often beaten back. Our ranks, although nobly assisted by the Forty-fourth, were becoming very much thinned. The enemy's dead lay in heaps, while he was seen to collect the bodies of his fallen slain and pile them for his protection from our fire. We felt almost overpowered from the fury and storm of shot poured into us. Yet, seeing our adversaries waver, we, in conjunction with the Forty-fourth New York Volunteers, decided to and did charge upon two of his regiments, drove them back, captured his colors, which was carried as a trophy by Orderly-Sergeant Wittich, who amid a shower of balls gallantly bore them off the field, and then fell back to the position we maintained and held for the two previous hours without a moment's cessation of battle and against vastly superior numbers, when to our utter joy the gallant Irish Brigade dashed onto the field in time to save our utter destruction. [*OR* 11, pt. 2, pp. 346–47.]

The Forty-fourth New York was committed to assist the Eighty-third Pennsylvania and went into position just to your left.

Report of Lieut. Col. James C. Rice, USA, Commanding Fourth-fourth New York, Third Brigade, First Division, Fifth Corps, Army of the Potomac

At about 5 o'clock in the afternoon the enemy attacked the left of our line with great vigor, and the general [Butterfield] moved up the Eighty-third Pennsylvania and the Sixteenth Michigan to support certain batteries in front, and soon afterward the Forty-fourth New York Volunteers was ordered to deploy and prepare for action. The Forty-fourth New York Volunteers immediately was ordered to advance, although the general was far in front and beyond sight, leading on the other regiments of his brigade. The Twelfth New York Volunteers followed, passing through the woods farther to our left. Onward the Forty-fourth marched in regular line of battle, with its colors far advanced, passing line after line of our troops, who loudly cheered our flag as we steadily and firmly pressed on, till at length, beyond the extreme front of our forces and within 100 yards of the enemy, the regiment was ordered to charge bayonets upon his lines. Scarcely had the regiment charged 50 yards toward the enemy before his lines broke and fell back, leaving his colors upon the field some 20 or 30 yards in front of our regiment. A dozen officers and soldiers sprang forward from our ranks to seize them, when a sergeant [Sergeant Wittich] of the Eighty-third Pennsylvania, which regiment we had passed on our right in the charge, fired to deeds of valor and daring by words spoken to him by the general, rushed forward, and running across the entire

The Crew House in the 1880s. *Century Magazine.*

right wing of our regiment, outstripped all his competitors in the race, seized the colors, bore them off, and handed them to the general.

Another brigade of the enemy was now advancing toward us. My command was ordered to halt and commence firing. For nearly half an hour the regiment held this brigade at bay by its constant and unerring fire, till the general commanding the corps personally led up re-enforcements to our relief, whose valor turned the fortunes of the day and secured a most signal victory to our arms.

The Forty-fourth New York entered this engagement with 225 men. Its loss was 11 killed, 84 wounded, and 4 missing. Among the wounded were Captain Shaffer and Lieutenant Woodworth, the latter mortally. At 10 o'clock at night, in company with Surgeon Frothingham and Assistant Surgeon Bissell, with a detachment from the regiment, I went over the field of battle, gathered together all our wounded, many of whom were lying among the wounded of the enemy, and carried them over a mile by hand in blankets to the hospital, there being no ambulances on the field. [*OR* 11, pt. 2, p. 342.]

> Return to the parking lot and walk east to Carter's Mill Road. Turn left and walk north along the side of the road, facing traffic, for seventy-five yards. Turn right and cross the road. Walk sixty yards to the artillery. When you reach the guns, stop and face left, back to the north and toward the Confederate line.

The Crew House today.

Position D—The Union Right

This is the position of Lieutenant Ames's Battery A, Fifth U.S. Artillery. To Ames's right was Lieutenant Kingsbury's Battery D, Fifth Artillery. One hundred yards behind these batteries were Captain Snow's Battery B, Maryland Artillery. All three of these batteries were from the Artillery Reserve. To the right of this artillery was Brigadier General Darius N. Couch's First Division, Fourth Corps. Couch deployed two of his three brigades forward with one brigade in a supporting role. However, by late afternoon all the regiments of the supporting brigade had been sent to the other brigades, and for all practical purposes all three brigades were deployed on the fighting line.

Couch's left brigade was located to the right of Lieutenant Kingsbury's battery. This was Brigadier General Innis N. Palmer's Third Brigade. Some distance to Palmer's right was Brigadier General Albion P. Howe's First Brigade. Initially, in a supporting position was Brigadier General John J. Abercrombie's Second Brigade. But as mentioned, the regiments were brought forward and essentially Abercrombie was in position as the center brigade. An additional artillery battery was positioned with Howe's brigade. When this battery was moved to another location it was replaced with Captain Snow's Battery B, Maryland Artillery. To Couch's right rear were Heintzelman's Third Corps, two divisions, and Sumner's Second Corps, two divisions. This force was deployed so as to extend the Union right flank along the line of Western Run and protect against a flanking attack.

Couch was in command of the field on the right of the road. His report gives an overview of the fighting on the Union right.

Report of Brig. Gen. Darius N. Couch, USA, Commanding First Division, Fourth Corps, Army of the Potomac

General Sumner, to whose support I had marched with two brigades the night previous, gave me orders to return to the position occupied the evening before on Malvern Hill. The brigades were posted on the right of the [Carter's Mill Road facing north]. The other brigade of the division—Abercrombie's—lay a few hundred yards to the rear. The Seventh Massachusetts and Second Rhode Island being on detached service much weakened the command. Part of Porter's corps was to my left across the road. Kingsbury's splendid battery,

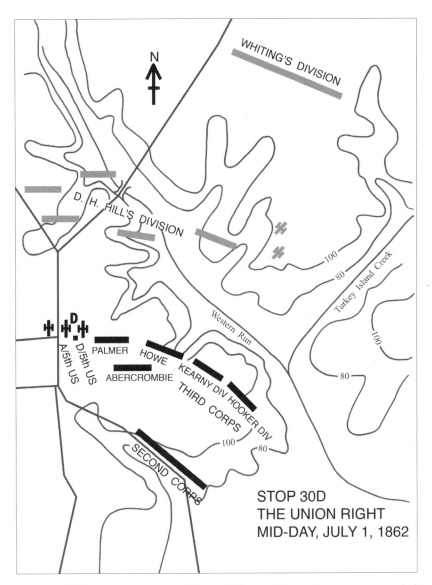

STOP 30D
THE UNION RIGHT
MID-DAY, JULY 1, 1862

formerly Griffin's, was on my left front; Palmer's brigade in a strong wooded ravine a little to the right of the battery, and running to the front 200 yards. One of Howe's regiments, Sixty-second New York, was strongly posted in a peach orchard to the rear and between the battery and Palmer. To the right of Palmer was an oat field, sloping to the front and skirted on the right by a tangled marsh and wooded bank.

This was my right and held by General Howe. In the course of the morning he was re-enforced by part of Abercrombie's command, and the balance

occupied the ground with Palmer. My own artillery being several miles to
the rear, General Heintzelman sent me a battery for my right, but afterward
withdrew it, to place it, probably, on his own front. To my right lay Kearny,
who during the day advanced two regiments of Robinson's brigade to sustain
Howe in case of need. The ground in front of me was open to within 100 to
500 yards from right to left. Across the road in front of Griffin the country was
open for three-fourths of a mile, making it very favorable for our artillery.

By 8 o'clock a.m. there were signs of the rebels in front. The rebels were
driven off by artillery alone. From this time until about 1 p.m. the contest
was on both sides in the hands of the artillerists; then they pushed forward
a column to carry the left of the line held by Griffin. They were driven back
disorganized and cut up by our artillery alone. Their batteries played upon
us without intermission, but owing to the care used in masking the men our
loss from it was not serious, with the exception of a battery to the right, that
enfiladed my position.

About 3 p.m. a brigade [*G. B. Anderson's*] broke through the opening
of the woods in front of Palmer and Abercrombie, but Kingsbury's battery,
together with the steady fire of the Tenth Massachusetts and a charge of the
Thirty-sixth New York, drove them back in confusion, the latter regiment
capturing the colors of the Fourteenth North Carolina. This movement of
the rebels was a rash one or a ruse to draw our troops on to disadvantageous
ground—undoubtedly the latter—and it did not succeed. The enemy were
now massing large columns on our front.

At about 4.30 p.m., after an incessant cannonade, they boldly pushed forward a large column from their right in the open field to carry Griffin's position. The fire of the three batteries was concentrated upon them. Kingsbury's
battery, having been withdrawn for ammunition, was relieved by three guns
of Battery C, Rhode Island Artillery, and two guns, [Hyde's], Fifth Massachusetts, under Captain Weeden. The attacking column kept on, continually
re-enforced, until within range of Griffin's rifles, when it was stopped and
formed line.

The action now being general, I assumed command of the whole line for
the time; ordered up the reserves on the left; placed in position regiments falling back, and halted those bravely moving forward, many of the regiments having already masked the fire of our artillery. Upon seeing the advance on the left
Abercrombie and Palmer pushed forward their brigades in front of the artillery,
in order to drive back the foe. The enemy continually re-enforced their column
of attack besides advancing heavy reserves in support. Abercrombie and Palmer
became engaged to their left and right. General Caldwell, of Richardson's division, having been sent to my support by General Sumner, now went into action,
joining my brave division, fiercely engaged. The enemy were making desperate efforts to drive in my right. General Heintzelman sent me Seeley's battery

[Battery K, Fourth U.S. Artillery], which, under De Russy, chief of his artillery, and with the advice of General Howe, was established on the ground held by this latter officer. It did its duty well.

General Porter came upon the ground about 6 p.m. Later General Sickles, of Hooker's division, reported to me with three regiments, leading his men directly into action, relieving some of my division whose ammunition was expended. At about 7 p.m. General Meagher, with his brigade, reported to me from General Sumner, and was posted on the left of Griffin's batteries.

Night closed upon us still fighting, the opposing forces only known by their lines of fire, that of the rebels gradually slackening until 8.30 p.m., after which an occasional cannon-shot from our batteries only broke the stillness that pervaded this bloody field. [*OR* 11, pt. 2, pp. 202–4.]

You are in the position of Battery A, Fifth U.S. Artillery. This battery was armed with six 12-pound Napoleon smoothbore cannon. Firing solid shot this gun had an effective range of approximately 1,500 yards. At ranges less than four hundred yards, with a 4.6-inch bore diameter and firing canister it was devastating. During the fighting this battery fired 1,392 rounds of ammunition. Each of the cannon would have had four ammunition chests, each chest capable of holding 32 rounds of ammunition. This would provide 128 rounds per cannon, or 768 rounds for all six cannon. Ames would have had to bring up a minimum of 624 more rounds, and he probably brought up more. To accomplish this his caissons and limbers must have been in constant motion back to the ammunition trains and then returning to the firing position.

Report of Lieut. Adelbert Ames, USA, Commanding Battery A, Fifth U.S. Artillery, Second Brigade, Artillery Reserve, Army of the Potomac

The battery was in position in a field at distances varying from 400 to 1,100 yards from woods occupied by the enemy. In the forenoon a heavy cannonading was opened upon us and continued at intervals during the day. Early in the afternoon the enemy charged a battery on our right, but were entirely cut up, with loss of their colors. In this instance our canister were very effective. Vigorous attempts were afterward made by heavy masses to turn our left. A heavy artillery fire was poured into them, canister being used from time to time. After night-fall all our ammunition but a few rounds of canister was expended. To use them to advantage we maintained our position for some time under a heavy musketry fire. During the battle 1,392 rounds of ammunition were expended. To obtain this quantity the caissons were sent to the rear as soon as emptied. [*OR* 11, pt. 2, p. 260.]

Soon after this battle Ames was promoted to colonel of volunteers. He departed to train his new regiment, the Twentieth Maine Infantry, and its new lieutenant colonel, Joshua L. Chamberlain.

Face right and walk east for thirty yards, stop, then face left so you are looking toward the Confederate position.

Position E—Palmer's Defense

You are at the position of Battery D, Fifth U.S. Artillery. This battery was armed with six ten-pound Parrott rifled guns. The rifled guns provided a higher degree of accuracy at longer ranges than the Napoleon. As such this battery was ideally armed for counter battery fire.

Report of Lieut. Henry W. Kingsbury, USA, Commanding Battery D, Fifth U.S. Artillery, First Division, Fifth Corps, Army of the Potomac

On July 1, at 9 a.m., the battery moved and took position on the right of that occupied by the battery of Lieutenant Ames. Our guns commanded the fork of the roads, one of which led to Richmond. Toward noon horsemen appeared to our front and right, distance 1,600 yards. Lieutenant Hazlett's section opened with shrapnel and percussion shell. The enemy immediately disappeared. Soon the enemy appeared in force to the front and left of Captain Livingston's battery [Battery F and K, Third U.S. Artillery], which was posted on the left of Lieutenant Ames. The three batteries at once opened with shrapnel, and the enemy were speedily driven back to the woods. Simultaneously with the appearance of this infantry a field battery opened on us from the [Carter's Mill] road. We returned the fire, and forced it apparently to change its position. Soon what I conceived to be two more batteries opened upon us from the same road. In connection with the other batteries we replied with shrapnel, range about 1,300 yards. In our front, distant 500 yards, there now appeared a mass of infantry preparing to charge. I ordered at once a brisk fire upon them with shrapnel. They advanced steadily until within 150 yards. Our canister then caused them to fly in confusion. They left a battle-flag behind them. This was picked up by an infantry officer some time later. Against these rebels a portion of a regiment on our right assisted. When they first formed I drew the attention of Lieutenant Ames to them. He, too, pointed some of his guns on them. We entered the fight in the morning with not less than 600 rounds of ammunition. Owing to the blowing up of our caissons on the 28th of June this began to fail. One hundred and fifty rounds, mostly shell, were sent us. This we used mostly in firing at masses of the enemy as they appeared in the distance.

I was now relieved [by other artillery], and went to the rear for ammunition. I left with 16 rounds to a piece, which I reserved for emergencies. . . . The effect of the firing upon our pieces was to enlarge materially the vents of three. No ammunition for 10-pounder Parrott guns was to be had, nor did we receive a supply until we reached Harrison's Landing. On the night of the battle the battery marched to Harrison's Landing, where we have since remained. [*OR* 11, pt. 2, pp. 287–88.]

> When Lieutenant Kingsbury withdrew his battery for ammunition resupply he was replaced by Battery C, First Rhode Island Artillery, with three guns and Battery E, First Massachusetts Artillery with two guns. Both of these batteries had initially been in position on the left half of the defensive line. Late in the fighting when these two batteries ran out of ammunition they were replaced with Captain Diederichs's Battery A and Captain Knieriem's Battery C, both from the First Battalion, New York Artillery.
>
> The infantry to the immediate right of this artillery position was Palmer's brigade. The other two brigades of Couch's division were to Palmer's right. The fighting done by Palmer was typical of the fighting done by remainder of Couch's division.

Report of Brig. Gen. Innis N. Palmer, USA, Commanding Third Brigade, First Division, Fifth Corps, Army of the Potomac

On the 30th ultimo two regiments of my command, the Second Rhode Island and the Seventh Massachusetts Volunteers, were detached by the order of Brigadier-General Couch, commanding the division, in order to take up a position near the Turkey Island Bridge, and they were unfortunately not present during the engagement. The remaining regiments of my brigade— the Tenth Massachusetts Volunteers, commanded by Major Miller, and the Thirty-sixth New York Volunteers, commanded by Major Raney—were on arriving on the battle ground placed in position under the direction of General Couch, and they were directed to hold the woods on the right of the

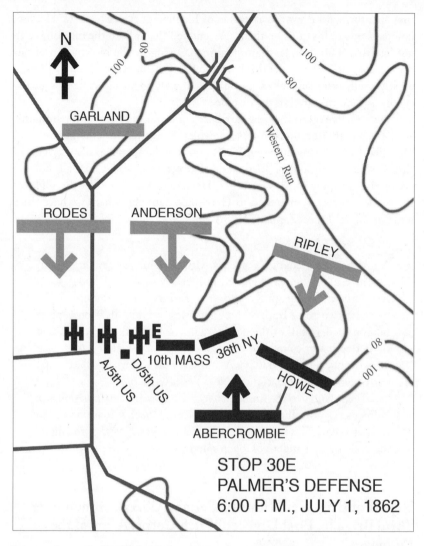

STOP 30E
PALMER'S DEFENSE
6:00 P. M., JULY 1, 1862

battery formerly Griffin's, and to act at the same time as the support to this battery. A company of the Tenth Massachusetts was detached as skirmishers to watch the ravine a little to the right and front of the battery, and four companies of the Thirty-sixth New York, under the command of Captain Walsh, were thrown out obliquely across the field on my right, in order to get a cross fire upon any force that might appear from the woods immediately in front of the battery.

Affairs remained in this state until about 3 o'clock p.m., when, after a sharp artillery fire from both sides, the enemy appeared in force on the right. This force proved to be a brigade of North Carolina troops, commanded by

General *Anderson,* and it advanced in good order until it was within about 350 yards of my men. A heavy fire was then opened upon it by the Tenth Massachusetts and the four companies under Captain Walsh. As soon as it was within the view of the battery a fire from it was opened, and I directed the remaining six companies of the Thirty-sixth New York to wheel from its position in the wood and open fire. This was done in gallant style, and after a sharp contest, which, however, lasted only a few minutes, the enemy broke and fled. After pursuing for some distance my command was recalled, as a pursuit would necessarily bring them in front of the batteries. In this short engagement the battle-flag of the Fourteenth North Carolina Regiment was captured by the Thirty-sixth New York Volunteers, and brought in by Captain Donoghue, of that regiment. The loss in my brigade was small in this affair.

This ended the first engagement of the day. Notice was immediately given to me by the general commanding the division, General Couch, that the enemy was receiving strong re-enforcements, and that the battle might be renewed at any moment. Nearly the same distribution of my command was made as before, and the renewal of the attack was awaited.

At about 6 p.m. the enemy again appeared in large force in front of Griffin's brigade, and one wing of that brigade immediately moved down upon them. This induced me to think that a charge would be made along the whole line, although I well knew that it was the intention of the general in command only to hold on to the line we had taken up, and not to interfere with the fire of the batteries. I ordered my command to move forward to support any troops that might be first engaged, not intending to get in front of the batteries. The firing commenced furiously along the line and other regiments of the division pressed forward, and soon my command was forced to move to the front of the batteries or remain inactive. The brigade moved in good order slowly to the front, keeping up the firing. Major Miller, commanding the Tenth Massachusetts, while gallantly leading and encouraging his men, fell mortally wounded, and the command of that regiment devolved on Captain Barton, who conducted it gallantly through the rest of the engagement. Major Raney led his regiment finely, and remained on the field until every cartridge was exhausted. I then directed him to take up a position in the rear of the regiments newly arrived on the ground. The Tenth Massachusetts, after several hours hard fighting, reported their ammunition exhausted, but they remained firmly on the field until after dark and until the enemy was everywhere repulsed. [*OR* 11, pt. 2, pp. 213–14.]

The coming of darkness brought the battle to a close. Malvern Hill was clearly a Union victory. When the firing stopped, the Union

The West House in the 1880s. The Crew House is in the distance. *Century Magazine.*

The West House today.

defenders still occupied their positions and *Lee* had been repulsed, with 5,650 casualties at a cost of 3,007 casualties for McClellan.

The defenders had taken advantage of the natural strengths of Malvern Hill. This naturally strong position had been made even stronger by the placement of infantry and artillery so as to cover the flanks. On the north side of the hill, where the gentle sloping ground provided good fields of fire, the infantry was positioned in depth. The artillery was positioned with the infantry so that they both supported each other and reserve artillery was readily available. Artillery positions were chosen that allowed more than one battery to fire upon a target. Union command and control at the corps level and down the chain of command provided the necessary directions for the infantry and artillery reserves to be employed where needed and in a timely manner.

As for the Confederates, command and control at army level had been poor. Early on *Lee* lost the ability to influence the battle when a series of random events culminated in only fourteen of his forty brigades attacking frontally, a strong defensive position. The attempt to suppress the Union artillery by massed Confederate batteries had failed. Poor command and control of the artillery and a flawed artillery organization brought an insufficient number of batteries into action. These were committed piecemeal, and under the weight of the Union artillery fire were driven from the field.

On the morning of July 2 *Lee* expected to again confront the Union defenses or to maneuver far enough to the east to threaten their supply line to Harrison's Landing on the James River. This threat might have turned the defenders out of their position and provided *Lee* with a favorable opportunity to attack again. However, this was not to be.

At daylight the Union army was gone from Malvern Hill. McClellan still in a retreat-oriented frame of mind threw away another opportunity to go over to the offense and take the initiative away from *Lee*. The position on Malvern Hill was an anchor from which McClellan could have maneuvered to his left or right. A maneuver to the left (west) by forces using Malvern Hill to cover their movement could have attacked *Holmes*'s Division along River Road and then hit the right flank of the Confederate units in front of Malvern Hill. This attack coordinated with a demonstration or attack by the defenders on Malvern Hill had the potential of inflicting major damage on *Lee*'s army. However, as in previous battles during the Seven Days, McClellan's mind was only on retreat to a safe enclave on the James River, and this opportunity was also allowed to pass.

Directions for returning to the major road network east of Richmond are at the end of chapter seven.

Chapter 7

The Aftermath

Daylight on July 2 revealed that the Union forces on Malvern Hill were gone as McClellan continued his retreat. Only a rearguard remained to protect the rear of the Army of the Potomac as it made its final move to a position on the James River. The commander of the rear guard was Colonel William W. Averell.

Report of Col. William W. Averell, USA, Commanding Third Pennsylvania Cavalry, Third Corps, Army of the Potomac

At 12 o'clock on the night of the 1st instant I received orders from the general commanding to take charge of the rear guard of the army. At daybreak on the 2d I took command of the rear guard, composed of the Third Pennsylvania Cavalry and four regiments of U.S. Infantry [the First Brigade of Sykes's Second Division, Fifth Corps], under Lieutenant-Colonel Buchanan. I found the [Sixty-fifth] New York Chasseurs on the field, and assumed command of them also.

Lieutenant-Colonel Buchanan informed me on my taking command that the enemy was threatening his pickets and advancing toward both his flanks. I sent an officer to the rear to direct the cavalry I had upon the road to push the trains forward with all dispatch and to collect those which could not be removed and prepare them for burning; then deployed three regiments of infantry with the Chasseurs along the front, which I immediately covered with a double line of skirmishers; then advanced the whole line as if for attack, pushing forward simultaneously from the right and left wings columns of cavalry and disposing parties of horsemen far to the right and left to divert the attention of the enemy and to give me information of their movements.

Observing that the feint was about to succeed, although the cavalry was suffering from the enemy's sharpshooters, I sent an officer to the rear to assure the rear of the army of its security, and to bring me back a battery of artillery, of which I was destitute. Captain Frank responded promptly to this call, and soon had four guns in good position in rear on a hill. While he was coming one of my squadrons by a skillful disposition of troopers in sections created a very good semblance of a battery which moved up under the crest of a hill in front, and went through the motions of going into action front. The enemy withdrew to the woods in their rear, and I held the position until 10 a.m. Parties of the enemy gaining confidence came out without arms and commenced collecting their dead, with which the fields in front were thickly strewn. At 10, hearing that the rear of the army was 2 miles away, I withdrew my artillery to another good position, with the reserve regiment of infantry; then withdrew the main body of the infantry, and then the line of skirmishers, screening these operations with galloping skirmishers of cavalry along the line in front. Two guns taken from the enemy the night before had to be spiked and the carriages broken for want of transportation.

From an early hour the rain commenced falling, and its increasing heaviness assisted to render my operations obscure to the enemy. As soon as the artillery and infantry were well upon the road I directed my cavalry, under Lieutenant-Colonel Owen, to withdraw, leaving 12 wagons without mules ready for them to destroy. The march was continued without incident until the rear crossed Turkey Island Bridge, which was destroyed. A mile farther on I found Brigadier-General Wessells in excellent position with his brigade, and a mile farther on Brigadier-General Naglee with a second line. [Both brigades were part of Brigadier General John J. Peck's Second Division, Fourth Corps.] Considering our rear perfectly secure, I passed through their lines with my wearied forces and came to this camp. [*OR* 11, pt. 2, pp. 235–36.]

In the 1880s Averell wrote an article for *Century Magazine* about his service with the Union cavalry on the Peninsula. In this article he gives a graphic description of the Confederate dead and wounded on Malvern Hill as he saw them in the early morning hours of July 2.

Narrative of Colonel William W. Averell, USA

By this time the leveling rays of the morning sun from our right were just penetrating the fog, and slowly lifting its clinging shreds and yellow masses. Our ears had been filled with agonizing cries from thousands [of wounded] before the fog was lifted, but now our eyes saw an appalling spectacle upon the slopes down to the woodlands half a mile away. Over five thousand dead and wounded men were on the ground, in every attitude of distress. A third of them were dead or dying, but enough were alive and moving to give to the field a singular crawling effect. [*Battles and Leaders of the Civil War* (Secaucus, N.J.: Castle Press), vol. 2, p. 432.]

On July 3 McClellan had his army in a defensive position eight miles southeast of Malvern Hill at Harrison's Landing on the James River. Harrison's Landing was the location of Berkley Plantation, which had been the home of the ninth president of the United States, William Henry Harrison. Here the Army of the Potomac went into position and began building fortifications. Two creeks and a swamp covering both flanks and part of the front added strength to this four-mile-long and one-mile-deep position.

The day after the Battle of Malvern Hill *Lee* dispatched his cavalry to determine the location of the Union army. Once he discovered the direction McClellan had gone, *Lee* ordered a continuation of the pursuit. Initially his intention was to again attack McClellan. The heavy rains of July 2 and the retreating Union forces had left the roads almost impassable and greatly slowed down the Confederate movements. It was not until July 4 that *Lee*'s army closed up to the Union defenses at Harrison's Landing. A reconnaissance convinced *Lee* of the futility of attacking McClellan's strong defenses, and on July 8 he withdrew his army and took up positions covering the roads to Richmond.

Report of Gen. *Robert E. Lee,* CSA, Commanding Army of Northern Virginia

On July 2 it was discovered that the enemy had withdrawn during the night, leaving the ground covered with his dead and wounded, and his route exhibiting abundant evidence of precipitate retreat. The pursuit was commenced, General *Stuart* with his cavalry in the advance, but a violent storm, which prevailed throughout the day, greatly retarded our progress. The enemy, harassed and closely followed by the cavalry, succeeded in gaining [Harrison's Landing], on James River, and the protection of his gunboats. He immediately began to fortify his position, which was one of great natural strength, flanked on each side by a creek, and the approach to his front commanded by the heavy guns of his shipping, in addition to those mounted in his intrenchments. It was deemed inexpedient to attack him, and in view of the condition of our troops, who had been marching and fighting almost incessantly for seven days under the most trying circumstances, it was determined to withdraw, in order to afford them the repose of which they stood so much in need.

Several days were spent in collecting arms and other property abandoned by the enemy, and in the mean time some artillery and cavalry were sent below Westover to annoy his transports.

On July 8 the army returned to the vicinity of Richmond.

Under ordinary circumstances the Federal Army should have been destroyed. Its escape was due to the causes already stated. Prominent among these is the want of correct and timely information. This fact, attributable chiefly to the character of the country, enabled General McClellan skillfully to conceal his retreat and to add much to the obstructions with which nature had beset the way of our pursuing columns; but regret that more was not accomplished gives way to gratitude to the Sovereign Ruler of the Universe for the results achieved. The siege of Richmond was raised, and the object of a campaign, which had been prosecuted after months of preparation at an enormous expenditure of men and money, completely frustrated. [*OR* 11, pt. 2, p. 497.]

Lee then used the rest of the month to reorganize his army. *Magruder* and *Holmes* were sent to the west while *Huger* went to a staff position. It was apparent to *Lee* that with nine infantry divisions reporting directly to him that his span of control was too great for one commander. Accordingly, he formed two commands. With corps organizations not yet authorized, he placed three divisions under *Jackson* and five divisions under *Longstreet,* while *D. H. Hill,* the cavalry, and reserve artillery reported directly to him.

Abraham Lincoln visited McClellan at Harrison's Landing on July 8. His purpose was to gain an appreciation of the condition of the army and to discuss future operations with McClellan. McClellan had been asking for additional reinforcements. With these reinforcements he proposed crossing his army to the south side of the James River and maneuver to cut the rail lines at Petersburg, which would sever most of the supply lines going into Richmond. This, he believed, would cause *Lee* to attack him on ground of his own choosing and allow him to defeat the Army of Northern Virginia.

Upon his return to Washington, Lincoln brought Major General Henry W. Halleck from the west and appointed him general-in-chief of all of the Union armies. Halleck visited McClellan on July 25. McClellan presented his new plan to move toward Petersburg. Halleck did not support this plan, and upon returning to Washington he ordered McClellan to begin evacuating his army from the Peninsula by water transport.

Washington, August 3, 1862—7.45 p.m.

Maj. Gen. GEORGE B. MCCLELLAN

It is determined to withdraw your army from the Peninsula to Aquia Creek. You will take immediate measures to effect this, covering the movement the best you can. Its real object and withdrawal should be concealed even from your own officers. Your material and transportation should be removed first. You will assume control of all the means of transportation within your reach, and apply to the naval forces for all the assistance they can render you. You will consult freely with the commander of these forces. The entire execution of the movement is left to your discretion and judgment.

You will leave such forces as you may deem proper at Fort Monroe, Norfolk, and other places, which we must occupy.

H. W. HALLECK,
Major-General,
Commanding U.S. Army

[*OR* 11, pt. 1, pp. 80–81.]

McClellan made an attempt to remain on the Peninsula and again move toward Richmond. He sent the following telegram to Halleck.

HEADQUARTERS ARMY OF THE POTOMAC
Berkeley, August 4, 1862—12 m.

Maj. Gen. H. W. HALLECK,
Commanding U.S. Army

Your telegram of last evening is received. I must confess that it has caused me the greatest pain I ever experienced, for I am convinced that the order to withdraw this army to Aquia Creek will prove disastrous to our cause. I fear it will be a fatal blow. Several days are necessary to complete the preparations for so important a movement as this, and while they are in progress I beg that careful consideration may be given to my statement.

This army is now in excellent discipline and condition. We hold a *debouche* on both banks of the James River, so that we are free to act in any direction; and with the assistance of the gunboats I consider our communications as now secure. We are 25 miles from Richmond, and are not likely to meet the enemy in force sufficient to fight a battle until we have marched 15 to 18 miles, which brings us practically within 10 miles of Richmond. Our longest line of land transportation would be from this point 25 miles, but with the aid of the gunboats we can supply the army by water during its advance certainly to within 12 miles of Richmond. At Aquia Creek we would be 75 miles from Richmond, with land transportation all the way. From here to Fort Monroe is a march of about 70 miles, for I regard it as impracticable to withdraw this army and its material except by land. The result of the movement would thus be a march of 145 miles to reach a point now only 25 miles distant, and to deprive ourselves entirely of the powerful aid of the gunboats and water transportation. Add to this the certain demoralization of this army which would ensue, the terribly depressing effect upon the people of the North, and the strong probability that it would influence foreign powers to recognize our adversaries, and these appear to me sufficient reasons to make it my imperative duty to urge in the strongest terms afforded by our language that this order may be rescinded, and that far from recalling this army, it may be promptly re-enforced to enable it to resume the offensive.

It may be said that there are no re-enforcements available. I point to Burnside's force; to that of Pope, not necessary to maintain a strict defensive in front of Washington and Harper's Ferry; to those portions of the Army of the West not required for a strict defensive there. Here, directly in front of this army, is the heart of the rebellion. It is here that all our resources should be collected to strike the blow which will determine the fate of the nation. All points of secondary importance elsewhere should be abandoned, and every available man brought here; a decided victory here and the military strength of the rebellion is crushed. It matters not what partial reverses we may meet with elsewhere. Here is the true defense of Washington. It is here, on the banks of the James, that the fate of the Union should be decided.

If my counsel does not prevail, I will with a sad heart obey your orders to the utmost of my power, directing to the movement, which I clearly foresee will be one of the utmost delicacy and difficulty, whatever skill I may possess. Whatever the result may be—and may God grant that I am mistaken in my forebodings—I shall at least have the internal satisfaction that I have written and spoken frankly, and have sought to do the best in my power to avert disaster from my country.

GEO. B. MCCLELLAN,
Major-General,
Commanding

[*OR* 11, pt. 1, pp. 81–82.]

Halleck, however, refused to be swayed by this appeal from McClellan and reaffirmed his decision with the following telegram.

Washington, August 4, 1862—12.45 p.m.
Maj. Gen. GEORGE B. MCCLELLAN

My telegram to you of yesterday will satisfy you in regard to future operations. It was expected that you would have sent off your sick as directed without waiting to know what were or would be the intentions of the Government respecting future movements. The President expects that the instructions which were sent you yesterday with his approval will be carried out with all possible dispatch and caution. The Quartermaster-General is sending to Fort Monroe all the transportation he can collect.

H. W. HALLECK,
Major-General

[*OR* 11, pt. 1, p. 82.]

In the meantime, on July 12 *Lee* had sent *Jackson* with two divisions northwest of Richmond to Gordonsville. A Union army, the Army of Virginia, had been formed in northern Virginia under the command of Major General John Pope. Pope advanced the lead elements of his army south toward Richmond. *Jackson*'s move was in response to this.

Jackson defeated Pope's advance forces at the Battle of Cedar Mountain on August 9. Four days later *Lee* began moving the remainder of his army to join *Jackson*.

On August 16 the last units of the Army of the Potomac left Harrison's Landing. Nine weeks earlier they had stood on the eastern edge of Richmond, close enough to hear the church bells ring on Sunday mornings, and now they were gone. It was over two years before the Army of the Potomac was again that close to Richmond.

This completes your tour of the Seven Days Battles. If you want to return to the major roads east of Richmond, follow these instructions:

Drive from the parking lot and turn right on Highway 156 (Carter's Mill Road), drive for 0.1 mile, and turn right. Drive west off Malvern Hill by following this road for 1.0 mile. Union officers called this the Richmond Road in their reports. In 1.0 mile this road will intersect with Highway 5 West. Turn right on to Highway 5 West (New Market Road) and drive for 4.1 miles to Interstate 295.

I-295 South will take you south of Richmond and to I-95 South. I-295 North will take you to East-West I-64 and eventually north of Richmond to I-95 North.

Appendix I

Union Order of Battle

ARMY OF THE POTOMAC
  MAJ. GEN. GEORGE B. MCCLELLAN

PROVOST MARSHALL AND HEADQUARTERS GUARD
  BRIG. GEN. ANDREW PORTER
  2d U.S. Cavalry (7 Co's) and McClellan Dragoons (2 Co's) Maj. Alfred
    Pleasonton
  93d New York (4 Co's) and Sturgis Rifles, Maj. Granville O. Haller
  8th U.S. Infantry (2 Co's), Capt. Royal T. Frank

ESCORT
  4th U.S. Cavalry (2 Co's) and Oneida (N.Y.) Cavalry, Capt. John B.
    McIntyre

SECOND ARMY CORPS
  BRIG. GEN. EDWIN V. SUMNER

CAVALRY
  6th New York Cavalry (4 Co's), Lieut. Col. Duncan McVicar

FIRST DIVISION
  BRIG. GEN. ISRAEL B. RICHARDSON

FIRST BRIGADE
  BRIG. GEN. JOHN C. CALDWELL
  5th New Hampshire, Lieut. Col. Samuel G. Langley, Capt. Edward E.
    Sturtevant
  7th New York, Col. George W. von Schack
  61st New York, Col. Francis C. Barlow
  81st Pennsylvania, Col. Charles F. Johnson (w), Lieut. Col. Eli T.
    Conner (k), Maj. H. Boyd McKeen

SECOND BRIGADE
    BRIG. GEN. THOMAS F. MEAGHER
    29th Massachusetts, Col. Ebenezer W. Pierce (w), Lieut. Col. Joseph H.
      Barnes
    63d New York, Col. John Burke (w), Lieut. Col. Henry Fowler, Capt.
      Joseph O'Neill
    69th New York, Col. Robert Nugent
    88th New York, Col. Henry M. Baker, Maj. James Quinlan

THIRD BRIGADE
    BRIG. GEN. WILLIAM H. FRENCH
    2d Delaware, Lieut. Col. William P. Baily, Capt. D. L. Stricker
    52d New York, Col. Paul Frank
    57th New York, Col. Samuel K. Zook
    64th New York, Col. Thomas J. Parker
    66th New York, Col. Joseph C. Pinckney
    53d Pennsylvania, Col. John R. Brooke

ARTILLERY
    CAPT. GEORGE W. HAZZARD (mw)
    Battery B, 1st New York Artillery, Capt. Rufus D. Pettit
    Batteries A and C, 4th U.S. Artillery, Capt. George W. Hazzard (mw),
      Lieut. Rufus King

SECOND DIVISION
    BRIG. GEN. JOHN SEDWICK

FIRST BRIGADE
    COL. ALFRED SULLY
    15th Massachusetts, Lieut. Col. John W. Kimball
    1st Minnesota, Lieut. Col. Stephan Miller
    34th New York, Col. James A. Suiter
    82d New York, Col. Henry W. Hudson
    1st Company Mass. Sharpshooters, Capt. John Saunders
    2d Company Minn. Sharpshooters, Capt. William F. Russell

SECOND BRIGADE
    BRIG. GEN. WILLIAM W. BURNS (w)
    69th Pennsylvania, Col. Joshua T. Owen
    71st Pennsylvania, Lieut. Col. William G. Jones
    72d Pennsylvania, Col. DeWitt C. Baxter
    106th Pennsylvania, Col. Turner G. Morehead

THIRD BRIGADE
    BRIG. GEN. NAPOLEON J. T. DANA
    19th Massachusetts, Col. Edward W. Hinks (w), Capt. Edmund Rice,
      Lieut. Col. Arthur F. Devereux
    20th Massachusetts, Col. William R. Lee

7th Michigan, Col. Ira R. Grosvenor
42d New York, Col. Edmund C. Charles (w, c), Lieut. Col. James J.
    Mooney

ARTILLERY
    COL. CHARLES H. TOMPKINS
    Battery A, 1st Rhode Island Artillery, Capt. John A. Tompkins
    Battery I, 1st U.S. Artillery, Lieut. Edmund Kirby

CORPS ARTILLERY RESERVE
    Battery G, 1st New York Artillery, Capt. John D. Frank
    Battery B, 1st Rhode Island Artillery, Capt. Walter O. Bartlett
    Battery G, 1st Rhode Island Artillery, Capt. Charles D. Owen

THIRD ARMY CORPS
    BRIG. GEN. SAMUEL P. HEINTZELMAN

CAVALRY
    3d Pennsylvania Cavalry, Col. William W. Averell

SECOND DIVISION
    BRIG. GEN. JOSEPH HOOKER

FIRST BRIGADE
    BRIG. GEN. CUVIER GROVER
    1st Massachusetts, Col. Robert Cowdin
    11th Massachusetts, Col. William Blaisdell
    16th Massachusetts, Col. Powell T. Wyman (k), Lieut. Col. George A.
        Meacham (w), Maj. Daniel S. Lamson
    2d New Hampshire, Col. Gilman Marston
    26th Pennsylvania, Lieut. Col. George D. Wells

SECOND BRIGADE
    BRIG. GEN. DANIEL E. SICKLES
    70th New York, Maj. Thomas Holt
    71st New York, Col. George B. Hall
    72d New York, Col. Nelson Taylor
    73d New York, Capt. Alfred A. Donalds
    74th New York, Col. Charles K. Graham

THIRD BRIGADE
    COL. JOSEPH B. CARR
    5th New Jersey, Maj. John Ramsey
    6th New Jersey, Col. Gershom Mott
    7th New Jersey, Col. Joseph W. Revere, Capt. Henry C. Bartlett
    8th New Jersey, Maj. William A. Henry
    2d New York, Lieut. Col. William A. Olmsted

Appendix I

ARTILLERY
Battery D, 1st New York Artillery, Capt. Thomas W. Osborn
4th Battery, New York Artillery, Lieut. Joseph E. Nairn
Battery H, 1st U.S. Artillery, Capt. Charles H. Webber

THIRD DIVISION
BRIG. GEN. PHILLIP KEARNY

FIRST BRIGADE
BRIG. GEN. JOHN C. ROBINSON
20th Indiana, Col. William Brown
87th New York, Lieut. Col. Richard A. Bachia
57th Pennsylvania, Lieut. Col. Elhanon W. Woods
63d Pennsylvania, Col. Alexander Hays
105th Pennsylvania, Col. Amor A. McKnight, Lieut. Col. William W.
    Corbet, Capt. Calvin A. Craig

SECOND BRIGADE
BRIG. GEN. DAVID B. BIRNEY
3d Maine, Lieut. Col. Charles A. L. Sampson, Maj. Edwin Burt
4th Maine, Col. Elijah Walker
38th New York, Col. Hobart Ward
40th New York, Col. Thomas W. Egan
101st New York, Col. Enrico Fardella

THIRD BRIGADE
BRIG. GEN. HIRAM G. BERRY
2d Michigan, Lieut. Col. Louis Dillman, Capt. William Humphrey
3d Michigan, Lieut. Col. Ambrose A. Stevens, Maj. Byron R. Pierce
5th Michigan, Maj. John D. Fairbanks (mw), Capt. Judson S. Farrer
1st New York, Col. Garrett Dyckman
37th New York, Col. Samuel B. Hayman

ARTILLERY
Battery E, 1st Rhode Island Artillery, Capt. George E. Randolph
Battery G, 2d U.S. Artillery, Capt. James Thompson

CORPS ARTILLERY RESERVE
CAPT. GUSTAVUS A. DERUSSY
6th Battery, New York Artillery, Capt. Walter M. Bramhall
2d Battery, New Jersey Artillery, Capt. John E. Beam (k), Lieut. John B.
    Monroe
Battery K, 4th U.S. Artillery, Lieut. Francis W. Seeley

FOURTH ARMY CORPS
BRIG. GEN. ERASMUS D. KEYES

CAVALRY
8th Pennsylvania Cavalry, Col. David McM. Gregg

FIRST DIVISION
BRIG. GEN. DARIUS N. COUCH

FIRST BRIGADE
BRIG. GEN. ALBION P. HOWE
55th New York, Lieut. Col. Louis Thourot
62d New York, Col. David J. Nevin
93d Pennsylvania, Capt. John S. Long
98th Pennsylvania, Col. John F. Ballier
102d Pennsylvania, Col. Thomas Rowley

SECOND BRIGADE
BRIG. GEN. JOHN J. ABERCROMBIE
65th New York (1st U.S. Chasseurs), Lieut. Col. Alexander Shaler
67th New York, (1st Long Island), Lieut. Col. Nelson Cross
23d Pennsylvania, Col. Thomas H. Neill
31st Pennsylvania, Col. David H. Williams
61st Pennsylvania, Lieut. Col. Frank Vallee

THIRD BRIGADE
BRIG. GEN. INNIS N. PALMER
7th Massachusetts, Col. David A. Russell
10th Massachusetts, Maj. Ozro Miller (mw), Capt. Frederick Barton
36th New York, Maj. James A. Raney
2d Rhode Island, Col. Frank Wheaton

ARTILLERY
Battery C, 1st Pennsylvania Artillery, Capt. Jeremiah McCarthy
Battery D, 1st Pennsylvania Artillery, Capt. Edward H. Flood

SECOND DIVISION
BRIG. GEN. JOHN J. PECK

FIRST BRIGADE
BRIG. GEN. HENRY M. NAGLEE
11th Maine, Col. Harris M. Plaisted
56th New York, Col. Charles H. Van Wyck
100th New York, Lieut. Col. Phineas Staunton
52d Pennsylvania, Lieut. Col. Henry M. Hoyt
104th Pennsylvania, Lieut. Col. John W. Nields

SECOND BRIGADE
BRIG. GEN. HENRY W. WESSELLS
81st New York, Col. Edwin Rose
85th New York, Col. Jonathan S. Belknap

92d New York, Lieut. Col. Hiram Anderson Jr.
96th New York, Col. James Fairman
98th New York, Lieut. Col. Charles Durkee
85th Pennsylvania, Col. Joshua B. Howell
101st Pennsylvania, Capt. Charles W. May
103d Pennsylvania, Col. Theodore F. Lehman

ARTILLERY
Battery H, 1st New York Artillery, Lieut. Charles E. Mink
7th Battery, New York Artillery, Capt. Peter C. Regan

CORPS ARTILLERY RESERVE
MAJ. ROBERT M. WEST
8th Battery, New York Artillery, Capt. Butler Fitch
Battery E, 1st Pennsylvania Artillery, Capt. Theodore Miller
Battery H, 1st Pennsylvania Artillery, Capt. James Brady
Battery M, 5th U.S. Artillery, Capt. James McKnight

FIFTH ARMY CORPS
BRIG. GEN. FITZ JOHN PORTER

CAVALRY
8th Illinois Cavalry, Col. John F. Farnsworth

FIRST DIVISION
BRIG. GEN. GEORGE W. MORELL

FIRST BRIGADE
BRIG. GEN. JOHN H. MARTINDALE
2d Maine, Col. Charles W. Roberts
22d Massachusetts, Col. Jesse A. Grove (k), Maj. William S. Tilton (w, c),
    Capt. Walter S. Sampson, Capt. David K. Wardwell
1st Michigan, Col. Horace S. Roberts
13th New York, Col. Elisha G. Marshall, Maj. Francis A. Schoeffel
25th New York, Maj. Edwin S. Gilbert (c), Capt. Shepard Gleason
2d Company Massachusetts Sharpshooters, Lieut. Charles D. Stiles

SECOND BRIGADE
BRIG. GEN. CHARLES GRIFFIN
9th Massachusetts, Col. Thomas Cass (mw), Lieut. Col. Patrick R. Guiney
4th Michigan, Col. Dwight A. Woodbury (k), Lieut. Col. Jonathan W.
    Childs (w), Capt. John M. Randolph
14th New York, Col. James McQuade
62d Pennsylvania, Col. Samuel W. Black (k), Lieut. Col. Jacob B. Sweitzer
    (w, c), Capt. James C. Hull

THIRD BRIGADE
BRIG. GEN. DANIEL BUTTERFIELD
12th New York, Lieut. Col. Robert M. Richardson

44th New York, Lieut. Col. James C. Rice
16th Michigan, Col. T. B. W. Stockton (c), Lieut. Col. John V. Ruehle
83d Pennsylvania, Col. John W. McLane (k), Capt. Hugh S. Campbell (w)
Brady's Company Michigan Sharpshooters, Capt. S. Dygert

ARTILLERY
CAPT. WILLIAM B. WEEDEN
3d (C) Battery, Massachusetts Artillery, Capt. Augustus P. Martin
5th (E) Battery Massachusetts Artillery, Lieut. John B. Hyde
Battery C, 1st Rhode Island Artillery, Lieut. Richard Waterman
Battery D, 5th U.S. Artillery, Lieut. Henry W. Kingsbury

SHARPSHOOTERS
1st U.S. Sharpshooters, Col. Hiram Berdan

SECOND DIVISION
BRIG. GEN. GEORGE SYKES

FIRST BRIGADE
COL. ROBERT C. BUCHANAN
3d U.S. Infantry, Maj. Nathan B. Rossell (k), Capt. Thomas W. Walker,
    Capt. John D. Wilkins
4th U.S. Infantry, Maj. Delozier Davidson (c), Capt. Joseph B. Collins
12th U.S. Infantry, Maj. Henry B. Clitz (w, c), Capt. John G. Read,
    Capt. Matthew M. Blunt
14th U.S. Infantry, Capt. John D. O'Connell

SECOND BRIGADE
LIEUT. COL. WILLIAM CHAPMAN
MAJ. CHARLES S. LOVELL
2d U.S. Infantry, Capt. Adolphus F. Bond, Lieut. John S. Poland
6th U.S. Infantry, Capt. Thomas Hendrickson
10th U.S. Infantry, Maj. Charles S. Lovell
11th U.S. Infantry, Maj. DeLancey Floyd-Jones
17th U.S. Infantry, Maj. George L. Andrews

THIRD BRIGADE
COL. GOUVERNEUR K. WARREN
5th New York, Lieut. Col. Hiram Duryea
10th New York, Col. John E. Bendix

ARTILLERY
CAPT. STEPHEN H. WEED
Batteries L and M, 3d U.S. Artillery, Capt. John Edwards
Battery I, 5th U.S. Artillery, Capt. Stephen H. Weed

THIRD DIVISION
BRIG. GEN. GEORGE A. McCALL (c)
BRIG. GEN. TRUMAN SEYMOUR

First Brigade
 Brig. Gen. John F. Reynolds (c)
 Col. Seneca G. Simmons (k)
 Col. R. Biddle Roberts
 1st Pennsylvania Reserves, Col. R. Biddle Roberts, Maj. Lemuel Todd
 2d Pennsylvania Reserves, Lieut. Col. William McCandless
 5th Pennsylvania Reserves, Col. Seneca G. Simmons (k), Lieut. Col.
  Joseph W. Fisher
 8th Pennsylvania Reserves, Col. George S. Hays
 13th Pennsylvania Reserves, Maj. Roy Stone

Second Brigade
 Brig. Gen. George G. Meade (w)
 Col. Albert L. Magilton
 3d Pennsylvania Reserves, Col. Horatio G. Sickel
 4th Pennsylvania Reserves, Col. Albert L. Magilton
 7th Pennsylvania Reserves, Col. Elisha B. Harvey
 11th Pennsylvania Reserves, Col. Thomas F. Gallagher (c), Capt. Daniel S.
  Porter

Third Brigade
 Brig. Gen. Truman Seymour
 Col. C. Feger Jackson
 9th Pennsylvania Reserves, Col. C. Feger Jackson, Capt. John
  Cuthbertson (w)
 10th Pennsylvania Reserves, Col. James T. Kirk
 12th Pennsylvania Reserves, Col. John H. Taggart

Artillery
 Battery A, 1st Pennsylvania Artillery, Capt. Hezekiah Easton (k), Lieut.
  Jacob L. Detrich, Lieut. John G. Simpson
 Battery B, 1st Pennsylvania Artillery, Capt. James H. Cooper
 Battery G, 1st Pennsylvania Artillery, Capt. Mark Kerns (w), Lieut.
  Frank P. Amsden
 Battery C, 5th U.S. Artillery, Capt. Henry V. DeHart (mw), Lieut.
  Eben G. Scott

Cavalry
 4th Pennsylvania Cavalry, Col. James H. Childs

Sixth Army Corps
 Brig. Gen. William B. Franklin

Cavalry
 1st New York Cavalry, Col. Andrew T. McReynolds

First Division
 Brig. Gen. Henry W. Slocum

FIRST BRIGADE
  BRIG. GEN. GEORGE W. TAYLOR
  1st New Jersey, Lieut. Col. Robert McAllister, Col. Alfred T. A. Torbert
  2d New Jersey, Col. Isaac M. Tucker (k), Maj. Henry O. Ryerson (w),
    Lieut. Col. Samuel L. Buck
  3d New Jersey, Col. Henry W. Brown
  4th New Jersey, Col. James H. Simpson

SECOND BRIGADE
  COL. JOSEPH J. BARTLETT
  5th Maine, Col. Nathaniel J. Jackson (w), Lieut. Col. William S. Heath (k),
    Capt. Clark S. Edwards
  16th New York, Col. Joseph Howland (w), Maj. Joel J. Seaver
  27th New York, Lieut. Col. Alexander D. Adams
  96th Pennsylvania, Col. Henry Cake

THIRD BRIGADE
  BRIG. GEN. JOHN NEWTON
  18th New York, Lieut. Col. George R. Myers, Maj. John C. Meginnis
  31st New York, Col. Calvin E. Pratt (w), Maj. Alexander Raszewski
  32d New York, Col. Roderick Matheson
  95th Pennsylvania, Col. John M. Gosline (mw), Lieut. Col. Gustavus W.
    Town

ARTILLERY
  CAPT. EDWARD R. PLATT
  1st Battery, Massachusetts Artillery, Capt. Josiah Porter
  1st Battery, New Jersey Artillery, Capt. William Hexamer
  Battery D, 2d U.S. Artillery, Lieut. Emory Upton

SECOND DIVISION
  BRIG. GEN. WILLIAM F. SMITH

FIRST BRIGADE
  BRIG. GEN. WINFIELD S. HANCOCK
  6th Maine, Col. Hiram Burnham
  43d New York, Col. Francis L. Vinton
  49th Pennsylvania, Col. William H. Irwin
  5th Wisconsin, Col. Amasa Cobb

SECOND BRIGADE
  BRIG. GEN. WILLIAM T. H. BROOKS
  2d Vermont, Col. Henry Whiting
  3d Vermont, Lieut. Col. Wheelock G. Veazey
  4th Vermont, Col. Edwin H. Stoughton
  5th Vermont, Lieut. Col. Lewis A. Grant
  6th Vermont, Col. Nathan Lord

THIRD BRIGADE
    BRIG. GEN. JOHN W. DAVIDSON
    7th Maine, Col. Edwin C. Mason
    20th New York, Col. Francis Weiss
    33d New York, Col. Robert F. Taylor
    49th New York, Col. Daniel D. Bidwell
    77th New York, Col. James B. McKean

ARTILLERY
    CAPT. ROMEYN B. AYRES
    Battery E, 1st New York Artillery, Capt. Charles C. Wheeler
    1st Battery, New York Artillery, Capt. Andrew Cowan
    3d Battery, New York Artillery, Capt. Thaddeus P. Mott
    Battery F, 5th U.S. Artillery, Capt. Romeyn B. Ayres

CAVALRY
    I and K Companies, 5th Pennsylvania Cavalry, Capt. John O'Farrell

ARMY ARTILLERY RESERVE
    COL. HENRY J. HUNT

FIRST BRIGADE
(Horse Artillery)
    LIEUT. COL. WILLIAM HAYS
    Battery A, 2d U.S. Artillery, Capt. John C. Tidball
    Batteries B and L, 2d U.S. Artillery, Capt. James M. Robertson
    Battery M, 2d Artillery, Capt. Henry Benson

SECOND BRIGADE
    LIEUT. COL. GEORGE W. GETTY
    Batteries E and G, 1st U.S. Artillery, Lieut. Alanson M. Randol
    Battery K, 1st U.S. Artillery, Lieut. Samuel S. Elder
    Battery G, 4th U.S. Artillery, Lieut. Charles H. Morgan
    Battery A, 5th U.S. Artillery, Lieut. Adelbert Ames
    Battery K, 5th U.S. Artillery, Capt. John R. Smead

THIRD BRIGADE
    MAJ. ALBERT ARNDT
    Battery A, 1st Battalion, New York Artillery, Capt. Otto Diederichs
    Battery B, 1st Battalion, New York Artillery, Capt. Adolph Voegelee
    Battery C, 1st Battalion, New York Artillery, Capt. John Knieriem
    Battery D, 1st Battalion, New York Artillery, Capt. Edward Grimm

FOURTH BRIGADE
    MAJ. EDWARD R. PETHERBRIDGE
    Battery A, Maryland Artillery, Capt. John W. Wolcott
    Battery B, Maryland Artillery, Capt. Alonzo Snow

FIFTH BRIGADE
CAPT. J. HOWARD CARLISLE
Battery E, 2d U.S. Artillery, Capt. J. Howard Carlisle
Batteries F and K, 3d U.S. Artillery, Capt. La Rhett L. Livingston

SIEGE TRAIN
1st Connecticut Heavy Artillery, Col. Robert O. Tyler

ARMY CAVALRY RESERVE
BRIG. GEN. PHILLIP ST. GEORGE COOKE

FIRST BRIGADE
BRIG GEN. WILLIAM H. EMORY
6th Pennsylvania Cavalry, Col. Richard H. Rush
5th U.S. Cavalry (5 Co's), Capt. Charles J. Whiting (c), Capt. Joseph H.
    McArthur

SECOND BRIGADE
COL. GEORGE A. H. BLAKE
1st U.S. Cavalry (4 Co's), Lieut. Col. William N. Grier
6th U.S. Cavalry (Detached), Capt. August V. Kautz

VOLUNTEER ENGINEER BRIGADE
BRIG. GEN. DANIEL P. WOODBURY
15th New York Engineers, Col. J. McLeod Murphy
50th New York Engineers, Col. Charles B. Stuart
Battalion U.S. Engineers, Capt. James C. Duane

CASEY'S COMMAND AT WHITE HOUSE
BRIG. GEN. SILAS CASEY
4th Pennsylvania Cavalry (Squadron), Capt. William Shorts
11th Pennsylvania Cavalry (5 Co's), Col. Josiah Harlan
93d New York (6 Co's), Col. Thomas F. Morris
Battery F, 1st New York Artillery, Capt. William R. Wilson
Batteries C and G, 3d U.S. Artillery, Capt. Horatio G. Gibson

[*OR* 11, pt. 2, pp. 24–482 and *B&L*, vol. 2, pp. 313–15.]

(k) Killed
(w) Wounded
(mw) Mortally wounded
(c) Captured

Appendix II

Confederate Order of Battle

ARMY OF NORTHERN VIRGINIA
  GEN. ROBERT E. LEE

JACKSON'S COMMAND
  MAJ. GEN. THOMAS J. JACKSON

WHITING'S DIVISION
  BRIG. GEN. WILLIAM H. C. WHITING

HOOD'S BRIGADE
  BRIG. GEN. JOHN B. HOOD
  18th Georgia, Lieut. Col. S. Z. Ruff
  1st Texas, Col. A. T. Rainey (w)
  4th Texas, Col. John Marshall (k), Capt. W. P. Townsend
  5th Texas, Col. Jerome B. Robertson
  Hampton Legion, Lieut. Col. M. W. Gary

LAW'S BRIGADE
  COL. EVANDER M. LAW
  4th Alabama, Lieut. Col. O. K. McLemore (w), Capt. L. H. Scruggs
  2d Mississippi, Col. J. M. Stone
  11th Mississippi, Col. P. F. Liddell
  6th North Carolina, Lieut. Col. Isaac E. Avery (w), Maj. Robert F. Webb

ARTILLERY
  Balthis's Battery, Staunton (Va.) Artillery, Capt. W. L. Balthis
  Reilly's Battery, Rowan (N.C.) Artillery, Capt. James Reilly

JACKSON'S DIVISION
  BRIG. GEN. CHARLES S. WINDER

WINDER'S BRIGADE
    BRIG. GEN. CHARLES S. WINDER
    2d Virginia, Col. J. W. Allen (k), Lieut. Col. Lawson Botts
    4th Virginia, Col. Charles A. Ronald
    5th Virginia, Col. William S. H. Baylor
    27th Virginia, Col. A. J. Grigsby (w), Capt. G. C. Smith
    33 Virginia, Col. John F. Neff
    Carpenter's (Va.) Battery, Lieut. John C. Carpenter
    Poague's Battery, Rockbridge (Va.) Artillery, Capt. William T. Poague

JONES'S BRIGADE
    BRIG. GEN. J. R. JONES (w)
    LIEUT. COL. R. H. CUNNINGHAM JR.
    21st Virginia, Lieut. Col. R. H. Cunningham, Maj. John B. Mosely
    42d Virginia, Lieut. Col. William Martin
    48th Virginia, Capt. John M. Vermillion
    1st Virginia Battalion (Irish), Capt. B. W. Leigh
    Caskie's Battery, Hampden (Va.) Artillery, Capt. William H. Caskie

FULKERSON'S BRIGADE
    COL. S. V. FULKERSON (mw)
    COL. E. T. H. WARREN
    BRIG. GEN. WADE HAMPTON
    10th Virginia, Col. E. T. H. Warren
    23d Virginia, Capt. A. V. Scott
    37th Virginia, Maj. T. V. Williams
    Wooding's Battery, Danville (Va.) Artillery, Capt. George W. Wooding

LAWTON'S BRIGADE
    BRIG. GEN. ALEXANDER R. LAWTON
    13th Georgia, Col. Marcellus Douglas
    26th Georgia, Col. E. N. Atkinson, Maj. E. S. Griffin
    31st Georgia, Col. C. A. Evans (w), Maj. J H. Lowe
    38th Georgia, Lieut. Col. L. J. Parr (w), Capt. William H. Battey
    60th Georgia, Lieut. Col. W. H. Stiles
    61st Georgia, Col. John H. Lamar

EWELL'S DIVISION
    MAJ. GEN. RICHARD S. EWELL

ELZEY'S BRIGADE
    BRIG. GEN. ARNOLD ELZEY
    COL. JAMES A. WALKER
    BRIG. GEN. JUBAL A. EARLY
    12th Georgia, Capt. James G. Rodgers
    13th Virginia, Col. James A. Walker
    25th Virginia, Lieut. Col. John C. Higginbotham
    31st Virginia, Col. John S. Hoffman

44th Virginia, Lieut. Col. Norvell Cobb
52d Virginia, Lieut. Col. J. H. Skinner
58th Virginia, Col. F. H. Board

TRIMBLE'S BRIGADE
   BRIG. GEN. ISAAC R. TRIMBLE
   15th Alabama, Col. James Cantey
   21st Georgia, Maj. Thomas W. Hooper (w)
   16th Mississippi, Col. Carnot Posey
   21st North Carolina, Lieut. Col. W. W. Kirkland
   1st North Carolina Battalion, Maj. Rufus W. Wharton
   Courtney's (Va.) Battery, Capt. A. R. Courtney

TAYLOR'S BRIGADE
   BRIG. GEN. RICHARD TAYLOR
   COL. I. G. SEYMOUR (k)
   COL. LEROY A. STAFFORD
   6th Louisiana, Col. I. G. Seymour (k)
   7th Louisiana, Lieut. Col. David B. Penn
   8th Louisiana, Col. Henry B. Kelly
   9th Louisiana, Col. Leroy A. Stafford
   1st Louisiana Special Battalion, Maj. Roberdeau Wheat (k)
   Carrington's Battery, Charlottesville (Va.) Artillery, Capt. J. McD.
      Carrington

MARYLAND LINE
   COL. BRADLEY T. JOHNSON
   First Maryland, Col. Bradley T. Johnson
   Brockenbrough's Battery, Baltimore (Md.) Artillery, Capt. J. B.
      Brockenbrough

D. H. HILL'S DIVISION
   MAJ. GEN. DANIEL H. HILL

RODES'S BRIGADE
   BRIG. GEN. ROBERT E. RODES
   COL. JOHN B. GORDON
   3d Alabama, Lieut. Col. Charles Forsyth, Maj. Robert Sands
   5th Alabama, Col. C. C. Pegues (mw), Maj. E. L. Hobson
   6th Alabama, Col. John B. Gordon, Maj. B. G. Baldwin
   12th Alabama, Col. B. B. Gayle
   26th Alabama, Col. E. A. O'Neal
   Carter's Battery, King William (Va.) Artillery, Capt. Thomas H. Carter

G. B. ANDERSON'S BRIGADE
   BRIG. GEN. GEORGE B. ANDERSON (w)
   COL. C. C. TEW
   2d North Carolina, Col. C. C. Tew

4th North Carolina, Col. E. A. Osborne
14th North Carolina, Lieut. Col. William A. Johnson
30th North Carolina, Col. Francis M. Parker
Hardaway's (Ala.) Battery, Capt. R. A. Hardaway

GARLAND'S BRIGADE
  BRIG. GEN. SAMUEL GARLAND
  5th North Carolina, Col. D. K. McRae
  12th North Carolina, Col. Benjamin O. Wade
  13th North Carolina, Col. Alfred M. Scales
  20th North Carolina, Col. Alfred Iverson (w), Lieut. Col. Franklin J. Faison
    (k), Maj. William H. Toon
  23d North Carolina, Col. Daniel H. Christie (w), Lieut. Isaac J. Young (w)
  Bondurant's Battery, Jeff. Davis (Ala.) Artillery, Capt. J. W. Bondurant

COLQUITT'S BRIGADE
  COL. ALFRED H. COLQUITT
  13th Alabama, Col. Birkett D. Fry
  6th Georgia, Col. J. M. Newton
  23d Georgia, Col. Emory F. Best
  27th Georgia, Col. Levi B. Smith
  28th Georgia, Col. T. J. Warthen
  Nelson's Battery, Hanover (Va.) Artillery, Capt. G. W. Nelson

RIPLEY'S BRIGADE
  BRIG. GEN. ROSWELL S. RIPLEY
  44th Georgia, Col. Robert A. Smith (mw), Capt. John W. Beck
  48th Georgia, Col. William Gibson
  1st North Carolina, Col. M. S. Stokes (k), Capt. H. A. Brown, Lieut. Col.
    William P. Bynum
  3d North Carolina, Col. Gaston Meares (k)

JONES' ARTILLERY BATTALION
  MAJ. HILARY P. JONES
  Clark's (Va.) Battery, Capt. P. H. Clark
  Peyton's Battery, Orange (Va.) Artillery, Lieut. C. W. Fry
  Rhett's (S.C.) Battery, Capt. A. Burnet Rhett

MAGRUDER'S COMMAND
  MAJ. GEN. JOHN B. MAGRUDER

FIRST DIVISION
  BRIG. GEN. DAVID R. JONES

TOOMBS' BRIGADE
  BRIG. GEN. ROBERT TOOMBS
  2d Georgia, Col. Edgar M. Butt (w), Lieut. Col. William R. Holmes

15th Georgia, Col. William M. McIntosh (mw), Lieut. Col. William T. Millican, Maj. T. J. Smith, Capt. Stephen Z. Hearnsberger
17th Georgia, Col. Henry L. Benning
20th Georgia, Col. J. B. Cumming

G. T. ANDERSON'S BRIGADE
COL. GEORGE T. ANDERSON
1st Georgia (Regulars), Col. William J. Magill
7th Georgia, Lieut. Col. W. W. White (w), Maj. E. W. Hoyle (w), Capt. George H. Carmical
8th Georgia, Col. L. M. Lamar (w, c), Capt. George O. Dawson
9th Georgia, Col. R. A. Turnipseed
11th Georgia, Lieut. Col. William Luffman

ARTILLERY
MAJ. JOHN J. GARNETT
Brown's Battery, Wise (Va.) Artillery, Capt. James S. Brown
Hart's Battery, Washington (S.C.) Artillery, Capt. James F. Hart
Lane's (Ga.) Battery, Capt. John Lane
Moody's (La.) Battery, Capt. George V. Moody
Woolfolk's Battery, Ashland (Va.) Artillery, Lieut. James Woolfolk

McLAW'S DIVISION
MAJ. GEN. LAFAYETTE McLAW

SEMMES'S BRIGADE
BRIG. GEN. PAUL J. SEMMES
10th Georgia, Col. Alfred Cumming (w), Capt. W. C. Holt
53d Georgia, Col. L. T. Doyal
5th Louisiana, Col. T. G. Hunt
10th Louisiana, Lieut. Col. Eugene Waggaman
15th Virginia, Col. T. P. August (w)
32d Virginia, Lieut. Col. William R. Willis
Manly's (N.C.) Battery, Capt. Basil C. Manly

KERSHAW'S BRIGADE
BRIG. GEN. JOSEPH B. KERSHAW
2d South Carolina, Col. John D. Kennedy, Maj. Franklin Gaillard
3d South Carolina, Col. James D. Nance
7th South Carolina, Col. D. Wyatt Aiken
8th South Carolina, Col. John W. Henagan
Kemper's Battery, Alexandria (Va.) Artillery, Capt. Del Kemper

MAGRUDER'S DIVISION

COBB'S BRIGADE
BRIG. GEN. HOWELL COBB
16th Georgia, Col. Goode Bryan

24th Georgia, Col. Robert McMillan
Cobb (Ga.) Legion, _____
2d Louisiana, Col. T. J. Norwood (w)
15th North Carolina, Col. Henry A. Dowd (w)
Troup (Ga.) Artillery, Capt. Henry H. Carlton

GRIFFITH'S BRIGADE
  BRIG. GEN. RICHARD GRIFFITH (mw)
  COL. WILLIAM BARKSDALE
  13th Mississippi, Col. William Barksdale, Lieut. Col. James W. Carter (w),
    Maj. Kennon McElroy
  17th Mississippi, Col. W. D. Holder (w), Lieut. Col. John C. Fiser
  18th Mississippi, Col. Thomas M. Griffin (w), Lieut. Col. William H. Luse
  21st Mississippi, Col. Benjamin G. Humphreys, Lieut. Col. W. L. Brandon
    (w), Capt. William C. F. Brooks
  McCarthy's (Va.) Battery, Capt. E. S. McCarthy

ARTILLERY
  COL. STEPHEN D. LEE
  Kirkpatrick's Battery, Amherst (Va.) Artillery, Capt. Thomas J. Kirkpatrick
  Page's Battery, Magruder (Va.) Artillery, Capt. T. Jeff Page
  Read's Battery, Pulaski (Ga.) Artillery, Capt. J. P. W. Read
  Richardson's Battery, Capt. L. W. Richardson

LONGSTREET'S DIVISION
  MAJ. GEN. JAMES LONGSTREET

KEMPER'S BRIGADE
  BRIG. GEN. JAMES L. KEMPER
  1st Virginia, Capt. G. F. Norton
  7th Virginia, Col. W. T. Patton
  11th Virginia, Capt. K. Otey
  17th Virginia, Col. M. D. Course
  24th Virginia, Lieut. Col. Peter Hairston
  Rogers's (Va.) Battery, Capt. Arthur L. Rogers

R. H. ANDERSON'S BRIGADE
  BRIG. GEN. RICHARD H. ANDERSON
  COL. MICAH JENKINS
  2d South Carolina Rifles, Col. J. V. Moore
  4th South Carolina, Maj. C. S. Mattison
  5th South Carolina, Lieut. Col. A. Jackson
  6th South Carolina, Col. John Bratton
  Palmetto (S.C.) Sharpshooters, Col. Micah Jenkins, Lieut. Col. Joseph Walker

PICKETT'S BRIGADE
  BRIG. GEN. GEORGE E. PICKETT (w)
  COL. EPPA HUNTON

Col. John B. Strange
8th Virginia, Col. Eppa Hunton
18th Virginia, Col. R. E. Withers (w)
19th Virginia, Col. John B. Strange
28th Virginia, Col. Robert C. Allen
56th Virginia, Col. W. D. Stuart

Wilcox's Brigade
Brig. Gen. Cadmus M. Wilcox
8th Alabama, Lieut. Col. Y. L. Royston (w)
9th Alabama, Maj. J. H. J. Williams, Capt. J. H. King (w)
10th Alabama, Col. John J. Woodward (k), Maj. John H. Caldwell (w)
11th Alabama, Lieut. Col. S. F. Hale (w), Capt. George Field (w)
Anderson's Battery, Thomas (Va.) Artillery, Capt. Edwin J. Anderson

Pryor's Brigade
Brig. Gen. Roger A. Pryor
14th Alabama, Lieut. Col. D. W. Baine (k)
2d Florida, Col. E. A. Perry
14th Louisiana, Col. Z. York
1st Louisiana Battalion, Lieut. Col. G. Coppens
3d Virginia, Lieut. Col. J. V. Scott (w)
Maurin's Battery, Donaldsonville (La.) Artillery, Capt. Victor Maurin

Featherston's brigade
Brig. Gen. Winfield S. Featherston (w)
12th Mississippi, Maj. W. H. Lilly (w), Capt. S. B. Thomas
19th Mississippi, Maj. John Mullins (w)
2d Mississippi Battalion, Lieut. Col. John G. Taylor
Smith's Battery, 3d Richmond Howitzers, Capt. Benjamin H. Smith

Artillery
Washington (La.) Battalion, Col. John B. Walton
Dearing's Battery (Lynchburg, Va.), Capt. James Dearing
Chapman's Battery (Dixie Artillery), Capt. W. H. Chapman

Huger's Division
Maj. Gen. Benjamin Huger

Mahone's Brigade
Brig. Gen. William Mahone
6th Virginia, Col. G. T. Rogers
12th Virginia, Col. D. A. Weisiger
16th Virginia, Lieut. Col. Joseph H. Ham
41st Virginia, Lieut. Col. William A. Parham (w)
49th Virginia, Col. William Smith
Grimes's (Va.) Battery, Capt. Casey F. Grimes
Moorman's (Va.) Battery, Capt. M. N. Moorman

Appendix II

WRIGHT'S BRIGADE
  BRIG. GEN. AMBROSE R. WRIGHT
  44th Alabama, Col. James Kent
  3d Georgia, Maj. John R. Sturges (k), Capt. R. B. Nisbet
  4th Georgia, Col. George Doles
  22d Georgia, Col. R. H. Jones, Maj. Joseph Wasden
  1st Louisiana, Lieut. Col. W. R. Shivers (w), Capt. M. Nolan
  Huger's (Va.) Battery, Capt. Frank Huger
  Ross's (Ga.) Battery, Capt. H. M. Ross

ARMISTEAD'S BRIGADE
  BRIG. GEN. LEWIS A. ARMISTEAD
  9th Virginia, Lieut. Col. James S. Gilliam
  14th Virginia, Col. James G. Hodges
  38th Virginia, Col. E. C. Edmonds
  53d Virginia, Col. H. B. Tomlin
  57th Virginia, Lieut. Col. Waddy T. James
  5th Virginia Battalion, Capt. William E. Alley
  Stribling's Battery, Fauquier (Va.) Artillery, Capt. Robert M. Stribling
  Turner's (Va.) Battery, Capt. William H. Turner

RANSOM'S BRIGADE (Attached)
  BRIG. GEN. ROBERT RANSOM JR.
  24th North Carolina, Col. William J. Clarke
  25th North Carolina, Col. Henry M. Rutledge
  26th North Carolina, Col. Z. B. Vance
  35th North Carolina, Col. M. W. Ransom (w), Lieut. Col. O. C. Petway (k)
  48th North Carolina, Col. Robert C. Hill
  49th North Carolina, Col. S. D. Ramseur

A. P. HILL'S (LIGHT) DIVISION
  MAJ. GEN. AMBROSE P. HILL

FIELD'S BRIGADE
  BRIG. GEN. CHARLES W. FIELD
  40th Virginia, Col. J. M. Brockenbrough
  47th Virginia, Col. Robert M. Mayo
  55th Virginia, Col. Francis Mallory
  60th Virginia, Col. William E. Starke (w), Lieut. Col. B. H. Jones, Maj.
    John C. Summers

GREGG'S BRIGADE
  BRIG. GEN. MAXCY GREGG
  1st South Carolina, Col. D. H. Hamilton
  1st South Carolina Rifles, Col. J. Foster Marshall
  12th South Carolina, Col. Dixon Barnes (w)
  13th South Carolina, Col. E. O. Edwards
  14th South Carolina, Col. Samuel McGowan

J. R. ANDERSON'S BRIGADE
BRIG. GEN. JOSEPH R. ANDERSON (w)
COL. EDWARD L. THOMAS
14th Georgia, Lieut. Col. Robert W. Folsom (w)
35th Georgia, Col. Edward Thomas
45th Georgia, Col. Thomas Hardeman (w)
49th Georgia, Col. A. J. Lane (w)
3d Louisiana Battalion, Lieut. Col. Edmund Pendleton

BRANCH'S BRIGADE
BRIG. GEN. LAWRENCE O'B. BRANCH
7th North Carolina, Col. Ruben P. Campbell (k), Lieut. Col. E. Graham
    Haywood (w), Maj. Junius L. Hill
18th North Carolina, Col. Robert Cowan
28th North Carolina, Col. James H. Lane
33d North Carolina, Lieut. Col. Robert F. Hoke
37th North Carolina, Col. Charles C. Lee (w), Lieut. Col. William Barbour

ARCHER'S BRIGADE
BRIG. GEN. JAMES J. ARCHER
5th Alabama Battalion, Capt. A. S. Van de Graaf (w)
19th Georgia, Lieut. Col. Thomas C. Johnson (k)
1st Tennessee, Lieut. Col. J. C. Shackelford (k)
7th Tennessee, Col. John F. Goodner (w)
14th Tennessee, Col. W. A. Forbes

PENDER'S BRIGADE
BRIG. GEN. WILLIAM D. PENDER
2d Arkansas Battalion, Maj. W. N. Bronaugh (k)
16th North Carolina, Lieut. Col. John S. McElroy
22d North Carolina, Col. James Conner (w), Lieut. Col. R. H. Gray
34th North Carolina, Col. Richard H. Riddick (w)
38th North Carolina, Col. William J. Hoke (w)
22d Virginia Battalion, Capt. J. C. Johnson

ARTILLERY
LIEUT. COL. LEWIS M. COLEMAN
Andrews's (Md.) Battery, Capt. R. Snowden Andrews
Bachman's (S.C.) Battery, Capt. William K. Bachman
Braxton's Battery, Fredericksburg (Va.) Artillery, Capt. Carter M. Braxton
Crenshaw's (Va.) Battery, Capt. William G. Crenshaw
Davidson's Battery, Letcher (Va.) Artillery, Capt. Greenlee Davidson
Johnson's (Va.) Battery, Capt. Marmaduke Johnson
McIntosh's Battery, Pee Dee (S.C.) Artillery, Capt. D. G. McIntosh
Purcell (Va.) Battery, Capt. William J. Pegram

HOLMES'S DIVISION
MAJ. GEN. THEOPHILUS H. HOLMES

Daniel's Brigade
Brig. Gen. Junius Daniel
43d North Carolina, Col. T. S. Kenan
45th North Carolina, Lieut. Col. J. H. Morehead
50th North Carolina, Col. M. D. Craton
Burroughs's Battalion (Cavalry), Maj. Edgar Burroughs

Walker's Brigade
Brig. Gen. John G. Walker
Col. Van H. Manning
3d Arkansas, Col. Van H. Manning
2d Georgia Battalion, Maj. George W. Ross
27th North Carolina, Col. John R. Cooke
46th North Carolina, Col. E. D. Hall
30th Virginia, Col. A. T. Harrison
Goodwyn's Cavalry Company, Capt. Edward A. Goodwyn

Artillery
Col. James Deshler
Branch's (Va.) Battery, Capt. James R. Branch
Brem's (N.C.) Battery, Capt. T. H. Brem
French's (Va.) Battery, Capt. David A. French
Graham's (Va.) Battery, Capt. Edward Graham
Grandy's (Va.) Battery, _____
Lloyd's (N.C.) Battery, _____

Wise's Command (Attached to Holmes's Division)
Brig. Gen. Henry A. Wise
26th Virginia, Col. P. R. Page
46th Virginia, Col. R. T. W. Duke
Andrews's (Va.) Battery, Capt. W. G. Andrews
Armistead's (Va.) Battery, _____
French's (Va.) Battery, Capt. David A. French
Rives's (Va.) Battery, Capt. J. H. Rives

Reserve Artillery
Brig. Gen. William N. Pendleton

First Virginia Artillery
Col. J. Thompson Brown
Coke's Williamsburg (Va.) Battery, Capt. John Coke
Macon's Battery, _____
Richardson's Battery, _____
Watson's Battery, Capt. David Watson

Jones's Battalion
Maj. H. P. Jones
Attached to D. H. Hill's Division

NELSON'S BATTALION
    MAJ. WILLIAM NELSON
    Huckstep's (Va.) Battery, Capt. Charles T. Huckstep
    Page's (Va.) Battery, Capt. R. C. M. Page

RICHARDSON'S BATTALION
    MAJ. CHARLES RICHARDSON
    Ancell's (Va.) Battery, Capt. John J. Ancell
    Milledge's (Ga.) Battery, Capt. John Milledge
    Masters's (Va.) Battery, Capt. L. Masters

SUMTER (GA.) BATTALION
    LIEUT. COL. A. S. CUTTS
    Blackshear's (Ga.) Battery, Capt. James A. Blackshear
    Price's (Ga.) Battery, Capt. John W. Price
    Hamilton's (Ga.) Battery, Capt. S. P. Hamilton

CAVALRY
    BRIG. GEN. JAMES E. B. STUART
    1st North Carolina, Col. Lawrence S. Baker
    1st Virginia. Col. Fitzhugh Lee
    3d Virginia, Col. Thomas F. Goode
    4th Virginia, Capt. F. W. Chamberlayne
    5th Virginia, Col. Thomas L. Rosser
    9th Virginia, Col. W. H. F. Lee
    10th Virginia, Col. J. Lucius David
    Cobb (Ga.) Legion, Col. Thomas R. Cobb
    Critcher's (Va.) Battalion, Maj. J. Critcher
    Hampton's (S.C.) Legion, Capt. Thomas E. Screven
    Jeff. Davis (Miss.) Legion, Lieut. Col. W. T. Martin
    Stuart Horse Artillery, Capt. John Pelham

[*OR* 11, pt. 2, pp. 483–918, and *B&L*, vol. 2, pp. 315–17.]

(k) Killed
(w) Wounded
(mw) Mortally wounded
(c) Captured

Appendix III

Casualties

Beaver Dam Creek

	Union	Confederate
Casualties	361	1,148
KIA	49	——
WIA	207	——
MIA	105	——

Gaines Mill

	Union	Confederate
Casualties	6,637	7,993
KIA	894	1,483
WIA	3,107	6,402
MIA	2,836	108

Savage Station

	Union	Confederate
Casualties	1,590	626
KIA	——	——
WIA	——	——
MIA	——	——

White Oak Swamp/Glendale

	Union	Confederate
Casualties	3,797	3,673
KIA	297	638
WIA	1,696	2,814
MIA	1,804	221

Malvern Hill

	Union	Confederate
Casualties	3,007	5,650
KIA	314	869
WIA	1,875	4,241
MIA	818	540

Total

	Union	Confederate
Casualties	15,795	20,204
KIA	1,743	3,494
WIA	8,006	15,758
MIA	6,055	952

Separate battles will not equal total. Total includes skirmishes between battles.

KIA, killed in action; WIA, wounded in action; MIA, missing in action.

[*OR* 11, pt. 2; Fox, *Regimental Losses.*]

Appendix IV

National Cemeteries

There are many National Cemeteries in and around the Richmond area. Three of them are on or close to the Seven Days route that you follow.

Cold Harbor National Cemetery

This cemetery is located on State Highway 156 between Stops 9 and 10. Established in 1866, the grounds encompass 1.4 acres. As of the writing of this book there are 2,110 veterans interned there.

Significant monuments are the Tomb of the Unknown Soldier, built in 1877 to remember the 889 unknown Union dead; the Pennsylvania Monument, built in 1909 to remember the Pennsylvania regiments who fought at Cold Harbor in 1864; Eighth New York Heavy Artillery Monument, built in 1909 to honor the 219 members of the regiment who died as a result of the Battle of Cold Harbor in 1864.

There is one recipient of the Medal of Honor. That individual is Sergeant Major August Barry of the Sixteenth U.S. Infantry of the Civil War. Sergeant Major Barry also was one of the early superintendents of the cemetery

Seven Pines National Cemetery

This cemetery is located on the Williamsburg Road, Highway U.S. 60, nine-tenths of a mile west of Stop 17. Established in 1866, the grounds encompass 2.1 acres. As of the writing of this book there are 1,808 veterans interned there.

Glendale National Cemetery

This cemetery is located on the Willis Church Road, State Highway 156, in the vicinity of Stop 24. Established in 1866, the grounds encompass 2.1 acres. As of the writing of this book there are 2,057 veterans interned there.

There is one recipient of the Medal of Honor. That individual is Corporal Michael F. Folland, Company D, 2d Battalion, 3d Infantry, 199th Infantry Brigade. The medal awarded posthumously for action in the Republic of South Vietnam in 1969.

Glendale National Cemetery.

Appendix V

Stuart's Reconnaissance, June 12–15, 1862

This appendix will take you on a tour and study of *Stuart*'s "Ride around McClellan." Total driving miles from the start point north of Richmond to the end point at the National Park Service Headquarters in southern Richmond is eighty miles.

 Robert E. Lee assumed command of the Army of Northern Virginia at the beginning of June. His first task was to establish his army firmly in the Richmond defensive works. He did this using a system of earth fortifications that allowed him to hold the defenses with a minimum number of troops while freeing part of his army for an attack against McClellan's Army of the Potomac. McClellan's army was deployed on both sides of the Chickahominy River and presented a lucrative target. *Lee* wanted to hold the left of the Union army south of the river and in front of Richmond and attack the right part north of the river. To increase his offensive combat power he planned to bring *Jackson*'s force from the Shenandoah Valley. However, in order to fully develop his plan *Lee* needed to know if McClellan's right flank extended beyond Mechanicsville and what forces might be available behind that position to reinforce.

 To obtain the information he needed, *Lee* dispatched Brigadier General *J. E. B. Stuart* with part of the army's cavalry on a reconnaissance of the area north of the Union right. The following order was issued to *Stuart*.

Headquarters, Dabb's Farm, Va., June 11, 1862

Brig. Gen. *J. E. B. STUART,*
Commanding Cavalry:

 GENERAL: You are desired to make a secret movement to the rear of the enemy, now posted on Chickahominy, with a view of gaining intelligence of his operations, communications, &c., of driving in his foraging parties, and securing such grain, cattle, &c., for ourselves as you can make arrangements to have driven in. Another object is to destroy his wagon trains, said to be daily passing from the Piping Tree road to his camp on the Chickahominy. The utmost vigilance on your part will be necessary to prevent any surprise to yourself, and the greatest caution must be practiced in keeping well in your front and flanks reliable scouts to give you information.

You will return as soon as the object of your expedition is accomplished, and you must bear constantly in mind, while endeavoring to execute the general purpose of your mission, not to hazard unnecessarily your command or to attempt what your judgment may not approve but be content to accomplish all the good you can without feeling it necessary to obtain all that might be desired. I recommend that you only take such men and horses as can stand the expedition, and that you take every means in your power to save and cherish those you do take. You must leave sufficient cavalry here for the service of this army, and remember that one of the chief objects of your expedition is to gain intelligence for the guidance of future operations.

Information received last evening, the points of which I sent you, lead me to infer that there is a stronger force on the enemy's right than was previously reported. A large body of infantry, as well as cavalry, was reported near the Central Railroad. Should you find upon investigation that the enemy is moving to his right, or is so strongly posted as to render your expedition inopportune—as its success, in my opinion, depends upon its secrecy—you will, after gaining all the information you can, resume your former position.

I am, with great respect, your obedient servant,

R. E. LEE,
General

[*OR* 11, pt. 3, pp. 590–91.]

To accomplish the mission assigned him, *Stuart* selected the following units from his cavalry force:

First Virginia Cavalry—Colonel *Fitzhugh Lee*
Ninth Virginia Cavalry—Colonel *William H. F. Lee*
Fourth Virginia Cavalry—Six companies divided between First and Ninth Cavalry
Jeff Davis Legion, two squadrons—Lieutenant Colonel *W. T. Martin*
Section (2 guns) *Stuart* Horse Artillery—Lieutenant *James Breathed*

Stuart began his reconnaissance in the early morning hours of June 12. He moved his column of horsemen from the northern outskirts of Richmond to Yellow Tavern. Two-tenths of a mile north of Yellow Tavern, where State Road 625 is today, he moved in a northwesterly direction to give the impression he was going to the Shenandoah Valley to reinforce *Jackson*. After marching northeast for seven miles he began to turn back to the northeast and then east and recrossed today's Highway U.S. 1 north of Ashland and marched east for two miles to the vicinity of the Winston's farm, where he went into bivouac. Instead of following this part of *Stuart*'s route, follow the instructions below and move directly north to the point where he crossed U.S. 1 north of Ashland then moved east to the vicinity of the bivouac site for the night of June 12–13.

From Richmond take I-95 North to Exit 92B. Drive west on State Highway 54 for 0.4 miles to Highway U.S. 1. Turn right on to U.S. 1 and drive 1.9 mile to State Highway 641. State Highway 641 is just past a historical marker about *Stuart*'s ride. Bear right at the fork in the road onto State Highway 641. Drive east on State Highway 641 for 0.8 mile to the intersection with State Highway 646, Hickory Hill Road. At State Highway 646 turn right and drive 2.2 miles to the intersection with State Highway 738, Old Ridge Road. At the intersection pull off to the side of the road and stop. Note: After you have driven for 1.2 mile State Highway 646 becomes a gravel road, but continue driving.

Position A—Bivouac Site, Night of June 12–13, 1862

Report of Brig. Gen *J. E. B. Stuart*, CSA, Commanding Cavalry Brigade, Army of Northern Virginia

The destination of the expedition was kept a profound secret (so essential to success) and was known to my command only as the actual march developed it. The force was quietly concentrated beyond the Chickahominy, near Kilby's Station, on the Richmond, Fredericksburg and Potomac Railroad, and moved thence parallel to and to the left of that road. Scouts were kept far to the right to ascertain the enemy's whereabouts, and advanced guard, flankers, and rear guard to secure our column against surprise. I purposely directed my first day's march toward Louisa [Court House], so as to favor the idea of re-enforcing *Jackson,* and encamped just opposite Hanover Court-House, near South Anna Bridge (Richmond, Fredericksburg and Potomac Railroad), 22 miles from Richmond.

Our noiseless bivouac was broken early next morning [June 13], and without flag or bugle-sound we resumed our march, none but one knew whither. I, however, immediately took occasion to make known my instructions and plans confidentially to the regimental commanders, so as to secure an intelligent action and co-operation in whatever might occur. Scouts had returned, indicating no serious obstacles to my march from that to Old Church, directly in rear of and on the overland avenue of communication to New Bridge and vicinity. [*OR* 11, pt. 1, p. 1036.]

Continue to drive on State Highway 646 for 3.5 miles to the intersection with State Highway 54, East Patrick Henry Road. Turn left and drive for 0.2 mile to the intersection with U.S. Highway 301. Turn right on to U.S. Highway 301 and drive 0.2 mile southeast on U.S. 301. Pull over to the side of the road and stop.

Position B—Hanover Court House, June 13

Here at Hanover Court House *Stuart* made his first contact with Union forces. A patrol from the Sixth U.S. Cavalry was covering the area. *Stuart*

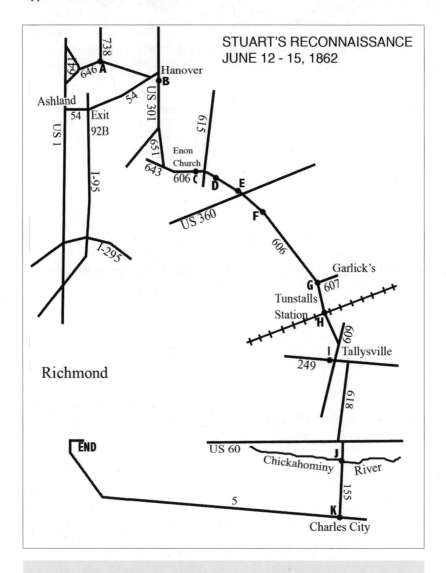

STUART'S RECONNAISSANCE
JUNE 12 - 15, 1862

deployed his force in an attempt to capture the patrol, but they were too fast for him and departed the area heading south.

Report of Brig. Gen *J. E. B. Stuart*, CSA [Continued]

Upon reaching the vicinity of Hanover Court-House I found it in possession of the enemy; but very little could be ascertained about the strength and nature of his force. I therefore sent Col. *Fitz. Lee*'s regiment (First Virginia Cavalry) to make a detour to the right and reach the enemy's route behind him, to ascertain his force here and crush it, if possible; but the enemy, proving afterward to be 150 cavalry, did not tarry long, but left, my column following slowly down, expecting every moment to hurl him upon *Lee;* but owing to a bad marsh Colonel *Lee* did not reach the intersection of roads in time, and the cavalry (the Regular Sixth) passed on in the direction of Mechanicsville. This course deviating too much from our direction, after the capture of a sergeant they were allowed to proceed without interruption on their way. [*OR* 11, pt. 1, p. 1036.]

Continue driving south on U.S. Highway 301 for 2.7 miles to Crosses Corner. Here take a left on to State Highway 651, Georgetown Road, and drive for 4 miles to the intersection of State Highway 643. When you cross Crumps Creek you are in the vicinity of Taliaferro's Mill. At 3.0 miles from Crosses Corner, the route *Stuart* took goes off to the left in a southeast direction. You will reconnect with his route in a few more miles. At the intersection with State Highway 643 turn left and drive for 0.9 mile to the intersection with State Highway 606, Studley Road. Turn left on to State Highway 606 and drive for 2 miles to Enon Church. Turn left into the Enon United Methodist Church parking area and park next to the Memorial for the Confederate Unknown. In this location *Stuart's* route rejoined the road you are on.

Position C—Leib's Reconnaissance, Morning, June 13

Lieutenant Edward H. Leib, with his Company F, Fifth U.S. Cavalry, had been sent toward Hanover Court House to watch over the area north of the Army of the Potomac's right flank. While conducting this reconnaissance, he sighted the advancing Confederate cavalry column.

Report of Brig. Gen. *J. E. B. Stuart,* CSA [Continued]

Our march led thence to Taliaferro's Mill and Enon Church to Hawes' Shop; here we encountered the first pickets, surprised and caught several vedettes, and pushed boldly forward, keeping advance guard well to the front. The regiment in front was the Ninth Virginia Cavalry (Col. *W. H. F. Lee*), whose advance guard, intrusted to the command of the adjutant (Lieutenant *Robins*), did admirable service, Lieutenant *Robins* handling it in the most skillful manner, managing to clear the way for the march with little delay, and infusing by a sudden dash at a picket such a wholesome terror that it never paused to take a second look. [*OR* 11, pt. 1, p. 1037.]

Report of Lieut. Edward H. Leib, USA, Commanding Company F, Fifth U.S. Cavalry, First Cavalry Brigade, Cavalry Reserve, Army of the Potomac

On the morning of the 13th I was ordered by Captain Royall, Fifth U.S. Cavalry, to make with my company a reconnaissance in the direction of Hanover

Court-House, and to proceed as far as that place, to ascertain the strength and position of the enemy, should he be found in that quarter. Leaving camp about 6 o'clock in the morning I advanced upon the Hanover road, throwing forward as an advance guard a non-commissioned officer and 8 men. Feeling my way cautiously I had advanced at 11 o'clock a.m. to within a half mile of Hanover Court-House, where I first caught sight of what I supposed to be the pickets of the enemy. Halting my main body and advance in a skirt of timber under cover and out of sight, I cautiously proceeded to reconnoiter in person the strength and position of the force in front. After a close observation I discovered a body of cavalry drawn up in line and numbering about two squadrons, together with a scattered advance of horsemen, amounting to about 15 men.

Having learned that a portion of the Sixth Cavalry had been sent forward in that direction I was uncertain as to whether it was they or the enemy. After halting a few moments I advanced alone to the banks of a small stream, upon the opposite side of which I could still see the horsemen in line. As I approached the stream an officer and 6 or 8 men came down the opposite side. Immediately upon seeing me they turned about and joined the main body. I then knew them to be the enemy. Returning to my advance, I informed them that the enemy were in front, and stationing them as a rear guard I returned to the main body, and immediately sent back one of my men to inform Captain Royall that I had met the enemy and that they were about two squadrons strong.

It was then about 11.30 o'clock, and having determined to fall back, I wheeled my company by fours, and giving my sergeant instructions to retire slowly and in order, regulating his gait by mine, I returned to the rear of my command, and leaving one man to keep the enemy in sight, I gave him instructions to regulate his gait by theirs. I then detached 6 men to keep this man in sight, and returned to the front and sent forward on the road an advance of 4 men, under a non-commissioned officer, to gather in the men which I had left to guard the different roads I had passed. After this I took my position between my company and my rear guard. The enemy did not immediately follow, and finding there was no immediate pursuit, I stationed a man upon a slight eminence, where the view was extended, and told him to wait for fifteen or twenty minutes, and if the enemy were not in sight by that time to join me at once. I still continued to retire until I reached our first pickets, stationed at a cross-road where were a few houses, known as Hall's [Haw's] Machine-Shop. Having heard from my scout I sent word to Captain Royall the enemy were not in sight, but repeated my first report, that I had seen two squadrons. After this I remained at the cross-roads and sent back my rear guard 1 1/2 miles on the road by which I had retired. [*OR* 11, pt. 1, pp. 1021–22.]

Turn left as you depart Enon United Methodist Church and continue on State Highway 606 for 0.8 mile. Just past State Highway 615, Williams Road, turn right in to the U.S. Post Office parking lot and park.

Position D—The Cavalry Fight Begins, 3 P.M., June 13

You are in the vicinity of the Haw's Shop mentioned in *Stuart*'s and Leib's reports. Here the advance guard of the Confederate column commanded by

Lieutenant *W. T. Robins* made contact with Lieutenant Edward H. Leib's Company F, Fifth U.S. Cavalry.

Report of Lieut. Edward H. Leib, USA [Continued]

After remaining at the cross-roads about an hour I received an order from Captain Royall to return to camp, and withdrawing my rear guard, I cautioned the pickets that the enemy were in my rear, and took up my march toward camp. About a mile from the cross-roads I was joined by Lieutenant McLean, in command of about 30 men of Company H, Fifth Cavalry, who again gave me Captain Royall's order to return to camp. Lieutenant McLean took command, and keeping his company in front, we in this manner retired half a mile, when I was informed by pickets that the enemy were about a quarter of a mile back, advancing rapidly. I immediately sent word to Lieutenant McLean, who was in front, and also to Captain Royall, to tell them the enemy were advancing upon us. Not hearing from Lieutenant McLean I drew up in line under the brow of a hill on the side of the road, intending if my force was sufficient to charge; if not, to keep them in check with the pistol; in either event to show a bold front and conceal as long as possible the small numbers of my command. The enemy came on in a few moments in large numbers. I held them in check at least twenty minutes, emptying during that time ten saddles (the horses coming over to my command). During this time I lost no men, but had several horses wounded.

It was at this point that I felt most seriously the superiority of the enemy, who were armed with rifles and shot-guns, and had my command been furnished with carbines I would have been able to do him more injury and hold him longer in check. After I had emptied all of my pistols I drew sabers and endeavored to charge, but finding they were coming up in greatly-superior force on either flank and in front, I thought it best to fall back on Lieutenant McLean's command, which at this time was halted on the opposite side of a small bridge. [*OR* 11, pt. 1, p. 1022.]

Stuart ordered *W. H. F. Lee* to bring his regiment forward to reinforce *Robins* and to attack the Union cavalry blocking the road. *Lee* ordered his leading squadron, commanded by Captain *S. A. Swann*, to attack.

Narrative of Lieut. *W. T. Robins*, CSA, Ninth Virginia Cavalry, Cavalry Brigade, Army of Northern Virginia

General *Stuart* at once ordered Colonel *W. H. F. Lee*, commanding the regiment leading the column, to throw forward a squadron to meet the enemy. Colonel *Lee* directed Captain *Swann*, chief of the leading squadron of his regiment, to charge with the saber. *Swann* moved off at a trot, and, turning a corner of the road saw the enemy's squadron about two hundred yards in front of him. The order to charge was given, and the men dashed forward in fine style. The onset was so sudden that the Federal cavalry broke and scattered in confusion. Now the road became very narrow, and the brush on either side was a place so favorable for an ambush that Captain *Swann* deemed it prudent to draw reign and recall his men. [*B&L*, vol. 2, p. 271.]

> Continue on State Highway 606 for 2.4 miles. Just after crossing the bridge, pull off to the side and stop. Note: There is a marker for *Stuart*'s ride on the near side of the bridge.
>
> ## Position E—The Cavalry Fight Continues
>
> Lieutenant Leib fell back from his initial position and joined Companies C and H of the Fifth U.S. Cavalry. This three-company force under command of Captain William B. Royal prepared to attack *Robins*'s advance guard. Seeing the size of the Union cavalry to his front, the commander of the Ninth Virginia Cavalry, Colonel *W. H. F. Lee*, ordered his next squadron in the column to attack and clear the road. Captain *William Latane* led his squadron in the attack. The fighting between these two forces ranged on and around the road for the next one-half mile as Royall's force was driven back. When it was over *Latane* wounded Royall and then Royall killed *Latane* with a pistol shot. The Union cavalry fell back toward the southeast.

Report of Brig. Gen *J. E. B. Stuart*, CSA [Continued]

Between Hawes' Shop and Old Church the advance guard reported the enemy's cavalry in force in front; it proved to be the Fifth Regular Cavalry. The leading squadron was ordered forward at a brisk gait, the main body following closely, and gave chase to the enemy for a mile or two, but not coming up with him. We crossed the Totopotomoy, a strong position of defense, which the enemy failed to hold, confessing a weakness. In such places half a squadron was deployed afoot as skirmishers till the point of danger was passed.

On, on dashed *Robins*, here skirting a field, there leaping a fence or ditch, and clearing the woods beyond, when not far from Old Church the enemy made a stand, having been re-enforced.

The only mode of attack being in column of fours along the road, I still preferred to oppose the enemy with one squadron at a time, remembering that he who brings on the field the last cavalry reserve wins the day. The next squadron therefore moved to the front under the lamented Captain *Latane*, making a most brilliant and successful charge with drawn sabers upon the picketed ground, and, after a hotly-contested hand-to-hand conflict, put him to flight, but not till the gallant captain had sealed his devotion to his native soil with his blood. The enemy's rout was complete; they dispersed in terror and confusion, leaving many dead on the field and blood in quantities in their tracks. Their commander, Captain Royall, was reported wounded. [*OR* 11, pt. 1, p. 1037.]

Report of Lieut. Edward H. Leib, USA [Continued]

I thought it best to fall back on Lieutenant McLean's command, which at this time was halted on the opposite side of a small bridge. [You crossed a creek where this bridge was 0.5 mile back.] From this point I again sent to Captain Royall an account of what had been done and what was then in progress. For some time I held the bridge, and the enemy fell back. I then found they were crossing the creek above and below the bridge, in order to surround and capture my small force. I was forced again to retire, which I did for 2 miles, disputing every inch of ground. The enemy gradually ceased to pursue, and to prevent them flanking me I continued to fall back until I reached the road, which here turns toward Richmond. At this point I determined to hold my position at all hazards, deeming it certain re-enforcements must soon come up. The enemy did not again attack, and after half an hour Captain Royall arrived and assumed command. [*OR* 11, pt. 1 pp. 1022–23.]

Narrative of Lieut. *W. T. Robins,* CSA [Continued]

Stuart, who had been marching steadily onward with the main body of the Confederate column, soon arrived at the front, and the advance-guard, which I had all long commanded, was directed to move forward again. I at once dismounted the men and pushed forward up a hill in my front. Just beyond the hill, I ran into a force of federal cavalry drawn up in column of fours, ready to charge. Just as my advance-guard was about to run into him, I heard their commanding officer give the order to charge. I fell back and immediately notified General *Stuart* of the presence of the enemy. Captain *Latane,* commanding a squadron of the 9th Virginia, was directed to move forward and clear the road. He moved up the hill at a trot, and when in sight of the enemy in the road gave the command to charge, and with a yell the men rushed forward. At the top of the hill, simultaneously with *Latane*'s order to charge, a company of Federal Cavalry, deployed as skirmishers in the woods on the right of the road, were stampeded, and rushed back into the woods to make good their retreat to their friends. The head of *Latane*'s squadron, then just fairly up the hill, was in the line of their retreat and was separated from the rest of the squadron, cut off by the rush of the federals, and borne along with them up the road towards the enemy. I was riding at the side of *Latane,* and just at the time when the Federal company rushed back into the road Captain *Latane* was shot dead. The rush of the federals separated myself and six of the leading files from our friends, and we were borne along by the flying Federals. Although the Federal cavalry both in front and rear were in full retreat, our situation was perilous in the extreme. Soon we were pushed by foes in our rear into the ranks of those in our front, and a series of hand-to hand combats ensued. Every one of my comrades was shot or cut down, and I alone escaped unhurt. After having been borne along by the retreating enemy for perhaps a quarter of a mile, I leaped my horse over the fence into a field and so got away.

Now came the rush of the Confederate column sweeping the road clear and capturing many prisoners. [*B&L*, vol. 2, pp. 271–72.]

Informed of the Confederate advance Captain Royal began moving reinforcement toward Leib and soon rode to the scene of the action and took personal command of all Union cavalry there.

Report of Capt. William B. Royall, USA, Commanding Squadron, Fifth U.S. Cavalry, First Cavalry Brigade, Cavalry Reserve, Army of the Potomac

One company was detailed daily to go in the direction of Hanover Court-House. On the morning of the 13th instant Lieut. Edward H. Leib was detailed for this duty. He left camp with his company (F) at an early hour. About 2 o'clock p.m. I received a message from him stating that the enemy were advancing in force from the direction of Hanover Court-House, and that he (Leib) was returning slowly toward camp. I immediately sent Lieut. William McLean, with his company (H), to support Lieutenant Leib, and prepared to follow myself with the remainder of my command, consisting of Company C, which was then being relieved from picket duty.

I started in person to join Lieutenant Leib. I found him about 1 mile from my camp, and he reported the enemy in force immediately in his front. This information I sent to the division commander by Lieut. Louis D. Watkins.

Wishing to satisfy myself from personal observation as to the strength and character of the enemy I ordered the command forward. I had proceeded but a short distance, not more than three-quarters of a mile, when I met the enemy's advance, which I charged and drove back. In a few minutes, however, I was attacked by a large force, consisting, I supposed, of six or seven squadrons of cavalry in front and on both flanks. My whole command did not exceed 100 men, and consequently I was driven back.

I wheeled my command twice on my retreat and arrested the overwhelming force that charged me, each time emptying three or four saddles. The last mile to camp I was not pursued closely, but on reaching my camp I was forced to turn over my command to Lieutenant Leib, having been exhausted from loss of blood from several saber wounds which I had received, instructing him not to risk another attack, but to remain there until the enemy approached, and then retire by the Cold Harbor road.

Lieutenant McLean, after fighting most gallantly, was wounded and taken prisoner. I had 4 men killed and I suppose 10 or 12 wounded. Most of the wounded were taken prisoners. Quite a number of Captain Harrison's company were captured whilst on picket, the enemy seeming to know exactly where they were posted, and I suppose cut off their retreat. Of the loss of the enemy I am unable to give an accurate account. We captured 8 or 10 horses, with their whole equipments. I know that quite a number must have been wounded, for in each of my encounters the saber was used freely by my command. [*OR* 11, pt. 1, pp. 1020–21.]

Continue on State Highway 606 for 2.6 miles to Old Church. Pull off to the side and stop.

Position F—The Decision Point, Late Afternoon, June 13

Royall's command retreated southeast along the road, through Linney, 1.7 miles back, to Old Church, which is where their camp was. Here the wounded Royall turned over command of the cavalry to Lieutenant Leib.

Report of Lieut. Edward H. Leib, USA [Continued]

After this the fighting gradually ceased, and I retired until we reached our camp. There, Captain Royall's wounds proving very severe; the command was turned over to me. Having sent word to General Cooke and sent out an advance to feel the enemy, at this point I was joined by Lieutenant Byrnes, with a part of Company C, Fifth Cavalry. I ordered him to form on the left of my line, and in this position I awaited the enemy for at least an hour. From this point I dispatched two non-commissioned officers—one to recall the picket at New Castle Landing and the other to turn back any wagons that might be coming from White House Landing. I also sent an express on the Cold Harbor road to ask for re-enforcements at the first camp he met. At last, in about an hour, the enemy attacked me on all sides, and such were his numbers I deemed it proper to order the command to retreat. [*OR* 11, pt. 1, p. 1023.]

Report of Brig. Gen *J. E. B. Stuart*, CSA [Continued]

Col. *Fitz. Lee*, burning with impatience to cross sabers with his old regiment, galloped to the front at this point and begged to be allowed to participate with his regiment (the First Virginia Cavalry) in the discomfiture of his old comrades, a request I readily granted, and his leading squadron pushed gallantly down the road to Old Church; but the fragments of Royall's command could not again be rallied, and Colonel *Lee*'s leading squadron charged without resistance into the enemy's camp, and took possession of a number of horses, a quantity of arms and stores of every kind, several officers and privates. The stores as well as the tents, in which everything had been left, were speedily burned, and the march resumed.

Here was the turning point of the expedition. Two routes were before me—the one to return by Hanover Court House, the other to pass around through New Kent, taking the chances of having to swim the Chickahominy and make a bold effort to cut the enemy's lines of communication. The Chickahominy was believed by my guide to be fordable near Forge Bridge. I was 14 miles from Hanover Court House, which I would have to pass. If I returned, the enemy had a much shorter distance to pass to intercept me there; besides, the South Anna was impassable, which still further narrowed the chances of escape in that direction; the enemy, too, would naturally expect me to take that route. These circumstances led me to look with more favor to my favorite scheme, disclosed to you [*Robert E. Lee*] before starting, of passing around. It was only 9 miles to Tunstall's Station, on the York River Railroad, and that point once passed I felt little apprehension beyond. The route was one of all others which I felt sure the enemy would never expect me to take. On that side of the Chickahominy infantry could not reach me before crossing, and I felt able to whip any cavalry force that could be brought against me. Once on the Charles City side, I knew you [*Lee*] would, when aware of my position, if necessary, order a diversion in my favor on the Charles City road, to prevent a move to intercept me from the direction of White Oak Swamp. Besides this, the hope of striking a serious blow at a boastful and insolent foe, which would make him tremble in his shoes, made more agreeable the alternative I chose. In a brief and frank interview with some of my officers I disclosed my views, but while none accorded a full assent, all assured me a hearty support in whatever I did.

With an abiding trust in God, and with such guarantees of success as the two *Lees* and *Martin* and their devoted followers, this enterprise I regarded as most promising. Taking care, therefore, more particularly, after this resolve, to inquire of the citizens the distance and the route to Hanover Court-House, I kept my horse's head steadily toward Tunstall's Station. [*OR* 11, pt. 1 pp. 1037–38.]

By this point in his reconnaissance *Stuart* had the information that *Lee* needed. *Stuart* had discovered that the Army of the Potomac's right (north) flank did not extend very far beyond Mechanicsville. *Lee* now knew that a Confederate force approaching from the northwest or north from the vicinity of Ashland would hit the Union army in the flank or would accomplish a turning movement as it went behind the defender's right and force them out of their prepared defenses at Mechanicsville and Beaver Dam Creek. This information was vital to *Lee*'s planning as to where he would attack and where he would bring *Stonewall Jackson*'s force from the Shenandoah Valley to the Richmond battlefield.

In the afternoon Union cavalry and infantry were gathered under the command of Brigadier General Phillip St. George Cooke, who was *Stuart*'s father-in-law. These Union units were in the vicinity of Cold Harbor, eight miles to the southwest. During the night this Union cavalry force, soon to be reinforced with infantry, arrived at Linney, 1.8 miles before this location. This force would have effectively cut *Stuart*'s return route had he decided to retrace his original route. From Linney, this force would conduct an ineffective pursuit of *Stuart*'s cavalry.

Continue on State Highway 606 for 7.8 miles to the intersection with State Highway 607, Steel Trap Road. Pull off to the side and stop.

Position G—Burning Union Boats and Supplies, 6 P.M., June 13

The road to the left today goes 0.9 mile to Putney's Mill on the Pamunkey River. In 1862 this was called Garlick's Landing. Late in the afternoon of June 13 squadrons from the First and Sixth Virginia Cavalry destroy Union wagons and two supply ships at Garlick's.

Report of Col. *W. H. F. Lee*, CSA, Commanding Ninth Virginia Cavalry, Cavalry Brigade, Army of Northern Virginia

I detached a part of two squadrons, Captain *Knight* and Lieutenant *Oliver* commanding, and directed them to go to Garlick's Landing and burn the vessels lying there, which they did very successfully, burning two transports laden with sutler's and quartermaster's stores. One escaped. Here they met with a slight resistance from a party of about 100 men, but a few shots soon brought the matter to an end, and they captured almost all of them. [*OR* 11, pt. 1 p. 1044.]

One of the details at Garlick's was a supply train for the First U.S. Cavalry with its escort.

Report of Lieut. Joseph S. Hoyer, USA, First U.S. Cavalry, Second Cavalry Brigade, Cavalry Reserve, Army of the Potomac

I proceeded to Garlick's Landing with an escort of a non-commissioned officer and 8 men, in charge of a supply train, consisting of 14 wagons and 1 ambulance. I arrived safely at the landing above mentioned about 2 o'clock p.m. on the same day, and having obtained the required supplies I ordered the horses unsaddled, and in accordance with orders encamped for the night on the banks of the Pamunkey River, near the landing.

About 6 o'clock p.m., whilst the animals were feeding and the men at supper, a platoon of the enemy's cavalry (deployed as skirmishers) unexpectedly attacked me. So sudden was their appearance that the men were unable to mount their horses. I therefore ordered them into line, which order was promptly executed, and upon being ordered to surrender we fired upon the enemy, when they retired, carrying with them 2 wounded. A squadron of their cavalry, however, subsequently charged upon us, when we were compelled to seek the underbrush for protection.

In connection with this I would state that a supply train from the Seventeenth and Forty-fourth New York Volunteer Regiments, although attended by an escort of 15 or more men, through some neglect were without arms. Had they been armed I might have repelled their attack with greater effect. The enemy meanwhile set fire to and destroyed the train and supplies, having previously turned loose and driven off the animals. Of 15 teamsters and 8 men I report a return to duty thus far of 10. To my knowledge 3 surrendered to the enemy, while the remainder [10] are yet missing. [*OR* 11, pt. 1, pp. 1027–28.]

Continue on State Highway 606 for 2 miles to Tunstall Station. Pull off to the side and stop.

Position H—Tunstall Station, Early Evening, June 13

Stuart arrived here just before dark. In 1862 the railroad was the Richmond and York River Railroad. The main Union supply base at White House is just 4.3 miles to the east.

Report of Brig. Gen *J. E. B. Stuart*, CSA [Continued]

[As the command approached Tunstall Station] 5 Co's of cavalry, escorting large wagon trains, were in sight and seemed at first disposed to dispute our progress, but the sight of our column, led by [*W. H. F.*] *Lee*, of the Ninth, boldly advancing to the combat, was enough. Content with a distant view, they fled, leaving their train in our hands. The party that reached the railroad at Tunstall's surprised the guard at the depot (15 or 20 infantry), captured them without their firing a gun, and set about obstructing the railroad, but before it could be thoroughly done, and just as the head of our column reached it, a train of cars came thundering down from the [Union] Army. It had troops on board and we prepared to attack it. The train swept off the obstructions without being thrown from the track, but our fire, delivered at only a few rods distance, either killed or caused to feign death every one on board, the engineer being one of the first victims from the unerring fire of Captain *Farley*. It is fair to presume that a serious collision took place on its arrival at the White House, for it made extraordinary speed in that direction. The railroad bridge over Black Creek was fired under the direction of Lieutenant *Burke,* and it being now dark, the burning of the immense wagon train and the extricating of the teams involved much labor and delay and illuminated the country for miles. [*OR* 11, pt. 1, pp. 1038–39.]

It was part of Colonel *W. H. F. Lee*'s command that rushed in and tried to stop the train that sped through the station.

Report of Col. *W. H. F. Lee*, CSA [Continued]

The advance guard had barely reached the York River Railroad, when a train was reported in sight. Lieutenant *Robins,* in command of the advance, tried to turn the switch, but found it locked. He had obstructions placed across the track, and I hurried a squadron forward, dismounted them, and as the train came down fired into it. A great many jumped off when the firing commenced. The conductor was killed or jumped off. The obstructions proved insufficient and the train escaped. There were some killed here and a number captured. [*OR* 11, pt. 1, p. 1044.]

Continue south on State Highway 606 for 2.6 miles to the intersection with State Highway 609. Veer right on to State Highway 609 and drive for 1.4 miles to Tallysville and the intersection with State Highway 249. Turn right on to State Highway 249. After you pass the historical markers on your left, turn around as soon as possible and return to the historical markers, now on your right. Stop at the historical markers. You are now facing southeast.

Position I—Tallysville, Evening, June 13

Upon reaching Tallysville *Stuart* halted his march so the column could close up and soldiers and horses could rest.

Report of Brig. Gen *J. E. B. Stuart*, CSA [Continued]

The roads at this point were far worse than ours, and the artillery had much difficulty in passing. Our march was finally continued by bright moonlight to Tallysville, where we halted 3 1/2 hours for the column to close up. At this point we passed a large hospital of 150 patients. I deemed it proper not to molest the surgeons and attendants in charge. [*OR* 11, pt. 1, p. 1039.]

Depart Tallysville by driving southeast, the direction you are facing, on State Highway 249. Drive for 0.6 mile to the intersection with State Highway 618, Olivet Church Road. It will be on your right. Turn right on to State Highway 618 and drive south for 6.2 miles to the intersection with U.S. Highway 60. Turn left on to U.S. Highway 60 and drive for 0.2 mile to the intersection with State Highway 155. Turn right on to State Highway 155 and drive south for 0.9 mile to the Chickahominy River. Just before the bridge pull off to the side and stop.

Position J—Chickahominy River, Morning, June 14

At dawn on June 14 *Stuart* reached the Chickahominy River. Expecting to be able to easily ford the river he was presented with a problem when he found it a barrier, as the river was flowing full and fast. After several attempts to cross it by fording, the soldiers rebuilt a damaged bridge using wood from a barn and they were able to cross before Union pursuers could catch up. The actual crossing site is about one mile to your left on private land.

Report of Brig. Gen *J. E. B. Stuart*, CSA [Continued]

At 12 o'clock at night the march was continued without incident under the most favorable auspices to Forge Bridge (8 miles), over the Chickahominy, where we arrived just at daylight. [*W.H.F.*] *Lee,* of the Ninth, by personal experiment having found the stream not fordable, axes were sent for and every means taken to overcome the difficulties by improvised bridges and swimming. I immediately dispatched to you [*Robert E. Lee*] information of my situation and asked for the diversion already referred to. The progress in crossing was very slow at the point chosen, just above Forge Bridge, and learning that at the bridge proper enough of the debris of the old bridge remained to facilitate the construction of another, material for which was afforded by a large warehouse adjacent, I moved to that point at once. Lieut. *Redmond Burke,* who in every sphere has rendered most valuable service and deserves the highest consideration at the hands of the Government, set to work with a party to construct the bridge. A footbridge was soon improvised, and the horses were crossed over as rapidly as possible by swimming. *Burke's* work proceeded like magic; in three hours it was ready to bear artillery and cavalry, and as half of the latter had not yet crossed, the bridge enabled the whole to reach the other bank by 1 p.m. Another branch of the Chickahominy still farther on was with some difficulty forded, and the march was continued without interruption toward Richmond. [*OR* 11, pt. 1, p. 1039.]

Continue south on State Highway 155 for 6.5 miles to Charles City and the intersection with State Highway 5. Pull off and stop just before the intersection.

Position K—Charles City, Evening, June 14

Stuart's column reached Charles City at sunset and went into camp to rest and eat. *Stuart* turned command of the force over to Colonel *Fitzhugh Lee* and with a small escort proceeded along the river road to Richmond in order to report the results of his reconnaissance to *Robert E. Lee.*

At 11:00 P.M. Colonel *Fitzhugh Lee* mounted up the column and proceeded along the River Road to Richmond. They rode throughout the night and reached the Confederate line east of Richmond on the morning of June 15.

Narrative of Lieut. *W. T. Robins,* CSA [Continued]

We were now twenty-five miles from Richmond on the James River Road. Had the enemy been aware of our position, it would have been easy for him to throw a force between us and Richmond, and so cut us off. But the Federal general was not very well served by his scouts, nor did his cavalry furnish him with accurate information of our movements. Relying upon the mistakes of the enemy, *Stuart* resolved to march straight on into Richmond by the River Road on which we now lay. To accomplish this with the greater safety, it was necessary for him to march at once. Accordingly, I was ordered to take the advance guard and move out. As soon as the cravings of hunger were appeased, sleep took possession of us. Although in the saddle and in motion, and aware that the safety of the expedition depended on great vigilance in case the enemy should be encountered, it was hard to keep awake. I was constantly falling asleep, and awaking with a start when almost [falling] off my horse. This was the condition of every man in the column.

The full moon lighted our way as we passed along the River Road, and frequently the windings of the road brought us near to the and in sight of the James River, where lay the enemy's fleet. At "Tighlman's" we could see the mast of the fleet, not far off. Happily for us, the banks were high, and I imagine they had no lookouts in the rigging, and we passed by unobserved. The sight of the enemy's fleet had aroused us somewhat, when "Who goes there?" rang out on the stillness of the early morning. The challenger proved to be a vidette of the 10th Virginia Cavalry, commanded by Colonel *J. Lucius Davis,* who was picketing the road. Then we crossed the stream by the jug factory, up towards New Market heights, by the drill-house, and about a mile beyond we called halt for a little rest and food. From this point the several regiments were dismissed to their respective camps. [*B&L*, vol. 2, p. 275.]

If you wish to follow the Confederate cavalry's route to Richmond follow these directions. Turn right on to State Road 5 and drive 28 miles back to Richmond. After you have driven 6.7 miles you will pass Berkley Plantation and Harrison's Landing. It was here that the Army of the Potomac retreated to, arriving there on July 2. In another 8.5 miles, 15.2 miles from Charles City, is Malvern Hill to the right, the site of the last of the Seven Days Battles. Continue on State Road 5 for another 12.9 miles to the intersection with 25th Street. Turn right on to 25th Street and drive for three blocks to Broad Street, U.S. Highway 60. Turn right on to Broad Street and drive eight blocks (0.4 mile) to Chimborazo Park, the Richmond National Battlefield Park Headquarters and Medical Museum. This is the end of your tour and study of *Stuart*'s reconnaissance.

Index

Echoes of Thunder was designed and typeset on a Macintosh computer system using InDesign software. The body text is set in 10/12 Adobe Caslon Pro and display type is set in Brittanic Bold. This book was designed and typeset by Stephanie Thompson and manufactured by Thomson-Shore, Inc.